Mike Dean John Hall
Antonino Rotolo Said Tabe

Semantic Web Rules

International Symposium, RuleML 2010
Washington, DC, USA, October 21-23, 2010
Proceedings

Springer

Volume Editors

Mike Dean
Raytheon BBN Technologies, 3658 Wagner Ridge Ct., Ann Arbor, MI 48103, USA
E-mail: mdean@bbn.com

John Hall
Model Systems, 15-19 Cavendish Place, London W1G 0DD, UK
E-mail: john.hall@modelsystems.co.uk

Antonino Rotolo
University of Bologna, CIRSFID, Via Galliera 3, 40121 Bologna, Italy
E-mail: antonino.rotolo@unibo.it

Said Tabet
Inferware Corporation, 24 Magnolia Road, Natick, MA 01760, USA
E-mail: stabet@comcast.net

Library of Congress Control Number: 2010935668

CR Subject Classification (1998): D.2, I.2, C.2.4, H.4, C.2, I.2.11

LNCS Sublibrary: SL 2 – Programming and Software Engineering

ISSN   0302-9743
ISBN-10 3-642-16288-6 Springer Berlin Heidelberg New York
ISBN-13 978-3-642-16288-6 Springer Berlin Heidelberg New York

springer.com

© Springer-Verlag Berlin Heidelberg 2010
Printed in Germany

Typesetting: Camera-ready by author, data conversion by Scientific Publishing Services, Chennai, India
Printed on acid-free paper   06/3180

Lecture Notes in Computer Science 6403

Commenced Publication in 1973
Founding and Former Series Editors:
Gerhard Goos, Juris Hartmanis, and Jan van Leeuwen

Preface

The 4th International Web Rule Symposium (RuleML 2010), co-located in Alexandria, Virginia, USA (near Washington, DC) with the 13th International Business Rules Forum Conference 2010, was organized to meet colleagues and to exchange ideas from all subareas of Web rule technology. The aims of RuleML 2010 were both to present new and interesting research results and to show successfully deployed rule-based applications. This annual symposium is the flagship event of the Rule Markup Language (RuleML) Initiative.

The RuleML Initiative (www.ruleml.org) is a non-profit umbrella organization of several technical groups organized by representatives from academia, industry and public sectors working on rule technologies and applications. Its aim is to promote the study, research and application of rules in heterogeneous distributed environments such as the Web. RuleML maintains effective links with other major international societies and acts as an intermediary between various "specialized" rule vendor, application, industrial and academic research groups, as well as standardization efforts including W3C, OMG and OASIS.

After a series of successful international RuleML workshops and conferences, the RuleML symposia, held since 2007, constitute a new kind of event where the Web rules and logic community joins the established, practically oriented business rules community (www.businessrulesforum.com). The symposium supports the idea that there is a successful path from high-quality research results to deployed applications. Hence, the RuleML Symposium is research-based and industry-focused: its main goal is to build a bridge between academia and industry in the field of Web rules, semantic technology, and business processes, and so to stimulate the cooperation and interoperability between business and research, by bringing together rule system providers, participants in rule standardization efforts, open source communities, practitioners and researchers.

The contributions in this volume include one abstract and one paper for the two invited keynote presentations, one extended abstract of an invited demo, one track paper (by Grigoris Antoniou and Antonis Bikakis, the track chairs, outlining a new research line for a topic not already presented in 2009) and a selection of 14 full papers and 7 short papers chosen from a pool of 42 submissions by authors from 22 countries. The accepted papers address a wide range of rule topics. In addition to some miscellaneous rule topics, most papers fall within the following track topics: Rules, Semantic Technology, and Cross-Industry Standards; Rule Transformation and Extraction; Rules and Uncertainty; Rules and Norms; Rules and Inferencing; Rule-Based Event Processing and Reaction Rules; and Rule-Based Distributed/Multi-Agent Systems.

The accepted papers were carefully selected after a rigorous peer-review process where each paper was evaluated by a panel of at least three members of the international Program Committee. We thank the reviewers for their effort and very valuable contribution; without them it would not be possible to maintain and improve the high scientific standard the symposium has now achieved. We thank the authors for submitting good papers, responding to the reviewers' comments, and abiding by our production schedule. We thank the keynote and invited demo speakers for their interesting presentations. And we thank the Business Rules Forum organizers for enabling this fruitful co-location of the 13th International Business Rules Forum Conference 2010 and RuleML 2010.

The real success of rule technology will be measured by the applications that use the technology rather than by the technology itself. To emphasize the practical use of rule technologies, RuleML 2010 continued the tradition of hosting the International Rule Challenge. The challenge offers participants the opportunity to demonstrate their commercial and open source tools, use cases, benchmarks, and applications. It was the ideal forum for those wanting to understand how rules technology can produce benefits, both technically and commercially.

The RuleML 2010 Symposium was financially supported by industrial companies and research institutes and was technically supported by several professional societies. We thank our sponsors, whose financial support helped us to organize this event, and whose technical support enabled us to attract many high-quality submissions.

August 2010   Mike Dean
                                                                   John Hall
                                                          Antonino Rotolo
                                                                  Said Tabet

Symposium Organization

General Chairs

Mike Dean   Raytheon BBN Technologies, USA
Said Tabet   Inferware Corp., USA

Program Chairs

John Hall   Model Systems, UK
Antonino Rotolo   University of Bologna, Italy

Liaison Chair

Mark Proctor   Red Hat, UK

Publicity Chair

Patrick Hung   University of Ontario Institute of Technology,
Canada

Rule Responder Chairs

Efstratios Kontopoulos   Aristotle University of Thessaloniki, Greece
Kalliopi Kravari   Aristotle University of Thessaloniki, Greece

Track Chairs

Rules, Semantic Technology, and Cross-Industry Standards

Tracy Bost   Valocity, USA
Robert Golan   DBMind, USA

Rule Transformation and Extraction

Mark Linehan   IBM, USA

Rules and Uncertainty

Davide Sottara   University of Bologna, Italy
Nikolaus Wulff   University of Münster, Germany

Rules and Norms

Thomas Gordon   Fraunhofer FOKUS, Germany
Guido Governatori   NICTA, Australia

Rules and Inferencing

Grigoris Antoniou   Information Systems Lab., FORTH, Greece
Antonis Bikakis   Information Systems Lab., FORTH, Greece

Rule-Based Event Processing and Reaction Rules

Alex Kozlenkov   Betfair Ltd., UK
Adrian Paschke   Free University Berlin, Germany

Rule-Based Distributed/Multi-Agent Systems

Nick Bassiliades   Aristotle University of Thessaloniki, Greece
Costin Badica   University of Craiova, Romania

RuleML Challenge

Enrico Francesconi   ITTIG-CNR, Italy
Monica Palmirani   University of Bologna, Italy
Omair Shafiq   University of Calgary, Canada
Fabio Vitali   University of Bologna, Italy

Program Committee

Hassan Ait-Kaci   Jürgen Dix
Sidney Bailin   Weichang Du
Matteo Baldoni   Schahram Dustdar
Claudio Bartolini   Andreas Eberhart
Bernhard Bauer   Jenny Eriksson Lundström
Mikael Berndtsson   Opher Etzion
Pedro Bizarro   Todd Everett
Jonathan Bnayahu   Maribel Fernandez
Guido Boella   Enrico Francesconi
Peter Bollen   Dragan Gasevic
Jordi Cabot   Adrian Giurca
Carlos Castro   Ioannis Hatzilygeroudis
Donald Chapin   Stijn Heymans
Federico Chesani   Yuh-Jong Hu
Horatiu Cirstea   Minsu Jang
Matteo Cristani   Yiannis Kompatsiaris
Claudia d'Amato   Manolis Koubarakis

Wolfgang Laun
Ian Mackie
Christopher Matheus
Craig McKenzie
Jing Mei
Zoran Milosevic
Anamaria Moreira
Leora Morgenstern
Jörg Müller
Chieko Nakabasami
Monica Palmirani
Alun Preece
Maher Rahmouni
Dave Reynolds
Graham Rong

Giovanni Sartor
Marco Seiriö
Silvie Spreeuwenberg
Giorgos Stamou
Giorgos Stoilos
Nenad Stojanovic
Umberto Straccia
Terrance Swift
Leon van der Torre
Jan Vanthienen
Fabio Vitali
George Vouros
Kewen Wang
Segev Wasserkrug
Ching-Long Yeh

External Reviewers

Gioele Barabucci
Sylvain Dehors
Irini Fundulaki
Roman Khazankin
Efstratios Kontopoulos
Elisa Marengo
George Meditskos
Gian Luca Pozzato

RuleML 2010 Sponsors and Partners

Gold Sponsors

Silver Sponsors

Bronze Sponsors

Partner Organizations

Media Partners

Table of Contents

Rule Transformation and Extraction

Rules, Semantic Technology, and Cross-Industry Standards

Rules and Norms

Rule-Based Distributed/Multi-Agent Systems

Miscellaneous Rule Topics

Logical Spreadsheets

Michael Genesereth

Stanford University, USA
genesereth@stanford.edu

Abstract. Logical spreadsheets are spreadsheets in which formulas are written as logical constraints rather than function definitions. Allowing logical constraints in spreadsheets substantially increases their utility. At the same time, it poses interesting technical challenges, notably the representation of logical constraints (both static and dynamic), query and update in the face of data incompleteness and inconsistency, and support for collaborative work on distributed spreadsheets. In this presentation, we describe logical spreadsheets in detail and offer some approaches to dealing with these underlying challenges.

While logical spreadsheet technology is useful in specialized applications, it is even more useful as a general technology for the World Wide Web, turning ordinary Web forms into logical forms (sometimes called websheets). Moreover, the concept and technology of collaborative websheets can be further generalized to collaborative management of arbitrary logical databases. We close with thoughts about how this generalized technology can be used to produce a key component of the Semantic Web, viz. a World Data Web in which concepts and relationships replace documents and links, in which rules replace code, and in which query and update replace keyword search and file management.

M. Dean et al. (Eds.): RuleML 2010, LNCS 6403, p. 1, 2010.

NIEM Canonical XML Dictionaries and Rule Engine Systems

David Webber

OASIS CAM TC Chair,
630 Boston Road, Suite M-102
Billerica, MA 01821,
United States of America
drrwebber@acm.org

Abstract. NIEM is the National Information Exchange Model strategy adopted in US government agencies to align their domain information exchanges. The aim is to provide government information exchanges that are consistent and interoperable by using the NIEM.gov approach that relies on repeatable and predictable patterns and techniques. This presents a range of challenges to implementers including mapping from domain vocabularies to NIEM and applying an appropriate rule validation framework. Also creating exchange schema structure definitions and generating testing data sample instances. How can rule engines assist in automating these processes? The methods NIEM advocates using have been criticized as being heavy-weight and cumbersome; how can rule-based techniques dramatically simplify the challenges that developers face in exploiting the NIEM-based approach?

Keywords: NIEM, dictionary, canonical, core, components, XML, exchange, validation, XSD, schema, template, framework, OASIS, CAM, content assembly, CCTS.

1 Introduction

Creating reliable information exchanges using the NIEM (National Information Exchange Model) approach presents a variety of challenges to developers. First there is the perceived complexity of the NIEM schemas themselves, which are deliberately over inclusive of components and thereby provide too much for the developer who is therefore required to select a subset mapping. For example, the components listed under "person" contain about 1.5Mbytes of structure and rule definition information for aspects relating to a person, their name, demographics, location, family, history, employment and so on. Indeed, mapping from a local application domain to the NIEM components is part of the initial barrier and is time consuming given the plethora of components and domain choices in NIEM. Therefore, mapping and component matching agents are one potential area to apply rule technologies. Otherwise, done manually the expedience is to use a semblance of obvious base component parts from NIEM rather than rigorous mapping (e.g. map to generic PersonName instead of locating and using BuildingOwnerName). In addition

M. Dean et al. (Eds.): RuleML 2010, LNCS 6403, pp. 2–15, 2010.

implementers then redundantly create local extensions for the remainder of an exchange structure leading to yet more abundance of component definitions.

Another area of challenge is the development of formal W3C XML Schema for NIEM. Again NIEM itself is using complex and arcane W3C XML Schema syntax to mimic modelling techniques and behaviours, whereas interoperable exchange schema require the opposite: simple clear and consistent syntax that can be implemented across any platform and system software of user partners. Software developers who are not adept in understanding of W3C XML Schema face a steep learning curve to assimilate NIEM techniques. This again presents an opportunity for the use of rule agents that can take simpler abstract representations of information exchange structures and components and automatically generate NIEM compatible W3C XML Schema without any specialized knowledge required of developers.

To enable this requires building neutral representation syntax dictionaries of these NIEM components for use by agent systems and for human use in discovery and search tools. These canonical XML component dictionaries [1] are the focus of this paper. A canonical collection contains the component parts without redundancy and hence represents the building blocks from which the desired information exchange structures can be assembled.

Related to the use of canonical components is the quality of their definitions. Hence the need for automatic evaluation of existing schema components to detect potential interoperability issues, and to apply the NIEM Naming and Design Rules (NDR) that are intended to ensure component definitions are consistent and more reusable. Spelling and abbreviation checks are important to avoid redundancy and ensure consistent discovery across collections. Agent tools can check rules far more reliably than manual inspection, especially of large and complex structures and schemas. Having consistent component definitions is essential for deriving canonical XML components in dictionaries.

Last but not least are the challenges of testing, test case generation and validation of actual exchange structure instances, including in an operational environment. These are traditional areas where rule agent technology has been applied.

Summarizing these areas for the application of canonical XML dictionary technology, we have needs for:

- Neutral representation dictionaries of NIEM components
- Mapping from domain vocabularies to NIEM schema components
- Automatic W3C XML Schema syntax generation to NIEM style guidelines
- NIEM Naming and Design Rule (NDR) and interoperability factors checking
- Test case generation, testing and validation framework

Each of these areas is reviewed here in turn and related to how canonical XML dictionaries are used. An introduction to the current state of available agent tools is provided with a focus particularly on those that are exploiting techniques and XML standards from the OASIS Content Assembly Mechanism (CAM) specifications. Specific references are made to the open source implementation of the CAM editor toolkit on Sourceforge.net and how those XSLT script tools are tackling these challenges.

Writing rule based agent components in XSLT with XPath expressions has proven to be an extremely powerful way of implementing the required XML handling and logic. We also touch on performance aspects relating to XML runtime rule evaluation and how approaches such as OASIS CAM templates provide can also facilitate use of external rule engines.

Unfortunately space restrictions limit the ability to consider the formal system design and approach in depth. An introduction and overview is provided here while more formal details can be found in the OASIS CAM specifications along with tutorial materials describing the reference Sourceforge implementation of the CAM toolkit itself. Similarly use cases are mentioned but a full worked example is out of scope. Again the Sourceforge resources provide plenty of examples of dictionary implementations for actual NIEM domain and other industry vocabularies that can be downloaded and examined.

2   NIEM Canonical Dictionaries and OASIS CAM

2.1 Neutral Assembly Component Dictionaries

Developing canonical XML dictionaries requires a target XML format for storing the semantic information about the components in the dictionary. The current OASIS CAM draft technical specification [2] provides a condensed dictionary structure that contains the semantics of information components and their relationships. This follows the main aspects of the UN/CEFACT Core Components Technical Specification (CCTS) [3] and the XML4CCTS Schema designed to present structure components and their model relationships. This OASIS dictionary specification is further designed to be compatible with use in spreadsheet formats so as to also aid human viewing and discovery of matching components. A dictionary pack is available as open source of the NIEM domain dictionaries expressed in the OASIS canonical XML format [4]. These were derived from the NIEM domain Schemas available from the NIEM web site (http://www.niem.gov). Each NIEM domain schema was processed initially into the OASIS CAM template format and then from there directly into the canonical XML dictionary format using XSLT processing scripts. These XSLT scripts are available with the open source CAM editor toolkit on Sourceforge, or directly from the project open source code repository there (http://www.sourceforge.net/projects/camprocessor). The scripts illustrate how agent technology can be successfully built using the XSLT scripting language and XPath expressions to operate on XML target content. These scripts have been refined over a three year period to the point now where they represent a very significant agent resource honed in processing W3C XML Schema syntax and the models and structures expressed using that. Over 5,000 lines of logic are now contained in the scripts and hundreds of rules for handling W3C XML Schema syntax and the vagaries of its use for expressing XML structure representations.

While the OASIS CAM template format is designed to provide equivalent constructs for much of W3C XML Schema syntax, however the many abstract modelling concepts from W3C XML Schema are stored as annotations within the template format and thus separate from the content rules. There is a clear delineation within the CAM template with three separate sections for *structure* layout, content *rules* and cardinality, and *definitions* as annotations and documentation elements (see diagram in Figure 2 below for illustration).

With regard to information loss between an original W3C XML Schema and the equivalent CAM template representation it is important to consider the roles; CAM templates are aimed at precisely defining actual contextual XML instances for business information exchanges, whereas W3C XML Schema provide a wider definition set of all possible structure variations that it may be possible to construct. Many of these structure variations however will undoubtedly be invalid for a given business information exchange context. W3C Schema does not address that whereas CAM templates have specific XPath rule constructs available for this. Also, by exploiting the canonical dictionary format approach, components can be harvested from across a set of W3C XML Schema and thus provide capabilities that are not present in W3C XML Schema (harvesting is discussed in following sections below).

Next here we consider the dictionary semantic content and format itself. Figure 1 here shows the conceptual information stored in the component dictionaries.

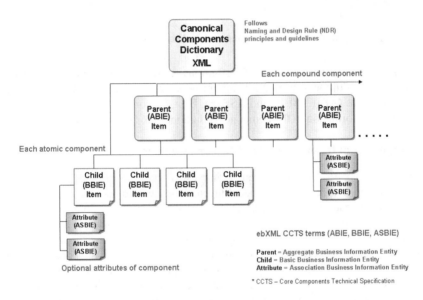

Fig. 1. Conceptual representation of schema components in a neutral format

Then this conceptual representation is mapped to the physical structure representation for each item as shown in Figure 2 below.

The physical dictionary components structure is persisted in XML elements and attributes that mirror this structure layout and named entities (see Appendix A). The full XML specification is available from the OASIS CAM committee web site downloads repository (http://www.oasis-open.org/committees/cam). Here we have provided a high level overview of how information is stored in a canonical XML dictionary according to the OASIS technical specifications (for an example of CAM

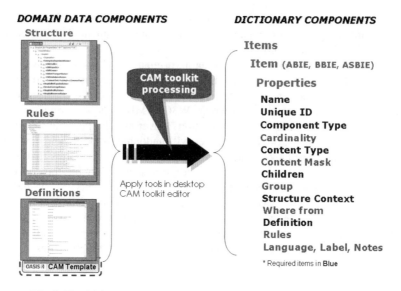

Fig. 2. Physical structure representation of schema components dictionary

template syntax for structure, rules and definitions shown here in Figure 2 please see Appendix B). In addition section 2.3 below provides more details on the component types shown above (ABIE, BBIE and ASBIE). First we consider how agent software can exploit the information in the components dictionary for mapping purposes.

2.2   Mapping from Domains to NIEM Schema Components

Lists of components for a domain can be harvested from a variety of sources. The primary preferred source is a data modelling tool that can export the definitions as W3C XML Schema (XSD) file formats. Alternatively existing domain exchange schema can be harvested for their components. Once a template is built of the components this can then be compared to the NIEM dictionary catalogue of components and a cross-reference spreadsheet built.   Currently this processing is implemented in XSLT scripting language using simple direct name pattern matching. However, significant work [5] has been done already in OASIS within the SET (Semantic Support for Electronic Business Document Interoperability) technical committee on using Java and OWL based presentations of component structures to do proximity and structure based matching by Professor Asuman Dodak's team at Ankara University in Turkey. Our plans include leveraging this work for future enhanced mapping capabilities and also for recommending changes and enhancements to NIEM itself to better facilitate mapping. Further work of interest in this area is the MITRE Corporation joint project with Google, Inc. on the OpenII toolset available as a Google open source project (http://projects.google.com/openii). Currently this is more focused on statistically analysing collections of components to determine potential alignment and proximity rather than directly supporting physical mapping. Clearly there is significant potential for further research on using agent technologies to facilitate mapping of related domain components in the future.

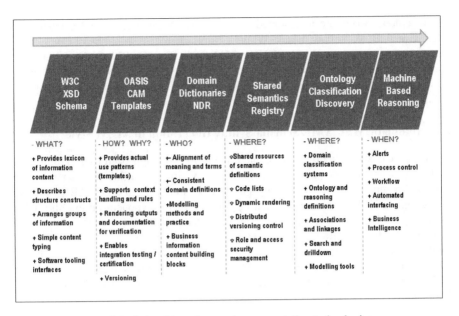

W3C XSD Schema	OASIS CAM Templates	Domain Dictionaries NDR	Shared Semantics Registry	Ontology Classification Discovery	Machine Based Reasoning
- WHAT?	- HOW? WHY?	- WHO?	- WHERE?	- WHERE?	- WHEN?
+ Provides lexicon of information content	+ Provides actual use patterns (templates)	← Alignment of meaning and terms	⊽Shared resources of semantic definitions	+ Domain classification systems	+ Alerts
+ Describes structure constructs	+ Supports context handling and rules	← Consistent domain definitions	⊽ Code lists	+ Ontology and reasoning definitions	+ Process control
+ Arranges groups of information	+ Rendering outputs and documentation for verification	+Modelling methods and practice	⊽ Dynamic rendering	+ Associations and linkages	+ Workflow
+ Simple content typing	+ Enables integration testing / certification	+ Business information content building blocks	⊽ Distributed versioning control	+ Search and drilldown	+ Automated interfacing
+ Software tooling interfaces	+ Versioning		⊽ Role and access security management	+ Modelling tools	+ Business Intelligence

Fig. 3. Relationships of semantic representation technologies

Figure 3 here shows how all these semantic technologies relate together.

The current approach is now only leveraging what is available in the first three columns in the diagram here (see "compare to dictionary" tool in the CAM toolkit download from Sourceforge). The potential is to incorporate technologies from all the columns to more effectively tackle the challenges of assisting mapping of domains to NIEM vocabularies and dictionaries of components.

2.3 Relating Schema Constructs to Neutral Syntax Components

As shown in Figure 2 above the dictionary components are organized as three related types. First there are atomic Basic Business Information Entities (BBIE) components. These equate to XML singleton elements without any child elements. Then there is Aggregate Business Information Entities (ABIE) that provides a container for one or more BBIE child elements along with the cardinality of those children (optional or repeatable), and can reference further ABIE components also. The third structure construct, Associated Business Information Entities (ASBIE) equate to XML attributes and hence may be found applied to a BBIE as children, or may be children of the parent element in an ABIE. The collection of ABIE, BBIE and ASBIE components are harvested below the root XML structure element. The ABIE's only shown nesting to the immediate one level below the parent. To augment the structure representation the *Structure Context* consists of XPath expressions that denote where a component may normally occur.

Associated with each component the facets and enumerations are captured in the *Content Type* and *Content Mask* neutral definition details. Unlike W3C XSD Schema syntax these are intended to be simple, atomic and human readable. So an enumerated list for colours would be represented as of *Content Type* "string" and *Content Mask* "Red, Green, Blue, Yellow, Black, White". Similarly a date would be of *Content Type* "date" and the *Content Mask* "YYYY-MM-DD". The OASIS CAM specification contains full details for these type and content representations. Next we look at how these representations are used to construct a schema definition from the component definitions.

2.4 Automatic W3C XML Schema Syntax Generation in NIEM Style

The canonical XML dictionaries enable a neutral syntax approach to designing XML exchange schema. This allows practitioners to simply outline the desired XML structure components by referencing parent component definitions (ABIE items) in the canonical XML dictionary. Then by running that component outline through an expander tool that references the desired dictionaries to expand each of the component schema definitions into a complete exchange schema structure. The CAM toolkit download from Sourceforge contains several working examples of these outline blueprints and the resulting full complete exchanges including NIEM and LEXS domain examples. Figure 4 here illustrates the components and tools needed to implement this process.

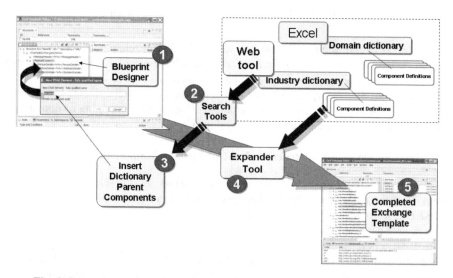

Fig. 4. Generating exchange structure from canonical XML dictionary components

Using the completed exchange template there is a further agent tool that then is able to generate the NIEM compatible W3C XML Schema representation of the structure and its content rules and definitions. This tool uses an XML configuration file that contains rules of how the various schemas are organized in physical folders and also details of namespaces for the various domains contained in the NIEM family of schema. Figure 5 illustrates a collection of schema generated automatically by the tool from a template representation similar to that in Figure 4.

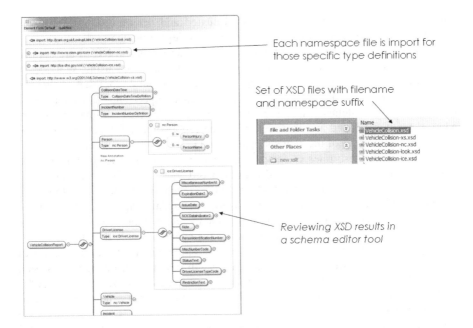

Each namespace file is import for those specific type definitions

Set of XSD files with filename and namespace suffix

Reviewing XSD results in a schema editor tool

Fig. 5. Generating exchange W3C XML Schema from template representation

The software agents written using XSLT scripts in this complete process are able to therefore assemble the desired exchange components from the neutral dictionary definitions and then from there to write the complex W3C XML Schema syntax required by NIEM across a collection of folders organized by namespace domains. To achieve this manually typically takes weeks of schema editing and can be achieved instead in a few hours of development and testing using the tooling automation. In addition the W3C XML Schema syntax written is conformant to the Naming and Design Rules (NDR) checks and more importantly is deliberately simple and concise so as to avoid using complex schema constructs that may be interoperability issues. The next section looks at the requirements for interoperability checking.

2.5 NIEM Naming and Design Rule (NDR) and Interoperability Factor Checking

When developing NIEM information exchange schema, there are a range of guidelines, principles and best practices that have been determined to significantly improve the quality of resulting production exchanges. NIEM itself has 193 NDR rules[1] specific to utilizing nuances of W3C XML Schema syntax. Many of these are complex and arcane. Producing agent software that is able to check for these automatically is therefore of high value for practitioners with NIEM development projects. For this specific implementation using OASIS CAM templates, we selected a subset if only 33 rules from the NIEM 193 rules. These represent those with the

---

[1] NIEM Naming and Design Rules (NIEM NDR) specification version 1.3 -
http://www.niem.gov/pdf/NIEM-NDR-1-3.pdf

highest value and also those that can be evaluated and determined by a software agent. Many of the NIEM NDR rules are subjective rules for human evaluation.

In addition to the 33 rules, an additional 6 rules that are not in NIEM are applied and these all relate to best practices from field experience with using W3C XML Schema to detect inconsistencies and logic errors. The evaluation tool that applies the rules reports errors, issues and warnings as a HTML report and also attempts to provide a scoring system where 10 represents no items detected and then points are deducted for items found and their severity. The report output can also be used for spell checking purposes of the element names used in the XML structure.

An example of these rules is comparing the name of an item to its content type definition. If a structure item is named with the word "date" in its item name, then the agent expects to see date content restrictions in the content definition and will produce a warning report if these are not present. Overall the agent script here implements a powerful set of checks that has proven invaluable in detecting and correcting a whole range of errors in exchange schema. In testing, the agent was able to detect errors in several popular industry standard schema sets that had gone unnoticed in some cases for over two years of widespread use worldwide. In other cases, the agent has been able to greatly improve the quality of industry standards that are currently under development, detecting inconsistencies and errors in initial draft schema, and further validating the approach.

In addition there is a renaming and rule alignment tool. This contains a powerful set of customizable rules that aim to ensure consistent naming of components and application of corresponding content rules. Rule sets include common typo and spelling errors (300 rules), NIEM domain abbreviations (several hundred), NIEM reference terms (25 content qualification terms such as number, name, date, Id, text, description and so on) and associated with these expected content restriction rules. The renaming tool can be utilized prior to running the NDR evaluation to correct common issues with Schema definitions. For example a Schema element may be named: *Lst_Calender_Upt_Dt* and this will be corrected by the renaming tools to be *LastCalendarUpdateDate* which will then correctly pass the NDR checking. A renaming spreadsheet is also produced so that spell checking can be performed and post-rename analysis. This allows fine tuning of the customizable rules and then iteration until a stable point is reached. This is particularly useful when harvesting dictionary components from enterprise data models or existing schema where correction of the original source may be problematic.

There is a governance and review process in place for evaluating NIEM exchange schema and the associated NIEM Information Exchange Package Documentation (IEPD). The renaming and NDR evaluation tools are used to assess quality of the resulting exchange schema and to recommend improvements and changes during the review process. This is deliberately flexible to permit developers to tailor exchanges to suit production requirements while also allowing them to avoid known pitfalls and interoperability issues early in the development cycle.

2.6 Test Case Generation, Testing and Validation Framework

Another area where the use of OASIS CAM templates with NIEM facilitates the use of agent technology is in test case generation and validation of example XML instances.

Previously, XML test case generator tools had been extremely simplistic and relied on manual editing to complete actual examples for testing purposes. The OASIS CAM template approach is a key facilitator because it uses actual physical structure instances in the definitions of the templates themselves. These then serve as master templates for the agent software to generate examples from. In addition, a content hinting mechanism is available that allows explicit real values to be provided to the agent scripts. These augment the rules that the agent script uses to make actual content match the definitions of the content rules in the template. The result is that the agent script is able to generate sets of realistic examples that are both valid and invalid. For testing purposes, being able to make invalid examples is equally if not more important than exercising anticipated valid logic paths.

To complete the validation framework here, the OASIS CAM specification allows for development of a fully featured validation engine. The open source CAMV engine has been developed for exactly this purpose. It is a fully self contained validation agent written in Java and is able to deploy in thread safe mode in application containers. IBM recently implemented a major automotive industry solution using this CAMV engine [7]. See the reference for complete implementation and design details. It should be noted that specific performance metrics are not provided although the solution has been able to operate without degrading the existing overall application throughput. Balancing concerns regarding the real time performance of any interpreted rule based approach compared to the desired production performance is an implementation and business needs decision. Additionally the CAMV engine architecture does permit calling external rule engines to augment the rule checking possible using the OASIS CAM rules syntax. Examples of rule engine extension are included in the Sourceforge CAM toolkit download.

With regard to NIEM applications, the key point to note is that the CAMV agent is able to implement selected validation by using context rules expressed in XPath syntax. The W3C XML Schema validation by contrast only permits one validation mode – error / fail. This means that W3C XML Schema based validation is extremely brittle in actual production environments and is often disabled or ignored because of the maintenance and support issues this would entail. By contrast the CAMV approach allows warnings and informational status reporting and outcomes, which results in a flexible and adaptive validation framework that can accept a wide range of input XML structure instances as valid.

For NIEM based applications this is of vital important when the information exchanges contain urgent content such as with emergency management applications. The worst case scenario is that a potential alert notification was blocked because it did not pass some arcane validation edit check that is embedded in middleware processing. Whereas in contrast a context rule based solution can report warnings instead of errors and therefore allow remediation and delivery to occur instead of rejection and failure to process.

3 Conclusion

We have presented here how using canonical XML dictionaries can provide multiple opportunities for using rule based associated agent technologies to support the implementation of complex extensive and multi-faceted software development approaches as found in NIEM.

Today's application development environments are increasingly complex and challenging for software development staff to assimilate and become proficient with. In Appendix C is provided a chart of the anticipated performance improvements that can be gained compared to current manual tasks involved in developing NIEM exchange schema. Additionally using agent based approaches can dramatically reduce the learning curve needed for practioners and ensure a consistent and reliable set of software products results. Furthermore the task faced by reviewers and the associated approval process can be automated to allow rigorous testing and evaluation. Without these tools, reviewers have little practical chance of successfully providing quality assurance given the demands of management to deliver solutions in a timely manner. Similarly developers also fail to maintain documentation artifacts.

Equally important is the use of open public standards and specifications and open source based software tools. These ensure that the criteria and approach can be peer reviewed and crosschecked or adapted to suit a particular development project's needs and domain idiosyncrasies. Making all of these aspects configurable through XML scripting technology and XML rule control files dramatically improves the usefulness and applicability of the overall toolkit solution.

4 Related Work

Schematron XML validation framework and ISO specification
http://www.schematron.com/resources.html
Reference Saxon XSLT engine implementation and Sourceforge project
http://saxon.sourceforge.net/

References

1. The Canonical, X.M.L.: dictionary definition from Wikipedia can be found at,
   http://www.wikipedia.org/canonical#dictionary
2. OASIS Content Assembly Mechanism (CAM) technical specification, version 1.1, published Boston, MA (2006), http://docs.oasis-open.org/cam
3. UN/CEFACT Core Components Technical Specification (CCTS) version 2.0, published Geneva, Switzerland (2002),
   http://www.unece.org/cefact/ebxml/CCTS_V2-01_Final.pdf
4. NIEM dictionary pack is available from Sourceforge (2010),
   http://www.sourceforge.net/projects/files#dictionary
5. NIEM Naming and Design Rules (NDR) 1.3 (2005),
   http://www.niem.gov/pdf/NIEM-NDR-1-3.pdf
6. OASIS SET TC work on automated component mapping,
   http://www.oasis-open.org/committees/set
7. Kathuria, P., Roberts, M.E., Webber, D.R.R. : XML Validation Framework using OASIS CAM (CAMV). In: IBM Developer Works (May 2010),
   http://www.ibm.com/developerworks/library/x-camval/index.html

Appendix A – Example NIEM Dictionary Entry XML

This section shows an example of the physical XML used to represent the items in a dictionary. In this case the example is taken from the NIEM International Trade (IT) domain. The XML syntax fragment shown below in Figure 6 illustrates the representation of NIEM components in a dictionary format. Items shown (prefixed with it:) include Stevedore ID Code, Previous Custom Document, Declaration Packaging, Duty Tax Fee, and Duty Tax Fee Assessment Basis Quantity.

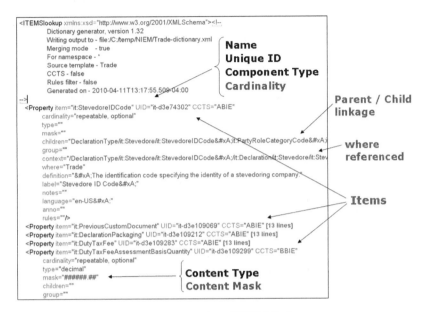

Fig. 6. XML syntax representation of NIEM dictionary components

The text in green is the comment produced by the XSLT script about the options and files used to generate the dictionary programmatically. Each Property element entry represents an Item. The description of each associated attribute of the element entry is provided next.

The **CCTS** attribute denotes Parent (ABIE) or Child (BBIE) entities. These are UN/CEFACT CCTS specification terms for collections of Business Information Entities. Some entries have been collapsed to show only the top line (13 lines).	**UID** is the Unique ID generated using the XSLT hashing algorithm. The prefix is the namespace for the dictionary.
Children are expressed as XPath terms, starting with the structure locator for the parent, followed by each of the child items.	**Group** can denote a logical abstract collection of items that this item belongs to.
Context is a collection of XPath locator terms for everywhere the item is used structurally by other items in the dictionary.	**Where** refers to external schema that the definitions are derived from. For dictionaries built by merging definitions across a collection of schema this helps identify the sources.
Definition is a textual description of the purpose of the item. It should not be self-referencing, but instead describe the context of its use in physical world.	**Label** is an aid to display the content on forms or reports.

The **Notes** attribute is an aid for user interfaces for content entry hints.	**Language** is the ISO code for the default content.
Anno is programmatic annotation derived from the CAM template that relates to this item.	**Rules** are programmatic XPath expressions that control the usage of this item and potentially relate to other items or control different picture masks for the content.

```
<as:CAM xmlns:as="http://www.oasis-open.org/committees/cam"
        xmlns:camed="http://jcam.org.uk/editor"
        xmlns:xsd="http://www.w3.org/2001/XMLSchema"
        xmlns:ram="urn:un:unece:uncefact:data:draft:Common:3"
        CAMlevel="1"
        version="1.0">
 <as:Header>
  <as:Description>Generated for AllRootLevelTypeDefinitions  by XSD 2 CAM generator v1.64</as:Description>
  <as:Owner>To be Completed</as:Owner>
  <as:Version>3.0</as:Version>
  <as:DateTime>2010-07-28T16:42:37.668-04:00</as:DateTime>
 </as:Header>
 <as:AssemblyStructure>
  <as:Structure taxonomy="XML" ID="AllRootLevelTypeDefinitions">
   <AllRootLevelTypeDefinitions>
    <QuantityType unitCode="%Token%" unitCodeListID="%Token%" unitCodeListAgencyID="%Token%"
                  unitCodeListAgencyName="%string%">%54321.00%</QuantityType>
    <AdvancePaymentType>
     <ram:PaidAmount>%54321.00%</ram:PaidAmount>
     <ram:ReceivedDateTime>%type=DateMandatoryDateTimeType%</ram:ReceivedDateTime>
    </AdvancePaymentType>
    <AppliedAllowanceChargeType>
     <ram:ActualAmount>%54321.00%</ram:ActualAmount>
     <ram:Description languageCode="%en-US%">%string%</ram:Description>
     <ram:CalculationPercent>%54321.00%</ram:CalculationPercent>
     <ram:ChargeIndicator>%false%</ram:ChargeIndicator>
    </AppliedAllowanceChargeType>
   </AllRootLevelTypeDefinitions>
  </as:Structure>
 </as:AssemblyStructure>
<as:BusinessUseContext>
 <as:Rules>
  <as:default>
   <as:context>
    <as:constraint action="setNumberMask(//QuantityType,###### ##)"/>
    <as:constraint action="makeOptional(//QuantityType/@unitCode)"/>
    <as:constraint action="datatype(//QuantityType/@unitCode,token)"/>
    <as:constraint action="makeOptional(//QuantityType/@unitCodeListID)"/>
    <as:constraint action="restrictValues(//AcknowledgementDocumentType/ram:TypeCode,'1'|'2'|'3'|'4'|'5'|'6'|'7'|'8'|'9'|'10')"/>
    <as:constraint action="makeOptional(//AcknowledgementDocumentType/ram:IssueDateTime)"/>
    <as:constraint condition="string-length(.) &lt;26 and(string-length(.) &gt;19)"
              action="setDateMask(//AcknowledgementDocumentType/ram:IssueDateTime,YYYY-MM-DD'T'HH:MI:SSZ)"/>
    <as:constraint condition="string-length(.) &gt;25"
              action="setDateMask(//AcknowledgementDocumentType/ram:IssueDateTime,YYYY-MM-DD'T'HH:MI:SS.SZ)"/>
    <as:constraint action="setNumberMask(//AppliedAllowanceChargeType/ram:BasisAmount,###### ##)"/>
    <as:constraint action="restrictValues(//AppliedAllowanceChargeType/ram:ChargeIndicator,'true'|'false')"/>
   </as:context>
  </as:default>
 </as:Rules>
</as:BusinessUseContext>
  <as:Extension name="uk.org.jcam.camed.extensions.StructureAnnotations">
   <camed:annotation item="//AllRootLevelTypeDefinitions/QuantityType">
    <camed:documentation type="Definition">
        ccts:Definition["A counted number of non-monetary units possibly including fractions."]
        ccts:PrimitiveType["decimal"]
    </camed:documentation>
   </camed:annotation>
   <camed:annotation item="//QuantityType/@unitCode">
    <camed:documentation type="Definition">
        ccts:Definition["The type of unit of measure."]
        ccts:PrimitiveType["string"]
    </camed:documentation>
   </camed:annotation>
   <camed:annotation item="//AppliedAllowanceChargeType/ram:ChargeIndicator">
    <camed:documentation type="Type">udt:IndicatorType</camed:documentation>
    <camed:documentation type="Definition">
        ccts:Definition["The indication of whether or not the applied allowance charge is a charge"]
    </camed:documentation>
    <camed:documentation type="Ref">AppliedAllowanceChargeType/ram:ChargeIndicator</camed:documentation>
   </camed:annotation>
  </as:Extension>
 </as:CAM>
```

Fig. 7. XML syntax representation of CAM Template

Appendix B – Example CAM Template XML

Here is shown below an example CAM template to illustrate the XML syntax and structure components from the OASIS CAM specification.

Appendix C – Comparing NIEM IEPD Timelines

Here below is shown two illustrative tables of the types of tasks required in a NIEM IEPD (Information Exchange Package Documentation) and the estimated potential impacts of using rule driven tools to automate much of the processes compared to existing manual practices.

Component	Manually Performed Tasks	Timings	Constraints
Collect exchange needs	Model information needs	Weeks	Spiral analysis
Perform XSD schema development with NIEM alignment	XSD syntax writing	Weeks	Complex with steep learning curve and limited practitioners.
Documentation of each element	Excel spreadsheet	Weeks	Manual preparation and review
Document NIEM element alignment (want list)	Excel spreadsheet	2 to 5 days	Manual preparation and review
Create test cases and examples	Sets of XML instances	Weeks	Manual hand editing of XML from XSD
Perform interoperability testing	Build test environments	Weeks	Test harnesses vary
Create IEPD document	Word documentation	Weeks	Manual preparation

Component	Agent Assisted Tasks	Timings	Constraints
Collect exchange needs	Model information needs	Days	Assisted analysis
Perform XSD schema development with NIEM alignment	XSD syntax writing	Hours	Remove need to know schema.
Documentation of each element	HTML report formats	Minutes	Automatic generation
Document NIEM element alignment (want list)	Excel spreadsheet	Minutes	Automatic generation
Create test cases and examples	Sets of XML instances	Hours	Automatic with content hinting
Perform interoperability testing	Build test environments	Hours	Test harnesses consistent
Create IEPD document	Word documentation	Days	Manual preparation

Fig. 8. NIEM IEPD Process Metrics Compared

Implementing SBVR with a Practitioner's Perspective

Donald Chapin

Business Semantics Ltd, London, United Kingdom
Donald.Chapin@BusinessSemantics.com

Abstract. The Object Management Group's "Semantics of Business Vocabulary and Business Rules (SBVR)" standard is a synthesis from four disciplines: terminology science, natural language grammar structures, formal logic and the practice of applying the business rules approach in organizations. The SBVR specification (like all OMG specifications) is directed primarily at tool developers. As a result some of SBVR's most important capabilities for practitioners are not self-evident from just reading the specification document. This paper will illustrate how a number of these SBVR features can be implemented in a tool to deliver significant value to SBVR users.

Building on a Foundation of Identifiable Business and Professional Communities

Clause 1: Scope of the SBVR specification says:

> This specification is applicable to the domain of business vocabularies and business rules of all kinds of business activities of all kinds of organizations. It is conceptualized optimally for business people rather than automated rules processing, and is designed to be used for business purposes, independent of information systems designs.

The terminology part of SBVR, which is built on the ISO TC 37 Terminology standards, is about documenting and managing the special purpose language of an organization, profession, discipline, or industry as an asset. This places terminology management within the well established field of Knowledge Management in which knowing what communities you belong to is a core technique.

An SBVR model—a 'body of shared meanings' comprising noun concepts, verb concepts and rules—is owned by a semantic community, typically a business or equivalent not-for-profit organization. Assumptions about meanings being the same very often turn out to be wrong, so it is important to establish semantic communities as boundaries across which no assumptions are made about semantic equivalents.

A business may be part of wider semantic communities such as shared interest groups, either by domain (healthcare, telecommunications, insurance, etc.) or by discipline (human resources, finance, project management etc.), from which it might adopt part of its SBVR model.

M. Dean et al. (Eds.): RuleML 2010, LNCS 6403, pp. 16–19, 2010.

An effective SBVR tool must support:

– Association of an SBVR model with its owning semantic community;
– Explicit adoption of all or integral parts of another semantic community's concepts, both from SBVR models and from authoritative non-SBVR sources such as industry glossaries and ontologies, standards and regulations;
– Ability to explicit assert that two meanings in different semantic communities are the same—of course, after sufficient analysis to demonstrate that is true.

In order to be shared, an SBVR model must have at least one representation— definitions and statements in text in a given natural language, icons, graphics, etc. Each representation is owned by a speech community, which is part of the semantic community that owns the model. A semantic community includes at least one speech community, and may include several, ranging from speakers of different natural languages to specialists such as lawyers, accountants and engineers who need specialized terminology for their disciplines.

An effective SBVR tool must support:

– Different representations of the same underlying model, including: i) different natural languages, and ii) synonyms, synonymous forms and homonyms that are connected to exactly one clearly-defined meaning in a given context within a given natural language;
– Association of a representation of an SBVR model with its owning speech community.

Separating Meaning from Its Expression

A common misconception is that SBVR Structured English (the styled subset of English used in the SBVR specification) is SBVR. It is not. SBVR Structured English is a non-normative notation for representing SBVR models. Other, equivalent, notations may be used, both in representing the models themselves, and in user interfaces with SBVR tools. An effective SBVR tool must maintain an internal model of an SBVR 'body of shared meanings' that is independent of the notations used for its representation.

This separation has to be built into the heart of the architecture of both the tool's database and software. In SBVR all of the connections that are used to construct meanings are made among meaning-model elements, independent of their representation in expressions. Implementing this is essential if an SBVR tool is to support the same, shared meaning across natural languages and different terms used by different speech communities in the same natural language.

While there are multiple speech communities for a given natural language, having one speech community identified as the core speech community for each language enables the speech communities for that language to add only those terms that are different for them. The same holds true in a tool's being able to identify and utilize a core language for each semantic community. That way, as terms for additional natural languages are added, they can be done first where there is least understanding of the core language, again added by exception as needed. This requires significant tool support when the tool decides which preferred terms to present to a given speech community.

Building Meanings Out of Their Component Parts and Not by Using Expression Syntax

A key aspect of making a clean separation of meaning from expression is to provide tool support for building up all of the semantics of each meaning from the components of that meaning and connections with other meaning constructs without any reference to expression syntax or grammar. In SBVR noun concepts are composed of characteristics, which are the meaning of adjectives and adjectival phrases. Verb Concepts are composed of noun concepts plus verbs, verb phrases and prepositions. Rules are composed of verb concepts and keywords ("rule" words). Good tool support leverages these meaning structures to enable exploration and navigation of meanings using the representation expressions of any chosen speech community.

Tying All Uses of Representation Expressions Directly to the Meanings They Represent

One of the biggest benefits of using defined terminology is that, with good tool support, it is possible to see the exact meaning the author of a document or a rule intended for each entry used from the terminology. The most easily used method is for the preferred definition in the language of the current speech community to be shown as a tooltip when the mouse hovers over the expression. XHTML and CSS are the most universal standards for providing this kind of capability. Using CSS systematically also enables a using organization to customize the way the representation expressions are displayed visually.

The ability to display changed representation expressions where ever they used on the next refresh of the input screen, report or document is evidence that tool is remembering the semantics of what the author intended. This is further illustrated in the ability to change the current speech community on the fly so that input screens, queries, and reports, as well as text documents, show the preferred terms of the new speech community immediately upon refreshing them.

Enabling Rule Authors to Have the Necessary Support from Terminology Authors

The majority of the work of creating formally defined business rules, as high as 80%, is the work of creating the terminology with which they are composed. Furthermore, terminology and business rules arise out of different business activities and are the responsibility of different groups of people. To enable the collaboration between business terminologists and business professionals who make policy, a tool needs to provide features that facilitate this collaboration between terminologists and policy-makers. Designs For Management^{TM} accomplishes this by providing the ability for policy-makers to compose new verb concepts out of existing nouns, verbs, and prepositions or request new ones in a way that they can be used while they are still only requests.

Providing Semantic Data Definitions Based on SBVR Terminology

The SBVR metamodel (defined in Clauses 8, 9, 11 & 12 of the specification) supports the documentation of the special purpose language used by business people to communicate with each other. However, the formal logic interpretation for SBVR (Clause 10 of the specification) is formulated in terms of the meaning of the data that will be supported in some IT application. While these two parts of SBVR are closely aligned, by definition a transformation is required between them. There is great IT value to be obtained from SBVR terminology in addition to its primary purpose of removing ambiguity from business communication. Tool support for this transformation to the not-standardized metamodel implied by SBVR Clause 10 can provide what is in effect a Semantic Data Dictionary, which removes ambiguity from Business Requirements for Application Software.

Bridging to IT System Design Tools

There exists in the marketplace a set of increasingly practical and platform-independent graphic modeling tools for IT systems design. Providing a transformation to the parts of these tools that are closest to the Business Requirements of Application Software adds a great deal of additional IT benefit. Key transforms are from the Semantic Data Dictionary to a logical data model and from automatable business rules to a rules language such as production rules.

A Practical Management of Fuzzy Truth-Degrees Using FLOPER*

Pedro J. Morcillo, Ginés Moreno, Jaime Penabad, and Carlos Vázquez

University of Castilla-La Mancha
Faculty of Computer Science Engineering
02071, Albacete, Spain
{pmorcillo,cvazquez}@dsi.uclm.es,
{Gines.Moreno,Jaime.Penabad}@uclm.es

Abstract. During the last two years, our developments regarding the design of the FLOPER tool ("Fuzzy LOgic Programming Environment for Research"), have been devoted to implant in its core a rule-based, easy representation of lattices representing fuzzy notions of truth degrees beyond the boolean case, in order to work with flexible programs belonging to the so-called *multi-adjoint logic approach*. Now, the system improves its initial running/debugging/tracing capabilities for managing this kind of fuzzy logic programs, with new options for manipulating in a classical Prolog style the mathematical foundations of the enrichment introduced by *multi-adjoint lattices*. In particular, we show that for a given program and query, many different answers can be obtained when changing the assumption of truth in a single work session. The experience related here evidences the expressive power of Prolog rules (i.e., clauses) for implementing rich versions of multi-adjoint lattices in a very easy way, as well as its crucial role in further fuzzy logic computations.

1 Introduction

Research in the fields of *Declarative Programming* and *Fuzzy Logic* have traditionally provided programming languages and techniques with important applications in the areas of AI, rule-based systems, and so on [3,17,21]. In particular, *Logic Programming* [16] has been widely used for problem solving and knowledge representation in the past. Nevertheless, traditional logic languages do not incorporate techniques or constructs to explicitly deal with uncertainty and approximate reasoning in a natural way.

To fulfill this gap, *Fuzzy Logic Programming* has emerged as an interesting and still growing research area trying to consolidate the efforts for introducing fuzzy logic into logic programming. During the last decades, several fuzzy logic programming systems have been developed, such as [2,4,6,15,13,27] and the many-valued logic programming language of [25,26], where the classical inference

---

* This work was supported by the EU (FEDER), and the Spanish Science and Innovation Ministry (MICIN) under grant TIN 2007-65749 and by the Castilla-La Mancha Administration under grant PII1I09-0117-4481.

M. Dean et al. (Eds.): RuleML 2010, LNCS 6403, pp. 20–34, 2010.

mechanism of SLD–Resolution has been replaced by a fuzzy variant which is able to handle partial truth and to reason with uncertainty.

This is the case of *multi-adjoint logic programming* [20,18,19], a powerful and promising approach in the area. In this framework, a program can be seen as a set of rules each one annotated by a truth degree and a goal is a query to the system plus a substitution (initially the empty substitution, denoted by *id*). *Admissible steps* (a generalization of the classical *modus ponens* inference rule) are systematically applied on goals in a similar way to classical resolution steps in pure logic programming, thus returning a state composed by a computed substitution together with an expression where all atoms have been exploited. Next, during the so called interpretive phase (see [10,22]), this expression is interpreted under a given lattice, hence returning a pair ⟨*truth degree*; *substitution*⟩ which is the fuzzy counterpart of the classical notion of computed answer used in pure logic programming.

The main goal of the present paper is to present our last developments performed on the FLOPER system (see [1,21,24] and visit `http://www.dsi.uclm.es/investigacion/dect/FLOPERpage.htm`) which enables the introduction of different notions of multi-adjoint lattices for managing truth degrees even in a single work-session without changing a given multi-adjoint logic program and goal. Nowadays, the tool provides facilities for executing and debugging (by generating declarative traces) such kind of fuzzy programs, by means of two main representation (high/low-level, Prolog-based) ways which are somehow antagonistics regarding simplicity and accuracy features.

The structure of the paper is as follows. In Section 2, we summarize the main features of multi-adjoint logic programming, both language syntax and procedural semantics. Section 3 presents a discussion on multi-adjoint lattices and their nice representation by using standard Prolog code, in order to facilitate its further assimilation inside the FLOPER tool, as described in Section 4. Finally, in Section 5 we give our conclusions and some lines of future work.

2   Multi-adjoint Logic Programming

This section summarizes the main features of multi-adjoint logic programming (see [20,18,19] for a complete formulation of this framework). In what follows, we will use the abbreviation MALP for referencing programs belonging to this setting.

2.1   MALP Syntax

We work with a first order language, $\mathcal{L}$, containing variables, constants, function symbols, predicate symbols, and several (arbitrary) connectives to increase language expressiveness: implication connectives ($\leftarrow_1, \leftarrow_2, \ldots$); conjunctive operators (denoted by $\&_1, \&_2, \ldots$), disjunctive operators ($\vee_1, \vee_2, \ldots$), and hybrid operators (usually denoted by $@_1, @_2, \ldots$), all of them are grouped under the name of "aggregators".

Aggregation operators are useful to describe/specify user preferences. An aggregation operator, when interpreted as a truth function, may be an arithmetic mean, a weighted sum or in general any monotone application whose arguments are values of a complete bounded lattice L. For example, if an aggregator @ is interpreted as $[\![@]\!](x, y, z) = (3x + 2y + z)/6$, we are giving the highest preference to the first argument, then to the second, being the third argument the least significant.

Although these connectives are binary operators, we usually generalize them as functions with an arbitrary number of arguments. So, we often write $@(x_1, \ldots, x_n)$ instead of $@(x_1, \ldots, @(x_{n-1}, x_n), \ldots)$. By definition, the truth function for an n-ary aggregation operator $[\![@]\!] : L^n \to L$ is required to be monotonous and fulfills $[\![@]\!](\top, \ldots, \top) = \top$, $[\![@]\!](\bot, \ldots, \bot) = \bot$.

Additionally, our language $\mathcal{L}$ contains the values of a multi-adjoint lattice $\langle L, \preceq, \leftarrow_1, \&_1, \ldots, \leftarrow_n, \&_n \rangle$, equipped with a collection of *adjoint pairs* $\langle \leftarrow_i, \&_i \rangle$, where each $\&_i$ is a conjunctor which is intended to the evaluation of *modus ponens* [20]. More exactly, in this setting the following items must be satisfied:

- $\langle L, \preceq \rangle$ is a bounded lattice, i.e. it has bottom and top elements, denoted by $\bot$ and $\top$, respectively.
- Each operation $\&_i$ is increasing in both arguments.
- Each operation $\leftarrow_i$ is increasing in the first argument and decreasing in the second.
- If $\langle \&_i, \leftarrow_i \rangle$ is an *adjoint pair* in $\langle L, \preceq \rangle$ then, for any $x, y, z \in L$, we have that: $x \preceq (y \leftarrow_i z)$ if and only if $(x \&_i z) \preceq y$.

This last condition, called *adjoint property*, could be considered the most important feature of the framework (in contrast with many other approaches) which justifies most of its properties regarding crucial results for soundness, completeness, applicability, etc.

In general, L may be the carrier of any complete bounded lattice where a L-expression is a well-formed expression composed by values and connectives of L, as well as variable symbols and *primitive operators* (i.e., arithmetic symbols such as $*, +, min$, etc...).

In what follows, we assume that the truth function of any connective @ in L is given by its corresponding *connective definition*, that is, an equation of the form $@(x_1, \ldots, x_n) \triangleq E$, where E is a L-expression not containing variable symbols apart from $x_1, \ldots, x_n$. For instance, in what follows we will be mainly concerned with the following classical set of adjoint pairs (conjunctors and implications) in $\langle [0, 1], \leq \rangle$, where labels L, G and P mean respectively *Łukasiewicz logic*, *Gödel intuitionistic logic* and *product logic* (which different capabilities for modeling *pessimist*, *optimist* and *realistic scenarios*, respectively):

$$\&_P(x, y) \triangleq x * y \qquad\qquad \leftarrow_P (x, y) \triangleq \min(1, x/y) \qquad\qquad Product$$

$$\&_G(x, y) \triangleq \min(x, y) \qquad\qquad \leftarrow_G (x, y) \triangleq \begin{cases} 1 & \text{if } y \leq x \\ x & \text{otherwise} \end{cases} \qquad Gödel$$

$$\&_L(x, y) \triangleq \max(0, x + y - 1) \qquad \leftarrow_L (x, y) \triangleq \min\{x - y + 1, 1\} \qquad Łukasiewicz$$

A *rule* is a formula $H \leftarrow_i \mathcal{B}$, where H is an atomic formula (usually called the *head*) and $\mathcal{B}$ (which is called the *body*) is a formula built from atomic formulas $B_1, \ldots, B_n$ — $n \geq 0$ —, truth values of L, conjunctions, disjunctions and aggregations. A *goal* is a body submitted as a query to the system. Roughly speaking, a multi-adjoint logic program is a set of pairs $\langle \mathcal{R}; \alpha \rangle$ (we often write "$\mathcal{R}$ *with* α"), where $\mathcal{R}$ is a rule and α is a *truth degree* (a value of L) expressing the confidence of a programmer in the truth of rule $\mathcal{R}$. By abuse of language, we sometimes refer a tuple $\langle \mathcal{R}; \alpha \rangle$ as a "rule".

2.2   MALP Procedural Semantics

The procedural semantics of the multi–adjoint logic language $\mathcal{L}$ can be thought of as an operational phase (based on admissible steps) followed by an interpretive one. In the following, $\mathcal{C}[A]$ denotes a formula where A is a sub-expression which occurs in the –possibly empty– context $\mathcal{C}[]$. Moreover, $\mathcal{C}[A/A']$ means the replacement of A by A' in context $\mathcal{C}[]$, whereas $\mathcal{V}ar(s)$ refers to the set of distinct variables occurring in the syntactic object s, and $\theta[\mathcal{V}ar(s)]$ denotes the substitution obtained from θ by restricting its domain to $\mathcal{V}ar(s)$.

Definition 1 (Admissible Step). *Let $\mathcal{Q}$ be a goal and let σ be a substitution. The pair $\langle \mathcal{Q}; \sigma \rangle$ is a state and we denote by $\mathcal{E}$ the set of states. Given a program $\mathcal{P}$, an admissible computation is formalized as a state transition system, whose transition relation $\rightarrow_{AS} \subseteq (\mathcal{E} \times \mathcal{E})$ is the smallest relation satisfying the following admissible rules (where we always consider that A is the selected atom in $\mathcal{Q}$ and $mgu(E)$ denotes the most general unifier of an equation set E [14]):*

1) $\langle \mathcal{Q}[A]; \sigma \rangle \quad \rightarrow_{AS} \quad \langle (\mathcal{Q}[A/v\&_i\mathcal{B}])\theta; \sigma\theta \rangle$,
   if $\theta = mgu(\{A' = A\})$, $\langle A' \leftarrow_i \mathcal{B}; v \rangle$ in $\mathcal{P}$ and $\mathcal{B}$ is not empty.

2) $\langle \mathcal{Q}[A]; \sigma \rangle \quad \rightarrow_{AS} \quad \langle (\mathcal{Q}[A/v])\theta; \sigma\theta \rangle$,
   if $\theta = mgu(\{A' = A\})$ and $\langle A' \leftarrow_i; v \rangle$ in $\mathcal{P}$.

Note that the second case could be subsumed by the first one, after expressing each fact $\langle A' \leftarrow_i; v \rangle$ as a program rule of the form $\langle A' \leftarrow_i \top; v \rangle$. As usual, rules are taken renamed apart. We shall use the symbols $\rightarrow_{AS1}$ and $\rightarrow_{AS2}$ to distinguish between computation steps performed by applying one of the specific admissible rules. Also, the application of a rule on a step will be annotated as a superscript of the $\rightarrow_{AS}$ symbol.

Definition 2. *Let $\mathcal{P}$ be a program, $\mathcal{Q}$ a goal and "id" the empty substitution. An admissible derivation is a sequence $\langle \mathcal{Q}; id \rangle \rightarrow_{AS} \ldots \rightarrow_{AS} \langle \mathcal{Q}'; \theta \rangle$. When $\mathcal{Q}'$ is a formula not containing atoms (i.e., a L-expression), the pair $\langle \mathcal{Q}'; \sigma \rangle$, where $\sigma = \theta[\mathcal{V}ar(\mathcal{Q})]$, is called an admissible computed answer (a.c.a.) for that derivation.*

Example 1. Let $\mathcal{P}$ be the multi-adjoint fuzzy logic program described in Figure 1 where the equation defining the average aggregator $@_{\mathtt{aver}}$ must obviously has the form: $@_{\mathtt{aver}}(x_1, x_2) \triangleq (x_1 + x_2)/2$. Now, we can generate the admissible

---

Multi-adjoint logic program $\mathcal{P}$:

$$\begin{array}{llll}
\mathcal{R}_1: & p(X) & \leftarrow_\mathsf{P} \quad \&_\mathsf{G}(q(X), @_{\mathrm{aver}}(r(X), s(X))) & \textit{with} \quad 0.9 \\
\mathcal{R}_2: & q(a) & \leftarrow & \textit{with} \quad 0.8 \\
\mathcal{R}_3: & r(X) & \leftarrow & \textit{with} \quad 0.7 \\
\mathcal{R}_4: & s(X) & \leftarrow & \textit{with} \quad 0.5
\end{array}$$

Admissible derivation:

$\langle \underline{p(X)};\ id \rangle \hspace{6.5cm} \rightarrow_{AS1} {}^{\mathcal{R}_1}$

$\langle \&_\mathsf{P}(0.9, \&_\mathsf{G}(\underline{q(X_1)}, @_{\mathrm{aver}}(r(X1), s(X1))));\ \{X/X_1\} \rangle \hspace{0.8cm} \rightarrow_{AS2} {}^{\mathcal{R}_2}$

$\langle \&_\mathsf{P}(0.9, \&_\mathsf{G}(0.8, @_{\mathrm{aver}}(\underline{r(a)}, s(a))));\ \{X/a, X_1/a\} \rangle \hspace{0.6cm} \rightarrow_{AS2} {}^{\mathcal{R}_3}$

$\langle \&_\mathsf{P}(0.9, \&_\mathsf{G}(0.8, @_{\mathrm{aver}}(0.7, \underline{s(a)})));\ \{X/a, X_1/a, X_2/a\} \rangle \hspace{0.2cm} \rightarrow_{AS2} {}^{\mathcal{R}_4}$

$\langle \&_\mathsf{P}(0.9, \&_\mathsf{G}(0.8, @_{\mathrm{aver}}(0.7, \underline{0.5})));\ \{X/a, X_1/a, X_2/a, X_3/a\} \rangle$

Interpretive derivation:

$\langle \&_\mathsf{P}(0.9, \&_\mathsf{G}(0.8, \underline{@_{\mathrm{aver}}(0.7, 0.5)}));\ \{X/a\} \rangle \rightarrow_{IS}$

$\langle \&_\mathsf{P}(0.9, \&_\mathsf{G}(0.8, \underline{0.6}));\ \{X/a\} \rangle \hspace{1.6cm} \rightarrow_{IS}$

$\langle \&_\mathsf{P}(0.9, \underline{0.6});\ \{X/a\} \rangle \hspace{2.5cm} \rightarrow_{IS}$

$\langle \underline{0.54};\ \{X/a\} \rangle.$

Fig. 1. MALP program $\mathcal{P}$ with admissible/interpretive derivations for goal $p(X)$

derivation shown in Figure 1 (we underline the selected atom in each step). So, the admissible computed answer (a.c.a.) in this case is composed by the pair: $\langle \&_\mathsf{P}(0.9, \&_\mathsf{G}(0.8, @_{\mathrm{aver}}(0.7, 0.5)));\ \theta \rangle$, where θ only refers to bindings related with variables in the goal, i.e., $\theta = \{X/a, X_1/a, X_2/a, X_3/a\}[\mathcal{V}ar(p(X))] = \{X/a\}$.

If we exploit all atoms of a given goal, by applying admissible steps as much as needed during the operational phase, then it becomes a formula with no atoms (a L-expression) which can be then directly interpreted w.r.t. lattice L by applying the following definition we initially presented in [10]:

Definition 3 (Interpretive Step). *Let $\mathcal{P}$ be a program, $\mathcal{Q}$ a goal and σ a substitution. Assume that $[\![@]\!]$ is the truth function of connective $@$ in the lattice $\langle L, \preceq \rangle$ associated to $\mathcal{P}$, such that, for values $r_1, \ldots, r_n, r_{n+1} \in L$, we have that $[\![@]\!](r_1, \ldots, r_n) = r_{n+1}$. Then, we formalize the notion of* interpretive computa- *tion as a state transition system, whose transition relation $\rightarrow_{IS} \subseteq (\mathcal{E} \times \mathcal{E})$ is defined as the least one satisfying:*

$$\langle \mathcal{Q}[@(r_1, \ldots, r_n)];\ \sigma \rangle \quad \rightarrow_{IS} \quad \langle \mathcal{Q}[@(r_1, \ldots, r_n)/r_{n+1}];\ \sigma \rangle$$

Definition 4. *Let* $\mathcal{P}$ *be a program and* $\langle \mathcal{Q}; \sigma \rangle$ *an a.c.a., that is,* $\mathcal{Q}$ *is a goal not containing atoms (i.e., a L-expression). An* interpretive derivation *is a sequence* $\langle \mathcal{Q}; \sigma \rangle \rightarrow_{IS} \ldots \rightarrow_{IS} \langle \mathcal{Q}'; \sigma \rangle$. *When* $\mathcal{Q}' = r \in L$, *being* $\langle L, \preceq \rangle$ *the lattice associated to* $\mathcal{P}$, *the state* $\langle r; \sigma \rangle$ *is called a* fuzzy computed answer *(f.c.a.) for that derivation.*

Example 2. If we complete the previous derivation of Example 1 by applying 3 interpretive steps in order to obtain the final f.c.a. $\langle 0.54; \{X/a\} \rangle$, we generate the interpretive derivation shown in Figure 1.

3   Truth-Degrees and Multi-adjoint Lattices in Practice

We have recently conceived a very easy way to model truth-degree lattices for being included into the FLOPER tool. All relevant components of each lattice can be encapsulated inside a Prolog file which must necessarily contain the definitions of a minimal set of predicates defining the set of valid elements (including special mentions to the "top" and "bottom" ones), the full or partial ordering established among them, as well as the repertoire of fuzzy connectives which can be used for their subsequent manipulation. In order to simplify our explanation, assume that file "bool.pl" refers to the simplest notion of (a binary) adjoint lattice, thus implementing the following set of predicates:

- member/1 which is satisfied when being called with a parameter representing a valid truth degree. In the case of finite lattices, it is also recommend to implement members/1 which returns in one go a list containing the whole set of truth degrees. For instance, in the Boolean case, both predicates can be simply modeled by the Prolog facts: member(0)., member(1). and members([0,1]).

- bot/1 and top/1 obviously answer with the top and bottom element of the lattice, respectively. Both are implemented into "bool.pl" as bot(0). and top(1).

- leq/2 models the ordering relation among all the possible pairs of truth degrees, and obviously it is only satisfied when it is invoked with two elements verifying that the first parameter is equal or smaller than the second one. So, in our example it suffices with including into "bool.pl" the facts: leq(0,X). and leq(X,1).

- Finally, given some fuzzy connectives of the form $\&_{label_1}$ (conjunction), $\vee_{label_2}$ (disjunction) or $@_{label_3}$ (aggregation) with arities n_1, n_2 and n_3 respectively, we must provide clauses defining the *connective predicates* "and_$label_1$/(n_1+1)", "or_$label_2$/(n_2+1)" and "agr_$label_3$/(n_3+1)", where the extra argument of each predicate is intended to contain the result achieved after the evaluation of the proper connective. For instance, in the Boolean case, the following two facts model in a very easy way the behaviour of the classical conjunction operation: and_bool(0,_,0). and_bool(1,X,X).

```
member(X) :- number(X),0=<X,X=<1.   %% no members/1 (infinite lattice)

bot(0).                 top(1).               leq(X,Y) :- X=<Y.

and\_luka(X,Y,Z) :- pri_add(X,Y,U1),pri_sub(U1,1,U2),pri_max(0,U2,Z).
and_godel(X,Y,Z):- pri_min(X,Y,Z).
and_prod(X,Y,Z) :- pri_prod(X,Y,Z).

or_luka(X,Y,Z)  :- pri_add(X,Y,U1),pri_min(U1,1,Z).
or_godel(X,Y,Z) :- pri_max(X,Y,Z).
or_prod(X,Y,Z)  :- pri_prod(X,Y,U1),pri_add(X,Y,U2),pri_sub(U2,U1,Z).

agr_aver(X,Y,Z) :- pri_add(X,Y,U),pri_div(U,2,Z).

pri_add(X,Y,Z)  :- Z is X+Y.    pri_min(X,Y,Z) :- (X=<Y,Z=X;X>Y,Z=Y).
pri_sub(X,Y,Z)  :- Z is X-Y.    pri_max(X,Y,Z) :- (X=<Y,Z=Y;X>Y,Z=X).
pri_prod(X,Y,Z) :- Z is X * Y.  pri_div(X,Y,Z) :- Z is X/Y.
```

Fig. 2. Multi-adjoint lattice modeling truth degrees in the real interval [0,1] ("num.pl")

The reader can easily check that the use of lattice "bool.pl" when working with MALP programs whose rules have the form:
$$"A \ \leftarrow_{bool} \ \&_{bool}(B_1, \ldots, B_n) \ with \ 1"$$
.... being A and B_i typical atoms[1], successfully mimics the behaviour of classical Prolog programs where clauses accomplish with the shape "$A \ : - \ B_1, \ldots, B_n$". As a novelty in the fuzzy setting, when evaluating goals according to the procedural semantics described in Section 2, each output will contain the corresponding Prolog's substitution (i.e., the *crisp* notion of computed answer obtained by means of classical SLD-resolution) together with the maximum truth degree 1.

On the other hand and following the Prolog style regulated by the previous guidelines, in file "num.lat" we have included the clauses shown in Figure 2. Here, we have modeled the more flexible lattice (that we will mainly use in our examples, beyond the boolean case) which enables the possibility of working with truth degrees in the infinite space (note that this condition disables the implementation of the consulting predicate "members/1") of the real numbers between 0 and 1, allowing too the possibility of using conjunction and disjunction operators recasted from the three typical fuzzy logics proposals described before (i.e., the *Łukasiewicz*, *Gödel* and *product* logics), as well as a useful description for the hybrid aggregator *average*.

Note also that we have included definitions for auxiliary predicates, whose names always begin with the prefix "pri_". All of them are intended to describe primitive/arithmetic operators (in our case +, −, *, /, *min* and *max*) in a Prolog style, for being appropriately called from the bodies of clauses defining predicates with higher levels of expressivity (this is the case for instance, of the

---

[1] Here we also assume that several versions of the classical conjunction operation have been implemented with different arities.

three kinds of fuzzy connectives we are considering: conjuntions, disjunctions and agreggations).

Since till now we have considered two classical, fully ordered lattices (with a finite and infinite number of elements, collected in files "bool.pl" and "num.pl", respectively), we wish now to introduce a different case coping with a very simple lattice where not always any pair of truth degrees are comparable. So, consider the following partially ordered multi-adjoint lattice in the diagram below for which the conjunction and implication connectives based on the *Gödel* intuistionistic logic described in Section 2 conform an adjoint pair.... but with the particularity now that, in the general case, the *Gödel*'s conjunction must be expressed as $\&_G(x,y) \triangleq inf(x,y)$, where it is important to note that we must replace the use of "*min*" by "*inf*" in the connective definition.

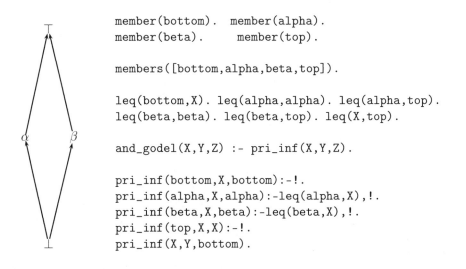

```
member(bottom).  member(alpha).
member(beta).    member(top).

members([bottom,alpha,beta,top]).

leq(bottom,X). leq(alpha,alpha). leq(alpha,top).
leq(beta,beta). leq(beta,top). leq(X,top).

and_godel(X,Y,Z) :- pri_inf(X,Y,Z).

pri_inf(bottom,X,bottom):-!.
pri_inf(alpha,X,alpha):-leq(alpha,X),!.
pri_inf(beta,X,beta):-leq(beta,X),!.
pri_inf(top,X,X):-!.
pri_inf(X,Y,bottom).
```

To this end, observe in the Prolog code accompanying the figure above that we have introduced five clauses defining the new primitive operator "pri_inf/3" which is intended to return the *infimum* of two elements. Related with this fact, we must point out the following aspects:

– Note that since truth degrees α and β (or their corresponding representations as Prolog terms "alpha" and "beta" used for instance in the definition(s) of "members(s)/1") are incomparable then, any call to goals of the form "?- leq(alpha,beta)." or "?- leq(beta,alpha)." will always fail.

– Fortunately, a goal of the form "?- pri_inf(alpha,beta,X).", or alternatively "?- pri_inf(beta,alpha,X).", instead of failing, successfully produces the desired result "X=bottom".

– Note anyway that the implementation of the "pri_inf/1" predicate is mandatory for coding the general definition of "and_godel/3".

4   The FLOPER System in Action

As detailed in [1,21], our parser has been implemented by using the classical DCG's (*Definite Clause Grammars*) resource of the Prolog language, since it is a convenient notation for expressing grammar rules. Once the application is loaded inside a Prolog interpreter (in our case, Sicstus Prolog v.3.12.5), it shows a menu which includes options for loading, parsing, listing and saving fuzzy programs, as well as for executing fuzzy goals (see Figure 3).

All these actions are based in the translation of the fuzzy code into standard Prolog code. The key point is to extend each atom with an extra argument, called *truth variable* of the form "_TV$_i$", which is intended to contain the truth degree obtained after the subsequent evaluation of the atom. For instance, the first clause in our target program is translated into:

```
p(X,_TV0)   :-  q(X,_TV1),
                r(X,_TV2),
                s(X,_TV3),
                agr_aver(_TV2,_TV3,_TV4),
                and_godel(_TV1,_TV4,_TV5),
                and_prod(0.9,_TV5,_TV0).
```

Moreover, the second clause in our target program, becomes the pure Prolog fact "q(a,0.8)" while a fuzzy goal like "p(X)", is translated into the pure Prolog goal: "p(X, Truth_degree)" (note that the last truth degree variable is not anonymous now) for which the Prolog interpreter returns the desired fuzzy computed answer [Truth_degree = 0.54, X = a]. The previous set of options suffices for running fuzzy programs (the "run" choice also uses the clauses contained in "num.pl", which represent the default lattice): all internal computations (including compiling and executing) are pure Prolog derivations whereas inputs (fuzzy programs and goals) and outputs (fuzzy computed answers) have always a fuzzy taste, thus producing the illusion on the final user of being working with a purely fuzzy logic programming tool.

On the other hand, as showed in the down-middle, dark part of Figure 3, FLOPER has been recently equipped with a new option, called "loadLat" for allowing the possibility of changing the multi-adjoint lattice associated to a given program. For instance, assume that "new_num.pl" contains the same Prolog code than "num.pl" with the exception of the definition regarding the average aggregator. Now, instead of computing the average of two truth degrees, let us consider the average between the results achieved after applying to both elements, the disjunctions operators described by Gödel and Łukasiewicz, that is: $@_{aver}(x_1, x_2) \triangleq (\vee_G(x_1, x_2) + \vee_L(x_1, x_2)) * 0.5$. The corresponding Prolog clause modeling such definition into the "new_num.pl" file could be:

```
agr_aver(X,Y,Z)   :-  or_godel(X,Y,Z1),
                      or_luka(X,Y,Z2),
                      pri_add(Z1,Z2,Z3),
                      pri_prod(Z3,0.5,Z).
```

Fig. 3. Example of a work session with FLOPER showing "Small Interpretive Steps" and program/goal menus

and now, by selecting again the "run" option (without changing the program and goal), the system would display the new solution: [Truth_degree = 0.72, X = a].

However, when trying to go beyond program execution, the previous method becomes insufficient. In particular, observe that we can only simulate complete fuzzy derivations (by performing the corresponding Prolog derivations based on SLD-resolution) but we can not generate partial derivations or even apply a single admissible step on a given fuzzy expression. This kind of low-level manipulations are mandatory when trying to incorporate to the tool some program transformation techniques such as those based on fold/unfold (i.e., contraction and expansion of sub-expressions of a program using the definitions of this program or of a preceding one, thus generating more efficient code) or partial evaluation we have described in [5,9,12]. For instance, our fuzzy unfolding transformation is defined as the replacement of a program rule $\mathcal{R} : (A \leftarrow_i B \text{ with } v)$ by the set of rules $\{A\sigma \leftarrow_i B' \text{ with } v \mid \langle B; id \rangle \rightarrow_{AS} \langle B'; \sigma \rangle\}$, which obviously requires the implementation of mechanisms for generating derivations of a single step, rearranging the body of a program rule, applying substitutions to its head, etc.

To this end, in [21] we have presented a new low-level representation for the fuzzy code which currently offers the possibility of performing debugging actions such as tracing a FLOPER work session. The idea is collect in detail all relevant components associated to each fuzzy rule, such as its number inside the program, composition of the atom conforming its head, kind of implication connecting the head and its body, details about connectives and atoms composing this body

and attached weight. For instance, after parsing the first rule of our program, we
obtain the following expression which is *asserted* into the interpreter's database
as a Prolog fact (which it is never executed directly, in contrast with the high-
level, Prolog-based representation, showed at the beginning of this section):

```
rule(1,
     head(atom(pred(p,1),[var('X')])),
     impl(prod),
     body(and(godel,2,
                     [ atom(pred(q,1),[var('X')]),
                       agr(aver,2,[ atom(pred(r,1),[var('X')]),
                                    atom(pred(s,1),[var('X')])
                                  ]
                          )
                     ]
               )
         ),
     td(0.9)
    ).
```

Two more examples: substitutions are modeled by lists of terms of the form
link(V, T) where V and T contains the code associated to an original variable
and its corresponding (linked) fuzzy term, respectively, whereas a state is represented by a term with functor state/2. We have implemented predicates for
manipulating such kind of code at a very low level in order to unify expressions,
compose substitutions, apply admisible/interpretive steps, etc...

Looking again to the darked part of Figure 3, observe in the FLOPER's
goal menu the "**tree**" and "**depth**" options, which are useful for tracing execution trees and fixing the maximum length allowed for their branches (initially
3), respectively. Working with these options is crucial when the "**run**" choice
fails: remember that this last option is based on the generation of pure logic
SLD-derivations which might fall in loop or directly fail in some cases as the
experiments of [21] show, in contrast with the traces (based on finite, non-failed,
admissible derivations) that the "**tree**" option displays. As we are going to
illustrate in what follows, the system displays states on different lines, appropriately indented to distinguish the proper relationship -parent/child/grandchild...-
among nodes on unfolding trees. Each node contains an state (composed by the
corresponding goal and substitution) preceded by the number of the program
rule used by the admissible step leading to it (root nodes always labeled with
the virtual, non existing rule R0).

Strongly related with these last options, the "**ismode**" choice showed at the
bottom of Figure 3, decides among three levels of detail when visualizing the
interpretive phase performed during the generation of "unfolding trees". It is important to remark that together with the possibility of introducing multi-adjoint
lattices, it represents our last record achieved in the development of the FLOPER
tool. When the user selects such choice, three options are offered:

• "Large" means to obtain the final result in one go. For instance, for our running example (with the second notion of "average") FLOPER draws:

```
R0 <p(X),{}>
 R1 <&prod(0.9,&godel(q(X1),@aver(r(X1),s(X1)))),{X/X1} >
  R2 <&prod(0.9,&godel(0.8,@aver(r(a),s(a)))),{X/a,X1/a}>
   R3 <&prod(0.9,&godel(0.8,@aver(0.7,s(a)))),{X/a,X1/a,X11/a}>
    R4 <&prod(0.9,&godel(0.8,@aver(0.7,0.5))),{X/a,X1/a,X11/a}>
     result < 0.7200000000000001,{X/a,X1/a,X11/a}>
```

• "Medium" implements the notion of "interpretive step" according Definition 3 [10] which in our case produces the picture (note here that those states produces during the interpretive phase are preceded by the word "is" instead of the number of a program rule, since no rules are exploited in this case in contrast with admissible steps):

```
R0 <p(X),{}>
 R1 <&prod(0.9,&godel(q(X1),@aver(r(X1),s(X1)))),{X/X1}>
  R2 <&prod(0.9,&godel(0.8,@aver(r(a),s(a)))),{X/a,X1/a}>
   R3 <&prod(0.9,&godel(0.8,@aver(0.7,s(a)))),{X/a,X1/a,X11/a}>
    R4 <&prod(0.9,&godel(0.8,@aver(0.7,0.5))),{X/a,X1/a,X11/a}>
     is <&prod(0.9,&godel(0.8,0.85)),{X/a,X1/a,X11/a,_16/a}>
      is <&prod(0.9,0.8),{X/a,X1/a,X11/a,_16/a}>
       is <0.7200000000000001,{X/a,X1/a,X11/a,_16/a}>
```

• "Small" allows to visualize in detail both the direct/indirect calls to connective definitions and primitive operators performed along the whole interpretive phase (see [22,24]). The reader can observe at the beginning of Figure 3, the aspect offered by FLOPER when visualizing in detail the behaviour of our running example, where the set of "small interpretive steps" are (we omit here the initial fourth states- associated to admissible steps- since they coincide with our two last illustrations above):

```
...
 R4 <&prod(0.9,&godel(0.8,@aver(0.7,0.5))),{X/a,X1/a,X11/a,_16/a}>
  sis1 <&prod(0.9,&godel(0.8,#prod(#add(|godel(0.7,0.5),|luka( ..
   sis1 <&prod(0.9,&godel(0.8,#prod(#add(#max(0.7,0.5),|luka(0.7.
    sis2 <&prod(0.9,&godel(0.8,#prod(#add(0.7,|luka(0.7,0.5)), ..
     sis1 <&prod(0.9,&godel(0.8,#prod(#add(0.7,#min(#add(0.7, ...
      sis2 <&prod(0.9,&godel(0.8,#prod(#add(0.7,#min(1.2,1)), ...
       sis2 <&prod(0.9,&godel(0.8,#prod(#add(0.7,1),0.5))), .....
        sis2 <&prod(0.9,&godel(0.8,#prod(1.7,0.5))), {X/a,X1/a ..
         sis2 <&prod(0.9,&godel(0.8,0.85)), {X/a,X1/a,X11/a, ....
          sis1 <&prod(0.9,#min(0.8,0.85)), {X/a,X1/a,X11/a, .....
           sis2 <&prod(0.9,0.8), {X/a,X1/a,X11/a,_16/a}>
            sis1 <#prod(0.9,0.8), {X/a,X1/a,X11/a,_16/a}>
             sis2 <0.7200000000000001, {X/a,X1/a,X11/a,_16/a}>
```

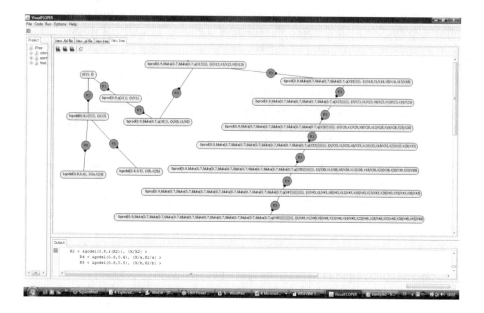

Fig. 4. Building a graphical interface for FLOPER

Observe in this last case that during the interpretive phase we apply "small interpretive steps" of kind $\rightarrow_{SIS1}$ or $\rightarrow_{SIS2}$ (according to [24]). The intuitive idea is that, whereas a $\rightarrow_{SIS1}$ step "expands" a connective definition on the next state, the role of evaluating primitive operators is played by $\rightarrow_{SIS2}$ steps. Notice in the figure that each primitive operators is always labeled by prefix "#"). These facts justify why in our Prolog-based implementation of multi-adjoint lattices, clauses defining connective predicates only perform calls to predicates of the form "and_*", "or_*", "agr_*" (useful for identifying further $\rightarrow_{SIS1}$ steps) or "pri_*" (associated to $\rightarrow_{SIS2}$ steps).

5   Conclusions and Future Work

The experience acquired in our research group regarding the design of techniques and methods based on fuzzy logic in close relationship with the so-called multi-adjoint logic programming approach ([10,5,9,11,12,7,8,22,23]), has motivated our interest for putting in practice all our developments around the design of the FLOPER environment [21,24]. Our philosophy is to friendly connect this fuzzy framework with Prolog programmers: our system, apart for being implemented in Prolog, also translates the fuzzy code to classical clauses (in two different representations) and, what is more, in this paper we have also shown that a wide range of lattices modeling powerful and flexible notions of truth degrees also admit a nice rule-based characterizations into Prolog.

Apart for our ongoing efforts devoted to providing FLOPER with a graphical interface as illustrated in Figure 4[2], nowadays we are especially interested in extending the tool with testing techniques for automatically checking that lattices modeled according the Prolog-based method established in this paper, verify the requirements of our fuzzy setting (with special mention to the *adjoint property*). For the future, we have in mind to provide an interface with rules written in Fuzzy-RuleML and other fuzzy languages like the ones presented in [26,13] (the XSB system supports GAP).

References

1. Abietar, J.M., Morcillo, P.J., Moreno, G.: Designing a software tool for fuzzy logic programming. In: Simos, T.E., Maroulis, G. (eds.) Proc. of the International Conference of Computational Methods in Sciences and Engineering ICCMSE 2007. Computation in Modern Science and Engineering, vol. 2, pp. 1117–1120. American Institute of Physics (distributed by Springer) (2007)
2. Baldwin, J.F., Martin, T.P., Pilsworth, B.W.: Fril- Fuzzy and Evidential Reasoning in Artificial Intelligence. John Wiley & Sons, Inc., Chichester (1995)
3. Bratko, I.: Prolog Programming for Artificial Intelligence. Addison Wesley, Reading (September 2000)
4. Guadarrama, S., Muñoz, S., Vaucheret, C.: Fuzzy Prolog: A new approach using soft constraints propagation. Fuzzy Sets and Systems 144(1), 127–150 (2004)
5. Guerrero, J.A., Moreno, G.: Optimizing fuzzy logic programs by unfolding, aggregation and folding. Electronic Notes in Theoretical Computer Science 219, 19–34 (2008)
6. Ishizuka, M., Kanai, N.: Prolog-ELF Incorporating Fuzzy Logic. In: Joshi, A.K. (ed.) Proceedings of the 9th Int. Joint Conference on Artificial Intelligence, IJCAI 1985, pp. 701–703. Morgan Kaufmann, San Francisco (1985)
7. Julián, P., Medina, J., Moreno, G., Ojeda, M.: Thresholded tabulation in a fuzzy logic setting. Electronic Notes in Theoretical Computer Science 248, 115–130 (2009)
8. Julián, P., Medina, J., Moreno, G., Ojeda, M.: Efficient thresholded tabulation for fuzzy query answering. Studies in Fuzziness and Soft Computing (Foundations of Reasoning under Uncertainty) 249, 125–141 (2010)
9. Julián, P., Moreno, G., Penabad, J.: On Fuzzy Unfolding. A Multi-adjoint Approach. Fuzzy Sets and Systems 154, 16–33 (2005)
10. Julián, P., Moreno, G., Penabad, J.: Operational/Interpretive Unfolding of Multi-adjoint Logic Programs. Journal of Universal Computer Science 12(11), 1679–1699 (2006)
11. Julián, P., Moreno, G., Penabad, J.: Measuring the interpretive cost in fuzzy logic computations. In: Masulli, F., Mitra, S., Pasi, G. (eds.) WILF 2007. LNCS (LNAI), vol. 4578, pp. 28–36. Springer, Heidelberg (2007)
12. Julián, P., Moreno, G., Penabad, J.: An Improved Reductant Calculus using Fuzzy Partial Evaluation Techniques. Fuzzy Sets and Systems 160, 162–181 (2009), doi:10.1016/j.fss.2008.05.006
13. Kifer, M., Subrahmanian, V.S.: Theory of generalized annotated logic programming and its applications. Journal of Logic Programming 12, 335–367 (1992)

---

[2] Here we show an unfolding tree evidencing an infinite branch where states are colored in yellow and program rules exploited in admissible steps are enclosed in circles.

14. Lassez, J.L., Maher, M.J., Marriott, K.: Unification Revisited. In: Minker, J. (ed.) Foundations of Deductive Databases and Logic Programming, pp. 587–625. Morgan Kaufmann, Los Altos (1988)
15. Li, D., Liu, D.: A fuzzy Prolog database system. John Wiley & Sons, Inc., Chichester (1990)
16. Lloyd, J.W.: Foundations of Logic Programming, 2nd edn. Springer, Berlin (1987)
17. Lloyd, J.W.: Declarative programming for artificial intelligence applications. SIG-PLAN Not. 42(9), 123–124 (2007)
18. Medina, J., Ojeda-Aciego, M., Vojtáš, P.: Multi-adjoint logic programming with continuous semantics. In: Eiter, T., Faber, W., Truszczyński, M. (eds.) LPNMR 2001. LNCS (LNAI), vol. 2173, pp. 351–364. Springer, Heidelberg (2001)
19. Medina, J., Ojeda-Aciego, M., Vojtáš, P.: A procedural semantics for multi-adjoint logic programming. In: Brazdil, P.B., Jorge, A.M. (eds.) EPIA 2001. LNCS (LNAI), vol. 2258, pp. 290–297. Springer, Heidelberg (2001)
20. Medina, J., Ojeda-Aciego, M., Vojtáš, P.: Similarity-based Unification: a multi-adjoint approach. Fuzzy Sets and Systems 146, 43–62 (2004)
21. Morcillo, P.J., Moreno, G.: Programming with Fuzzy Logic Rules by using the FLOPER Tool. In: Bassiliades, N., Governatori, G., Paschke, A. (eds.) RuleML 2008. LNCS, vol. 5321, pp. 119–126. Springer, Heidelberg (2008)
22. Morcillo, P.J., Moreno, G.: Modeling interpretive steps in fuzzy logic computations. In: Di Gesù, V., Pal, S.K., Petrosino, A. (eds.) WILF 2009. LNCS (LNAI), vol. 5571, pp. 44–51. Springer, Heidelberg (2009)
23. Morcillo, P.J., Moreno, G.: On cost estimations for executing fuzzy logic programs. In: Arabnia, H.R., de la Fuente, D., Olivas, J.A. (eds.) Proceedings of the 11th International Conference on Artificial Intelligence, ICAI 2009, Las Vegas, Nevada, USA, July 13-16, pp. 217–223. CSREA Press (2009)
24. Morcillo, P.J., Moreno, G., Penabad, J., Vázquez, C.: Modeling interpretive steps into the FLOPER environment. In: Proceedings of the 12th International Conference on Artificial Intelligence, ICAI 2010, Las Vegas, Nevada, USA, July 12-15, CSREA Press (2010) (accepted for publication)
25. Straccia, U.: Query answering in normal logic programs under uncertainty. In: Godo, L. (ed.) ECSQARU 2005. LNCS (LNAI), vol. 3571, pp. 687–700. Springer, Heidelberg (2005)
26. Straccia, U.: Managing uncertainty and vagueness in description logics, logic programs and description logic programs. In: Baroglio, C., Bonatti, P.A., Małuszyński, J., Marchiori, M., Polleres, A., Schaffert, S. (eds.) Reasoning Web. LNCS, vol. 5224, pp. 54–103. Springer, Heidelberg (2008)
27. Vojtáš, P.: Fuzzy Logic Programming. Fuzzy Sets and Systems 124(1), 361–370 (2001)

A Rule-Based Implementation of Fuzzy Tableau Reasoning

Stefano Bragaglia, Federico Chesani, Paola Mello, and Davide Sottara

DEIS, University of Bologna,
Viale Risorgimento, 2
40136 - Bologna, Italy
name.surname@unibo.it

Abstract. The integration of distinct reasoning styles such as the ones exploited by description logics and rule-based systems is still an open challenge because of the differences among them. Such integration may be achieved by following two complementary approaches: loose integration vs. tight integration. Loosely integrated hybrid systems couple existing tools, so they have to handle mutual interactions and keep their models aligned. Tightly-coupled hybrid systems, instead, are based on a unified model supporting both reasoning styles.

In this paper we present a basic implementation of a fuzzy tableau algorithm for description logics by means of rules. It is a step towards tight integration because it requires only one rule engine while preserving the semantics of both reasoning styles. In particular, the adoption of a fuzzy tableau in a fuzzy rule engine allowed us to extend the expressiveness of the latter while handling description logics reasoning coherently.

Keywords: Rule-Based Systems, Description Logic, Tableau Reasoning, Fuzzy Systems.

1 Introduction

Recently, there has been a growing interest about the combination of domain representation systems based on some type of Description Logics, and rule-based systems, mainly in the context of the Semantic Web technologies.

Description Logics (and the Semantic Web initiative) already provide languages and tools for representing and reasoning upon a certain domain. In particular, formal languages for knowledge representation are given, together with algorithms for detecting inconsistencies, for classifying new concepts (w.r.t. previous knowledge), and for recognizing individuals w.r.t. to a given set (hierarchy) of concepts. Rule-based systems, instead, have been largely used to express applications logic in terms of rules, thus easing the process of coding the high-level logic (the *business* logic) into a procedural-like, executable specification. Rule-based systems take as input external stimuli (the happening of events) and react (by triggering the rules) producing some effects. The causal relation between observed facts (inputs) and the observed effects (outcomes) is defined by the rules that the user specifies as "knowledge base".

M. Dean et al. (Eds.): RuleML 2010, LNCS 6403, pp. 35–49, 2010.

As both these technologies are reaching a good maturity level, the need for a comprehensive and unifying approach is emerging. As recognized also in [1,9,26], domain-based applications could greatly benefit from such integration, at both the levels of language expressiveness, as well as at the level of algorithms and reasoning tools. Several solutions have been already proposed in the literature, either achieving this integration in a *loosely* manner [12,2], or with a more *tighter* integration [17,28]. However, such attempts have been limited by many theoretical issues. To cite one, Description Logics are usually based on the *Open World Assumption* (OWA), while rule-based reasoners often assume the *Close World Assumption* (CWA) hypothesis: combining both the assumptions without providing a comprehensive semantics turns to be very hard. Moreover, a further aspect is emerging as of fundamental importance when dealing with real-life domains: the Description Logics adopted within the Semantic Web initiative support only "crisp" concepts and formulas, but more realistic models should also allow for imperfection [30]. Indeed, several works have already tried to integrate the different concepts: technological integration of rule-based and DL-based systems has been studied [3,10] and even implemented within several existing frameworks. Similarly, many researches has been carried out on the integration of imperfect reasoning and logic-based system, both rule-based and description-oriented. In the latter case, in particular, both probabilistic and/or fuzzy extensions of DL have been proposed: a detailed survey can be found in [31]. To the best of our knowledge, however, no mainstream tool supporting ontological reasoning, rule-based reasoning, and fuzzy reasoning at the same time is currently available.

In this paper, we present our preliminary results about a more comprehensive approach to all these aspects. Building on previous works [8], we aim to achieve a tighter integration, where a single reasoner accommodates for rule-based, DL-aware, and fuzzy-based reasoning. To this end, we start from Drools Chance [22], a fuzzy-capable extension of the state-of-the-art rule-based reasoner Drools[1]. By means of a semantics based on many-valued fuzzy logic, we can model both the OWA and the CWA reasoning styles in terms of fuzzy intervals attached to each conclusion. Moreover, our framework allows for a unified, single representation of rules, A-Box and T-Box facts/axioms.

The paper is organized as follows: Section 2 is dedicated to an analysis of the related works and existing solutions; Section 3, instead, describes the proposed solution and discusses some examples.

2   Integrating RBSs with DLs

2.1   Rule-based vs. Description-Oriented Reasoning

In general, integrating different reasoning styles is a rather difficult task, since quite often the assumptions made by one of them does not meet the requirements of the others, and vice versa. In particular, [13,24,29] has determined that the

---

[1] http://jboss.org/drools

combination of ontological and rule-based reasoning is especially tricky because of the *Open World Assumption* and the *Closed World Assumption*.

As explained by [27], rule-based systems are typically based on the Closed World Assumption, which basically says that everything not explicitly asserted as true has to be considered as false. This assumption allows to infer the most information possible from available data. However, it makes the inference non--monotonic, in the sense that any new information may invalidate some of the deduction done so far. So, this type of inference can be applied when the available facts are reasonably stable, i.e., all the information available at a certain time has already been collected. On the contrary, ontologies and description logics in general adhere to the Open World Assumption, which only considers true (or false) what can be effectively determined as such. This kind of inference is actually safer than the previous one since new conclusions never contradict the rest of the knowledge, but the price to pay is that some formulas can neither be proven to be true, nor false.

Technically speaking, a successful integration is also difficult to achieve because it soon leads to undecidability. As depicted by [19], in fact, DL models are often infinite and, being their knowledge incomplete, they can be completed in several ways. Rule languages, instead, are meant to query finite knowledge bases or, in the worst case, finitely enumerable structures. Problems, then, may arise when knowledge is not restricted properly since it may prevent the system mixing both reasoning styles from being decidable. Nevertheless, [1,9,26] showed that the combination of such reasoning paradigms is a fundamental case in many domains.

2.2   Loose vs. Tight Integration

From a methodological point of view, the possible integration approaches can be reduced to three [10]: two of them, namely *loose* and *tight* integration, are complementary while the third, *embedded* integration, can be seen a compromise between the other two. Loosely-coupled systems delegate each reasoning task they support to different sub-systems, so they require a preliminary study to identify which reasoners are available and their peculiarity in terms of expressiveness and ease of integration: once the most appropriate set of tool has been identified, a unifying framework has to be created to enable interoperability between tools by means of entailment, to keep the knowledge within their models aligned and finally to hide the implementative details.

The implementation of tightly-coupled systems, instead, involves (i) the definition of a coherent theory enough complex to support all the desired reasoning styles; and (ii) the development of a single reasoner able to understand its language and semantics, and to manage the expressed knowledge accordingly.

As we had the opportunity to experience in a previous work ([8] in which we developed an initial loosely-integrated solution based on Drools, Pellet and FuzzyDL), tightly--integrated systems typically show better expressiveness and performance at the cost of a higher degree of complexity whereas loosely-integrated ones are simpler but still challenging due to aligning issues.

Eventually, embedded solutions tend to combine the simplicity of the approaches based on loose integration with the expressiveness (and possibly the efficiency) of tightly-coupled systems by implanting several reasoning behaviours into a unique system exploiting a unified formalism.

2.3 Existing Approaches

There exist several concrete solutions combining rule- and DL-based reasoning at the same time.

Jena[2] is a flexible framework adopting mainly a loosely-based approach: it includes a hybrid forward/backward chaining rule engine, but also allows to plug in different reasoners to support the other required reasoning styles. Likewise, SweetRules[3], is an even richer integrated toolkit for semantic web revolving around RuleML and many other W3C standards that works with ontologies. Algernon[4], instead, is a forward/backward chaining rule reasoner embedded in Protégé: the rule engine processes and manipulates the facts inferred from the ontology, possibly expanding it. Similarly, the *CLASSIC DL* reasoner adopts simple procedural rules (equivalent to plain horn rules), on top of an ontology which can be exploited to evaluate such rules [12].

A tighter approach has been adopted in O-Device [21], where the axioms of DL are converted in FOL and then rewritten using rules. As will be discussed in Section 3, however, this approach poses some additional limitations.

An even tighter level of integration requires the definition of a common logic framework: the intersection of logic programs and description logics, rooted in the common origins of first order logic, has been found and named *Description Logics Program (DLP)* by [14] and a translation procedure has been proposed by [18]. Thanks to those advancements, [25] has developed *dlpconvert*, a tool that converts and handles the DLP fragment of OWL ontologies to Datalog clauses. In [23] and [20], the authors define practices to reason upon large amount of individuals within description logics by exploiting respectively bottom-up Datalog and Deductive Database inference (with $\mathcal{SHOIN}$ expressiveness) and top-down Prolog resolution (with $\mathcal{SHIQ}$ expressiveness). Moreover, since Deductive Database supports rules natively, an extension capable of full rule handling can be achieved by simply appending rules to the existing knowledge base.

Despite their remarkable expressive power, none of these systems supports non-boolean reasoning natively. Actually, there exist several tools supporting "fuzzy logic", but one has to distinguish between the ones implementing "fuzzy logic in a broad sense" [15], from those which intend fuzzy logic in the mathematical sense. Nevertheless, in the context of rule-based reasoning, Clips and Jess had a proper fuzzy extension (FuzzyClips[5] and FuzzyJess[6] respectively), in addition to other attempts to integrate generic logic programming and fuzzy

---

[2] http://jena.sourceforge.net/

[3] http://sweetrules.semwebcentral.org

[4] http://algernon-j.sourceforge.net/

[5] http://www.nrc-cnrc.gc.ca/eng/projects/iit/fuzzy-reasoning.html

[6] http://www.csie.ntu.edu.tw/~sylee/courses/FuzzyJ/FuzzyJess.htm

logic such as FRIL [5], a prolog-like language and interpreter. In parallel, many theoretical works [31] show the possibility to integrate an uncertain semantic in several families of DLs, but only a few concrete systems actually exist, such as DeLorean[7], FiRe[8] and FuzzyDL[9].

3   Embedding (Fuzzy) DL Reasoning in Production Rules

3.1   A Few Considerations on Integration Issues

Recently, Business Logic Integration Platforms (BLIP) have become relevant tools for the modelling of business processes and to provide support during their execution, possibly in distributed and heterogeneous contexts such as the world wide web. Most of such tools use rules to encode the business logic and exploit (production) rule engines to execute them, finding applications in fields - just to cite some of the ones we are involved in - ranging from environmental defence to tourism to medicine. When different parties are involved, it is convenient to share a common language allowing to exchange information: while initiatives such as RuleML and RIF provide a solution at the syntactic level, defining a standard language, an appealing way to share semantics is to build rules on top of some mutually recognized ontology.

The integration of an ontology in a rule-based system, then, poses several issues: (i) there should be a way for the engine to import an existing ontology as well as a way to define it internally; (ii) the engine should be capable to query the ontology, since an ontology usually asserts a compact model which allows to infer additional implicit information; (iii) the conditions expressed in the rules should be defined using the concepts from the ontology T-Box and evaluated against entities in the ontology A-Box.

Drools is possibly the only open source BLIP offering many of the advanced functionalities useful for the development of business applications, from workflow to event to planning capabilities, but unfortunately lacks support for "semantic" applications. One of the goals of this paper, then, is to use it as a case study, showing a possible way to embed DL reasoning natively in the object-oriented production rule system.

The theoretical possibility of integrating a rule-based system with an ontologic description has been discussed in [3], where it is shown that basic RDF and RDFS reasoning can be performed using an appropriate set of rules, transforming the axioms in an appropriate set of FOL formulas which, in turn, can be translated into rules. Moreover, the same procedure can be applied to OWL axioms, obtaining rules which use transitivity, symmetry, domain/range, inverse, type and inheritance relations to compute the closure of a (descriptive) knowledge base. A concrete implementation of this approach using a a RETE-based engine is described in [21].

---

[7] http://webdiis.unizar.es/~fbobillo/delorean.php

[8] http://www.image.ece.ntua.gr/~nsimou/FiRE/

[9] http://gaia.isti.cnr.it/~straccia/software/fuzzyDL/fuzzyDL.html

This implementation of DL reasoning, however, has a few relevant differences from its counterpart in more dedicated "semantic" reasoners. First of all, the former adopts the CWA while the latter uses the OWA: this means, for example, that an individual x could be considered a member, say, of a class defined by the concept $\forall R.C$ by a rule-based reasoner, but not by a semantic one, because even if all the known instances y such that $R(x, y)$ holds have type C, there could always exist another R-related element z for which $C(z)$ does not hold. While this "pragmatic" behaviour may be desirable in some cases, the user should be allowed to choose which approach to use according to the application's needs.

Moreover, while (CWA) *testing* (i.e. deciding whether an entity belongs to a class defined by a concept) and thus *recognition* (i.e. finding the most specific concept(s) an instance is member of) involve a particular A-box instance, a pure T-box problem such as *subsumption* (i.e. deciding whether a concept is a subconcept of another or not) and then *classification* (i.e. reconstructing the minimal hierarchy given a set of concepts) [4] can't be performed safely and soundly using only the limited population of individuals present in the A-box at a given moment.

These problems motivated the search for a way to integrate the reasoning style of a semantic engine in a rule-based one, in addition to importing the facts and concepts contained in a semantic rule base. Given that reasoning under OWA can be modelled more naturally using a 3-valued logic instead of a boolean one, the choice of Drools becomes even more convenient because such a logic is supported using the Drools Chance extension [22] which is currently being developed as a part of the core engine. Moreover, the same extension supports different (interval) many-valued fuzzy logics: in the rest of this section, then, we will discuss how this feature allows to integrate a simple many-valued description logic and its related reasoning framework in a seamless way.

3.2   Proposed Architecture

Loose Integration. In a previous work [8], we experimented with a loose integration of rule-based and semantic reasoning, using Drools as main system and invoking the subordinated reasoners - Pellet and FuzzyDL - as needed. Drools offers two convenient ways to do so : custom evaluators - pluggable interfaces for predicate evaluation functions - and fact pulling using the featured keyword from. Exploiting the Jena framework and the JenaBeans API, as in rule 1.1, it is possible to invoke a reasoner like Pellet for recognition purposes whenever a fact is matched against a pattern. Jena automatically serializes an annotated (Java) object into its description, feeds it to Pellet, performs the query and recovers the result. A similar approach allows to interact with FuzzyDL, but the (de)serialization operations have to be performed manually. The second alternative, instead, is to retrieve previously inferred facts from the external reasoner's working memory, exposed by Jena as a collection.

This trivial approach turned out to be unsatisfactory from many point of views: each one of the different reasoners uses a private knowledge base and a private working memory, which must be kept aligned at the cost of some communication overhead; moreover, the initial mapping requires a considerable effort from the user.

Listing 1.1. Loose integration example

```
rule "Loose1"
when
    $o : Object( this isA "SomeConcept" )
    $p : Statement( predicate == "Prop", ... )
        from inferredModel
then ... end
```

Embedded Integration Overview. To avoid these additional costs, we studied the possibility of emulating the behaviour of a semantic reasoner using production rules, thus allowing to share knowledge and data between the reasoners - in fact, using only one reasoner and allowing the user to choose the desired behaviour. It turns out that a fuzzy tableau algorithm such as the one proposed by Straccia and Bobillo in [7] can easily be adapted and integrated in a RETE network according to the procedure described in this section. More properly, one can consider a family of related tableaux algorithms which depend on two main degrees of freedom: the expressiveness of the description logic used to *construct* the formulas and the family of many-valued logic used to *evaluate* them.

The latter issue is already addressed in Drools Chance, which can be configured to use different "imperfect" logic frameworks (e.g. many-valued or probabilistic logic) combined with different models of generalized truth degrees (e.g. real values, intervals, fuzzy numbers, ...). Being natively supported in the rule engine working memory, the fuzzy tableau rules can draw the fuzzy facts directly from it; likewise, the inferred semantic facts can trigger other rules naturally, with their associated degrees combined and propagated in a transparent way. The proposed architecture, then, can be outlined as shown in Figure 1:

1. A set of semantic concept definitions, expressed using an extended version of Drools' native DRL language, is parsed. The same intermediate Abstract Sytntax Tree (AST) representation could be obtained by parsing a T-Box expressed in some more standard language.
2. The resulting AST is visited to build a set of rules which, all together, implement a (fuzzy) tableau. In particular, appropriate rule templates are instantiated as will be discussed in Section 3.3
3. The same intermediate AST can be built from the parsing of other standard ontology languages
4. Optionally, the AST can be used to build CWA recognition rules, as in [21]
5. Optionally, the AST can be used to build dynamic beans, as in [21]. This feature is currently under development
6. The rules are compiled and merged in the main RETE

Language extensions. While there exist several families of Description Logics[10] with different expressiveness and complexity, at the moment our prototype supports only a many-valued extension of $\mathcal{ALC}$, where derived concepts are defined by equivalence within an acyclic T-Box based on Lukasiewicz's logic. The

---

[10] http://dl.kr.org

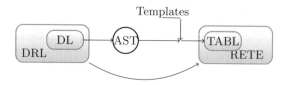

Fig. 1. Architecture Outline

language and the semantics of its fuzzy extension are the usual as can be found in [32] and [7]. The limitations on the language, which will be addressed in future works, reduce its expressiveness, but guarantee the correctness of several reasoning algorithms [6].

To be compatible with the existing Drools language, we decided to extend the DRL `declare` feature, adopting the Manchester syntax [16]. Originally, this construct had been designed to declare beans "on-the-fly" by listing the fields and their types. In [21], it has been shown that this is equivalent to a fragment of $\mathcal{ALC}$ with number restriction and concrete datatypes: in fact, the declaration of a field F of type T is equivalent to the constructor $\exists_{\leq 1} F.T$.

So, legacy declarations can be assimilated to a conjunction of $\exists R.C$ statements[11]. Extended ones, instead, can exploit the standard connective constructors, mapped using the keywords `and`, `or` and `not`, and the quantified ones, mapped using the keywords `some` and `all`. For example, consider the (not so realistic) definition of the concept "Engineering professor": a subset of professors characterized by having at least one male student. The corresponding DL formulas $EngineeringProfessor \equiv Professor \sqcap \exists HasStudent.Male$ can be written as shown in rule 1.2. Additional information, such as namespaces, can be provided using metadata annotations.

Listing 1.2. Example declaration

```
declare  EngineeringProfessor  @[ ns=... ]
    as  Professor
        and  HasStudent  some  Male
end
```

3.3   (Fuzzy) Tableau Algorithm

A tableau algorithm [4] is a procedure to verify the consistency of a given knowledge base: in fact, it has been shown that all other common tableau problems, including recognition and subsumption, can be transformed to a consistency verification problem. The algorithm uses a generative procedure to search for a consistent interpretation, applying rules, ordered by priority, corresponding to DL constructors. The implementation of a tableau algorithm in a production rule system, however, is not trivial because such systems do not normally support explicit logical negation (i.e. it is not possible to state that a fact is

---

[11] Notice that, at the moment, the mapping is not perfect.

false) and, more importantly, do not support the backtracking mechanism required by the non-deterministic tableau rules. However, both problems can be circumvented using the fuzzy tableau algorithm present in [7], which is also a generalization of and thus compatible with the boolean case. The algorithm reduces the consistency check to a numeric optimization problem, solved using a dedicated component. The actual class of this problem depends on the family of (many-valued) logic adopted: since Lukasiewicz's operators are linear, choosing them causes the problem to fall within the Mixed Integer Linear Programming (MILP) class.

While Drools does have a Solver module, at the moment it does not support MILP problems, so we resorted to the open source solver GLPK[12], invoked through the interface Java ILP[13], planning to do a tighter integration at a later time. This interface offers the convenient abstraction of `Problems`, `Constraints`, `Variables` and `Linear` combinations thereof. The main advantage of this approach is that all the non-determinism is delegated to the solver: the tableau generation, then, becomes deterministic and suitable for a production rule implementation.

As already noted, a tableau implicitly makes the open-world assumption: in many-valued logic, this means that it is not possible to entail an exact truth value, but only a lower or an upper bound (the latter by entailment of the negation of a formula). The `IDegree` interface of Drools Chance allows to model many-valued truth degrees with interval-bounded variables (see also [32]): these variable degrees, compatible with JavaILP `Variables`, are generated and combined in the tableau. At each step, a generation rule processes a DL constructor (a logical connective or a quantifier). The degrees associated to the operands, then, are connected using an abstract operator whose implementation is provided by an external `Factory` - the same which generates the operators for the normal production rules.

In order to practically implement the rule-based tableau, each concept declaration is first parsed to obtain an AST tree, then negations are resolved by cancelling double negations and embedding the surviving ones in their operands' nodes using a dedicated flag. Eventually, the tree is further split into a set of elementary sub-trees: to do so, every operator/quantifier node is replaced by a uniquely identified "mock" type node. This node is instantiated twice: one copy is attached to the former operator node's father, while the other replaces the operator node itself and is connected to its children. An example is shown in figure 2.

Every elementary tree is then used to instantiate a pair of rule templates, choosing the templates according to the type of the original operator. The mock types are used to chain and propagate information during the generation process: whenever an instance of a mock type is generated, its children are generated and their associated `Variables` are combined and constrained appropriately to their parent's one. Whenever a variable-degree `Type` fact is about to be generated by

---

[12] http://www.gnu.org/software/glpk/

[13] http://javailp.sourceforge.net/

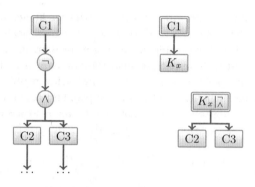

Fig. 2. AST Splitting

the tableau, the system exploits the engine's insertion and merging features to look whether an equivalent fact for the same object and type is already present, so that the existing degrees can be imported as bounds for the variable in the optimization problem. Notice that since assertions can be positive or negative, there must exist two distinct rules for each mock type.

For example, the **and** tree of Figure 2 yields a (positive) rule shown in pseudo-code in 1.3. Values between brackets are parametric and derived from the AST; the **and** constraint, generated by an appropriate `Factory`, depends instead on the parent's degree and is extracted using the `degree()` helper method. The additional fact in the premise, finally, is used to associate each rule activation and the temporary facts it generates to a specific tableau instance, allowing multiple queries to be performed at the same time as well as clearing the WM after a problem has been solved.

Listing 1.3. Tableau Rule example

```
rule "AND_[klass_x]"
salience ...  //used to enforce priority
when
    QueryContext( $prob : problem )
    Type( $xlab : label , $neg : negated == [false],
        $x : subject, object == "[klass_x]")
then
    String [] chClass = new String [] { [ ... ] };
    boolean [] chNeg = new boolean [] { [ ... ] };

    // for each Child[j]
    //    generate/collect Type(x, chClass[j], chNeg[j])
    //    generate variable degrees

    Object parentVar = $neg ? degree() : degree().neg();
    ConstraintFactory.addAndConstraint(
                        chldVars, parentVar, $prob);
end
```

All the dynamically generated rules are appended to a common header which contains, among other things, the rule which invokes the `solve()` method on a query `problem` and generates the final response.

3.4 Tableau Queries : Comparing OWA and CWA

The tableau, even in its rule-based version, works by (fuzzy) refutation. In order to prove that the "real" truth degree ε_A of a formula A is true to at least degree τ, it minimizes τ under the constraint $\varepsilon_{\neg A} \leq 1 - \tau$ [7]. The value τ can be considered the fuzzy degree of *necessity* of A being true: the minimization of $1 - \tau$, then, is a refutation in the sense that it maximizes the necessity of $\neg A$ or, equivalently [11], that it finds the minimum allowed degree of *possibility* for A. Informally: since it is not possible for ε to be lower than that value, that one is the best necessity bound.

The problems of *test* and *subsumption*, then, can be reduced to finding the greatest necessity (lower) bound for the formulas $A(x)$ and $A(\cdot) \rightarrow B(\cdot)$ respectively. In their rule-based version, the former is triggered by the insertion of a `Query` fact, the test fact `Type(x,"not A")`, where x is the individual to be tested, and the constraint $\varepsilon_{Type} \leq 1 - \tau$. The latter, instead, requires a `Query` fact, the test facts `Type(x,"A")/`τ_1 and `Type(x,"B")/`τ_2 (where, in this case, x is a new mock object) and the constraint $\neg(\tau_1 \rightarrow \tau_2) \leq 1 - \tau$, which in Łukasiewicz's logic reduces to $\tau_1 - \tau_2 \leq 1 - \tau$.

The same tableau rules can also be used to compute the upper bound $1 - \varphi$ of a formula [32], i.e. the *possibility* of its being true. To do so, it is sufficient to compute the necessity φ of the negation of a formula: for test problems the objective becomes `Type(x,"A")` constrained by $/(1 - \varphi)$, while in the case of subsumption the only difference is in the constraint, which is based on the implication-equivalent disjunction $\neg A \vee B$ instead of the conjunction $A \wedge \neg B$ (in practice, $\varphi_2 - \varphi_1 \geq 1 - \varphi$).

To better exploit this feature, Drools Chance is configured to use $[\tau, 1 - \varphi]$ intervals as truth degrees: the tableau query, then, produces facts such as `Type(x,"A")` and `SubConceptOf("A","B")` whose interval degree derives from the two tableau queries. These facts are indistinguishable from the others in the WM and can be used as needed. Moreover, the possibilistic interval representation is a generalization of three-valued logic[14], so it can take into account the cases when the tableau can't provide a definite answer for neither the positive nor the negative query.

Recovering the default behaviour. A further advantage of this approach is the possibility to reduce the fuzzy intervals to simpler cases. If the lower bound alone is considered, the result of a tableau query coincides with a traditional inference under OWA; the upper bound, instead, is normally constrained by the existing facts and thus connected to an inference under CWA. Hence, the fuzzy interval attached to each conclusion brings both the results of applying CWA and OWA to the same query. Note, however, that although we map both CWA and OWA

---

[14] The "third" value is easily modelled by $[0, 1]$.

to fuzzy intervals, it is not possible to map such fuzzy intervals to CWA/OWA. In the general case, in fact, fuzzy intervals retain much more information than the CWA/OWA models. This means that each computed result (in the general case) can be interpreted only in terms of the underlying fuzzy logic. It is up to the user to decide how to reduce the rich information represented by the fuzzy interval in terms of a boolean conclusion under CWA/OWA.

To support the user in such a task, we propose two unary pattern operators, nec and pos, which return a precise degree instead of an interval and thus are compatible with simpler degree representations. Their definitions are, respectively:

- nec: $[\tau, 1 - \varphi] \mapsto [\tau, \tau]$
- pos: $[\tau, 1 - \varphi] \mapsto [1 - \varphi, 1 - \varphi]$.

Using either in front of a tableau-generated pattern not only allows to choose between closed- and open-world assumption, but also to use the tableau rules in a system where simple fuzzy values are used in place of intervals, at the expense of being forced to choose either assumption every time. Although the formal connection to (fuzzy) modal logic is still object of study, we have also defined the related operators $T \equiv$ nec ("true"), $F \equiv$ not nec ("false") and $U \equiv$ pos and not nec ("unknown"), returning respectively τ, φ and $\varphi - \tau$. The degrees, while intuitively acceptable, introduce a second-order evaluation feature which we haven't studied thoroughly yet.

4 Examples

As an example, consider the problem of testing whether an individual x matches with the concept EngineeringProfessor described in 1.2. If no other individual exists in the WM, the $\exists HasStudent.Male$ evaluates to $[0, 1]$: while it is possible for one to exist, it is not necessary because no existing object makes the contrary impossible. Assume, instead, that other rules have generated the facts HasStudent(x,y)$_{[0.7,0.8]}$, Male(y)$_{[0.8,1]}$, HasStudent(x,z)$_{[0.3,0.4]}$ and, finally, Male(z)$_{[0,0.2]}$. In this case, the existential part of the concept evaluates to $[0.5, 1]$. Since it relies on the OWA, the possibility remains unchanged, but the necessity is now conditioned by the best of the available facts, i.e. the one for which the relation HasStudent and the type Male condition hold simultaneously. To get a non-trivial answer, it is also necessary to have the fact Professor(x) in the WM. If, for example, it is associated to the degree $[0.9, 0.95]$, the result of the test query will be Type(x,EngineeringProfessor$_{[0.4,0.95]}$. Notice that the lower bound (i.e. nec Type(...)) would be equivalent to the one returned by the reactive test rule 1.4 which could be generated trivially from the DL definition. The upper bound, instead, remains different in the two cases: the exist quantifier in the CWA rule, in fact, returns 0.8 (leading to 0.75 in the final result), which is different from the upper bound computed using the OWA.

Given the current level of expressiveness of the language, instead, the fuzzy subsumption queries are coherent with the corresponding boolean ones since there is no way to express partial subsumption relations between concepts. It is important to remark, however, that with a trivial rule-based approach such queries are not possible. While the rules involving **Type** relations discussed in [21] can be generated and applied at run-time, they operate and complete the A-box, but can hardly reason on the T-box. Likewise, a CWA subsumption rule such as 1.5 is not safe because it is not based on the analysis of the description of the two concepts, but on the analysis of the properties of a (limited) number of individuals present in the WM at a given time.

Listing 1.4. CWA Test Rule

```
rule "EngineeringProfessor"
when
    $t : Type( $x : subject , object == "Prof" )
    exists ( HasStudent( subject == $x, $y : object )
             Type( subject == $y, object == "Male" )
then insert( new Type($x, "EngProf", degree()) ); end
```

Listing 1.5. CWA Subsumption Rule - Unsafe

```
rule "Human -> Mortal"
when
    forall ( $t : Type( $x : subject , object == "Human" )
             ( Type( subject == $x, object == "Human" )
             implies
             Type( subject == $x, object == "Mortal" )
then insert(
    new SubConceptOf("Human", "Mortal", degree()) );
end
```

5   Conclusions and Future Developments

This work has shown a possible way to integrate many-valued logics, description logics and production rules in the context of a single engine. Although the current implementation of our prototype is limited to the expressiveness provided by the $\mathcal{ALC}$ DL family, it supersedes previous attempts in many aspects. It provides a single, unified model for facts, concepts and rules, letting the user to specify within the same context both the ontological knowledge as well as the operational knowledge. Since the data model - the Working Memory - is shared, we managed to avoid the interfacing, coherency and communication problems connected to the use of different reasoners in the same architecture. Moreover, the tool supports fuzzy extensions to both aspects, and through such extensions it tries to avoid the dichotomy between OWA and CWA reasoning styles. The next step will be the upgrade of the expressiveness of the supported logics, both in term of DL features and in term of fuzzy logic families. To do so, the tableau rules will have to be expanded and, possibly, a more powerful solver will have to be integrated. As the expressiveness increases, it will be possible to implement more powerful recognition and classification algorithms which, in our plans, will also allow us to define a better mapping between the declared concepts and the (Java) classes used to implement the individuals. In parallel, a more compact and efficient way to use semantic predicates in rules and to evaluate them in RETE nodes is being studied to improve readability and performance.

The prototype, developed in a branch of Drools, is to be integrated in the next version of the engine and will be made available in the SVN repository at http://anonsvn.jboss.org/repos/labs/labs/jbossrules/

Acknowledgements

We wish to thank the anonymous reviewers for the precious comments on how to improve the quality of this work and the future ones. This work has been partially supported by the Italian MIUR PRIN 2007 project No. 20077WWCR8.

References

1. Analyti, A., Antoniou, G., Damásio, C.: A principled framework for modular web rule bases and its semantics. In: Proc. KR 2008, pp. 390–400 (2008)
2. Antoniou, G.: Nonmonotonic rule systems on top of ontology layers. In: Horrocks, I., Hendler, J. (eds.) ISWC 2002. LNCS, vol. 2342, pp. 394–398. Springer, Heidelberg (2002)
3. Antoniou, G., Damasio, C., Grosof, B., Horrocks, I., Kifer, M., Maluszynski, J., Patel-Schneider, P.: Combining Rules and Ontologies. A Survey. Tech. Rep., Rewerse Project (2005)
4. Baader, F., Sattler, U.: Tableau algorithms for description logics. Studia Logica 69, 5–40 (2001)
5. Baldwin, J., Martin, T., Pilsworth, B.: Fril-fuzzy and evidential reasoning in artificial intelligence. John Wiley & Sons, Inc., New York (1995)
6. Bobillo, F., Bou, F., Straccia, U.: On the failure of the finite model property in some fuzzy description logics. CoRR abs/1003.1588 (2010)
7. Bobillo, F., Straccia, U.: Fuzzy description logics with general t-norms and datatypes. Fuzzy Sets Syst. 160(23), 3382–3402 (2009)
8. Bragaglia, S., Chesani, F., Ciampolini, A., Mello, P., Montali, M., Sottara, D.: An Hybrid Architecture Integrating Forward Rules with Fuzzy Ontological Reasoning. Architecture (2010)
9. Damásio, C., Analyti, A., Antoniou, G., Wagner, G.: Supporting open and closed world reasoning on the web. Principles and Practice of Semantic Web Reasoning pp. 149–163 (2006)
10. De Bruijn, J., Bonnard, P., Citeau, H., Dehors, S., Heymans, S., Korf, R., Pührer, J., Eiter, T.: State-of-the-art survey of issues. Tech. rep., ONTORULE (2009), http://ontorule-project.eu/project/workpackages/wp-3-execution-and-inference/d31
11. Dubois, D., Lang, J., Prade, H.: Possibilistic logic (1992)
12. Eiter, T., Ianni, G., Lukasiewicz, T., Schindlauer, R., Tompits, H.: Combining answer set programming with description logics for the semantic web. Artificial Intelligence 172(12-13), 1495–1539 (2008)
13. Eiter, T., Ianni, G., Polleres, A., Schindlauer, R., Tompits, H.: Reasoning with rules and ontologies. In: Barahona, P., Bry, F., Franconi, E., Henze, N., Sattler, U. (eds.) Reasoning Web 2006. LNCS, vol. 4126, pp. 93–127. Springer, Heidelberg (2006)

14. Grosof, B., Horrocks, I., Volz, R., Decker, S.: Description logic programs: Combining logic programs with description logic. In: Proceedings of the 12th International Conference on World Wide Web, p. 57. ACM, New York (2003)
15. Hájek, P.: Metamathematics of Fuzzy Logic (Trends in Logic). Springer, Heidelberg (2001)
16. Horridge, M., Drummond, N., Goodwin, J., Rector, A., Stevens, R., Wang, H.: The manchester owl syntax. In: OWLED 2006 Second Workshop on OWL Experiences and Directions, Athens, GA, USA (2006)
17. Horrocks, I., Patel-Schneider, P.: A proposal for an OWL rules language. In: Proc. 13th International Conference on World Wide Web, p. 731. ACM, New York (2004)
18. Hustadt, U., Motik, B., Sattler, U.: Reducing SHIQ- description logic to disjunctive datalog programs. In: Proc. KR, vol. 4, pp. 152–162 (2004)
19. Levy, A., Rousset, M.: Combining Horn rules and description logics in CARIN. Artificial Intelligence 104(1-2), 165–209 (1998)
20. Lukácsy, G., Szeredi, P., Kádár, B.: Prolog based description logic reasoning. In: Garcia de la Banda, M., Pontelli, E. (eds.) ICLP 2008. LNCS, vol. 5366, pp. 455–469. Springer, Heidelberg (2008)
21. Meditskos, G., Bassiliades, N.: A rule-based object-oriented owl reasoner. IEEE Trans. on Knowl. and Data Eng. 20(3), 397–410 (2008)
22. Mello, P., Proctor, M., Sottara, D.: A configurable RETE-OO engine for reasoning with different types of imperfect information. IEEE Transactions on Knowledge and Data Engineering (TKDE) - Special Issue on Rule Representation, Interchange and Reasoning in Distributed, Heterogeneous Environments (2010) (article in Press)
23. Motik, B.: Reasoning in description logics using resolution and deductive databases. PhD theis, University Karlsruhe, Germany (2006)
24. Motik, B., Horrocks, I., Rosati, R., Sattler, U.: Can OWL and Logic Programming live together happily ever after? In: Cruz, I., Decker, S., Allemang, D., Preist, C., Schwabe, D., Mika, P., Uschold, M., Aroyo, L.M. (eds.) ISWC 2006. LNCS, vol. 4273, pp. 501–514. Springer, Heidelberg (2006)
25. Motik, B., Vrandečić, D., Hitzler, P., Studer, R.: dlpconvert–converting OWL DLP statements to logic programs. In: European Semantic Web Conference 2005 Demos and Posters, Citeseer (2005)
26. Polleres, A., Feier, C., Harth, A.: Rules with contextually scoped negation. In: Sure, Y., Domingue, J. (eds.) ESWC 2006. LNCS, vol. 4011, pp. 332–347. Springer, Heidelberg (2006)
27. Reiter, R.: On closed world data bases. Morgan Kaufmann Publishers Inc., San Francisco (1987)
28. Rosati, R.: On the decidability and complexity of integrating ontologies and rules. Web Semantics: Science, Services and Agents on the World Wide Web 3(1), 61–73 (2005)
29. Rosati, R.: Integrating ontologies and rules: Semantic and computational issues. In: Barahona, P., Bry, F., Franconi, E., Henze, N., Sattler, U. (eds.) Reasoning Web 2006. LNCS, vol. 4126, pp. 128–151. Springer, Heidelberg (2006)
30. Smets, P.: Imperfect Information: Imprecision and Uncertainty (1996)
31. Straccia, U.: Managing uncertainty and vagueness in description logics, Logic Programs and Description logic Programs, 54–103 (2008)
32. Zhao, J., Boley, H., Du, W.: Knowledge Representation and Consistency Checking in a Norm-Parameterized Fuzzy Description Logic. In: Huang, D.-S., Jo, K.-H., Lee, H.-H., Kang, H.-J., Bevilacqua, V. (eds.) ICIC 2009. LNCS, vol. 5755, pp. 111–123. Springer, Heidelberg (2009)

Ensuring Compliance with Semantic Constraints in Process Adaptation with Rule-Based Event Processing

Akhil Kumar[1], Wen Yao[2], Chao-Hsien Chu[2], and Zang Li[2]

[1] Smeal College of Business, Penn State University,
University Park, PA 16802, USA
[2] College of Information Sciences and Technology, Penn State University,
University Park, PA 16802, USA
{akhil,wxy119,chc4,zul110}@psu.edu

Abstract. An Adaptive Process Management System (APMS) allows for flexible, dynamic and even ad hoc adaptation of business processes based on case data, context and events. It is also important that APMS technology ensure error-free process execution and compliance with semantic constraints. However, most process design tools tend to be rigid or they handle only syntactic constraints. This restricts their value in real-world applications considerably. This paper presents a new approach to validate process change operations against semantic constraints using an integer programming formulation. The formulation allows us to describe existential as well as coordination (such as before-after ordering sequence) relationships between tasks in a process in a common way. It can then be solved to not only check full or strong compliance, but also determine the minimum set of additional process changes required to ensure weak compliance. Notions of strong and weak compliance are discussed and illustrated with a detailed example. We argue that this approach is more elegant and superior to a pure logic based approach.

Keywords: business process adaptation, semantic constraints, rules, ECA, complex events, change patterns, weak compliance, strong compliance.

1 Introduction

Today's organizations often face continuous and unprecedented changes in their business environment. Hence, there is a strong demand for Adaptive Process Management Systems (APMS) that allow flexible adaptation of processes. Process adaptation is a strategy to deal with exceptional situations during workflow execution. Thus, if such exception can be captured and modeled, business processes can adapt to it automatically without human intervention. In addition, APMS technology should ensure error-free process execution and compliance to external regulations and internal business policies. Thus, two *conflicting goals* need to be balanced – the need for *control* versus the need to provide sufficient *flexibility* for workflows to adapt to a constantly changing environment.

Process adaptation is defined as the capability to react to uncertainty in a process model through change or a running process instance through deviation. The

M. Dean et al. (Eds.): RuleML 2010, LNCS 6403, pp. 50–65, 2010.

uncertainty may arise from the case data, context, and real-time events. There are several ways to incorporate flexibility into a process design. First, *ECA (Event-condition-action) rules* are a popular approach to catch unanticipated events and adapt to exceptions [1]. This can allow an APMS to deviate from normal execution. Second, process flexibility is provided by *under-specification*. An underspecified model is described as a list of tasks to be executed and a set of constraints that apply to them. At run time, any instance that satisfies the constraints is valid. A third notion of flexibility is based on *separation of business policy from process control flow* by parameterizing aspects of the process description with business policy elements instead of hard-coding them.

Of course, it is very important that process flexibility should not violate structural and semantic constraints. *Structural constraints* refer to the control of process execution at the structural level. For example, by verifying the absence of deadlocks and inconsistent data in a process model at design time, an APMS can determine that a process is structurally correct. This is necessary to guarantee error-free execution of a workflow both before and after making changes. *Semantic constraints* stem from domain specific requirements and express dependencies, incompatibilities, and existence conditions between activities [2]. As an example, such a constraint may state that: *possible drug interaction between amoxicillin and oral contraceptives prohibits a patient from taking both medications within, say, 7 days of each other.* In addition, similar constraints are also required to ensure that the process models are compliant with policies and regulations (both internal and external) as well. Hence, an APMS must guarantee that process changes will not violate both structural and semantic constraints. The work in reference [2] provides a useful inspiration for our work, but it focuses more on a constraint framework for compliance support and formal compliance criteria. It also does not discuss a constraint language, instead relying on natural language examples.

The main focus of our paper is on developing techniques for detecting and handling semantic constraint violations. We assume that process change operations are generated by ECA-like rules that are triggered when certain events occur, or context related conditions in the environment are satisfied. Our main contributions are: (1) giving a formal language to describe a variety of semantic constraints; (2) expressing semantic constraints as an integer programming (IP) formulation; and, (3) showing how an IP formulation is solved and analyzed to determine and correct violations.

This paper is organized as follows. In section 2, we give background on business process management notation and introduce semantic constraints. Section 3 presents a framework for ECA rules and discusses various change operations or actions for adapting a process produced by such rules in response to events based on case data and context. Then in section 4, we present a formal specification of semantic constraints and show how the problem of checking compliance of constraints to change operations checking can be formulated as in integer program (IP). We also show how the IP can be solved and solution analyzed. We discuss related work and our advantages in section 5. Lastly, section 6 concludes the paper and presents future work.

2   Preliminaries

2.1   Basic Notations in Business Process Management

A business process is mainly formed by tasks that need to be performed by resources to complete the process. To support the execution of each process, a *process model* needs to be defined by a formal language (e.g., BPMN, BPEL). Let $M = (T, N, E, Res, Dat)$ to denote a process model, where T denotes the set of all tasks, N denotes the set of all control nodes, E represents the set of all edges connecting tasks and control nodes, *Res* denotes a set of all resources, and *Dat* denotes related data. The node $N \in$ *{start, end, sequence, parallel, choice, loop}* means it has six types. The start node and end node are required for each process model to specify the beginning and the end of a process. In this paper, we also use *process type* or *process template* to refer to process model since they are often used interchangeably.

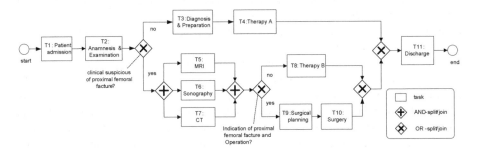

Fig. 1. A simplified clinical process for proximal femoral fracture, adapted from [3]

Fig. 1 presents a simplified clinical pathway for proximal femoral fracture in BPMN notation [4]. This process model is coordinated by a series of tasks. After patient admission (T1), the task anamnesis & examination (T2) is conducted. Then, depending upon the result of examination, if the patient has clinical suspicious of proximal femoral facture, she has to take imaging diagnosis, which is composed of three parallel tasks: MRI (T5), Sonography (T6), and CT (T7); otherwise, she is diagnosed and prepared for therapy (T3), followed by customized therapy (T4). Further, depending on the results of her imaging diagnosis, she is either treated with therapy (T8) or surgery (T9 and T10).

Finally, the patient will be discharged and documented (T11). The ordering relationship of tasks can be easily told from this process model. For example, T1 is followed by T2, implying the sequential control flow. T5, T6, and T7 are executed in parallel, denoted by AND-split and AND-join. T8 and T9 are executed in choice, denoted by OR-split and OR-join. The semantics of an OR-split node is that one or more branches can be pursued at this node. Hence, it is like a multi-choice structure. All the paths initiated at the OR-split node must finish and meet at the corresponding OR-join node. At an AND-split node, all branches are followed and they meet at an AND-join.

Based on the process model, at run time a *process instance* is created and executed for a specific case. *A process instance records an actual execution of a process model*. For example, a patient named Mary was admitted by the hospital, and then underwent anamnesis and examination. The result indicated that she was not suspicious of proximal femoral fracture, thus she did not need imaging diagnosis. However, her symptom was further examined and diagnosed. After that, she took a therapy and was discharged. This is a typical process instance following the process model in Fig.1. The actual execution path of this instance can be recorded as {start, T1, T2, T3, T4, T11, end}. For a running process instance, a task can have the following status values: *activated, executing, done, aborted, suspended,* and *not activated*. One process model may have hundreds or thousands of process instances running at the same time.

2.2   Semantic Constraints

A process is balanced by control (through constraints) and flexibility (through change operations). Traditional APMS only consider structural constraints that deal with structural correctness of the modified process, such as deadlock and infinite loop. A large number of studies have been devoted towards this research effort, and handled this problem very well. Thus, in this paper we only focus on semantic constraints. *We define semantic constraint as a domain specific restriction on business processes which needs to be compliant with during process execution.* A process model or instance that violates semantic constraints may be still syntactically correct, but not applicable to a real world scenario because it is semantically wrong. This is particularly important for a knowledge-intensive environment where domain knowledge plays a critical role in process design. For example, a patient with bacterial infection is usually administered with amoxicillin or clindamycin. In addition, we should add a semantic constraint that medication of amoxicillin is forbidden for patients who are hypersensitive to penicillin. In an application, a doctor may handle a number of cases each day and she may not recall specific patients. A certain patient may be sensitive to amoxicillin and react badly to it. Thus, the APMS should provide compliance checking mechanism to avoid these problems. Other examples for semantic constraints include:

- Symptom examination and diagnosis should be performed before therapy.
- A patient with a cardiac pacemaker is not allowed to have a MRI test.
- A patient must not be administered Aspirin and Marcumar within 5 days of each other to avoid possible interactions.

During process design, the semantic constraints for a particular business process should be acquired from domain experts written in English-like language and then transformed into a language understandable by computers. The original process model is usually verified and compliant with predefined constraints. However, when change or deviation takes place, such semantic constraints can be easily violated. Our paper aims to propose a formal definition for semantic constraints and provide a compliance checking mechanism to ensure no process change or adaptation will violate these constraints. This mechanism is also incorporated into an ECA framework.

3   An Extended-ECA Model for Compliant Process Adaptation

In this section, we present an extended-ECA framework for automatically adapting business processes and checking compliance with semantic constraints.

3.1   Rule Specification

Rules (or *production rules*) are usually expressed in the format of "If condition Then action" to encode appropriate knowledge. They are usually invoked by a user or an application and then processed by the rule engine. *Reaction rules* are represented in the format of *Event-Condition-Action (ECA)* and they can be automatically triggered when the specified event occurs. In APMS, reaction rules have been used to handle deviations [5, 6], which allow a process instance to deviate temporarily from its associated standard process templates for exception cases. An *ECA rule* can react to events in real time. After an event (E) occurs, a condition clause (C) is checked. If it is satisfied, then the action (A) is performed. An example ECA rule is:

> ECA (
>   *event* (PatientConditionUpdate),
>   *condition* (Patient.isPregnant == true),
>   *Action* (Delete(CTScan), Delete(X-ray test))

In this rule, as soon as a patient's condition is updated an event is generated. Then, a condition ("pregnancy") is tested and if true, then any CT scan or X-ray tasks are removed from the process.

ECA rules are a flexible way to achieve process adaptation, in contrast to, say, a series of nested if-then-else statements that hurt workflow readability. There are a variety of rule-based event processing languages, e.g., Drools [7] and Reaction RuleML [8]. For a comprehensive survey on existing event processing languages (EPL) in terms of their syntax, application domain, and features, see reference [9]. A variant of ECA called ECA-LP formalism [10] handles more advanced rules represented as a 6-ary tuple [10]: *ECA (T, E, C, A, P, EL)*. In addition to the three elements above, it also includes *T (time)*, *P (post condition)* and *EL (else action)*. *Time* is absolute ("5pm of July 29th, 2010"), relative ("5 hours from 'now'"), or periodic ("every 10 seconds"). *EL* represents an alternative action if the condition is false, while the post condition is checked for satisfaction after the action is finished.

The ECA-LP formalism provides a richer syntax than ECA for expressing rules to model the needs of a flexible process designer. Moreover, many efforts are being devoted to developing such a homogeneous language and transforming it into RuleML [11], which is becoming a standard in the rule research community. Many languages also support *complex events* based on *conjunction, disjunction* and *negation* of events. Moreover, temporal relationships between events, such as: *before, after, during, at,* etc. may also be stated. In this paper, we assume that in general, the action part of an ECA-like rule specifies an action to be performed to modify or adapt a business process. This action may be a change operation to insert, delete, move, replace, or swap certain tasks in the process. We discuss such change operations next.

3.2 Change Operations

Process change operations (or adaptation patterns) are actions from triggered ECA-like rules in reaction to complex events. To enable maximum flexibility, a variety of adaptation patterns should be designed and supported in APMS. A comprehensive survey of available change patterns and change support features was described in reference [12] based on empirical evidence from large case studies. In addition, reference [5] presented a variety of operations that can be done to change a process model or instance. We define *primitive change operations* (see Table 1) as atomic operations at the task level since they are indivisible units of making changes to a process, and serve as a foundation for composing more advanced adaptation patterns.

Table 1. Primitive change operations

Expression	Meaning
insert $(T, N_1, N_2, [cond^*])$	Insert T between N_1 and N_2, i.e. after N_1 and before N_2
delete (T)	Remove T from the process
move $(T, N_1, N_2, [cond])$	Move T to a new position between N_1 and N_2
replace (T_1, T_2)	Replace T_1 with T_2
swap (T_1, T_2)	Swap the position of T_1 and T_2 in the process
repeat(T, t)	Repeat task T for time period t

*cond is an optional parameter that should be specified as the condition if T is inserted as a choice or loop structure; same for the move operation

These operations can provide process flexibility both at the process model and instance levels. A change can be associated with a specific process model identified by a *process_ID*, or with a process instance by a *instance_ID*. Permitting change at the process model level allows long-term flexibility in the standard operations; while, change at the process instance level permits short-term flexibility so that an instance can deviate temporarily from a standard process model. For example, applying delete(T) on a process instance only allows the current instance to skip task T while other process instances are still executing T. If we apply this change on a process model, then it will remove task T permanently from this model and all instances derived from this model will be affected accordingly.

Detailed steps for performing change operations, and validation of change conflicts at the structural level, are discussed in reference [6]. For example, if both delete(T) and move(T, T_1, T_2) should be carried out to the same process, it will cause a conflict because task T can either be deleted or moved, but not both. An incompatibility table is created to check whether any two are operations compatible. However, compliance of change operations against semantic constraints is not possible with this mechanism. Also note that this list of change operations is typical, but not exhaustive. It is difficult to make a claim of completeness since notions of completeness are also domain specific. Other change operations we plan to add in later work are *postpone*, *prepone*, and *repeat* actions.

In the next section, we address how to handle semantic constraints which is a key contribution of this paper. Our goal is to be able to check if a set of primitive, non-conflicting change operations that are correct at the structural level are also compliant with a given set of semantic constraints.

4   Compliance Checking with Semantic Constraints Using IP

The importance of semantic constraints has been mentioned in reference [13], but only two types of semantic constraints (i.e., dependency and exclusion) are considered there. We adapt the constraints used to specify interdependencies of tasks and validate process variants from reference [14], and use them to model semantic constraints, since the underlying semantics are the same. Further, our study provides a formal definition for specifying these constraints, and a novel approach based on integer programming (IP) for compliance checking.

4.1   Specification and Property of Semantic Constraints

Table 2 presents a comprehensive set of semantic constraints and their meanings. To enable the validity checking of a constraint set and the compliance checking of change operations, we propose a formal definition to semantic constraints so as to enable automatic checking. Each task T_i is considered a propositional variable ranging over domain $D_i = \{0, 1\}$. Let $T_i = 1$ indicate the presence of task T_i, and $T_i = 0$ its absence. With this notation, we can use equations or inequalities to present other constraints such as *coexist, ex-choice*, etc. In addition, we define the sequential relationship of T_i and T_j as $S_{i,j}$ with domain $D_{i,j} = \{0, 1\}$. $S_{i,j} = 1$ means T_j must be executed after T_i. $S_{i,j} = 0$ means T_j can be executed before or in parallel with T_i. Obviously, we must ensure $S_{i,j} + S_{j,i} \leq 1$. This set of constraints represents most common scenarios, but a claim of completeness is difficult to make.

Table 2. Formal specification of semantic constraints

Constraint	Meaning	Formal Specification	Property *
mandatory (*T*)	*T* must be executed.	$T = 1$	N/A
forbidden (*T*)	*T* is not allowed to be executed.	$T = 0$	N/A
coexist (T_1, T_2)	T_1 and T_2 must be both selected or be both unselected.	$T_1 = T_2$	M, T
choice (T_1, T_2)	Only one of T_1 and T_2 must be executed.	$T_1 + T_2 = 1$	M
choice ($T_1, T_2, ...,$ T_n, m) [n ≥ m]	Exactly *m* of $T_1, T_2, ..., T_n$ should be executed.	$T_1 + T_2 + ... + T_n = m$	N/A
dependency (T_1, T_2)	The presence of T_1 also imposes the restriction that T_2 must be included.	$T_1 \leq T_2$	T
exclusion (T_1, T_2)	The presence of T_1 imposes the restriction that T_2 must be excluded.	$T_1 + T_2 \leq 1$	M
cardinality (*T, min, max*) [max ≥ min]	The execution time of *T* is between *min* and *max*.	N/A	N/A
sequence (T_1, T_2)	T_2 must be executed after T_1.	$S_{1,2} = 1$	T

*M: commutative; T: transitive

Some semantic constraints are *commutative* and/or *transitive*. Our definitions provide a well-founded representation of these properties that lends itself well to reasoning. For example:

For commutativity:
C1: coexist $(T_1, T_2) \leftrightarrow$ coexist (T_2, T_1) is equivalent to $T_1 = T_2 \leftrightarrow T_2 = T_1$
C2: choice $(T_1, T_2) \leftrightarrow$ choice (T_2, T_1) is equivalent to $T_1 + T_2 = 1 \leftrightarrow T_2 + T_1 = 1$
C3: exclusion $(T_1, T_2) \leftrightarrow$ exclusive (T_2, T_1) is equivalent to $T_1 + T_2 \leq 1 \leftrightarrow T_2 + T_1 \leq 1$

For transitivity:
T1: coexist (T_1, T_2), coexist $(T_2, T_3) \rightarrow$ coexist (T_1, T_3) is equivalent to:
  $T_1 = T_2, T_2 = T_3 \rightarrow T_1 = T_3$
T2: dependency (T_1, T_2), dependency $(T_2, T_3) \rightarrow$ dependency (T_1, T_3) is equivalent to:
  $T_1 \leq T_2, T_2 \leq T_3 \rightarrow T_1 \leq T_3$
T3: sequence (T_i, T_j) and sequence $(T_j, T_k) \rightarrow$ sequence (T_i, T_k) is equivalent to:
  $S_{i,k} \geq S_{i,j} + S_{j,k} - 1, S_{i,k} \leq S_{i,j}, S_{i,k} \leq S_{j,k}$

Thus, coexistence, dependency and sequence relationships between multiple tasks can thus be easily represented because of the transitivity property.

4.2   Implicit, Redundant and Conflicting Constraints

To describe a process model, an end user will consult with domain experts and define a set of semantic constraints, among which implicit, redundant, and conflicting constraints may exist. Thus, we propose an algorithm to infer implicit constraints, and resolve redundancy and conflict issues. This provides the foundation for further compliance checking of change operations.

Two constraints C1, C2 can be composed together to derive new constraints. Such *implicit constraints* can be inferred using the definition of constraints as a system of equations. For example, say,

  C1: T_1 and T_2 must coexist (i.e., $T_1 = T_2$),
  C2: T_2 is dependent on T_3 (i.e., $T_2 \leq T_3$).

From the equations representing C1 and C2, one can derive a new expression $T_1 \leq T_3$. Semantically, this means that T_1 is also dependent on T_3. Detection of such implicit constraints can help remove redundancy. For the above example, if an explicit constraint, C3: $T_1 \leq T_3$ were defined, then it can be removed because it creates a redundancy. Conflicting constraints on the other hand will lead to inconsistencies and must be resolved before they can be applied. For the above example, if an explicit constraint C3: $T_3 \leq T_1$ were defined, it would create a conflict since $T_1 \leq T_3$ and $T_3 \leq T_1$ cannot be both true.

When the constraint set is large, we need an algorithm to resolve the redundancies and conflicts. Table 3 gives the listing of such an algorithm. The composition of two constraints, say, C1 and C2 can be represented as C1 $\otimes$ C2. In the above example,

  C1 $\otimes$ C2 $= (T_1 \leq T_3)$,
  C1 $\otimes$ C2 $\otimes$ C3 = fail.

If two constraints conflict (line 4), then a message is generated by the algorithm to notify the user (line 5), while if they are redundant (line 7) then one of them is removed (line10). We don't discuss details of which one of the redundant constraints to remove. If they are independent, their composition is $\emptyset$ and no action is needed (line 14). For example $(T_1 = T_2) \otimes (T_3 + T_4 \leq 1) = \emptyset$. The time complexity for this algorithm is $\Theta(n^3)$, where n denotes the number of semantic constraints. Thus, the composition of two constraints produces a value of $\emptyset$ or "fail", if a result is not found.

Table 3. Algorithm for validating the constraint set

Input: initial constraint set vector SC,
Output: complete and sound constraint set vector SC
Constraint_validation (parameter: SC)
1:    Define n = SC.size
2:    FOR i = 1 to n   // go through all the constraints in the set
3:        FOR j = i+1 to n
4:            IF SC[i] $\otimes$ SC[j] = fail   // composition failed from a constraint conflict
5:                Print "constraints SC[i] and SC[j] conflict."
6:                break;
7:            ELSE IF SC[i] $\otimes$ SC[j] $\neq \emptyset$ // redundant constraints
8:                FOR k = j+1 to n
9:                    IF SC[k] == SC[i] $\otimes$ SC[j]
10:                        SC.remove (SC[k])   // remove the redundant constraint
11:                    END IF
12:                END FOR
13:            ELSE
14:                do nothing;   // independent constraints
15:            END IF
16:        END FOR
17: END FOR

4.3   Compliance Checking for Change Operations

During process adaptation, the triggered change operations need to be validated to ensure their compliance to predefined semantic constraints. Here, we assume that the semantic constraint set has been validated using the algorithm in Table 3, and it is sound and conflict-free. In this section, we introduce how compliance checking can be handled as a standard integer programming (IP) problem, using the definitions above.

At a specific point in time when a complex event is detected, let us denote a process instance as $P = (T, D, SC, CP)$, where $T = \{T_1, T_2, ..., T_n\}$ denote the set of all tasks, $D = \{D_1, D_2, ..., D_n\}$, $D_i \in \{0, 1\}$, $i \in [1, n]$, denote the respective domain for task set T, $SC = \{SC_1, SC_2, ..., SC_k\}$ denote a set of semantic constraints defined for P, and $CP = \{OP_1, OP_2, ..., OP_m\}$ denote a set of change operations to be applied on P. We assume the current state of P is compliant with SC (i.e., $P \vDash SC$) and our goal is to:

(1) decide whether CP is compliant with SC;
(2) if CP is not totally compliant find:

(a) the *maximal* subset of *CP* that is compliant with *SC*.
(b) the *minimum* set of *additions to CP* to make CP compliant with *SC*.

Since our goal is to get the cumulative effects of a series of change operations, we can decompose this problem by verifying each operation *OP* against *SC*. Let Δ_{op} denote the compensation needed for *OP* to be compliant with *SC*. We can identify three types of *OP* in terms of compliance.

$$f\left(P \xrightarrow{CP+\Delta_{op}} P'\right) = \begin{cases} P' \vDash SC, \Delta_{op} = \emptyset & (a) \\ P' \vDash SC, \Delta_{op} \neq \emptyset & (b) \\ P' \nvDash SC, \Delta_{op} = \emptyset & (c) \end{cases}$$

(a) **Strong compliance.** *CP* is compliant with *SC* without compensation;
(b) **Weak compliance** (with compensation operations). *CP* is compliant with *SC*, providing that Δ_{op} is carried out in addition to *CP*, so that $P' \vDash SC$.
(c) **Non-compliance.** *CP* is non-compliant with *SC*. In other words, no compensable operations Δ_{op} can be found so that $P' \vDash SC$.

Our goal is to find the *optimal compliant change pattern* (OCPA), defined as $CP' = CP \cup \Delta_{op}$, where Δ_{op} represents the minimal (in terms of size) compensation required to CP in order to make the change strongly compliant, or, if not, then weakly compliant.

Now, the problem to find Δ_{op} is formulated as an integer program and solved with the LPSolve tool [15], to verify that all semantic constraints are satisfied. For each task T_i, variables X_i and Y_i are defined to denote the allowed changes in its status (i.e., presence or absence), and $X_{i,j}$ and $Y_{i,j}$ to denote the allowed change for task execution sequence (i.e., in sequence or not). Their meaning is defined as follows:

$$X_i = \begin{cases} 1, & if\ T_i\ flips\ from\ 0\ to\ 1 \\ 0, & if\ no\ flip \end{cases} \qquad Y_i = \begin{cases} 1, & if\ T_i\ flips\ from\ 1\ to\ 0 \\ 0, & if\ no\ flip \end{cases}$$

$$X_{i,j} = \begin{cases} 1, & if\ S_{i,j}\ flips\ from\ 0\ to\ 1 \\ 0, & if\ no\ flip \end{cases} \qquad Y_{i,j} = \begin{cases} 1, & if\ S_{i,j}\ flips\ from\ 1\ to\ 0 \\ 0, & if\ no\ flip \end{cases}$$

An X_i or $X_{i,j}$ above represents a change from 0 to 1 (i.e. a task or a sequence relationship is added), while a Y_i or $Y_{i,j}$ represents a removal of a task or a sequence relationship. Both types of changes are possible. Then, we define $T_i \leftarrow T_i + X_i - Y_i$, $0 \leq T_i + X_i - Y_i \leq 1$ to represent the new task status after possible changes, and define $S_{i,j} \leftarrow S_{i,j} + X_{i,j} - Y_{i,j}$, $0 \leq S_{i,j} + X_{i,j} - Y_{i,j} \leq 1$ to reflect the new task pair execution sequence after possible changes. Our objective is to find if there is a solution to minimize the total number of changes represented by the objective function $\sum_{i=1}^{n} \sum_{j=1}^{n} (X_i + Y_i + X_{i,j} + Y_{i,j})$. Three results are possible in accordance with the above three cases:

(1) a solution is found with all variable values 0, and the objective function also 0;
(2) a non-zero solution is found with non-zero values assigned to some variables;
(3) no feasible solution is found.

The feasible solution for X_i, Y_i, $X_{i,j}$ and $Y_{i,j}$, denotes the status and sequential changes required task or sequential relationship. As shown in Table 4, the change operations can be specified in the same formalism as semantic constraints to check their compliance.

Table 4. Specification of change operations for compliance checking

Change operations	Formal constraint specification
insert (T, N_1, N_2): insert task T between tasks N_1 and N_2	$T = 1$, $S_{N_1,T} = 1$, $S_{T,N_2} = 1$
delete (T): delete task T	$T = 0$
move (T, N_1, N_2): move task T to between node N_1 and N_2	$S_{N_1,T} = 1$, $S_{T,N_2} = 1$; remove any sequence status constraints for the former position of T
replace (T_1, T_2): replace T_1 by T_2	$T_1 = 0$, $T_2 = 1$, $S_{N_1,T_2} = 1$, $S_{T_2,N_2} = 1$ (note: $[N_1, N_2]$ denotes the original position for T_1)
swap (T_1, T_2): swap tasks T_1 and T_2	$S_{N_3,T_1} = 1$, $S_{T_1,N_4} = 1$, $S_{N_1,T_2} = 1$, $S_{T_2,N_2} = 1$ (note: $[N_1, N_2]$ and $[N_3, N_4]$ denotes the original positions for T_1 and T_2)

4.4 Example

To illustrate our approach, we continue with the example in Fig. 1. In addition, we define two new tasks: task T_{12} as "amoxicillin medication", and T_{13} as "Therapy C". Thus, $T = \{T_1, T_2, ..., T_{13}\}$. We can define a validated set of semantic constraints for this process (i.e., with no redundancy or conflict): SC = $\{SC_1, SC_2, ..., SC_7\}$. Their description and formal definitions are provided in Table 5.

Table 5. Semantic constraints for clinical process in Fig. 1

#	Semantic meaning	Definition
SC_1	T_3 (diagnosis & preparation) is dependent on T_4 (therapy A)	$T_3 \leq T_4$
SC_2	T_9 (surgical planning) and T_{10} (surgery) must coexist	$T_9 = T_{10}$
SC_3	T_3 (diagnosis & preparation) must be done before T_4 (therapy A)	$S_{3,4} = 1$
SC_4	T_2 (anamnesis & examination) is mandatory	$T_2 = 1$
SC_5	T_{12} (medication of amoxicillin) and T_{13} (Therapy C) are exclusive since they have the same function	$T_{12} + T_{13} \leq 1$
SC_6	At least 2 imaging diagnoses are needed to ensure accuracy.	$T_5 + T_6 + T_7 \geq 2$
SC_7	T_9 (surgical planning) must be executed before T_{10} (surgery)	$S_{9,10} = 1$

Now we use the process described in the above section to check the compliance of change operations. Say, upon completion of T_2, a patient status change is triggered because the system detects this patient is pregnant, hypersensitive to penicillin, and has a bacterial infection. This necessitates therapy and medication changes. Moreover, because of the equipment availability schedule, the surgery step T_{10} has to be advanced to before the surgical planning step. Hence, a set of five change operations is triggered:

$CP = \{OP_0, OP_1, OP_2, OP_3, OP_4\}$, where:

$OP_0 =$ delete (T_7), i.e. delete CT scan task (T7).

$OP_1 =$ delete (T_4), i.e. delete the Therapy A task.

$OP_2 =$ insert (T_{12}, T_2), i.e. insert 'amoxicillin medication' task after T2

$OP_3 =$ swap (T_9, T_{10}), i.e. swap 'surgical planning' and 'surgery' tasks

$OP_4 =$ replace (T_8, T_{13}), replace the task 'Therapy B' with 'Therapy C'

We use the notation introduced in section 4.3 to define variables and can construct the following formulation:

Objective: Minimize $\sum_{i=1}^{13} \sum_{j=1}^{13} (X_i + Y_i + X_{i,j} + Y_{i,j})$

Such that:

Semantic constraints:

$$T_4 + X_4 - Y_4 \leq T_3 + X_3 - Y_3 \qquad \dots SC_1$$
$$T_9 + X_9 - Y_9 = T_{10} + X_{10} - Y_{10} \qquad \dots SC_2$$
$$S_{3,4} + X_{3,4} - Y_{3,4} = 1; \quad S_{3,4} + S_{4,3} \leq 1 \qquad \dots SC_3$$
$$T_2 = 1 \qquad \dots SC_4$$
$$T_{12} + X_{12} - Y_{12} + T_{13} + X_{13} - Y_{13} \leq 1 \qquad \dots SC_5$$
$$T_5 + X_5 - Y_5 + T_6 + X_6 - Y_6 + T_7 + X_7 - Y_7 \geq 2 \qquad \dots SC_6$$
$$S_{9,10} + X_{9,10} - Y_{9,10} = 1; \quad S_{9,10} + S_{10,9} \leq 1 \qquad \dots SC_7$$

Task status constraints (from known values):

$$T_1 = 1; \ T_2 = 1; \ T_3 = 1; \ T_4 = 1; \ T_5 = 1; \ T_6 = 1; \qquad \dots TS1$$
$$T_7 = 1; \ T_8 = 1; \ T_9 = 1; \ T_{10} = 1; \ T_{11} = 1; \ T_{12} = 0; \ T_{13} = 0;$$

Sequence status constraints:

$$S_{1,2} = 1; \ S_{2,3} = 1; \ S_{2,5} = 1; \ S_{2,6} = 1; \ S_{2,7} = 1; \ S_{3,4} = 1; \ \dots SS1$$
$$S_{3,4} = 1; S_{3,4} = 1; S_{4,11} = 1; \dots.$$
$$S_{5,8} = 1; \ S_{6,8} = 1; S_{7,8} = 1; S_{9,10} = 1; \ S_{10,11} = 1;$$

We can solve this formulation in the LPSolve tool [15]. We found a feasible solution with the objective and all variable values 0. These constraints capture the existing process description and the semantic constraints that apply to it.

4.5   Analysis of the Example and Results

Now, the change operations are also converted into constraints as follows:

Change operations:

$OP0$: $T_7 = 0$

$OP1$: $T_4 = 0$

$OP2$: $T_{12} = 1, S_{2,12} = 1$

$OP3$: $S_{10,9} = 1$

$OP4$: $T_8 = 0; T_{13} = 1; \quad S_{3,13} = 1; \ S_{13,11} = 1$

For each operation we modify the IP formulation using the change_IP algorithm:

Algorithm change_IP

(1) <u>Semantic constraints</u>: for each operation pertaining to task T_i, replace $T_i + X_i - Y_i$ with the value assigned to T_i in the change operation.

(2) <u>Semantic constraints</u>: similarly, for a sequence variable $S_{i,j}$, replace $S_{i,j} + X_{i,j} - Y_{i,j}$ with the value assigned to $S_{i,j}$ in the change operation.

(3) <u>Task status constraints</u>: update the constraint to assign the new value as per the change operation. If T_i was 1, but is to be deleted then set $T_i = 0$.

(4) <u>Sequence status constraints</u>: If a deleted task, say T_i appears in a sequence constraint as $S_{i,j}$ or $S_{j,i}$, then delete this constraint since the task is deleted. If task T_i is replaced by task T_k, then replace all i occurrences by k in $S_{i,j}$ or $S_{j,i}$, for all j.

After these modifications, we solve the new IP formulation using LPSolve. Table 6 shows the results of adding the operations one at a time. The last column gives the values of the objective function (Obj), and the non-zero variables in the solution. In row 1, Obj is 0; thus, the operation is allowed. In row 2, Obj and Y_3 are both 1. This indicates that task T3 should be deleted. This is a *compensation* operation for task T4 because T3 is dependent on T4. Moreover, OP3 is *infeasible*, while OP2 and OP4 are *allowed*. Thus, $\Delta_{op} = \{\text{delete}(T_3), \text{cancel}(OP3)\}$. Thus, by applying Δ_{op}, it is possible to take the process into a state with no constraint violations.

Table 6. Results of analyzing change operations using the IP approach

Change operation	New constraint(s)	Result
OP0: Delete task T_7	$T_7 = 0$	Obj = 0; the operation is *allowed*
OP1: Delete task T_4	$T_4 = 0$	Obj = 1; Y_3 =1; *compensate*: i.e. delete task T3
OP2: insert (T_{12}, T_2)	$T_{12} = 1, S_{3,12} = 1,$ $S_{12,4} = 1$	Obj = 0; the operation is *allowed*
OP3: swap (T_9, T_{10})	$S_{10,9} = 1$	Obj = 2; operation is *infeasible*
OP4: replace (T_8, T_{13})	$T_8 = 0; T_{13} = 1;$ $S_{5,13}$ =1; $S_{6,13}$ =1; $S_{7,13}$ =1;	Obj = 0; operation is *allowed*

5   Discussion and Related Work

The integer programming (IP) based approach has several advantages over a logic based approach, such as first order predicate logic. First, it is very difficult to express m-of-n constraints in logic such as SC_6 in Table 5. Second, logic does not allow us to find an optimal solution to ensure weak compliance as we can do with the IP method. Thirdly, commutative and transitive relationships can be expressed more simply and elegantly in the proposed formalism as compared to that with logic. Finally, IP formulations can be solved very efficiently using a variety of open source tools. A more exhaustive evaluation is out of our current scope and is left for future work.

Two streams of research efforts are involved in the flexible process modeling area: the *imperative* (or *change-based*) *approach* which provides a variety of change patterns (e.g., delete or insert a task) that can be applied to the process model or instance, and the *declarative* (or *constraint-based*) *approach* which uses constraints to restrict possible task execution options. The imperative approach adds the exception handling capability to existing workflow management systems [16-18]. Among research prototypes, ADEPT$_{flex}$ [19] supports a comprehensive set of operations for dynamic workflow adaptation at both the process model and instance level. It is based on a manual approach where the user has to decide which events constitute logical failures and which adaptations have to be performed. CBRFlow [20] uses a case-based reasoning approach to support adaptations of predefined workflow models to changing circumstances by allowing annotation of business rules during runtime via incremental evaluation of the user. However, users must be actively involved in the inference process during each case. The manual approaches do not scale because they are time consuming and error prone.

Recent studies on adaptation are useful but also have limitations. AgentWork [6] provides the ability to modify process instances by dropping and adding individual tasks based on events, and ECA rules. It also gives a table for checking compatibility of various operations. However, semantic issues are neglected. FLOWer [21] is a case handling paradigm which describes only the preferred way of doing things and a variety of mechanism are offered to allow users to deviate in a controlled manner.

The declarative approach limits the process flexibility by enforcing required constraints among tasks. To increase flexibility in an imperative process, more execution paths have to be modeled explicitly, whereas increasing the flexibility in declarative processes is accomplished by reducing the number of constraints, or weakening the existing constraints [22]. Other studies using the declarative approach, such as [23], present a foundation set of constraints which allows ad hoc changes to workflows for highly flexible processes, based on the concept of "pockets of flexibility". They also provide a discussion on both static verification (i.e., conflict validation) and dynamic verification (i.e., template validation). Reference [14] proposed constraint modeling including selection and scheduling constraints. Selection constraints are used to conceptually express task selection requirements and scheduling constraints model the temporal property of each task in a process template. Although they mentioned validation of constraints and process templates, they do not provide a formalized mechanism for validation. The *Declare* framework [24] is developed to address the full spectrum of flexibility while at the same time supporting the user with recommendations and other process-mining-based diagnostics.

6   Conclusion

Increasingly, processes that arise in healthcare and other applications need flexibility and ease of adaptability to changes and events in the environment. They cannot be treated as rigid production processes. Rule based approaches, such as ECA, lend themselves well to the design of such processes. However, it is also important to ensure that changes conform to semantic constraints. We propose a new approach for detecting and correcting any violations to such constraints. It is based on a formal language for describing constraints that captures a large set of existential and coordination relationships among tasks, an integer programming formulation, and solution and analysis techniques. When change operations occur, by using a notion of weak compliance, we can determine a minimum set of additional process changes required to restore compliance. This feature is not possible with first-order logic.

So far we only have a basic proof of concept. But in future work our goal is to have a more complete implementation, and integrate it within a BPM environment with suitable plug-ins. We plan to do more exhaustive testing with larger examples. In particular, we would like to include transitivity of the sequence relationship in the examples, and show how our approach can identify transitivity problems that arise from change operations. Finally, we plan to align our approach with the new Rule Interchange Format (RIF) that has become a W3C standard in June 2010 [25].

References

1. Bae, J., et al.: Automatic control of workflow processes using ECA rules. IEEE Transactions on Knowledge and Data Engineering 16, 1010–1023 (2004)
2. Ly, L., et al.: On enabling integrated process compliance with semantic constraints in process management systems. Information Systems Frontiers (2009)
3. Blaser, R., et al.: Improving pathway compliance and clinician performance by using information technology. International Journal of Medical Informatics 76, 151–156 (2007)
4. OMG: Business Process Modeling Notation (BPMN) Version 1.0. OMG Final Adopted Specification. Object Management Group (2006)
5. Kumar, A., Yao, W.: Process Materialization Using Templates and Rules to Design Flexible Process Models. In: Governatori, G., Hall, J., Paschke, A. (eds.) RuleML 2009. LNCS, vol. 5858, pp. 122–136. Springer, Heidelberg (2009)
6. Müller, R., Greiner, U., Rahm, E.: Agentwork: a workflow system supporting rule-based workflow adaptation. Data & Knowledge Engineering 51, 223–256 (2004)
7. jBoss: Drools, http://jboss.org/drools/
8. Reaction RuleML, http://reaction.ruleml.org
9. Paschke, A., Kozlenkov, A.: Rule-Based Event Processing and Reaction Rules. In: Governatori, G., Hall, J., Paschke, A. (eds.) RuleML 2009. LNCS, vol. 5858, pp. 53–66. Springer, Heidelberg (2009)
10. Paschke, A., Kozlenkov, A., Boley, H.: A homogenous reaction rule language for complex event processing. In: Proc. 2nd International Workshop on Event Drive Architecture and Event Processing Systems, EDA-PS 2007 (2007)
11. Paschke, A.: ECA-RuleML: An Approach combining ECA Rules with temporal interval-based KR Event/Action Logics and Transactional Update Logics. Arxiv preprint cs/0610167 (2006)
12. Weber, B., Reichert, M., Rinderle-Ma, S.: Change patterns and change support features-enhancing flexibility in process-aware information systems. DKE 66, 438–466 (2008)
13. Ly, L.T., Rinderle, S., Dadam, P.: Integration and verification of semantic constraints in adaptive process management systems. Data & Knowledge Engineering 64, 3–23 (2008)
14. Lu, R., Sadiq, S., Governatori, G.: On managing business processes variants. Data & Knowledge Engineering 68, 642–664 (2009)
15. Berkelaar, M., Eikland, K., Notebaert, P.: lp solve
16. Chiu, D.K.W., Li, Q., Karlapalem, K.: A meta modeling approach to workflow management systems supporting exception handling* 1. Information Systems 24, 159–184 (1999)

17. Hagen, C., Alonso, G.: Exception handling in workflow management systems. IEEE Transactions on Software Engineering 26, 943–958 (2000)
18. Luo, Z., et al.: Exception handling in workflow systems. Applied Intelligence 13, 125–147 (2000)
19. Reichert, M., Dadam, P.: ADEPT flex—supporting dynamic changes of workflows without losing control. Journal of Intelligent Information Systems 10, 93–129 (1998)
20. Weber, B., Wild, W., Breu, R.: CBRFlow: Enabling adaptive workflow management through conversational case-based reasoning. In: Funk, P., González Calero, P.A. (eds.) ECCBR 2004. LNCS (LNAI), vol. 3155, pp. 89–101. Springer, Heidelberg (2004)
21. van der Aalst, W.M.P., Weske, M., Grünbauer, D.: Case handling: a new paradigm for business process support. Data & Knowledge Engineering 53, 129–162 (2005)
22. Schonenberg, M.H., et al.: Towards a taxonomy of process flexibility (extended version). BPM Center Report BPM-07-11, BPMcenter. org. (2007)
23. Sadiq, S.W., Orlowska, M.E., Sadiq, W.: Specification and validation of process constraints for flexible workflows. Information Systems 30, 349–378 (2005)
24. van der Aalst, W., Pesic, M., Schonenberg, H.: Declarative workflows: Balancing between flexibility and support. Computer Science - Research and Development 23, 99–113 (2009)
25. W3C: Rule Interchange Format, RIF (2010),
    http://www.w3.org/TR/rif-overview/

Establishing a Procedure Model for Combining and Synergistically Aligning Business Rules and Processes within Ontologies

Alexander Sellner[1], Adrian Paschke[2], and Erwin Zinser[1]

[1] FH JOANNEUM University of Applied Sciences, Department of Information Management
Alte Poststrasse 147, 8020 Graz, Austria
`{Alexander.Sellner,Erwin.Zinser}@fh-joanneum.at`
[2] Freie Universitaet Berlin, Institut for Computer Science, AG Corporate Semantic Web
Koenigin-Luise-Str. 24/26, 14195 Berlin, Germany
`Paschke@inf.fu-berlin.de`

Abstract. Business Rule Management (BRM) and Business Process Management (BPM) present two viable strategies for improving organizational efficiency and effectiveness as well as achieving enterprise agility. In addition, both approaches aim at establishing a close IT-business alignment. Recently, semantic paradigms have been introduced in order to achieve a close relationship and automated understanding between BRM/BPM models and natural language. This paper presents a prototypical approach for integrating business rules into a natural language-like and strongly IT-supported subject-predicate-object notation of subject oriented business process models based on a shared organizational semantic vocabulary. Scientific findings derived from this approach are used to establish a consistent procedure model for representing and linking business rules and processes within ontologies.

Keywords: Rule-based Event Processing and Reaction Rules, Subject oriented business process modeling, Ontologies.

1 Introduction

The areas of business rules and business process management (BPM) can be seen as two different perspectives for achieving IT-business alignment and enterprise agility [1]. Business rules are required to be derived from an organization's strategy and need to be kept well separated from business processes [2]. Nevertheless, business rules are often implicitly included when modeling business processes according to BPM principles. Another challenge is the establishment of a shared business vocabulary within decision-intensive and process focused organizations as well as to preserve consistency and integrity within the contents of this 'organizational dictionary'. Recent approaches for defining and interchanging natural language based business vocabulary and business rules intensively relate to the OMG standard Semantic of Business Vocabulary and Rules (SBVR)[1]. SBVR realizes a core principle of the

---

[1] SBVR `http://www.omg.org/spec/SBVR/`

M. Dean et al. (Eds.): RuleML 2010, LNCS 6403, pp. 66–73, 2010.

business rules approach by expressing rules with fact types being built on concepts expressed by terms. As a result, controlled natural language definitions such as SBVR Structured English can be used to establish meta models for establishing business rules [3].

In the area of business process management, the use of natural language is not necessarily seen as the starting point for building models. This paper presents a first approach for applying the business rules concept to the subject oriented business process modeling (S-BPM) approach. The main motivation is that both concepts are easy to understand and focus on using the natural language as basis for creating models, leading to the assumption for the general feasibility of a rule and process integration within that environment. A prototype was developed using the jCOM1 BPM Suite[2] as S-BPM modeling tool and the Rules Composer component of Microsoft BizTalk Server[3] for defining business rules. Deductions taken from this approach led to a procedure model for representing and linking business rules and processes within ontologies.

The paper is structured as follows: Section 2 briefly explains the concepts of business rules, S-BPM and areas of application for ontologies. Section 3 focuses on establishing a prototype for rule enactment within S-BPM. Section 4 presents a consistent procedure model for representing and linking business rules and processes by use of ontologies. Section 5 concludes the paper.

2 Background

2.1 S-BPM Approach

Subject oriented business process modeling (S-BPM) brings together the two concepts of flow-based and object oriented process descriptions. The idea is to present an easy to learn and reusable approach where real-life processes can be immediately captured in an abstract form [4].

The underlying concept is to describe business processes starting from written definitions in the natural language by using the generic elements of human communication, namely subject, predicate, and object. As this modeling language is very easy to learn and understand by non-IT personnel, it can help a lot in order to close the gap between business-oriented and IT-focused environments. Moreover, the mapping into the machine-understandable Semantic Web RDF triple syntax of "subject predicate object" becomes easier. Having a look at the Business Process Modeling Notation (BPMN), it shows that although it is one of the most commonly used modeling standards, only a few modeling symbols are actually used in practice [5], pointing to a too high degree of complexity.

As already revealed by the name, S-BPM primarily focuses on all subjects being involved in a process. The subjects exhibit internal behaviors to transform data objects and trigger interactions which are grammatically equivalent to predicates.

---

[2] jCOM1 S-BPM Suite - http://jcom1.com/cms/index.php?id=152&L=1
[3] Microsoft BizTalk Server –
http://www.microsoft.com/biztalk/en/us/default.aspx

Consequently, the use of predicates leads to the need for objects as elements being affected by subject interactions.

Following these principles, the basic grammatical constituents of the sequence flows *"Customer (subject1) sends (predicate1) request (object1)"* and *"Vendor (subject2) creates (predicate2) offer (object2)"* can be modeled within the S-BPM approach, before they are combined to a generic process (see Figure 1).

Having a look at the jCOM1 BPM suite as the practical application of S-BPM, the basic elements are expressed in the following way:

- Subjects are directly expressed by a modeling shape
- Objects are comparable to messages. They can be represented as so called "business objects" making use of XML schemas representing data structures
- Predicates are defined by the internal behavior of subjects, making use of three basic modeling shapes: send action, receive action, and internal function.

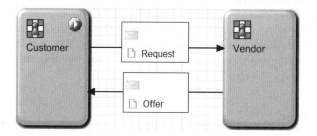

Fig. 1. Sample S-BPM process model within the jCOM1 BPM suite

One of the major advantages of the jCOM1 BPM suite is also that process models can be immediately validated meaning they can be executed on a web server during design time. This enables direct workflow integration and facilitates modifications or changes to S-BPM processes.

2.2 Business Rules Approach

In general, business rules are instructions or restrictions triggered by business events. Hence, they represent derivatives from a company's strategy and aim at establishing unified descriptions of a company's business activities in order to achieve customer satisfaction and an effective use of resources [6].

To give an example, a business rule might be defined as follows: *If the total amount of an order exceeds $5000, a rebate of 5% is granted.* The example illustrates that, similar to the S-BPM approach described above, business rules are also defined using natural language aiming at providing a fully integrated approach for executing business directives defined by people with business background within IT systems.

An important prerequisite for the integration of the business rules approach is the definition of a business vocabulary. This ensures a consistent use of language terms throughout the whole company [7]. Typically, business rules in IT environments are expressed as reaction rules, relating to the general definitions of rules [8]:

- Normative rules: They serve as constraints on data structures to ensure consistency and compliance with business logic.
- Reaction rules: They are used for programming rule-based, reactive systems and can be classified in Event-Condition-Action (ECA) rules and production rules [9].
- Derivation rules: These rules serve to derive knowledge from knowledge. They can, for instance, act as a filter on a large amount of data. Derivation rules can occur in combination with normative and reactive rules and also serve to derive implicit facts using forward or backward reasoning [10].

2.3 Ontologies

Over the last years, various aspects have been discovered of how ontologies can lead to improvements within the area of information systems such as for evaluating business process modeling languages [11], bringing together languages describing software systems [12] or serving as meta model to validate the correctness of business process models based on natural language [13]. Different types of ontologies have been developed which can serve as organizational reference ontology such as top level ontologies (e.g. TOVE [14]), business model ontologies (e.g. REA [15]) or other upper level ontologies (e.g. SUMO [16]).

3 Rule Enactment within S-BPM

An overview of the technical concept for linking business rules and S-BPM is presented in Figure 2. The general approach was to establish a shared business vocabulary by establishing a commonly used XML schema. Regarding rule, enactment, the BizTalk Rules composer was selected to serve as repository for providing business rules to jCOM1 BPM suite where processes and integrated rules could be instantly validated and executed.

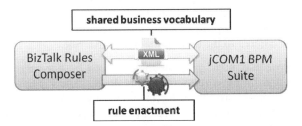

Fig. 2. Technical concept of linking business rules and S-BPM

The most feasible approach identified when creating the prototype was to create code snippets with a general structure of the rules, based on the rule data model and to define dynamic parts of the rules such as business objects names and values from this structure. By allowing database queries for modifications to these parts during runtime, a flexible rule integration within S-BPM models was achieved.

The overall approach for modeling and enacting business rules within S-BPM is graphically displayed in Figure 3:

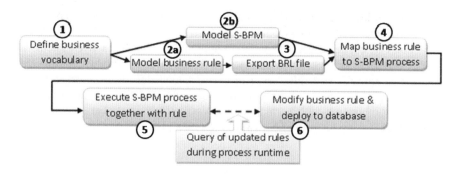

Fig. 3. Enacting business rules in S-BPM notations

4 Procedure Model for Representing and Linking Business Rules and Processes within Ontologies

The evaluation of the approach clearly revealed challenges regarding the discovery of common standards, the definition of a complex business vocabulary and the avoidance of semantic gaps within this vocabulary. These challenges can be overcome, having a look at the general attributes of ontologies:

- Ontologies serving as meta models can help to overcome problems regarding different modeling standards. As soon as models can be exported in a way that enables annotation, the ontology serves as common basis for the models.
- Regarding the definition and maintenance of a complex business vocabulary, ontologies provide ideal support by providing methods for validation and verification of semantic environments.
- Based on findings and prototypes regarding the representation reactive business rules in ontologies [17], solutions to the problems of having semantic gaps in heterogeneous modeling environments and ECA statements which are not entirely decoupled from business processes are identified by establishing ontologies that are specifically tailored to the description of reactive rules.

The following procedure model presents the approach for a synergistic alignment of business process and business rules within ontologies (see Figure 4). The model is based on an initial procedure model for integrated modeling of rules and processes [18], an execution environment for semantic process modeling [19] and the procedure used for the integration of S-BPM and business rules presented earlier in this paper.

The first step is to define overall business objectives which will be expressed by rules and processes. The experiences derived from the implementation of business rules into S-BPM have shown that it is essential to establish a common business vocabulary. The definition of business objectives will lead to the definition of such a business vocabulary describing business objects and activities involved. At this early stage, a reference ontology needs to be adopted according to the capabilities required for the semantic representation of the semantic business environment. Such a reference ontology, can also be a combination of top and upper level ontologies, which have been presented earlier in this paper [20].

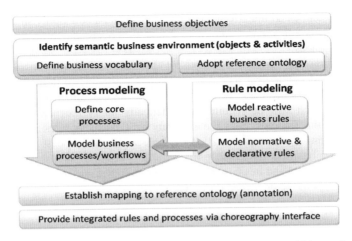

Fig. 4. Procedure model for linking business rules and processes within ontologies

After the adoption of a reference ontology, modeling of rules and processes can be carried out. The idea is to allow the use of independent modeling environment and to establish links directly within the ontology. On the process side, core processes are identified and initial process models are drafted. Within the S-BPM modeling approach of the jCOM1 suite, this would mean to capture the core processes in written or electronic form by collaborating with all people being involved in the process. On the rules side, reactive business rules are modeled. Modeling of rules and processes is done according to the already established business vocabulary, which can of course be extended if necessary.

Based on the core process definitions, modeling of business processes can be performed at workflow level. At this point, in order to preserve consistency and integrity within the ontological definitions, normative and declarative rules need to be put in place. Following the goal of unified rule modeling, it is advisable to define normative ontological rules being valid for business processes in the same environment as executable business rules. A continuous cross-checking needs to be performed between these rules and workflow-enabled business processes.

Mapping of rules and processes is continuously carried out using the respective annotation to the reference ontology. Hence, the models need to be exported in a standardized format before they are ontologically annotated.

Regarding the actual execution of integrated business processes and rules within IT environments, the goal is to provide the rules and processes model as distributed semantic web services via a standardized choreography interfaces [21].

5 Conclusions and Future Work

Prototypic work has shown that the concepts of subject oriented process modeling and business rules, both being based on natural language statements, can be combined, leading towards the goal of achieving enterprise agility. When aiming for a common integration of business rules and processes, several questions arise in context of keeping consistency and integrity within the models and a commonly shared business vocabulary. The application of ontologies can help to overcome these conceptual and technical challenges.

By following the general concepts of business rules and business process management and ontological modeling, it becomes possible to develop a procedure model for combining business rules and processes within ontologies.

Further research will be required to practically apply the presented procedure model. Taken the findings from the integration of business rules into the S-BPM approach, an ontological representation of subject oriented process models together with integrated business rules will provide further insights into the potential of the integration of S-BPM and business rules within ontologies and will serve as a proof of the practicability of the presented procedure model.

References

1. Harmon, P.: Business Rules and Business Processes. In: Business Process Trends, http://www.bptrends.com/ (accessed November 17, 2009)
2. von Halle, B., Goldberg, L.: The Business Rule Revolution. Happy About, Silicon Valley (2006)
3. Spreeuwenberg, S., Gerrits, R.: Business Rules in the Semantic Web, Are There Any or Are They Different? In: Barahona, P., Bry, F., Franconi, E., Henze, N., Sattler, U. (eds.) Reasoning Web 2006. LNCS, vol. 4126, pp. 152–163. Springer, Heidelberg (2006)
4. Schmidt, W., Fleischmann, A., Gilbert, O.: Subjektorientiertes Geschäftsprozessmanagement. Praxis der Wirtschaftsinformatik (2009)
5. zur Muehlen, M., Recker, J.: How Much Language is Enough? Theoretical and Practical Use of the Business Process Modeling Notation. In: Bellahsène, Z., Léonard, M. (eds.) CAiSE 2008. LNCS, vol. 5074, pp. 465–479. Springer, Heidelberg (2008)
6. Morgan, T.: Business Rules and Information Systems. Addison-Wesley, Indianapolis (2002)
7. Ross, R.: Business Rule Concepts: Getting to the Point of Knowledge. Business Rule Solutions (2009)
8. Boley, H., Kifer, M., Patranjan, P.-L., Polleres, A.: Rule Interchange on the Web. In: Antoniou, G., Aßmann, U., Baroglio, C., Decker, S., Henze, N., Patranjan, P.-L., Tolksdorf, R. (eds.) Reasoning Web. LNCS, vol. 4636, pp. 269–309. Springer, Heidelberg (2007)
9. Paschke, A., Boley, H.: Rules Capturing Event and Reactivity. In: Handbook of Research on Emerging Rule-Based Languages and Technologies: Open Solutions and Approaches (2009)
10. Paschke, A.: ECA-RuleML: An approach combining ECA rules with temporal interval-based KR event logics and transactional update logics. Technical Report 11, Technische Universität München (2005)
11. Van Nuffel, D., Mulder, H., Van Kervel, S.: Enhancing the formal Foundations of BPMN by Enterprise Ontology. Advances in Enterprise Engineering III (2009)
12. Bräuer, M., Lochmann, H.: Towards Semantic Integration of Multiple. Domain-Specific Languages Using Ontological Foundations. In: Proceedings of 4th International Workshop on (Software) Language Engineering (ATEM 2007) co-located with MoDELS 2007 (2007)

13. Di Francescomarino, C., Ghidini, C., Rospocher, M., Serafini, L., Tonella, P.: Semantically-aided business process modeling. In: International Semantic Web Conference (2009)
14. Fox, M.: The TOVE Project: A Common-sense Model of the Enterprise. In: Belli, F., Radermacher, F.J. (eds.) IEA/AIE 1992. LNCS, vol. 604. Springer, Heidelberg (1992)
15. McCarthy, W.: The REA Accounting Model: A Generalized Framework for Accounting Systems in a Shared Data Environment. The Accounting Review (1982)
16. Niles, I., Pease, A.: Towards a Standard Upper Ontology. In: Proceedings of the International Conference on Formal Ontology in Information Systems (2001)
17. Alferes, J., Amador, R.: r3– A Foundational Ontology for Reactive Rules. In: Meersman, R., Tari, Z. (eds.) OTM 2007, Part I. LNCS, vol. 4803, pp. 933–952. Springer, Heidelberg (2007)
18. zur Muehlen, M., Indulska, M., Kittel, K.: Towards Integrated Modeling of Business Processes and Business Rules. In: 19th Australasian Conference on Information Systems (2008)
19. Barnickel, N., Böttcher, J., Paschke, A.: Incorporating Semantic Bridges into Information Flow of Cross-Organizational Business Process Models. In: I-Semantics 2010 (2010)
20. Andersson, B., Bergholtz, M., Edirisuriya, A., Ilayperuma, T., Johannesson, P., Gordijn, J., Grégoire, B., Schmitt, M., Dubois, E., Abels, S., Hahn, A., Wangler, B., Weigand, H.: Towards a Reference Ontology for Business Models. In: Embley, D.W., Olivé, A., Ram, S. (eds.) ER 2006. LNCS, vol. 4215, pp. 482–496. Springer, Heidelberg (2006)
21. Paschke, A., Teymourian, K.: Rule Based Business Process Execution with BPEL+. In: I-Semantics 2009 (2009)

Rule-Based Contextual Reasoning
in Ambient Intelligence

Antonis Bikakis and Grigoris Antoniou

Institute of Computer Science, FO.R.T.H., Vassilika Voutwn
P.O. Box 1385, GR 71110, Heraklion, Greece
{bikakis,antoniou}@ics.forth.gr

Abstract. *Context*, *Context Representation* and *Contextual Reasoning* constitute central notions in the Ambient Intelligence vision to transform our living and working environments into '*intelligent spaces*'. Ontology-based models have been argued to satisfy all demands concerning context representation. Rule-based reasoning has already been successfully integrated in ontology-based applications for domains with similar requirements (e.g. the Web), while it offers significant advantages concerning its deployment in the Ambient Intelligence domain. In this paper, we analyze the general challenges of contextual reasoning, argue about the suitability of rule-based reasoning, and describe the deployment of such methods in two different settings; in a centralized semantics-based context management framework for Ambient Intelligence, and in a totally distributed system of logic-based abient agents.

1 Introduction

Rules and Inferencing constitutes a subfield of Artificial Intelligence, which studies logic-based models, methods and tools aimed at automating inference in computer systems. Over the last years a great number of studies have focused on different forms of rule-based inferencing, including classical, modal, deontic, defeasible, spatiotemporal and contextual reasoning, as well as on their applications to several domains, with Business Rule Processing and Web-Centered Reasoning being the most prominent and successful examples. This paper focuses on another domain with much more demanding requirements and challenges, where rules are expected to play a significant role; the Ambient Intelligence domain.

Ambient Intelligence constitutes a new paradigm of interaction between agents acting on behalf of humans, smart objects and devices. Its ultimate goal is the transformation of our living and working environments into '*intelligent spaces*', which are able to adapt to changes in contexts as well as to their users' needs and desires. This requires augmenting the environments with sensing, computing, communicating and reasoning capabilities. Ambient Intelligence environments are expected to support humans in their every day tasks and activities in a personalized, adaptive, seamless and unobtrusive fashion. To achieve this, an Ambient Intelligence system, either if this has the form of a stand-alone application or of a system of agents lying on a variety of devices, must have a thorough understanding of its context, namely of any information that may be relevant to the interaction between the user and the system. Methods and technologies

M. Dean et al. (Eds.): RuleML 2010, LNCS 6403, pp. 74–88, 2010.

from the fields of Knowledge and Reasoning are expected to provide valuable tools in these efforts.

As it becomes obvious, *context* is a central notion in the field of Ambient Intelligence. Context is typically derived from heterogeneous information sources and includes various concepts, such as the roles of people interacting with the environment, their profiles, the devices that they use and their capabilities, their interests, relationships, tasks, activities, intentions and current state, as well as the state of the environment itself, its spatial and temporal dimensions and others. The fact that this information comes at heterogeneous formats prevents applications from interpreting and using it without prior knowledge of the context representation. As a consequence, the need for a *semantically explicit context representation* has emerged, in order for independently developed applications to be able to comprehend it in a common manner and to interoperate within a integrated environment. The approaches for context representation have been classified by [1] to six main categories:

1. *key-value models*, e.g. [2], where services are described with a list of simple attributes in a key-value manner;
2. *markup scheme models*, e.g. the *CC/PP Context Extension* proposed in [3], a XML-based format for exchanging context descriptions;
3. *graphical models*, e.g. the *Context Modeling Language* proposed in [4];
4. *object oriented models*, e.g. the *Active Object Model* of the GUIDE project [5], where all context data is encapsulated within active objects;
5. *logic-based models*, e.g. the First Order Logic-based model used in Gaia [6];
6. *ontology-based models*, which is the most common approach.

Ontologies meet the representation requirements set by many studies in terms of type and level of formality, expressiveness, flexibility and extensibility, generality, granularity and valid context constraining [1,7,8].

On top of the context representation model, appropriate reasoning mechanisms are required to exploit the available context information and add intelligence to the systems. The general aim of contextual reasoning is to derive meaningful high-level information from the available raw context data, and based on this knowledge to determine the appropriate system behavior in order to adapt to its context and to the user's needs and desires. The challenges to this direction are numerous and are mainly caused by the imperfect nature of context and the special characteristics of the environments and the devices that operate in them. The various approaches that have been proposed so far for contextual reasoning on top of ontology-based context models may be classified to the following categories:

1. *ontological reasoning*, where a set of Description Logic rules are primarily used to derive implicit knowledge from the context knowledge base (e.g. [9,10]). Although they naturally integrate with the underlying ontology-based representation model, they offer limited expressive and reasoning capabilities;
2. *rule-based reasoning*, where richer reasoning models are enabled by more expressive rule languages, such as First Order Logic (e.g. [6]), Logic Programming (e.g. [11,12]) and Defeasible Logic (e.g. [13]);

3. *probabilistic reasoning*, which integrates ontology-based models with probabilistic models, such as Bayesian networks [14], in order to explicitly model uncertainty in the context data, confidence in the available sources, and causal relationships between various contexts. The rich expressive capabilities constitute the main advantage of such approaches, while their high complexity and the requirement to explicitly and precisely define uncertainty are their main limitations concerning their deployment in Ambient Intelligence systems.

In the rest of the paper, we focus our attention on rule-based reasoning approaches. Specifically, in Section 2, we analyze the general challenges of contextual reasoning and discuss how rule-based methods may offer efficient solutions. In Sections 3 and 4, we discuss two different directions of contextual reasoning with respect to the allocation of the reasoning tasks. In Section 3, we describe the centralized rule-based approach that we have followed in a context management framework for Ambient Intelligence, while Section 4 describes a totally distributed reasoning framework, where the reasoning tasks are distributed among a set of logic-based agents, interacting through a set of bridge rules. Section 5 concludes with a comparison of the two approaches and with a discussion on open problems and possible future research directions with respect to contextual reasoning in Ambient Intelligence.

2   Rule-based Contextual Reasoning: Challenges and Benefits

The challenges of contextual reasoning in Ambient Intelligence environments result mainly from the imperfect nature of context. Henricksen and Indulska in [15] characterize four types of imperfect context information: *unknown*, *ambiguous*, *imprecise*, and *erroneous*. Sensor or connectivity failures (which are inevitable in wireless connections) result in situations, that not all context data is available at any time. When data about a context property comes from multiple sources, then context may become ambiguous. Imprecision is common in sensor-derived information, while erroneous context arises as a result of human or hardware errors. Moreover, the entities that operate in such environments are expected to have different goals, experiences and perceptive capabilities. They typically have restricted computing capabilities and may use distinct vocabularies to describe their context. Due to the highly dynamic and open nature of the environment (various entities join and leave the environment at random times) and the unreliable and restricted by the range of the transmitters wireless communications, ambient agents do not typically know a priori all other entities that are present at a specific time instance nor can they communicate directly with all of them. The problem becomes even more challenging if we also consider the potentially vast amount of available context information, the distribution of this knowledge to several heterogenous distributed entities and the need for quick adaptation to changes in context.

Rule-based reasoning has already been applied with success to several domains with similar challenges and requirements, such as the Web. Assuming an ontology-based underlying representational model, the main benefits of adopting a rule-based reasoning model are:

1. **Simplicity and flexibility.** Rules are, in general, easy to write and comprehend as most rule languages adopt a natural-language-like syntax. Moreover, they offer

flexibility in the sense that they are easy to adapt, alter and maintain, making them an attractive solution for non-expert users. The development of Ambient Intelligence systems requires cooperation between people with different research backgrounds who must be enabled to easily design the operational behavior of ambient agents, and such features are of great importance.

2. **Formality.** Rule languages are based on formal logics and have a well-defined syntax and semantics. In Ambient Intelligence environments, using formal expressions allows heterogenous agents to communicate, and share and combine their knowledge and beliefs avoiding ambiguities and mistranslation.

3. **Expressivity.** Among the desirable features of contextual reasoning in Ambient Intelligence systems is also the rich expressive capabilities of the underlying language. Compared to ontology languages, rule languages have much more expressive power. For the domain of Ambient Intelligence, some important features that rule languages may support include: (a) *reactivity*, using Event Condition Action rules; (b) *uncertainty*, supported mainly by nonmonotonic rule languages; and (c) *modularity*, which we further analyze below.

4. **Modularity.** Modularity in the rule bases may be a great benefit for context-based systems. It provides better maintainability of the rule base, enables detecting the causes or effects of specific changes in context, and allows managing rules either in a single rule base as well as in several rule bases possibly distributed over several different ambient agents.

5. **High-level abstraction - Information hiding.** In Ambient Intelligence systems, where most information sources are sensors that provide raw low-level context data, the reasoning mechanisms must enable combining this data to infer higher-level context knowledge, and prescribing the system behavior using higher-level abstractions. Rule languages and systems provide such mechanisms, allowing to define several levels of reasoning, which share a limited part of the available knowledge hiding meaningless, not relevant or protected (e.g. by privacy policies) information.

6. **Integration with ontology models.** The integration of rules and ontologies has been extensively studied in the recent years, resulting in several Semantic Web rule languages (e.g. SWRL [16], TRIPLE [17], DLP [18]) and rule systems (e.g. Jena[1], Jess[2], DLV [19], SweetJess [20], DR-DEVICE[21], DR-Prolog[22]), and offering several efficient and ready-to-use solutions with respect to rule-based reasoning on top of ontology-based context models. Furthermore, the research efforts of (a) the RuleML Markup Initiative [3] and (b) the Rule Interchange Format Working Group primarily deal with the standardization of rules for the Semantic Web, which will provide a more formal and steady basis for knowledge sharing between distributed agents.

In the following sections, we describe how rule-based contextual reasoning is used in practice in two different implementations, which are built upon two completely different architectures.

---

[1] Jena, http://jena.sourceforge.net/index.html

[2] Jess, http://www.jessrules.com

[3] RuleML, http://www.ruleml.org/

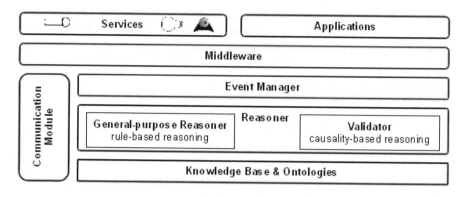

Fig. 1. Context Management Framework for Ambient Intelligence

3   A Centralized Approach

In this section, we describe the rule-based methods that we have employed in a centralized reasoning framework for Ambient Intelligence. The design goals of the framework have been the efficient representation, monitoring and dissemination of any low- or high-level context information, as well as the support for a number of general-purpose and domain-specific inferencing tasks.

The reasoning framework is part of a large-scale Ambient Intelligence facility that is being implemented in ICS-FORTH and has completed its first year of life. It expands in a three-room set up, where a multitude of different -hardware and software- technologies contribute services, such as camera network support for 2D person localization and 3D head pose estimation, RFID, iris and audio sensors for person identification and speech recognition, and multi-protocol wireless communications.

The framework is based on a hybrid event-based reasoning architecture depicted in Fig. 1 (a more detailed description of the system architecture is available at [23]), which comprises four main components:

- the *Event Manager*, which receives and processes incoming events from the ambient infrastructure;
- the rule-based *Reasoning Engine*, which undertakes all required inferencing and reasoning tasks;
- the *Context Knowledge Base*, which stores context information on top of an ontology-based representation model;
- the *Communication Module*, which forwards Reasoning Engine requests for action execution to appropriate services.

A middleware layer acts as a medium for information flow between heterogeneous services and applications. Services denote standalone entities that implement specific functionalities and provide low-level context information about world aspects, such as voice recognition, localization and light management, whereas applications group together service instances to provide an Ambient Intelligence experience in smart rooms. As obvious, the system is built upon a centralized architecture; all relevant context information is provided by services to the central context management framework, which has the full responsibility to process, combine and transform this information into higher-level context knowledge, store this knowledge in the central knowledge base, and apply an appropriate set of rules to achieve a context-aware behavior.

At the core of the system architecture stands an OWL context knowledge base, which captures the meaning and relations of concepts regarding low-level context acquired from sensors, high-level context inferred through reasoning, user and device profiling information, spatial features and resource characteristics. The rule-based reasoning engine is implemented in Jess and enables reasoning tasks of several types, such as high-level context inference, query answering and reactive to context changes decision making. The rules have an Event-Condition-Action (ECA) form; on a specific Event arrival, Conditions are evaluated and if they hold, Action is executed.

Three specific requirements that we wanted to address using this centralized reasoning architecture are: (a) seamless interaction with the supported context-aware services, (b) real-time handling of the potentially vast amount of available context information; and (c) resolution of conflicts that may arise by competing policies, which may represent user preferences, system behavior policies or application policies.

Seamless interaction. Enabling service provision is an anywhere, any-time and for all fashion is among the primary goals of Ambient Intelligence. Systems should always be able to deliver services to the user, but also to adjust services to the user's context. In our system, this is achieved through sensing, high-level context inference and context-aware reasoning. The system keeps track of the user's context, which is obtained by the available sensors, and records all context changes in the central context knowledge base. The inferencing mechanism of the Reasoner enables detecting specific situations. In this way, we can draw conclusions of the form: 'the user is sleeping' or 'the user is having a phone call conversation'. For each of the supported services, we have pre-defined policies in the form of rules that describe the way that the service should be delivered to the user. Consider, for example, the user of a web application (e.g. e-mail application), who is moving between the rooms of his apartment. While in his office, he accesses the application through his desktop PC. When he moves to other rooms, where there is no PC available, the system provides access to the application through his mobile phone, unless there is a screen available that can be used for viewing purposes. In any case, the system provides seamless interaction with the application, adapting the type of interaction to the user's context.

Vast amount of available context information. The volume of sensory data in smart environments may be potentially vast, while the rates of context change are high. A system must be able to process this data on the fly in order to achieve a reactive behavior. We handle such problems using two general methods:

(a) *Context Classification.* The system supports multiple levels of knowledge structuring, and each system component registers only to the appropriate abstraction. In this way, while the localization subsystem uses data from the installed cameras to evaluate a user's location in a room, a map service receives only two coordinates for each detected person at a rate of three messages per second. The context knowledge base, on the other hand, records only substantial changes in the user's position, i.e. the id of each new map area that the user enters, as this is evaluated by the map service.

(b) *Context segmentation*. The intuition behind this method is that not all context data is relevant in every state. In a state that the lights in a room with cameras are off, the data derived from a camera-based localization subsystem should be ignored and the rules that take into account the user's position should not be considered. To this direction, we have deployed a module-based mechanism, which enables dividing the whole set of rules into rule subsets, i.e. modes that prescribe alternate system behavior. Each rule set is assigned to a particular predefined context state, and certain rules allow for the shifting between states when certain context changes are recorded.

Inconsistency resolution. In a setting that several different types of policies may be applied (e.g. user preferences, system behavior policy, application policies etc.), inconsistencies between competing policies are to be expected. Consider, for example, the case that two different users are located in the same room. The policies that prescribe the system's behavior may be conflicting for the two users. The system must be able to resolve such types of conflicts in a principled way. Our solution is based on a priority-based mechanism that classifies rules in sets of different priority using the salience value feature of Jess. Rules with highest priority always fire first, while those with lowest priority do not fire unless all the others do.

4 Contextual Defeasible Reasoning, a Totally Distributed Approach

A totally distributed rule-based approach for contextual reasoning is the *Contextual Defeasible Reasoning (CDL)* approach proposed in [24]. CDL adopts ideas from:

- *Defeasible Logic* [25] - it is rule-based, skeptical, and uses priorities to resolve conflicts among rules;
- *Multi-Context Systems* [26,27], which can be abstractedly defined as a set of contexts, which can be thought of as logic theories, and a set of inference rules (known as mapping or bridge rules) that enable information flow between different contexts.

4.1 Main Features

In CDL, the Multi-Context Systems model is enriched through defeasible rules, and a preference relation reflecting the trust each context assigns to other contexts. Specifically, CDL defines a MCS C as a collection of distributed context theories C_i: A context C_i is defined as a tuple of the form (V_i, R_i, T_i), where V_i is the vocabulary used by C_i, R_i is a set of rules, and T_i is a preference ordering on C. V_i is a set of positive and negative literals, and it is assumed that each context uses a distinct vocabulary.

R_i consists of two sets of rules: the set of local rules and the set of mapping rules. The body of a local rule is a conjunction of *local* literals (literals that are contained in V_i), while its head contains a local literal. There are two types of local rules:

- Strict rules, of the form

$$r_i^l : a_i^1, a_i^2, ...a_i^{n-1} \rightarrow a_i^n$$

They express sound local knowledge and are interpreted in the classical sense: whenever the literals in the body of the rule ($a_i^1, a_i^2, ...a_i^{n-1}$) are strict consequences of the local theory, then so is the conclusion of the rule (a_i^n). Strict rules with empty body denote factual knowledge.

- Defeasible rules, of the form

$$r_i^d : b_i^1, b_i^2, ...b_i^{n-1} \Rightarrow b_i^n$$

They are used to express uncertainty, in the sense that a defeasible rule (r_i^d) cannot be applied to support its conclusion (b_i^n) if there is adequate contrary evidence.

Mapping rules associate literals from the local vocabulary V_i (*local literals*) with literals from the vocabularies of other contexts (*foreign literals*). The body of each such rule is a conjunction of local and foreign literals, while its head contains a single local literal. Mapping rules are modeled as defeasible rules of the form:

$$r_i^m : a_i^1, a_j^2, ...a_k^{n-1} \Rightarrow a_i^n$$

r_i^m associates local literals of C_i (e.g. a_i^1) with local literals of C_j (a_j^2), C_k (a_k^{n-1}) and possibly other contexts. a_i^n is a local literal of the theory that has defined r_i^m (C_i).

Finally, each context C_i defines a strict total preference ordering T_i on C to express its confidence on the knowledge it imports from other contexts. This is of the form:

$$T_i = [C_k, C_l, ..., C_n]$$

According to T_i, C_k is preferred to C_l by C_i, if the rank of C_k is lower than the rank of C_l in T_i. The strict total preference ordering enables resolving all potential conflicts that may arise from the interaction of contexts through their mapping rules.

Contextual reasoning proceeds roughly as follows (more details are available in [24]): when a context C_i processes a query q, it may query through bridge rules other contexts, which in turn may pass on queries to further contexts. Based on the information collected, C_i builds a support set and a blocking set for the query q; these sets contain information about the contexts from which (supporting or attacking) information was received. These are compared to each other, based on the preference order T_i, and a positive or negative conclusion is drawn.

In the simplest case, a context C_j responses to a query issued by context C_i only with true/false. In more complex strategies [28], C_j returns more information regarding the support and blocking sets it built in order to evaluate the appropriate answer. The intuition behind these strategies is that imported knowledge should be evaluated not only based on their 'source', e.g. C_j, but also on the way that the 'source' acquired this knowledge. Specifically, the three alternative strategies rely on the exchange of additional information describing respectively:

- whether the answer is based on local knowledge of C_j, or on combined knowledge of C_j and other contexts. Answers based on local knowledge are always preferred in this case.

- the contexts that are involved in the derivation of the returned answer. Specifically, C_j in this case returns the support set / blocking set for the query, which represents its best justification for the answer.
- the contexts that are involved in all possible derivations of the answer. In this case, the support set / blocking set, which is returned by C_j, contains information about all possible justifications for the answer.

Selection of the right strategy depends, among others, on the requirements regarding efficiency and privacy protection. With respect to complexity, it is obvious that the latter strategies (especially the last one) impose a much heavier overhead in terms of *size of messages* exchanged between the system contexts and *computational complexity* of the algorithm used for query evaluation.

Privacy, on the other hand, is also an important issue in such environments. The latter two strategies require the agents to disclose the identities of the agents that are involved in the derivation of their knowledge. We argue, that in real Ambient Intelligence environments or similar settings that our methods can be applied (e.g. social networks), disclosing this type of information to third parties may be part of an agreement that the agents make, and possibly depends on the privacy policies of the involved agents. For example, an agent may agree to disclose part of its knowledge to another trusted agent, but disagree with the fact that the other agent may reveal its identity to a third party that it may not a priori know or trust. In this case, the latter two strategies are not acceptable, and the agents should resort to one of the first two strategies.

4.2   Application to Ambient Intelligence

CDL has already been applied in real scenarios of several domains, including the Semantic Web [29], Social Networks [30] and Ambient Intelligence [31]. All scenarios require the deployment of CDL algorithms in a variety of stationary and mobile devices. This is achieved using an implementation of CDL methods in Prolog and lightweight Prolog systems. Figure 2 depicts a layered overview of a system node.

- The *Reasoning and Inference* layer is where contextual reasoning is performed. Its implementation is based on the Java 2 Micro edition (J2ME) programming language, which enables java applications on any mobile device that features a Java Virtual Machine - nowadays the vast majority of cell phones, PDAs and set top boxes. The layer implements Contextual Defeasible Logic using a Prolog implementation of the distributed query evalaution algorithms described in [24] and a lightweight Prolog engine, TuProlog [32]. The latter is based on ideas of the logic metaprogram that simulates the proof theoretic semantics of Defeasible Logic [33].
- The *Profile and Knowledge Management* layer stores the local context knowledge of the node, which can be also accessed remotely through the communication layer.
- The *Communications* layer provides a protocol for handling all incoming or outgoing communication of the application using any networking capabilities provided by a given device. The system currently supports (a) access to the Internet through WiFi, GPRS or 3G, (b) access to other devices using P2P connections based on Bluetooth, and (c) use of GSM cellular network to send and receive SMSs.

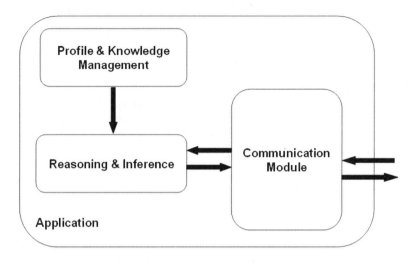

Fig. 2. System Node Layered Architecture

- On top of all layers lies the *Application* layer, which orchestrates all underlying component interactions.

In [31], we describe a use case scenario that highlights the benefits of CDL in the Ambient Intelligence domain. The scenario involves a context-aware mobile phone, which has been configured by its owner, Professor Amber, to take decisions about whether it should ring in case of incoming calls based on his preferences and context. Prof. Amber has the following preferences: His phone should ring in case of an incoming call, unless it is in silent mode or he is giving a lecture. Such preferences are represented by two local defeasible rules:

$r_{11}^{d} : incoming\_call_1, \neg lecture_1 \Rightarrow ring_1$
$r_{12}^{d} : silent\_mode_1 \Rightarrow \neg ring_1$

Suppose that Prof. Amber is currently located in a university classroom. It is class time, but he has just finished with a course lecture, and still remains in the classroom reading his emails on his laptop. The mobile phone receives an incoming call, while it is in normal mode. The local knowledge of the mobile phone (C_1), which includes information about the mode of the phone and incoming calls, is encoded in the following strict local rules.

$r_{13}^{l} :\rightarrow incoming\_call_1$
$r_{14}^{l} :\rightarrow normal_1$

In case the mobile phone cannot reach a decision based on its local knowledge, it imports knowledge from other ambient agents. In this case, to determine whether Prof. Amber is giving a lecture, it connects through the university wireless network with Prof. Amber's laptop (C_2), a localization service (C_3) and the classroom manager (C_4, a stationary computer installed in the university classroom), and imports information about

Prof. Amber's scheduled events, location, and the classroom state through mapping rules r_{15}^m and r_{16}^m.

$r_{15}^m : classtime_2, location\_class_3 \Rightarrow lecture_1$

$r_{16}^m : \neg class\_activity_4 \Rightarrow \neg lecture_1$

The local context knowledge of the laptop, the localization service, and the classroom manager is encoded in rules r_{21}^l, r_{31}^l and r_{41}^l, respectively. The classroom manager infers whether there is active class activity based on information it imports (through rule r_{42}^m) about the number of people detected in the classroom ($detected$) from a person detection service (C_5).

$r_{21}^l :\rightarrow classtime_2$

$r_{31}^l :\rightarrow location\_class_3$

$r_{41}^l :\rightarrow detected(1)_4$

$r_{42}^m : detected(1)_5 \Rightarrow \neg class\_activity_4$

The mobile phone is configured to give highest priority to information imported from the classroom manager and lowest priority to information imported from the laptop (in the sense that Prof. Amber considers that his calendar information is inaccurate). This is encoded in preference ordering $T_1 = [C_4, C_3, C_5, C_2]$. This ordering is used by the mobile phone to resolve the conflict caused by competing rules r_{15}^m and r_{16}^m. Following the simplest strategy, the system will give priority to r_{16}^m, as this involves knowledge from the classroom manager (C_4), which is preferred to knowledge from contexts C_2 (laptop) and C_3 (localization service). Using the conclusion of r_{16}^m, the system will eventually reach the decision to ring.

The second strategy, however, will lead to the contrary decision. The information that it is class time and that Prof. Amber is located in a university classroom, is part of the local knowledge of contexts C_2 (laptop) and C_3 (localization service), respectively. On the other hand, the conclusion that there is no class activity is derived by C_4 (classroom manager) based on external information about the presence of people in the classroom, which it imports from C_5 (person detection service). Therefore, rule r_{15} will override rule r_{16}, the mobile phone will infer that Prof. Amber is currently giving a lecture and the phone will not ring.

Following the third or fourth strategy, the classroom manager will inform the mobile phone about its conclusion that there is no class activity and will additionally send the list of contexts that were involved in this inference, which actually contains only context C_5 (person detection service). In order to resolve the conflict caused by rules r_{15} and r_{16}, the mobile phone will compare contexts C_2 and C_3, which support the *lecture* conclusion, with contexts C_4 and C_5, which support the contrary conclusion, based on T_1. As C_2 is in the end of this preference list, the phone will infer that there is no lecture, and will eventually reach the decision to ring.

5 Discussion

Rule based approaches have already been applied to several Ambient Intelligence systems, offering many benefits including flexibility, formality, modularity, reactivity, information hiding and efficient support by reasoning engines. The approaches that we presented in the previous two sections, although based on totally different reasoning architectures, highlight how such features can be beneficial for contextual reasoning. Below, we discuss how the reasoning architecture itself is also very important in Ambient Intelligence systems, based on the comparison of the two approaches with respect to the special characteristics and requirements of the specific domain.

- *Distribution of knowledge.* In ambient environments, knowledge is typically distributed among several different entities. For this reason, distributed reasoning solutions are more natural, since centralized approaches require periodically collecting all available information in a central entity. When the frequency of context change is high, which is the typical case for such environments, updating the central knowledge base may become a critical challenge.
- *Reasoning with the 'whole picture'.* On the other hand, collecting all available information in a central place ensures reasoning with the *'whole picture'*, which may provide with more useful conclusions about the state of the system. In the distributed case, where agents share only part of their local knowledge, the final conclusions that ambient agents reach may not be based on all available knowledge.
- *Scalability.* In centralized reasoning architectures, we assume that a central entity is enabled to communicate with all involved entities and reason with all available information. Even if we assume that a powerful central computer can undertake all the required reasoning tasks, the communication with the central entity cannot always be guaranteed due to the restrictions posed by wireless communications. Therefore, if we consider environments that are broader than closed areas, such as rooms, offices or houses, we cannot rely on centralized architectures.
- *Computational issues.* As mentioned above, centralized architectures require the existence of a powerful central reasoning engine. In such environments, the amount of available information may be potentially vast, therefore we must ensure that the central engine has the computational power to efficiently process all available information and react in time to changes in context. On the other hand, distributing the reasoning tasks to all involved entities requires adding reasoning capabilities to devices with limited computing power, such as mobile phones. However, as we described in Section 4, using lightweight reasoning algorithms and lightweight reasoning engines, such as TuProlog, may offer efficient solutions.
- *Communication issues.* If we focus on indoor environments, where there are no communication restrictions, another issue is the communication overhead in terms of size and number of messages. Centralized solutions require updating the central knowledge base with all context changes, which may result in long update messages to the central node. On the other hand, distributed solutions such as Contextual Defeasible Reasoning require (in the simplest form) the exchange of single boolean values between the ambient agents. The number of messages, though, for a single query evaluation process, may be exponential to the number of nodes. However, in contrast with centralized approaches that require agents to send updates to the central base whenever they detect changes in their context, in CDL communication is imposed only when an external query is posed to a system node.
- *Points of failure.* Centralized approaches have always the disadvantage of the *single point of failure*. A single failure to the central entity may be enough to disable the entire system. Distributed approaches, on the other hand, can afford such failures.

Failing to communicate with a system node will only restrict the access to the local knowledge of this node, narrowing the underlying distributed knowledge base.

– *Privacy*. This is a very critical issue, which has not yet been adequately studied in the Ambient Intelligence domain. Collecting all available knowledge from an ambient agent, e.g. the user's personal agent, may be in contrast with the agent's privacy policy. In centralized approaches, this actually means that the system is able to reason with part of this agent's knowledge; the one that it is permitted to share. In distributed approaches, information hiding and localized reasoning ensures that this part of the agent's knowledge may be used in the reasoning process without disclosing it to the other parties.

Choosing the best reasoning approach with respect to the allocation of the reasoning tasks depends on several parameters, such as the targeted environment, the available means of communication, the computational, communication and reasoning capabilities of the involved devices, and the specific needs and requirements of the use cases that we want to support. Although the two described approaches clearly demonstrate how rule-based inferencing can address specific problems with respect to contextual reasoning in Ambient Intelligence, the list of open problems is still long, and we have identified several opportunities for future research in this area. Below, we list some critical issues along with possible future research directions.

– *Privacy and Security*. Retaining the user's privacy and providing a secure environment for collaboration between ambient agents are key issues for Ambient Intelligence. Due to the open nature of the environments, and the unnoticeable ways in which various sensors may access the user's personal data, these issues become critical and require principled solutions. From our perspective, an access-control language and framework would be significant contributions to such efforts.

– *Planning*. Ambient agents are expected to have their individual capabilities, desires and goals. However, the ultimate goal of Ambient Intelligence is to enable agents forming teams in order to achieve common objectives that are in line with the users' desires. Ambient agents must not only be able to communicate and share their knowledge, but also develop common plans, and coordinate their actions in order to execute these plans effectively. The heterogeneity of the involved devices, the restrictions of wireless communications, and the imperfection and distribution of the available knowledge make distributed planning in such environments a really challenging problem that cannot be handled by classical planning approaches.

– *Learning*. Based on the experience from other domains, we argue that the intelligence of a system is to a large extent determined by its learning capabilities. An Ambient Intelligence system should learn from the user's behavior so as to be able to identify the user's needs and desires. Learning can also be used for computational reasons. Learning how other agents act in certain situations, may help an agent to conduct conclusions about other agents' state, needs and objectives based only on its experience, avoiding unnecessary communication and computations.

Overall, the Ambient Intelligence domain, apart from its key role in facilitating our every day tasks, may also serve as an interesting test bed for AI methods. Rules and Inferencing are already in the mainstream of such efforts enabling the development of formal models and methods for context representation and reasoning, while their combination with other fields of AI, such activity recognition, reasoning about action, agent coordination, distributed planning and learning is expected to provide valuable solutions to the critical challenges of the domain.

References

1. Strang, T., Linnhoff-Popien, C.: A context modeling survey. In: First International Workshop on Advanced Context Modelling, Reasoning And Management (2004)
2. Samulowitz, M., Michahelles, F., Linnhoff-Popien, C.: CAPEUS: An Architecture for Context-Aware Selection and Execution of Services. In: Proceedings of the IFIP TC6 / WG6.1 Third International Working Conference on New Developments in Distributed Applications and Interoperable Systems, Deventer, The Netherlands, pp. 23–40. Kluwer, B.V., Dordrecht (2001)
3. Indulska, J., Robinson, R., Rakotonirainy, A., Henricksen, K.: Experiences in Using CC/PP in Context-Aware Systems. In: Chen, M.-S., Chrysanthis, P.K., Sloman, M., Zaslavsky, A. (eds.) MDM 2003. LNCS, vol. 2574, pp. 247–261. Springer, Heidelberg (2003)
4. Henricksen, K., Indulska, J.: A Software Engineering Framework for Context-Aware Pervasive Computing. In: Proceedings of PERCOM 2004: Proceedings of the Second IEEE International Conference on Pervasive Computing and Communications (PerCom 2004), Washington, DC, USA. IEEE Computer Society Press, Los Alamitos (2004)
5. Cheverst, K., Mitchell, K., Davies, N.: Design of an object model for a context sensitive tourist GUIDE. Computers & Graphics 23(6), 883–891 (1999)
6. Ranganathan, A., Campbell, R.H.: An infrastructure for context-awareness based on first order logic. Personal Ubiquitous Comput. 7(6), 353–364 (2003)
7. Bolchini, C., Curino, C.A., Quintarelli, E., Schreiber, F.A., Tanca, L.: A data-oriented survey of context models. SIGMOD Rec. 36(4), 19–26 (2007)
8. Bettini, C., Brdiczka, O., Henricksen, K., Indulska, J., Nicklas, D., Ranganathan, A., Riboni, D.: A survey of context modelling and reasoning techniques. Pervasive and Mobile Computing 6(2), 161–180 (2010)
9. von Hessling, A., Kleemann, T., Sinner, A.: Semantic User Profiles and their Applications in a Mobile Environment. Fachberichte Informatik 2–2005, Universität Koblenz-Landau (2005)
10. Turhan, A.Y., Springer, T., Berger, M.: Pushing Doors for Modeling Contexts with OWL DL a Case Study. In: PERCOMW 2006: Proceedings of the 4th annual IEEE International Conference on Pervasive Computing and Communications Workshops, Washington, DC, USA. IEEE Computer Society Press, Los Alamitos (2006)
11. Toninelli, A., Montanari, R., Kagal, L., Lassila, O.: A Semantic Context-Aware Access Control Framework for Secure Collaborations in Pervasive Computing Environments. In: Cruz, I., Decker, S., Allemang, D., Preist, C., Schwabe, D., Mika, P., Uschold, M., Aroyo, L.M. (eds.) ISWC 2006. LNCS, vol. 4273, pp. 5–9. Springer, Heidelberg (2006)
12. Agostini, A., Bettini, C., Riboni, D.: Experience Report: Ontological Reasoning for Context-aware Internet Services. In: PERCOMW 2006: Proceedings of the 4th annual IEEE International Conference on Pervasive Computing and Communications Workshops, Washington, DC, USA. IEEE Computer Society, Los Alamitos (2006)
13. Antoniou, G., Bikakis, A., Karamolegou, A., Papachristodoulou, N., Stratakis, M.: A context-aware meeting alert using semantic web and rule technology. International Journal of Metadata Semantics and Ontologies 2(3), 147–156 (2007)
14. Gu, T., Pung, H.K., Zhang, D.Q.: A Bayesian Approach for Dealing with Uncertain Contexts. In: Proceedings of the Second International Conference on Pervasive Computing, Vienna, Austria, Austrian Computing Society (2004)
15. Henricksen, K., Indulska, J.: Modelling and Using Imperfect Context Information. In: Proceedings of PERCOMW 2004, Washington, DC, USA, pp. 33–37. IEEE Computer Society, Los Alamitos (2004)

16. Horrocks, I., Patel-Schneider, P.F.: A proposal for an OWL rules language. In: Proceedings of the 13th International Conference on World Wide Web, WWW 2004, May 17-20, pp. 723–731. ACM, New York (2004)
17. Sintek, M., Decker, S.: TRIPLE - A Query, Inference, and Transformation Language for the Semantic Web. In: Horrocks, I., Hendler, J. (eds.) ISWC 2002. LNCS, vol. 2342, pp. 364–378. Springer, Heidelberg (2002)
18. Grosof, B.N., Horrocks, I., Volz, R., Decker, S.: Description logic programs: combining logic programs with description logic. In: WWW, pp. 48–57 (2003)
19. Leone, N., Pfeifer, G., Faber, W., Eiter, T., Gottlob, G., Perri, S., Scarcello, F.: The DLV system for knowledge representation and reasoning. ACM Transactions on Computational Logic 7(3), 499–562 (2006)
20. Grosof, B.N., Gandhe, M.D., Finin, T.W.: SweetJess: Translating DAMLRuleML to JESS. In: RuleML. CEUR Workshop Proceedings, vol. 60. CEUR-WS.org. (2002)
21. Bassiliades, N., Antoniou, G., Vlahavas, I.P.: DR-DEVICE: A Defeasible Logic System for the Semantic Web. In: Ohlbach, H.J., Schaffert, S. (eds.) PPSWR 2004. LNCS, vol. 3208, pp. 134–148. Springer, Heidelberg (2004)
22. Antoniou, G., Bikakis, A.: DR-Prolog: A System for Defeasible Reasoning with Rules and Ontologies on the Semantic Web. IEEE Transactions on Knowledge and Data Engineering 19(2), 233–245 (2007)
23. Patkos, T., Chrysakis, I., Bikakis, A., Plexousakis, D., Antoniou, G.: A Reasoning Framework for Ambient Intelligence. In: Konstantopoulos, S., Perantonis, S., Karkaletsis, V., Spyropoulos, C.D., Vouros, G. (eds.) SETN 2010. LNCS, vol. 6040, pp. 213–222. Springer, Heidelberg (2010)
24. Bikakis, A., Antoniou, G.: Contextual Argumentation in Ambient Intelligence. In: Erdem, E., Lin, F., Schaub, T. (eds.) LPNMR 2009. LNCS, vol. 5753, pp. 30–43. Springer, Heidelberg (2009); an extended version of this paper has been accepted for publication in IEEE Transactions on Knowledge and Data Engineering
25. Antoniou, G., Billington, D., Governatori, G., Maher, M.J.: Representation results for defeasible logic. ACM Transactions on Computational Logic 2(2), 255–287 (2001)
26. Giunchiglia, F., Serafini, L.: Multilanguage hierarchical logics, or: how we can do without modal logics. Artificial Intelligence 65(1) (1994)
27. Ghidini, C., Giunchiglia, F.: Local Models Semantics, or contextual reasoning=locality+compatibility. Artificial Intelligence 127(2), 221–259 (2001)
28. Bikakis, A., Antoniou, G., Hassapis, P.: Alternative strategies for conflict resolution in multicontext systems. In: AIAI, pp. 31–40 (2009); an extended version of this paper has been accepted for publication in Knowledge and Information Systems
29. Bikakis, A., Antoniou, G.: Local and Distributed Defeasible Reasoning in Multi-Context Systems. In: Bassiliades, N., Governatori, G., Paschke, A. (eds.) RuleML 2008. LNCS, vol. 5321, pp. 135–149. Springer, Heidelberg (2008)
30. Antoniou, G., Papatheodorou, C., Bikakis, A.: Reasoning about Context in Ambient Intelligence Environments: A Report from the Field. In: KR, pp. 557–559. AAAI Press, Menlo Park (2010)
31. Bikakis, A., Antoniou, G.: Distributed Defeasible Contextual Reasoning in Ambient Computing. In: Aarts, E., Crowley, J.L., de Ruyter, B., Gerhäuser, H., Pflaum, A., Schmidt, J., Wichert, R. (eds.) AmI 2008. LNCS, vol. 5355, pp. 308–325. Springer, Heidelberg (2008)
32. Denti, E., Omicini, A., Ricci, A.: tu Prolog: A Light-Weight Prolog for Internet Applications and Infrastructures. In: Ramakrishnan, I.V. (ed.) PADL 2001. LNCS, vol. 1990, pp. 184–198. Springer, Heidelberg (2001)
33. Antoniou, G., Billington, D., Governatori, G., Maher, M.J.: Embedding Defeasible Logic into Logic Programming. Theory Pract. Log. Program. 6(6), 703–735 (2006)

Enhancing a Smart Space with Answer Set Programming

Vesa Luukkala[1] and Ilkka Niemelä[2]

[1] Nokia Research Center Helsinki, P.O. Box 407, FI-00045 NOKIA GROUP, Finland
vesa.luukkala@nokia.com
[2] Aalto University, Department of Information and Computer Science
P.O. Box 15400, FI-00076 AALTO, Finland
ilkka.niemela@tkk.fi

Abstract. The background for this work lies in the visions of ubiquitous systems and semantic web. To realize this vision in embedded domains we have implemented an interoperability platform called Smart-M3, which allows sharing of RDF information. In this paper we investigate integrating reasoning capabilities to this platform for solving problems arising from resource allocation and conflict resolution under preferences in dynamic context sensitive environments. Additional goals for our work is to take into account requirements for efficiency, scalability and localized reasoning. For this we are investigating Answer Set Programming (ASP) techniques in particular. We present an integration framework for using an ASP solver Smodels with Smart-M3 and we demonstrate its use within a use case. Both the framework and the rules described in this paper are available for trial.

1 Introduction

The background for this work lies in the visions of ubiquitous systems and semantic web. We expect that the amount of devices and objects with computers having digital communcation facilities embedded in the environment will continue its growth. These devices contain information and functionality which is then available for other devices like mobile devices or personal computers. The line between various types and roles of devices will also blur. Together these devices form a *smart space*, an abstract entity, which makes services available for the user in a seamless way using the most suitable available resources. This is a realization of the *ubiquitous computing* vision [30].

To guarantee interoperability between the participants, a common ground needs to be defined. Typically this has been achieved by standardization but the number of participating devices, vendors, product domains, and produced information is large and, thus, creating a common standard is hard as is changing an existing one [4].

Semantic Web [1] approaches offer one solution to this by mechanisms which allow handling and representing semistructured information. At the lowest level, the Resource Description Framework [22] (RDF) is used to present the information as a set of triples. The structures which are built on top of RDF can be specified by knowledge representation languages such as RDF-Schema [23] (RDFS) or web ontology language [21] (OWL). These languages are used to define ontologies which describe the shared vocabulary for modeling a particular domain. Exhaustively defining and agreeing on

M. Dean et al. (Eds.): RuleML 2010, LNCS 6403, pp. 89–103, 2010.

ontologies for all or most domains and participants is a similar effort to standardization but the semantic web approach gives the possibility of leaving information only partially defined.

The semantic web route to interoperability assumes that the relevant information is published as RDF so that participants of a smart space can handle that information. The original semantic web vision was that the semantic information would accompany web pages and be fairly tied to the web infrastructure. We assume that the web infrastructure may not be the most suitable mechanism for smart spaces because of privacy and efficiency reasons. This has been the motivation for implementing Smart-M3 [20], an interoperability platform which allows devices to share and access local semantic information, while also allowing the more global semantic information to be available. Logically, Smart-M3 has two kinds of elements: a single *Semantic Information Broker*, *SIB*, a blackboard like RDF-store to which several *nodes* can connect and exchange information. It may be that a logical SIB spans over several devices, internally handling the required synchronization. Smart-M3 provides a set of primitives for manipulating the RDF content and ontologies can be used to define larger structures in the published information. However, for applications which need to allocate resources and resolve conflicts, these means are not sufficient and additional mechanisms are required.

In this paper the aim is to develop a methodology for handling resource allocation and conflict resolution on top of Smart-M3. This is a very dynamic and context sensitive setting because typically the availability of resources and their usage depends on various dynamically changing conditions and because resources and users are frequently added or removed. We put forward rule-based constraint programming and, in particular, Answer Set Programming (ASP) [19,17,15] as an interesting framework for developing such a methodology.

In Smart-M3 the required information is in the RDF format which matches well with the rule-based approach. Each RDF triple can be interpreted as a fact of arity two and, hence, it is straightforward to represent RDF content in a rule base and to include RDF triples as first class components in rules. When new information is derived by deducing new facts, the information can easily be rendered in the RDF native format. Moreover, rules provide a natural way of defining new concepts (views) from the underlying RDF information base. Furthermore, the rules themselves can easily be represented using RDF. Having the behavior description given in the rule form as data opens up possibilities for modifying and augmenting the behavior. Hence, the rule-based approach offers well-suited features for the application area and, e.g., Wielemaker et. al [31] have proposed Prolog to be fundament for application development for the semantic web.

ASP is a rule-based approach that enjoys a number of properties which makes it an attractive alternative for handling resource allocation and conflict resolution. Rule based constraints in ASP provide a natural way of expressing dynamic context dependent constraints needed in this area. When compared to Prolog, ASP rules are fully declarative. This facilitates considerably maintaining, extending, combining and distributing constraint sets. When compared to description logics, ASP supports well the setting where resource allocation and conflict resolution typically have multiple possible solutions and where preferences and optimization techniques are used to select the most suitable solution.

Moreover, the rule format provides an attractive approach between rigid standard based solutions and completely ad hoc ways for handling resource allocation and conflict resolution. Using rules it is possible, e.g., to tailor resource allocation by providing new rules giving preferences or other additional constraints important to the user and to combine them with other constraints required by the environment, technical properties of the device, or the intended business logic.

Our target of defining common structures for coordination is similar to workflows [2] and a data-oriented approach [5] but we rely on a simpler execution model and on defining data structures by means of ontologies. Our update mechanism is similar to earlier efforts in combining rule-based approaches with updates to an underlying database [16,2] but our update semantics is separated from the used rule language itself. The work is also related to efforts on combining rules and semantic web [3] where the approach using dlvhex being perhaps the closest. However, we are aim at using ASP techniques local in a node such that nodes communicate asynchronously through the SIB whereas the related work is more aiming at using rules to integrate difference information sources. The idea of combining semantic web technologies to a blackboard-type system is not new. Khushraj et al. [10] present a framework combining tuple spaces with a service framework, where service descriptions and other information are published as tuples, which can then be matched by means of an ontology based mechanism and description logic reasoner. Simperl et al. [25] also describe an extension to tuple spaces and they describe a similar access protocol as Smart-M3. Mrohs et al. [18] present a service framework with distributed service and reasoning resources. There are also several approaches like [11,12] in which a blackboard-like system is used for sharing context information. The key difference is that our framework is conceptually simpler, based on an declarative ASP rule language allowing flexible extensibility and having a single logical blackboard for all information.

The rest of the paper is structured as follows. Section 2 introduces the Smart-M3 system and Section 3 two uses cases that will used to illustrate how typical resource allocation and conflict resolution tasks in smart spaces can be solved using the proposed techniques. Section 4 summarizes the key relevant features of ASP for this work. Section 5 presents our approach to integrating ASP to Smart-M3 and then demonstrates how resource allocation and conflict resolution problems can be solved using the ASP enhanced Smart-M3 system. Section 6 provides information on the implementation of the integrated system and Section 7 concludes the paper.

2   Smart-M3

The Smart-M3 system provides a set of primitives for a node participating in a smart space to manipulate the RDF triples on the SIB: *insert* and *delete* both use a list of triples which are atomically committed or removed from the SIB. An *update* uses two lists, one for deletion, another for insertion. The commit is done atomically, first performing deletes and then inserts. This resolves possible conflicts in deleting and inserting the same triple content. Further primitives are a *query* and a *subscription* (a persistent query). The queries can consist of a set of triples where one or more of the elements may be an "any" element as well as SPARQL [28] or WQL [13] queries. It is guaranteed that for a single node, the operations are done in the same order as they were performed by the node. For operations performed by parallel or distributed nodes, the only guarantee given is that for a received operation, the SIB will process no operation received later before processing the earlier operations.

Currently, none of the operations will fail due to the information content but we expect that an upcoming access control mechanism will change this. Before a node can use the primitives to manipulate information it must join a particular named smart space and at the same time provide credentials. This allows tagging information with ownership and access rights and the idea is to extend Smart-M3 with privacy mechanisms using these features. Also we expect that we will implement a "test-and-set" type of primitive which allows basic synchronization. Without the latter, there is no guarantee of information persistence between primitives.

The definition of a Smart-M3 application is very loose: it is the result of the combined actions of the participating nodes, which may appear and disappear spontaneously. Each node can always operate on the triple level, however, if the node has an understanding of an ontology pertaining to the triples, they may be interpreted as forming larger conceptual entities. Figure 1 shows an example logical architecture of such a system consisting of several nodes which are logically separate but may reside physically in the same device or in several devices. The SIB appears logically as one entity but it may also be physically distributed across multiple devices. The distribution of the SIB is not handled in this work. Each participating node may be able to interpret the RDF information according to predefined ontologies.

This approach works well when there are nodes which only write information and the potential mash up and further processing of available information is done in one reader node internally. However, when nodes compete for the same resources and need to synchronize with each other, the loose coupling becomes more challenging and for this work we assume that the nodes do share a common small ontology.

The implementations of the nodes themselves are not limited to any particular system or runtime, as long as the platform has an implementation of the SSA protocol. The SSA protocol operates on the triple level but it is also possible to build the application logic on different ontologies and libraries generated from them, which allows working on a higher abstraction level. In principle a node can choose its own used ontologies independently, but especially when there is a need for synchronization a common vocabulary on the triple or ontology level is needed.

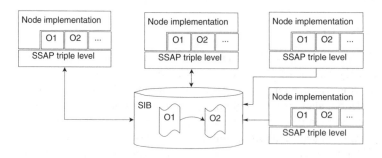

Fig. 1. A diagram of logical architecture with multiple nodes and the SIB

3   Use Cases

The general operation by entities that wish to participate in the smart space is that they publish information to the SIB about their capabilities, resources, and state and use similar information other nodes have published for their operation. Not all the state of the node needs to be published but we expect the nodes to behave sensibly so that they keep their published state consistent with their internal state and also that the nodes observe and react to the information on the SIB. Note that this partial visibility and controllability of the node also carries the possibility of later introducing more of each.

Specifically, we are interested in ubiquitous computing-like scenarios. In such a setting there are several computing resources that can be used by the participants of a specific smart space to fulfil more abstract functionalities also represented in the smart space. The resource usage and availability may change dynamically and there may be preferences according which the resources are allocated in competing situations.

For a concrete example we have defined two use cases "music follows user" and "read aloud message", whose mashup we think covers a relevant subset of the typical patterns of use. The narration for the "music follows user" use case is that a user starts listening to music on her mobile device (MD), using the loudspeaker and keypad of the MD to listen and control. When entering her car, she can seamlessly use the car loudspeakers and the steering wheel buttons and when exiting the car, she can continue the listening but only with the resources of the MD. The intuition behind this is that the user should have the best available resources at her disposal. The "read aloud message" use case consists of monitoring an account for messages and upon receiving one, using a text-to-speech functionality to read the content of the message for the user. In the car this would be useful for delivering traffic announcements. Both of the use cases exist in the same smart space and compete for the use of audio resources, not necessarily for the same individual resource but for the user's attention.

Whenever a device joins this smart space, it publishes information about its capabilities and resources. In this case both the MD and the car publish information about themselves and their capabilities as instances of predefined classes to the SIB. Here we use the SPICE mobile ontologies [29] and specifically classes `dcs:Device`, `dcs:AcousticModalityCapability` and `dcs:KeypadInputCapability` whose names are self describing. We assume for simplicity that once the connection between the device and the SIB disappears, the published information is removed as well. We could modify the SPICE ontologies and the messaging ontologies to directly include additional bookkeeping information but this is not scalable for other use cases as each of them may need some specific information. Instead we define generic concepts including bookkeeping and just refer to the use case specific ones by means of relations.

When a node wishes to use the capabilities of a device, it publishes an instance of the `Activity` class (hence Activity), using the `uses` property to target the desired Capability. An Activity has a state, `active`, which indicates whether it is running or not. Additional, non-essential properties for an Activity include `importance`, containing a free form value and `requires`, which targets a type of a Capability. It is expected that the creator of the Activity monitors the `active` property and honors it so that when it has value "no", the behaviour is in paused state. A Capability which is targeted by the `uses` relation may commit to the use by publishing a `commits` relation between itself and the Activity which uses it. Once all `uses` relations have been committed to, the Activity is ready to operate and its `active` property can be changed to "yes".

There is also a `Preference` class which associates a free text entry to a numeric value. The preferences may be aggregated to a named collection and there may be several such collections. It is expected that these are provided by the user but it might also be sensible to have some default values, which may even be hardcoded by the system designer. For equally valued preferences, we expect a nondeterministic choice. Devices, Capabilities, Preferences and Activities with their associated relations form a common ontology that we expect each participating entity to share. One of the expectations for this and other similar systems is that there may be an unpredictable number of Capabilities appearing and disappearing dynamically and that these are not necessarily owned by the users. For example, the same "music follows user" use case should be valid in the user's home environment or in cars of other people. The underlying idea is that the same implementation for the use case is valid in many environments.

The potential transient nature, large number, and ownership of the Capabilities means that it is not sensible to have a single global arbiter which manages the Capabilities and the Activities. We expect that each Capability manages itself, that is, decides independently on whether it commits itself. At this point policies may be in effect regarding what kind of entities may use the Capability.

4   Answer Set Programming

Logic programs with the stable model semantics [8] have emerged as an attractive knowledge representation formalism and as an approach to solving search problems using the *answer set programming* (ASP) paradigm [19,17,15]. The basic idea is to encode a given search problem as a set of rules such that the stable models of the rules correspond to the solutions of the original problem. Hence, a solution to a given problem can be found by giving the logic program encoding as input to an ASP solver which computes a stable model of the encoding and then a solution of the original problem can be extracted from the computed stable model.

The basic idea in this paradigm is to interpret the rules of a program as constraints on a solution set for the program. A solution set is a set of atoms, and a normal logic program rule of the form

$$a :- b_1, \ldots, b_m, \text{not } c_1, \ldots, \text{not } c_n. \tag{1}$$

is seen as a constraint on this set stating that if $b_1, \ldots, b_m$ are in the solution set and none of $c_1, \ldots, c_n$ are included, then a must be included in the set. A very natural definition for the solution sets is provided by *stable models* [8]. Models of a program are sets of ground atoms. A set of atoms Δ is said to satisfy an atom a if $a \in \Delta$ and a negative literal $\text{not } a$ if $a \notin \Delta$. A rule r of the form (1) is satisfied by Δ if the head a is satisfied whenever every body literal $b_1, \ldots, \text{not } c_n$ is satisfied by Δ and a program Π is satisfied by Δ if each rule in Π is satisfied by Δ.

Stable models of a program are sets of ground atoms which satisfy all the rules of the program and are justified by the rules. This is captured using the concept of a *reduct*. For a program Π and a set of atoms Δ, the reduct Π^Δ is defined by

$$\Pi^\Delta = \{a \; \text{:-} \; b_1, \ldots, b_m. \mid a \; \text{:-} \; b_1, \ldots, b_m, \text{not } c_1, \ldots, \text{not } c_n. \in \Pi,$$
$$\{c_1, \ldots, c_n\} \cap \Delta = \emptyset\}$$

i.e., a reduct Π^Δ does not contain any negative literals and, hence, has a unique subset minimal set of atoms satisfying it.

Definition 1. *A set of atoms Δ is a stable model of a program Π iff Δ is the unique minimal set of atoms satisfying Π^Δ.*

Current answer set programming systems such as Smodels [24], dlv [14], and clasp [7] support a richer modelling language than normal logic programs. In particular, Smodels supports, for example, *integrity constraints, choice rules, cardinality and weight constraints, rules with variables,* and *conditional literals*.

- A *integrity constraint* (denial) of the form :- $b_1, \ldots, \text{not } b_k$. excludes any stable model where the body holds.
- A *choice rule* of the form $\{a_1, \ldots, a_l\}$:- $b_1, \ldots, \text{not } b_k$. allows to include a subset of $\{a_1, \ldots, a_l\}$ to a stable model whenever the body of the rule holds in the model.
- A *cardinality constraint* of the form $l\{b_1, \ldots, b_m, \text{not } c_1, \ldots, \text{not } c_n\}u$ is satisfied in a model if at least l and at most u of the literals $\{b_1, \ldots, \text{not } c_n\}$ are satisfied in the model where $l < u$ are integers.
- A *weight constraint* $l\{b_1 = w_{b_1}, \ldots, b_m = w_{b_m}, \text{not } c_1 = w_{c_1}, \ldots, \text{not } c_n = w_{c_n}\}u$ is a generalization where each literal b_i is assigned a (positive) integer weight w_{b_i} and such a constraint is satisfied in a model if the sum of weights of the satisfied literals in the model is at least l but at most u.
- For *rules with variables* the semantics is based on Herbrand interpretations where a rule with variables is interpreted as the set of its ground instantiations such that the variables are substituted by ground terms from the Herbrand universe of the program. In order to guarantee that determining stable model existence remains decidable, typically ASP systems require some kind of a safeness condition for rules with variables. For the Smodels system the rules are required to be *domain restricted* which makes it possible to use function symbols but to preserve decidability. A domain restricted program can be thought of as being divided into two parts: Π_{Defs} defining *domain predicates* and Π_{Cs} containing all other rules. The rules Π_{Defs} for the domain predicates form a stratified program (i.e., no recursion through negation) and all the rules in Π are domain-restricted in the sense that every variable in a rule must appear in a domain predicate which appears positively in the body of the rule.
- *Conditional literals* are of the form $l : d$ where l is a literal and the conditional part d is a domain predicate and they are required to be *domain-restricted* in the sense

that each variable in the rule appears in a domain predicate which is a positive body predicate or the conditional part of some conditional literal in the rule.

When using conditional literals we need to distinguish between *local* and *global* variables in a rule. The idea is that global variables quantify over the whole rule but the scope of a local variable is a single conditional literal. We do not introduce any notation to make the distinction explicit but use the following convention: a variable is local to a conditional literal if it appears only in this literal in the rule and all other variables are global to the rule.

Example 1. Consider the graph colorability problem where a problem instance is given by a set of facts vertex/1, edge/2, color/1, for the vertices and edges of the graph and the available colors, respectively. Then the ASP encoding of the problem is

```
1 {colored(X,C):color(C) } 1 :- vertex(X).
:- edge(X,Y), colored(X,C), colored(Y,C), color(C).
```

where the first rule includes for each vertex x exactly one atom colored(x,c) such that c is one of the available colors and the second rule is an integrity constraint saying that there is no model such that there is an edge (x,y) with end points assigned the same color. Here vertex/1, edge/2, color/1 are domain predicates but colored/2 is not. In the first rule X is a global variable while C is a local one for the conditional literal.

Now given a set of facts describing a graph and the available colors, this set of facts and the two rules have a stable model exactly when the graph is colorable using the available colors and the coloring can be read directly from a stable model (the atoms of the form colored(x,c)).

5   Integrating ASP to Smart-M3

The integration of a rule engine to Smart-M3 is based on a simple execution model. A node makes a query on the SIB content. Then the rules and the rule base constructed from the SIB contents are executed by the ASP system and facts with predetermined names in the resulting stable model are interpreted by an external entity possibly leading to facts being committed or deleted atomically in the SIB. We have limited support for reactivity so that the above cycle can be triggered by changes in the SIB contents. For simplicity we assume that the described rules are executed for every change in the SIB. Hence, the overall execution of a set of nodes is an asynchronous process where the nodes query the SIB, do some inferences and then make atomic updates in the SIB in an interleaved fashion.

Below we illustrate the use of ASP techniques in solving resource allocation and conflict resolution problems in the two use cases introduced in Section 3. In ASP such a problem is solved by constructing a set of rules such that the stable models of the rule set corresponds to the solutions of the original problem.

We have two levels of rule sets: the Capability specific level, which allows Capabilities to manage themselves individually, and the higher level rules which pertain to Activities and allow policies and decisions related to aggregates of the defined entities.

This is a part of the partitioning mechanism, which we expect to enhance scalability. We assume that a relatively small number of Capabilities (e.g. associated to a particular device) are managed by a single rule engine containing the rules in a set called resource.lp. This rule engine may execute in the same physical device as the Capabilities. The association between the Capabilities and the rule engine managing them is arbitrary, however. It may be that for a limited resource device the managing rules are executed on another device. The mechanism for assigning rule engines to particular entities is not in the scope of this paper. For the Activities we have another set of rules activity.lp, which can be associated with several Activities.

As explained in Section 3, it may be that there will be a uses relation between an Activity instance and Capability instance indicating that the Activity wants to use the Capability. If the Capability accepts this, it makes a commits relation between the same instances. The rules in resource.lp deal with managing this from the point of view of a Capability. The predicate to_commit is designed to choose a set of capability-activity pairs satisfying the following principles for a managed Capability:

1. All available capacity should be used if needed.
2. Activities with higher preference should be given priority.
3. Activities already committed to should be kept if they are not replaced by Activities with higher preference.

Below we illustrate how ASP can be used to express these kinds of typical resource allocation constraints by walking through the rules implementing the principles above.

We start with a rule that chooses from the used Capabilities any number of capability-activity pairs to the relation to_commit indicating the chosen commitments after the rule execution. We employ the Smodels choice rule to implement the choice of at most M to_commit facts limited by the Capability specific maximum M (via max_users relation).

```
{to_commit(Cap,Act):used(Cap,Act)} M :- max_users(Cap,M),
    non_dangling(Cap), managed_cap(Cap).
```

Then the three principles given above to restrict the choices can be implemented by denials (integrity constraints). First, we consider the condition that all available capacity should be used if needed. It can be expressed as a denial stating that for a Capability specific maximum M, it cannot be that up to M − 1 commits have been chosen but there is an Activity Act1 which requests access (indicated by the predicate used) and Act1 is not among the chosen Activities to be committed by the Capability:

```
:- {to_commit(Cap,Act):used(Cap,Act)} M-1, used(Cap,Act1),
    not to_commit(Cap,Act1), max_users(Cap,M).
```

The second principle, Activities with higher preference should be given priority, can be stated with a denial saying that it cannot be the case that a used Activity ActBad has been chosen to be committed (1-2) but another used Activity ActGood has not been chosen for commitment (3-4) and ActGood has higher preference than ActBad, i.e., the preference value of ActGood is smaller than that of ActBad (5-7).

```
:- to_commit(Cap,ActBad),                % 1
   used(Cap,ActBad),                     % 2
   not to_commit(Cap,ActGood),           % 3
   used(Cap,ActGood),                    % 4
   available_option(P,X,ActGood),        % 5
   available_option(P,Y,ActBad),         % 6
   X < Y.                                % 7
```

The third principle (Activities already committed to should be kept if they are not replaced by Activities with higher preference) can be stated similar to the second principle: it cannot be the case that a used Activity ActBad not already committed to is chosen to be committed (1-3) but a used Activity ActGood already committed to is not chosen to be committed (4-6) and ActGood is at least as preferable as ActBad (7-9).

```
:- to_commit(Cap,ActBad),                % 1
   not committed_to(Cap,ActBad),         % 2
   used(Cap,ActBad),                     % 3
   committed_to(Cap,ActGood),            % 4
   not to_commit(Cap,ActGood),           % 5
   used(Cap,ActGood),                    % 6
   available_option(P,X,ActGood),        % 7
   available_option(P,Y,ActBad),         % 8
   X <= Y.                               % 9
```

Figure 2 illustrates some auxiliary predicates. For Capabilities which have dangling commits, we define a predicate retract which will be used to trigger the removal of the particular commit. The rule for predicate committed_to captures the pairs of (Cap, Act) where a particular managed Capability instance Cap has committed itself to an Activity Act (indicated by the uses -commits pair of relations). Similarly, the rule for used captures managed capability-entity pairs in the uses relation but posing no constrains on type or other properties of the entity. For the predicate dangling capturing the capability-activity pairs where the Capability has committed to the Activity but the Activity has removed the uses relation, we employ *the closed world assumption* on the SIB information, i.e., if there is no information on the "wp1:uses" relation in the SIB for a particular Activity-Capability pair, we assume that this instance of the predicate is false. Using this predicate also the predicate non_dangling can be easily defined.

The preference mechanism is based on having a free text importance property in the Activity instance. We expect that the information store contains a mapping ranking between the string and a numerical value. Technically, the importance and the credentials of the Activity is related to the uses relation, which can be thought of as the connection request. From the RDF point of view we could have associated them with the relation itself, but for this work it is more straightforward to have it in the Activity. The available_option combines the ranking which maps the importance string to a numerical value with a given Activity. The first argument P is the name of string-value mappings, which can later be used to enable multiple mappings.

```
retract(Cap,Act) :-                    used(Cap,X) :-
    managed_cap(Cap),                      managed_cap(Cap),
    dangling(Cap,Act).                     "rdf:type"(Cap,
                                                "dcs:Capability"),
committed_to(Cap,Act) :-                   "wp1:uses"(X,Cap).
    managed_cap(Cap),
    "rdf:type"(Cap,                    dangling(Cap,X) :-
         "dcs:Capability"),                managed_cap(Cap),
    "wp1:uses"(Act,Cap),                   "rdf:type"(Cap,
    "wp1:commits"(Cap,Act).                     "dcs:Capability"),
                                           "wp1:commits"(Cap,X),
                                           not "wp1:uses"(X,Cap).
```

Fig. 2. Examples of auxiliary predicates

```
available_option(P,I,Act) :-
    ranking(P,ImpStr,I), available(Act,ImpStr).
```

Finally, we can connect the primitives for inserting and deleting particular triples to the store with the derived facts. For example, we insert a "wp1:commits" triple for a Capability and Activity to commit but not yet committed to.

```
i(Cap,"wp1:commits",Act) :-
    managed_cap(Cap), "rdf:type"(Act,"wp1:Activity"),
    not committed_to(Cap,Act), to_commit(Cap,Act).
```

It is possible to define rules over the i and d predicates, which may preprocess them independently. This can be a way of implementing common policies over the insertions and deletions. A possibility is that we interpret predicates i and d outside of the ASP solver and leave the further actions up to the external interpreter, which may resolve the conflict, for example, by triggering another higher level rule set.

Many of the above rules contain the managed_cap/1 relation stating whether a Capability instance is being "managed" by the rules. In this paper we expect it to be defined outside of the described rules as a parametrization for the rule engine. We could read this parametrization from the SIB, but this requires more synchronization. Here we expect that any Capability sets up a rule engine for itself. However, the managed_cap/1 mechanism allows for many Capabilities to express their desire to be managed, so it is possible to have several Capabilities handled by one instance of the rule engine.

Similar as for Capabilities we have a set of rules which pertain to Activities as a whole in activities.lp, as entities which may have multiple requests towards Capabilities. At simplest the rules detect whenever all uses relations have a corresponding commits relation and then set the active property to "yes". We expect that the entities which created the Activity instance monitor this property and do not engage in further behaviour before that. Likewise, if the active property is changed to "no", they should honor that as well. This enables a primitive co-operative multi-tasking scheduling, where the rules act as the scheduler. These rules can be bound to individual Activity instances using a similar mechanism as for the Capabilities and this approach is scalable as it only observes properties directly associated with the Activity.

Activities use the same priority mechanism as Capabilities, so it is possible to compare and select between any two Activity instances. Conflicts between Activities with different priorities for the same Capabilities are automatically handled by the mechanism explained above.

```
deadlock(A):-                        waiting_closure(A1,A3) :-
    "rdf:type"(A,"wp1:Activity"),      "rdf:type"(A1,"wp1:Activity"),
    waiting_closure(A,A).              "rdf:type"(A2,"wp1:Activity"),
waiting_closure(A1,A2) :-             "rdf:type"(A3,"wp1:Activity"),
    "rdf:type"(A1,"wp1:Activity"),    waitingfor(A1,A2),
    "rdf:type"(A2,"wp1:Activity"),    waiting_closure(A2,A3).
    waitingfor(A1,A2).
```

Fig. 3. Rules for detecting deadlocked Activities

However, we may want to check that multiple Activities with more than one `uses` relation are not mutually deadlocked, in a similar manner as in the dining philosophers problem. In practice this should be resolved by Activity specific timers, which would trigger retracting the `uses` relations and retrying later. In Figure 3 we present another solution, where we detect this kinds of deadlocks based on `waitingfor` relation between two arbitrary Activities A1 and A2 where A1 is waiting for a fully booked Capability already committed to A2. For the circular chain of waiting Activities, we pick one which we temporarily put to sleep in order to break the deadlock. In our case we optimistically awaken the sleeping Activity by the next time the rules fire. At this point there is no guarantee that the same state would not reoccur. The downside of these rules is that they are not bound for a limited number of Activities but need to access potentially all of them, which can be detrimental for scalability.

6   Implementation

The implementation of the Smart-M3 is publicly available [20] and we have used this platform in multiple use cases. It is also used as the reference platform within the EU Artemis/SOFIA project [27], which aims to produce an ecosystem for semantic interoperability. The use case implementations exist on a range of platforms and runtimes including i386 and Armel; Windows, Linux and Symbian; Python, C, C++ and C#. So far our experience consists of implementations using procedural and object-oriented languages [20,9,6,26]. In all these cases a part of the behaviour could have been straightforwardly implemented or expressed by means of rules and a part of the implementations essentially implements a simple rule set and its support mechanisms.

For the integration we use a command-line tool `ssls` giving access to Smart-M3 operations with some additional convenience features as well as a possibility of interfacing external tools to operate on the results of the operations. We use `ssls` to integrate ASP with Smart-M3 as a node of the system and `ssls` interprets certain facts such that the SIB contents will be manipulated. The facts for adding triples to insert and delete buffers are correspondingly i and d, both of arity three. Note that both i and d are ssls commands for adding triples to the buffers, which are then committed by the SSAP command update. After all generated facts have been parsed the update command is issued which will cause atomically the deletions to occur, followed by the insertions. As the ASP systems we have used the Smodels systems available at http://www.tcs.hut.fi/Software/smodels/.

As an example of the behaviour Figure 4 shows how the rules operate in a simple case. The vertical timelines correspond to the instances on the SIB. We have two Capabilities, a keypad and a loudspeaker and initially one Activity for playing. The "player" activity places a uses relations between itself and both capabilities. This triggers the execution of the resource.lp rules for both Capabilities and they commit to the "player". After this the activity.lp rules are executed and the "player" is set to be active. Once another Activity, "messaging", appears, it places a uses relation targeting the loudspeaker. In this example the capabilities only serve one user, so this is a conflict. The resource.lp rules are triggered for the

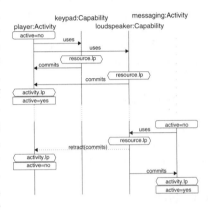

Fig. 4. An illustration of the behaviour of rules

loudspeaker and the previous commit is retracted and the "messaging" is committed to. This triggeres the activity.lp rules, which make "player" inactive and "messaging" active. Note that here we do not make any distinction on where the entities and the rule execution physically resides. Both ssls and the rules described in this paper are available along with an example setup to illustrate their behaviour, including the above example at http://sourceforge.net/projects/ssls/files/ (both ruleml090710.tar.gz and dated ssls).

7   Conclusions and Future Work

We have presented a rule-based approach to locally deciding resource allocation in a dynamic and distributed environment. We have made a prototype implementation available and plan to use it in future case studies. We see the role of the ASP techniques to provide a powerful reasoning engine for resource allocation and related conflict resolution and configuration tasks. We expect that for more low-level tasks related to node management, communication, and coordination, a more procedural host platform is needed. The current ssls tool seems already quite adequate but it is interesting to see what extensions are needed in future applications.

Our approach to local decision making is motivated by the expected large amount of available information. The other guidelines we have followed have arisen from the reactive nature of the system: our rules have been written in a defensive manner to operate in a changing environment. In addition to trialing this approach within use cases, we aim to create a test setup to verify the scalability of our approach with measurements. Furthermore, we aim to optimize the amount of traffic between an individual rule engine node and the SIB based on analyzing the rules themselves.

The second major work item is to take advantage of the ASP features of optimization and deriving several possible answers. We aim to produce mechanisms which would enable optimized solutions either locally or within a controlled amount of locality. We expect that the upcoming synchronization mechanism for M3 will require and enable new features in these rules. Finally, it may be that the we start defining process structures similar to [5]. Combination of this approach with (partial) publishing the rules on the SIB itself would allow us to coordinate the distributed execution of the rules.

Acknowledgement

This research has been supported by Tekes (the Finnish Funding Agency for Technology and Innovation), the European Commission under the SOFIA (Smart Objects For Intelligent Applications) project, and the Academy of Finland under project 122399.

References

1. Berners-Lee, T., Hendler, J., Lassila, O.: The semantic web. Scientific American (May 2001)
2. Bonner, A.J.: Workflow, transactions and datalog. In: Proceedings of the Eighteenth ACM SIGMOD-SIGACT-SIGART Symposium on Principles of Database Systems (PODS 1999), pp. 294–305. ACM, New York (1999)
3. Eiter, T., Ianni, G., Krennwallner, T., Polleres, A.: Rules and ontologies for the semantic web. In: Baroglio, C., Bonatti, P.A., Małuszyński, J., Marchiori, M., Polleres, A., Schaffert, S. (eds.) Reasoning Web 2008. LNCS, vol. 5224, pp. 1–53. Springer, Heidelberg (2008)
4. Farrell, J., Saloner, G.: Standardization, compatibility, and innovation. RAND Journal of Economics 16(1), 70–83 ((Spring 1985), http://ideas.repec.org/a/rje/randje/v16y1985ispringp70-83.html
5. Field, J., Marinescu, M.C.V., Stefansen, C.: Reactors: A data-oriented synchronous/asynchronous programming model for distributed applications. Theor. Comput. Sci. 410(2-3), 168–201 (2009)
6. Främling, K., Oliver, I., Honkola, J., Nyman, J.: Smart spaces for ubiquitously smart buildings. In: Proceedings of the 3rd International Conference on Mobile Ubiquitous Computing, Systems, Services and Technologies, UBICOM 2009 (October 2009)
7. Gebser, M., Kaufmann, B., Neumann, A., Schaub, T.: *clasp*: A conflict-driven answer set solver. In: Baral, C., Brewka, G., Schlipf, J. (eds.) LPNMR 2007. LNCS (LNAI), vol. 4483, pp. 260–265. Springer, Heidelberg (2007)
8. Gelfond, M., Lifschitz, V.: The stable model semantics for logic programming. In: Proceedings of the 5th International Conference on Logic Programming, pp. 1070–1080. The MIT Press, Seattle (August 1988)
9. Honkola, J., Laine, H., Brown, R., Oliver, I.: Cross-domain interoperability: A case study. In: Balandin, S., Moltchanov, D., Koucheryavy, Y. (eds.) ruSMART 2009. LNCS, vol. 5764, pp. 22–31. Springer, Heidelberg (2009)
10. Khushraj, D., Lassila, O., Finin, T.W.: stuples: Semantic tuple spaces. In: Proceedings of the 1st Annual International Conference on Mobile and Ubiquitous Systems: Networking and Services (MobiQuitous 2004), pp. 268–277 (2004)

11. Korpipää, P., Mäntyjärvi, J., Kela, J., Keränen, H., Malm, E.J.: Managing context information in mobile devices. IEEE, Pervasive Computing 2(3), 42–51 (2003), http://dx.doi.org/10.1109/MPRV.2003.1228526
12. Krummenacher, R., Kopecký, J., Strang, T.: Sharing context information in semantic spaces. In: On the Move to Meaningful Internet Systems (OTM Workshops 2005), pp. 229–232 (2005)
13. Lassila, O.: Programming Semantic Web Applications: A Synthesis of Knowledge Representation and Semi-Structured Data. Ph.D. thesis, Helsinki University of Technology (November 2007)
14. Leone, N., Pfeifer, G., Faber, W., Eiter, T., Gottlob, G., Perri, S., Scarcello, F.: The dlv system for knowledge representation and reasoning. ACM Trans. Comput. Log. 7(3), 499–562 (2006)
15. Lifschitz, V.: Answer set planning. In: Proceedings of the 16th International Conference on Logic Programming, pp. 25–37. The MIT Press, Las Cruces (December 1999)
16. Liu, M.: Extending datalog with declarative updates. J. Intell. Inf. Syst. 20(2), 107–129 (2003)
17. Marek, W., Truszczyński, M.: Stable models and an alternative logic programming paradigm. In: The Logic Programming Paradigm: a 25-Year Perspective, pp. 375–398. Springer, Heidelberg (1999)
18. Mrohs, B., Luther, M., Vaidya, R., Wagner, M., Steglich, S., Kellerer, W., Arbanowski, S.: OWL-SF—a distributed semantic service framework. In: Proceedings of the Workshop on Context Awareness for Proactive Systems (CAPS 2005), Helsinki, Finland (June 2005)
19. Niemelä, I.: Logic programs with stable model semantics as a constraint programming paradigm. Annals of Mathematics and Artificial Intelligence 25(3,4), 241–273 (1999)
20. Openm3 release, http://sourceforge.net/projects/smart-m3/
21. Web ontology language, http://www.w3.org/2004/OWL/
22. Resource description framework, http://www.w3.org/RDF/
23. Rdf vocabulary description language, http://www.w3.org/TR/rdf-schema
24. Simons, P., Niemelä, I., Soininen, T.: Extending and implementing the stable model semantics. Artificial Intelligence 138(1-2), 181–234 (2002)
25. Simperl, E., Krummenacher, R., Nixon, L.: A coordination model for triplespace computing. In: Murphy, A.L., Vitek, J. (eds.) COORDINATION 2007. LNCS, vol. 4467, pp. 1–18. Springer, Heidelberg (2007)
26. Smirnov, A., Kashevnik, A., Shilov, N., Oliver, I., Balandin, S., Boldyrev, S.: Anonymous agent coordination in smart spaces: State-of-the-art. In: Balandin, S., Moltchanov, D., Koucheryavy, Y. (eds.) ruSMART 2009. LNCS, vol. 5764, pp. 42–51. Springer, Heidelberg (2009)
27. Sofia project, http://www.sofia-project.eu
28. W3C recommendation: SPARQL query language for RDF, http://www.w3.org/TR/2008/REC-rdf-sparql-query-20080115
29. Villalonga, C.: et al.: Mobile ontology: Towards a standardized semantic model for the mobile domain. In: Proceedings of the 1st International Workshop on Telecom Service Oriented Architectures (TSOA 2007) (September 2007)
30. Weiser, M.: The computer for the twenty-first century. Scientific American 265(3), 94–104 (1991)
31. Wielemaker, J., Hildebrand, M., van Ossenbruggen, J.: Using Prolog as the fundament for applications on the semantic web. In: Proceedings of the 2nd Workshop on Applicatiions of Logic Programming and to the Web, Semantic Web and Semantic Web Services. CEUR Workshop Proceedings, vol. 287, pp. 84–98. CEUR-WS.org. (2007)

Superiority Based Revision of Defeasible Theories

Guido Governatori[2], Francesco Olivieri[1,2],
Simone Scannapieco[1,2], and Matteo Cristani[1]

[1] Department of Computer Science, University of Verona, Italy
[2] NICTA, Queensland Research Laboratory, Australia

Abstract. We propose a systematic investigation on how to modify a preference relation in a defeasible logic theory to change the conclusions of the theory itself. We argue that the approach we adopt is applicable to legal reasoning, where users, in general, cannot change facts and rules, but can propose their preferences about the relative strength of the rules.

We provide a comprehensive study of the possible combinatorial cases and we identify and analyse the cases where the revision process is successful.

1 Introduction

Typically skeptical non-monotonic formalisms are equipped with techniques to address conflicts, where a conflict is a combination of reasoning chains leading to a contradiction. The most common device to handle conflicts is a preference or superiority relation over the elements used by the formalism to reason. These elements can be formulae, axioms, rules or arguments, and the preference relation states that one of such elements is to be preferred to another one when both can be used.

In this research we concentrate on a specific rule-based non-monotonic formalism, Defeasible Logic, but the motivation behind the particular technical development applies in general to other rule-based formalisms. In a rule based formalism, typically knowledge is described in *facts* (describing immutable propositions/statements about a case), *rules* (describing relationships between a set of premises and a conclusion), and *preference relation* or *superiority relation* (describing the relative strength of rules). A revision operation transforms a theory by changing some of its elements, that is: facts, rules and superiority relation. Revision based on change of facts corresponds to an update operation [1], revision based on modification of rules has been investigated in [2], to the best of our knowledge, revision of non-monotonic theories based on modifications of the underlying superiority relation has been neglected so far. In this paper we concentrate on this issue, and we argue that, while little attention has been dedicated to this topic, it has natural correspondences to reasoning patterns in legal reasoning.

The paper is organised as follows: In Section 2 we motivate that reasoning over preferences on rules and on how to modify the preferences is a natural reasoning pattern in legal reasoning. Then in Section 3 we introduce Defeasible Logic, the formalism chosen for our investigation; in particular we introduce new auxiliary proof tags to describe derivations in Defeasible logic. The new proof tags do not modify the expressive power of the logic, but they identify patterns where instances of the superiority relation contribute to the derivation of a conclusion. Armed with this technical machinery,

M. Dean et al. (Eds.): RuleML 2010, LNCS 6403, pp. 104–118, 2010.

we provide an exhaustive analysis of the cases and conditions under which revision operation modifying only the superiority relation are successful (Section 4). Section 5 concludes the paper with a short discussion of related and future wok.

2   Norms and Preferences in Legal Reasoning

It has been argued [3] that some aspects of legal reasoning can be captured by non-monotonic rule based formalisms. The main intuition is that norms can be represented by rules, facts to the evidence in cases, and the superiority relation is induced by legal principles determining how to solve conflicts between norms.

We take the stance that, typically in the legal reasoning domain, we do not have control over the rules (norms) and on how to modify them, but there is some control on how they can be used. A normal single citizen has no power to change the Law, and has no power on what norms are effective in the jurisdiction she is situated in. These powers instead are reserved to persons, entities and institutions specifically designated to do so, for example, the parliament, and, under some given constraints, also by judges (in Common Law juridical system, especially).

However, a citizen can argue that a norm instead of another norm applies in a specific case. This amounts to say that one norm is to be preferred to the other in the case.

Prima-facie conflicts appear in legal systems for a few main reasons, among which we can easily identify three major representatives: (1) norms from different sources, (2) norms emitted at different times, and (3) exceptions. These phenomena are well understood and principles to solve such issues existed for a long time in legal theory, and are still used, for instance, as an argument to drive constitutional judgement against a given norm or a given sentence. Here we list the three major legal principles, expressing preferences among rules to be applied [4].

Lex Superior. When there is a conflict between two norms from different sources, the norms originating from the legislative source higher in the legislative source hierarchy takes precedence over the other norm.

Lex Posterior. According to this principle a norm emitted after another norm takes precedence over the older norm.

Lex Specialis. This principle states that when a norm is limited to a specific set of admissible circumstances, and under more general conditions another norm applies, the most specific norm prevails.

Besides the above principles a legislator can explicitly establish that one norm prevails over a conflicting norm.

The intuition behind the above principles (and eventually others) is that when there are two conflicting norms, and the two norms are applicable in a specific case, we can apply one of these principles to create an instance of a superiority relation that discriminates between the two conflicting norms. However, there is further complication. What about if several principles apply and these produce opposite preferences? This is when revision of preferences is relevant. The following example illustrates this situation.

Charlie is an immigrant living in Italy, who is interested in joining the Italian Army, based on Law 91 of 1992. However, his application is rejected, based upon a constitutional norm (Article 51 of the Italian Constitution). The two norms Law 91 and Article

51 are in conflict thus the Army's decision is based on the *lex superior* principle. Charlies appeals against the decision in court. The facts of the case are undisputed, and so are the norms to be applied and their interpretation. Thus the only chance for Bob, Charlie's lawyer, to overturn the decision is to argue that Law 91 overrides Article 51 of the constitution. Thus Bob, Charlie's advocate, counter-argues appealing to the *lex specialis* principle since Law 91 of 1992 explicitly covers the case of a foreigner who applies for joining the Army for the purpose of obtaining citizenship.

The two arguments do not discuss about facts and rules that hold in the case. They disagree about which rule prevails over the other, Article 51 of the Constitution or Law 91. In particular, Bob's argument can be see as an argument where the relative strength of the two rules is reversed compared to the argument of the Army's lawyer, and it is an argument to revise the previous decision.

The mechanism sketched above attains at the notion of strategic reasoning, where a discussant looks at the best argument to be used in a case to prove a given claim.

In the current literature about formalisms apt to model normative and legal reasoning, a simple and efficient non-monotonic formalism which has been discussed in the community is *defeasible logic*. This system is described in detail in the next section.

One of the strong aspects of defeasible logic is its characterisation in terms of argumentation semantics [5]. In other words, it is possible to relate it to general reasoning structure in non-monotonic reasoning, that is based on the notion of admissible reasoning chain. An admissible reasoning chain is an argument in favour of a thesis. For these reasons, much research effort has been spent upon defeasible logic, and once formulated in a complete way it encompasses other (skeptical) formalisms proposed for legal reasoning [5,6].

Most interestingly, in defeasible logic we can reach positive conclusions as well as negative conclusions, thus it gives understanding to both accept a conclusion as well as reject a conclusion. This is particularly advantageous when trying to address the issues determined by reasoning conflicts.

This paper provides a comprehensive study of the conditions under which it is possible to revise a defeasible theory by changing the superiority relation of the theory, that is changing the relative strength of conflicting rules.

3   Defeasible Logics

A defeasible theory consists of five different kinds of knowledge: facts, strict rules, defeasible rules, defeaters, and a superiority relation [7]. Examples of facts and rules below are standard in the literature of the field.

Facts denote simple pieces of information that are considered always to be true. For example, a fact is that Sylvester is a cat: $cat(Sylvester)$. A *rule r* consists of its *antecedent* $A(r)$ which is a finite set of literals, an *arrow*, and its *consequent* (or *head*) $C(r)$, which is a single literal. A *strict rule* is a rule in which whenever the premises are indisputable (e.g. facts) then so is the conclusion, e.g.

$$cat(X) \rightarrow mammal(X),$$

which means "Every cat is a mammal". A *defeasible rule* is a rule that can be defeated by contrary evidence: "Cats typically eat birds", written formally:

$$cat(X) \Rightarrow eatBirds(X).$$

The underlying idea is that if we know that something is a cat, then we may conclude that it eats birds, unless there is other evidence that it may not. Defeasible rules with an empty antecedent are "almost" facts. *Defeaters* are rules that can not be used to draw any conclusions. Their only use is to prevent some conclusions, i.e. to defeat defeasible rules by producing evidence to the contrary. An example is "If a cat has just fed itself, then it might not eat birds", formally

$$justFed(X) \rightsquigarrow \neg eatBirds(X).$$

The *superiority relation* among rules is used to define where one rule may override the conclusion of another one, e.g. given the defeasible rules

$$r : cat(X) \Rightarrow eatBirds(X)$$
$$r' : domesticCat(X) \Rightarrow \neg eatBirds(X)$$

which would contradict one another if Sylvester is both a cat and a domestic cat, they do not if we state that $r' > r$, leading Sylvester not to eat birds. Notice that in defeasible logic the superiority relation determines the relative strength of two conflicting rules.

Like in [7], we consider only a propositional version of this logic, and we do not take in account function symbols. Every expression with variables represents the finite set of its variable-free instances.

A *defeasible theory D* is a triple $(F, R, >)$, where F is a finite consistent set of literals called *facts*, R is a finite set of rules, and $>$ is an acyclic superiority relation on R. The set of all strict rules in R is denoted by R_s, and the set of strict and defeasible rules by R_{sd}. We name $R[q]$ the rule set in R with head q. A *conclusion* of D is a tagged literal and can have one of the following forms:

1. $+\Delta q$, which means that q is definitely provable in D, i.e. there is a definite proof for q, that is a proof using facts, and strict rules only;
2. $-\Delta q$, which means that q definitely not provable in D (i.e., a definite proof for q does not exist);
3. $+\partial q$, which means that q is defeasibly provable in D;
4. $-\partial q$, which means that q is defeasibly not provable in D.

A *proof* (or *derivation*) is a finite sequence $P = (P(1), \ldots, P(i))$ of tagged literals where for each n, $0 \leq n \leq i$ the following conditions (proof conditions) are satisfied.[1]

$+\Delta$: If $P(n+1) = +\Delta q$ then
    (1) $q \in F$ or
    (2) $\exists r \in R_s[q] \forall a \in A(r) : +\Delta a \in P(1..n)$

---

[1] $P(1..i)$ denotes the initial part of the sequence of length i, and $\sim p$ the complement of a literal p.

$-\Delta$: If $P(n+1) = -\Delta q$ then
    (1) $q \notin F$ and
    (2) $\forall r \in R_s[q] \exists a \in A(r) : -\Delta a \in P(1..n)$

The proof conditions just given are meant to represent forward chaining of facts and strict rules $(+\Delta)$, and that it is not possible to obtain a conclusion just by using forward chaining of facts and strict rules $(-\Delta)$.

$+\partial$: If $P(n+1) = +\partial q$ then either
    (1) $+\Delta q \in P(1..n)$ or
    (2) (2.1) $\exists r \in R_{sd}[q] \forall a \in A(r) : +\partial a \in P(1..n)$ and
        (2.2) $-\Delta \sim q \in P(1..n)$ and
        (2.3) $\forall s \in R[\sim q]$ either
            (2.3.1) $\exists a \in A(s) : -\partial a \in P(1..n)$ or
            (2.3.2) $\exists t \in R_{sd}[q]$ such that
                $\forall a \in A(t) : +\partial a \in P(1..n)$ and $t > s$.

$-\partial$: If $P(n+1) = -\partial q$ then
    (1) $-\Delta q \in P(1..n)$ and
    (2) (2.1) $\forall r \in R_{sd}[q] \exists a \in A(r) : -\partial a \in P(1..n)$ or
        (2.2) $+\Delta \sim q \in P(1..n)$ or
        (2.3) $\exists s \in R[\sim q]$ such that
            (2.3.1) $\forall a \in A(s) : +\partial a \in P(1..n)$ and
            (2.3.2) $\forall t \in R_{sd}[q]$ either
                $\exists a \in A(t) : -\partial a \in P(1..n)$ or $t \not> s$.

The main idea of the conditions for a defeasible proof $(+\partial)$ is that there is an applicable rule, i.e., a rule whose all antecedents are already defeasibly provable and for every rule for the opposite conclusion either the rule is discarded, i.e., one of the antecedents is not defeasibly provable, or the rule is defeated by a stronger applicable rule for the conclusion we want to prove. The conditions for $-\partial$ show that any systematic attempt to defeasibly prove the conclusion fails.

In this paper, we do not make use of strict rules, nor defeaters[2], since every revision changes only priority among defeasible rules (the only rules that act in our framework), but we need to introduce eight new types of tagged literals. As it will be clear in the rest of the paper, they would be of significant utility in simplifying the categorisation process, and consequently, the revision calculus.

5. $+\Sigma q$, which means there is a reasoning chain supporting q;
6. $-\Sigma q$, which means there is not a reasoning chain supporting q;
7. $+\sigma q$, which means there exists a reasoning chain supporting q that is not defeated by any applicable reasoning chain attacking it;

---

[2] The restriction does not result in any loss of generality: (1) the superiority relation does not play any role in proving definite conclusions, and (2) for defeasible conclusions [7] proves that it is always possible to remove (a) strict rules from the superiority relation and (b) defeaters from the theory to obtain an equivalent theory without defeaters and where the strict rules are not involved in the superiority relation.

8. $-\sigma q$, which means that every reasoning chain supporting q is attacked by an applicable reasoning chain;
9. $+\varphi q$, which means there exists a reasoning chain that defeasibly proves q made of elements such that there does not exist any rule for the opposite conclusion;
10. $-\varphi q$, which means that for every reasoning chain supporting q there exists an element such that a rule for the opposite conclusion could fire;
11. $+\omega q$, which means there exists a reasoning chain supporting q that defeasibly proves every its antecedent;
12. $-\omega q$, which means that in every reasoning chain supporting q, at least one of its antecedents is not defeasibly provable.

The tagged literals can be formally defined by the following proof conditions as:

$+\Sigma$: If $P(n+1) = +\Sigma q$ then
    (1) $q \in F$ or
    (2) $\exists r \in R_{sd}[q] \forall a \in A(r) : +\Sigma a \in P(1..n)$

$-\Sigma$: If $P(n+1) = -\Sigma q$ then
    (1) $q \notin F$ and
    (2) $\forall r \in R_{sd}[q] \exists a \in A(r) : -\Sigma a \in P(1..n)$

$+\sigma$: If $P(n+1) = +\sigma q$ then
    (1) $q \in F$ or
    (2) (2.1) $\exists r \in R_{sd}[q] \forall a \in A(r) : +\sigma a \in P(1..n)$ and
       (2.2) $\forall s \in R[\sim q] \exists a \in A(s)$ such that
          $-\partial a \in P(1..n)$ or $s \not> r$.

$-\sigma$: If $P(n+1) = -\sigma q$ then
    (1) $q \notin F$ and
    (2) (2.1) $\forall r \in R_{sd}[q] \exists a \in A(r) : -\sigma a \in P(1..n)$ or
       (2.2) $\exists s \in R[\sim q]$ such that
          $\forall a \in A(s) : +\partial a \in P(1..n)$ and $s > r$.

Notice that the definitions given above for $\pm\sigma$ are weak forms of the notion of support proposed in [8,9] for the definition of an ambiguity propagating variant of defeasible logic, in the sense that these definitions are less selective than the ones of [8].

$+\varphi$: If $P(n+1) = +\varphi q$ then
    (1) $q \in F$ or
    (2) (2.1) $\exists r \in R_{sd}[q] \forall a \in A(r) : +\varphi a \in P(1..n)$ and
       (2.2) $\forall s \in R[\sim q] \exists a \in A(s) : -\Sigma a \in P(1..n)$.

$-\varphi$: If $P(n+1) = -\varphi q$ then
    (1) $q \notin F$ and
    (2) (2.1) $\forall r \in R_{sd}[q] \exists a \in A(r) : -\varphi a \in P(1..n)$ or
       (2.2) $\exists s \in R[\sim q] \forall a \in A(s) : +\Sigma a \in P(1..n)$.

$+\omega$: If $P(n+1) = +\omega q$ then
    (1) $q \in F$ or
    (2) $\exists r \in R_{sd}[q] \forall a \in A(r) : +\partial a \in P(1..n)$.

$-\omega$: If $P(n+1) = -\omega q$ then
  (1) $q \notin F$ and
  (2) $\forall r \in R_{sd}[q] \exists a \in A(r) : -\partial a \in P(1..n)$.

By the above definitions, it is straightforward to derive the implication chains reported below in Figure a -(b) .

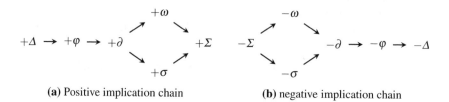

(a) Positive implication chain   **(b)** negative implication chain

Fig. 1. Implication chains

One could think that $+\sigma$ implies $+\omega$ (and symmetrically, $-\omega$ implies $-\sigma$). It is not so. To better explain this fact, and the meaning of the proof conditions, we present an illustrative example.

Example 1

$$\Rightarrow_{r_1} a \Rightarrow_{r_2} c \Rightarrow_{r_3} d$$
$$\vee \qquad\qquad \wedge$$
$$\Rightarrow_{r_4} \neg a \qquad\qquad \Rightarrow_{r_5} \neg d \Rightarrow_{r_6} p$$

$$\Rightarrow_{r_7} b \Rightarrow_{r_8} \neg c$$

$$\Rightarrow_{r_9} \neg b$$

$$\Rightarrow_{r_{10}} e \Rightarrow_{r_{11}} f$$

with $r_1 > r_4$, and $r_5 > r_3$. In this theory, we can obtain the following conclusions:

	a	b	c	d	e	f	p
+	$+\partial$	$+\sigma$	$+\partial$	$+\omega$	$+\phi$	$+\phi$	$+\partial$
−	$-\phi$	$-\partial$	$-\partial$	$-\sigma$			$-\phi$

	$\neg a$	$\neg b$	$\neg c$	$\neg d$	$\neg e$	$\neg f$	$\neg p$
+	$+\omega$	$+\sigma$	$+\sigma$	$+\partial$			
−	$-\partial$	$-\partial$	$-\omega$	$-\phi$	$-\Sigma$	$-\Sigma$	$-\Sigma$

From the definitions above and the example, we can take some theoretical results about the proof tags that will be used during the revision process described in Section 4.

Proposition 1. *Given a consistent defeasible theory D, if we have $+\phi p$ for a literal p, then $-\Sigma \sim p$.*

Proof. Let us suppose D is a consistent defeasible theory, and $+\varphi p$ holds for a literal p. Now, if we assume that $+\Sigma \sim p$, we say that there exists a reasoning chain supporting $\sim p$ which fails somewhere, leading also to $-\varphi p$ to hold, against the hypothesis.[3] A contradiction.

The opposite does not hold (literal p in Example 1). The next proposition states formally the following idea: if we can defeasibly prove a literal p, and we know also that there exists a chain leading to $\sim p$ with all the antecedents defeasibly proved, then such a chain has to be defeated by a priority rule at the last proof step (by the rule proving p).

Proposition 2. *Given a consistent defeasible theory D, if $+\partial p \wedge +\omega \sim p$ holds for a literal p, then $-\sigma \sim p$.*

Proof. By definition of $+\partial$, we have that condition below

(2.3) $\forall s \in R[\sim q]$ either
$\quad$ (2.3.1) $\exists a \in A(s): -\partial a \in P(1..n)$ or
$\quad$ (2.3.2) $\exists t \in R_{sd}[q]$ such that
$\quad\quad \forall a \in A(t): +\partial a \in P(1..n)$ and $t > s$.

holds for p. In fact condition (2.3.2) has to be true since we know condition (2.3.1) is not, because

$$\left. \begin{array}{l} +\partial p \implies \exists r \in R[p].\forall a \in A(r): +\partial a \\ +\omega \sim p \implies \exists s \in R[\sim p].\forall a \in A(s): +\partial a \end{array} \right\} \implies$$

$$\exists t \in R[p].\forall a \in A(t): +\partial a \text{ and } t > s.$$

This is the definition of $-\sigma \sim p$. Since all the premises of $\sim p$ are defeasibly proved by hypothesis, and we have proved that the chain is defeated, then it has to loose on the last proof step.

4   Preference Defeasible Revision

Here we analyse the processes of revision in a defeasible theory, when no changes to the rules and facts are allowed. Henceforth, when no confusion arises, every time we speak about a (revision) transformation we refer to a (revision) transformation acting only on the superiority relation.

$\quad$ In the legal domain, when two lawyers dispute a case, there are four situations in which each of them can be if she revises the superiority relation employed by the other one.

(a) The revision process supports the argument of *reasonable doubt*. Someone proves that the rules imply a given conclusion. If the preference is revised then we can derive that this is not the case, showing thus that the conclusion was not beyond reasonable doubt.

---

[3] All proof conditions given in this paper obey the principle of strong negation, thus for any literal p and any proof tag # it is not possible to have both $+\#p$ and $-\#p$. [9]

(b) The revision process beats the argument of *beyond reasonable doubt*. Analogously to situation (a), someone proves that the rules do not imply a given conclusion. If the preference is revised then we can derive that this is indeed the case.
(c) The revision process supports the argument of *proof of innocence/guilt*. Someone proves that the rules imply a given conclusion. If the preference is revised then we can derive that the opposite holds.
(d) The revision process cannot support a given thesis.

Revising a defeasible theory by changing only the priority among its rules means studying how an hypothetic revision operator works in the three cases reported below:

(1) how to obtain $-\partial p$, starting from $+\partial p$;
(2) how to obtain $+\partial \sim p$, starting from $+\partial p$;
(3) how to obtain $+\partial p$, starting from $-\partial p$.

We name these three revisions *canonical*. We provide an exhaustive analysis, based on the definitions above, in the next subsections.

The situation (a) is represented by the canonical case (1). The situation (b) is represented by the canonical case (3). Situation (c) is represented by the canonical case (2). The situation (d) arises when the condition $+\varphi p$ holds.

In this case, if one of the parties argues in favour of a thesis in a defeasible way, then the counter-part cannot exhibit a proof of the opposite, independently of the changes in the superiority relation.

In the cases (1) and (2) analysed below, we know that $-\partial \neg p$ holds, since D is a consistent theory in which $+\partial p$ holds. Furthermore, Proposition 3 allows us not to consider a tree with branches tagged by $\pm \varphi$.

Notice that some revisions do not indeed modify the knowledge in the system. For instance, revising a theory from $+\partial p$ to $-\partial \sim p$ is useless.

The above reasoning proves that we have canonical revisions, revisions that are equivalent to canonical ones and useless revisions, thus we have the following theorem.

Theorem 1. *The revision of the preference relation in a defeasible theory is either canonical or useless.*

Proposition 3 states that if there is no way to defeat a chain supporting a literal p, there is no revision transformation which leads to defeasibly derive $\sim p$.

Proposition 3. *Given a consistent defeasible theory D, if for a literal p holds $+\varphi p$, then there does not exist a transformation to obtain $+\partial \sim p$.*

Proof. Given any theory, to obtain a defeasible proof of a literal q, there must exist at least a reasoning chain for q, i.e. $+\Sigma q$. This is in contradiction with Proposition 1 which states that if $+\varphi \sim q$ holds, also $-\Sigma \sim q$ does.

For every consistent theory, $+\partial p \implies -\partial \sim p$, [7], Proposition 3 states also that with the same premises it is impossible to revise the theory in order to obtain $-\partial p$.

We are now ready to go onto the systematic analysis of the combinations arising from the above defined model. We list the cases by tagging each macroscopic case by the name *Canonical case* and the combinations depending upon the analytical schema introduced above by the name *Instance*.

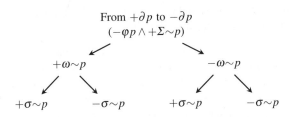

Fig. 2. From $+\partial p$ to $-\partial p$: revision cases

4.1   Canonical Case: From $+\partial p$ to $-\partial p$

Instance $-\Sigma{\sim}p \wedge +\partial p$: This first case is not reported in Figure 2 since the premises are not true ($-\Sigma{\sim}p$ holds). This means there is no supporting chains for ${\sim}p$, so we can not operate on them. Holding $-\varphi p$, this means there exists at least one of its premises that could be defeated by a rule leading to the opposite conclusion. Thus, in order to obtain $-\partial p$, we have to revise the theory putting at least one of such rules be able to fire (to defeat, or at least to have the same power of a rule which actually proves one of the antecedents in the chain supporting p).

Instance $+\omega{\sim}p \wedge +\sigma{\sim}p$: As stated in Proposition 2 this branch represents an impossible case for any consistent defeasible theory.

Instance $+\omega{\sim}p \wedge -\sigma{\sim}p$: By the straightforward implication of Proposition 2, the chain supporting ${\sim}p$ fails on the last proof step defeated by priorities for rules which defeasibly prove p. Thus, we have only to erase these priorities.

Instance $-\omega{\sim}p \wedge +\sigma{\sim}p$: Since there exists a chain P_{np} (whilst P_p denotes the proof for p) supporting ${\sim}p$ which is never defeated ($-\omega{\sim}p$ condition tells us only that such a chain fails before the last proof step), a revision process does not have to operate on a chain supporting p. We have to strengthen P_{np} changing so many priorities to let a rule in P_{np}, which leads to an opposite conclusion of a rule in P_p, have at least the same strength of such a rule in P_p. In this process, we do not remove any priority rule among elements in P_p, but only add priority rules to let a rule in P_{np} win.

Instance $-\omega{\sim}p \wedge -\sigma{\sim}p$: The reasoning chain P_{np} supporting ${\sim}p$ is defeated, but not necessarily by a chain proving p (P_p). The case is analogous of the above, but: probably we have to act not only on P_{np}, but also on P_p; we do not have only to introduce priority rules, but also to erase (invert) them. This case represents the most general situation, where less information is given: a revision is possible, but we do not know *a priori* where to change the theory.

4.2   Canonical Case: From $+\partial p$ to $+\partial {\sim}p$

We follow the cases depicted in the search tree in Figure 2, in order to explain how a revision operator should work. We change the root label when revising from $+\partial p$ to $+\partial {\sim}p$, taking in account the same premises ($-\varphi p \wedge +\Sigma{\sim}p$). Once more, our revision tree does not take in account tags $\pm\varphi$ for the same reasons explained in Section 4.

Instance $+\omega{\sim}p \wedge +\sigma{\sim}p$: As stated in Proposition 2 this branch represents an impossible case for any consistent defeasible theory.

Instance $+\omega{\sim}p \wedge -\sigma{\sim}p$: Proposition 2 states that the chain supporting ${\sim}p$ fails on the last proof step. This, combined with $-\sigma{\sim}p$, implies this last step is defeated by a priority for the rule which defeasibly proves p. In fact, there would exist more than one chain that fails on the last step, and also more than one chain which proves p. We propose two different approaches. We name P the set of chains proving defeasibly p, $P_{ls} \subseteq P$ the chains that prove defeasibly p for which there is a priority rule that applies at the last proof step (against a chain that proves ${\sim}p$), and N the set of chains for which the premises hold:

1. We choose a chain in N. We invert the priority rule for every chain in P_{ls} that wins at the last proof step. We introduce a new priority for making it win against any remaining chain in P.
2. In this approach we have two neatly distinguished cases:
   (a) $||P_{ls}|| > ||N||$: for every chain in N we invert the priority rules on the last proof step. For every remaining chain in P, we add a priority rule between the defeasible rule used in the last proof step of a chain in N and the rule used in the last proof step of a chain in P (possibly different for each chain in N) such that the chain in P looses.
   (b) $||N|| > ||P_{ls}||$: firstly we choose a number $||P_{ls}||$ of chains in N and invert the priority rule on the step that makes them loose. If at the end of this step there are still chains in P that defeasibly prove p, we go on with the method used for the case (2)(a), only looking at the subset of chains in N on which we operated at the first step.

The two approaches rely on different underlying ideas. In the first case we want a unique winning chain. This makes the revision procedure faster than the second method, we do not have to choose every time a different chain where to act. Moreover, it guarantees to make at most many changes as the second one (in general, it revises the theory with the minimum number of changes).

The strength of the second method relies on the concept of *team defeaters*: we give power not only to a single element, but to a team of rules. Thus, in the first method if the only winning chain would be defeated, the entire revision process must be repeated, whilst in the second method if one of the winning rule would be beaten, we have to repair only for it, but not for all the other chains that continue to win.

Let us consider the following simple example:

$$
\begin{array}{cc}
\Rightarrow_{r_1} p & \Rightarrow_{r_2} p \\
\vee & \vee \\
\Rightarrow_{r_3} \neg p & \Rightarrow_{r_4} \neg p
\end{array}
$$

The first approach would give in output: $\{r_1 > r_3, r_4 > r_1, r_4 > r_2\}$ (if the second chain for $\neg p$ would be chosen to win), erasing one priority rule and introducing two, whilst the second approach would lead to have the following priority rule set: $\{r_3 > r_1, r_4 > r_2\}$, erasing two priority rules, and introducing two. It is easy to see that if r_4 would be defeated by a rule r_s, in the first case we have to entirely revise the theory, for example, let r_3 win among r_1 and r_2, while in the second case we have only to introduce $r_3 > r_2$.

Instance $-\omega \sim p \wedge +\sigma \sim p$**:** There exists at least a chain supporting $\sim p$, which is not defeated. To revise the theory, we have to choose one of them and, starting from $\sim p$ go back in the chain to the ambiguity point (where holds $P(i) = +\partial p_i \wedge P(i+1) = -\partial p_{i+1}$), strengthen the chain adding a priority rule where a rule leading to an antecedent in the chain for $\sim p$ and a rule for the opposite have the same strength.

Instance $-\omega \sim p \wedge -\sigma \sim p$**:** Every chain supporting $\sim p$ is defeated at least one time. A first approach one could be tempted to use is to go back in the chain searching for the point where $P(i) = +\sigma p_i \wedge P(i+1) = -\sigma p_{i+1}$. Note that this is not enough to guarantee the chain to win. Let us consider the following example.

$$\begin{array}{ccc}
\text{From} +\partial \text{ to } -\partial & \text{From} +\sigma \text{ to } -\sigma & \\
\Rightarrow_{r_1} \qquad a \Rightarrow_{r_2} b & \Rightarrow_{r_3} \qquad c \Rightarrow_{r_4} p \\
& \wedge & \\
\Rightarrow_{r_5} \qquad \neg a & \Rightarrow_{r_6} \qquad \neg c &
\end{array}$$

As it can be easily seen, letting r_3 win over r_6 is not sufficient. We have also to introduce a priority rule between r_1 and r_5. Thus, we have to act exactly as in the previous case, with the solely difference that every time a rule in the chain supporting $\neg p$ is defeated, the priority rule has to be inverted.

4.3   Canonical Case: From $-\partial p$ to $+\partial p$

We start this case, saying that $-\partial \sim p$ has to hold since, if it is not so, the case is analogous of the previous revision from $+\partial q$ to $+\partial \sim q$. Moreover, we do not take in consideration the case when $-\Sigma p$ holds, as if there are no chains leading to p, there will be no revision to obtain $+\partial p$. The cases are the ones reported in Figure 3.

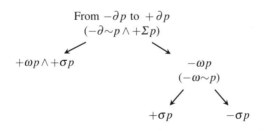

Fig. 3. From $-\partial p$ to $+\partial p$: revision cases

Note that $+\omega p$ and $-\sigma p$ can not hold at the same time: as all the premises for p are proven, the chain has to fail on the last step, i.e. it has to be defeated by a firing rule for $\sim p$. This would defeasibly prove $\sim p$, but this can not happen since we have stated that $-\partial \sim p$ holds. Furthermore, $-\omega p$ implies that also $-\omega \sim p$ holds, since if it is not so, we have either $+\omega p$, or $+\partial \sim p$, both of them against the hypothesis.

Instance $+\omega p \wedge +\sigma p$: Since there would exist more than one chain such that $+\omega p \wedge +\sigma p$ holds, we have to choose one of them, and introduce as many priority rules as the number of chains where $+\omega \sim p$ holds.

Instance $-\omega p \wedge +\sigma p$: This case is analogous to the revision case: From $+\partial p$ to $+\partial \sim p$: $-\omega \sim p \wedge +\sigma \sim p$.

Instance $-\omega p \wedge -\sigma p$: This case is analogous to the case: From $+\partial p$ to $+\partial \sim p$: $-\omega \sim p \wedge -\sigma \sim p$.

We have to remark that conditions $\pm\sigma \sim p$ do not give information on the revision process, since they do not tell if the changes will apply on chains for $\sim p$, or not. Referring to the example proposed below, we can see that, holding $+\sigma \sim p$, there exists a revision which involves the chain for $\sim p$ (introducing $r_1 > r_3$, and $r_2 > r_4$), and the other one that does not (introducing $r_5 > r_6$).

$$\Rightarrow_{r_1} a \Rightarrow_{r_2} p$$
$$\Rightarrow_{r_3} \neg a \Rightarrow_{r_4} \neg p$$

$$\Rightarrow_{r_5} b \Rightarrow_{r_6} p$$
$$\Rightarrow_{r_6} \neg b$$

An analogous situation can be proposed for $-\sigma \sim p$.

$$\Rightarrow_{r_1} a \Rightarrow_{r_2} p$$
$$\Rightarrow_{r_3} \neg a \Rightarrow_{r_4} b \Rightarrow_{r_5} \neg p$$
$$\wedge$$
$$\Rightarrow_{r_6} \neg b$$
$$\Rightarrow_{r_7} c \Rightarrow_{r_8} p$$
$$\Rightarrow_{r_9} \neg c$$

In here, there exist two revisions: one introducing $r_1 > r_3$ and $r_2 > r_4$, and the other one which introduces $r_7 > r_9$.

Note that in all the canonical cases, the revision mechanism guarantees that no new cycle can be introduced. We can formulate the above result, that is a straightforward consequence of the case analysis presented here.

Theorem 2. *Revising superiority relation generates a superiority relation.*

5   Conclusions and Further Work

A large number of real-life cases in legal reasoning, information security, digital forensic, and even engineering or medical diagnosis, exhibit the two circumstances: (a) different persons have different preferences, and (b) decision making depends upon the order the rules are applied. When defeasible rules are in conflict, and then potentially generate inconsistencies, decision making may require preferences. In the same way, belief revision in presence of inconsistent information requires preference revision.

Notice that in non-monotonic reasoning, revision is not necessarily triggered by inconsistencies. [2] investigates revision for defeasible logic and relationships with AGM postulates. While the ultimate aim is similar to that of the present paper – i.e., transforming a theory to make a previously provable (resp. non provable), non provable (resp. provable) – the approach is different, and more akin to standard belief revision. More precisely, revision is achieved by introducing new exceptional rules. Furthermore they discuss how to adapt the AGM postulates for non-monotonic reasoning.

In this work we are not interested in examining conformance with the AGM postulates. [10] show that, typically, belief revision methodologies are not suitable to changes in theories intended for legal reasoning, and similarly they show that it is possible to revise theories fully satisfying the AGM postulates, but then the outcome is totally meaningless from a legal point of view. Anyway, to investigate the relationships between AGM and the approach presented here one has to adjust the AGM postulates to be meaningful (e.g., what is the meaning of expansion or contraction, when the operation is defined on instances of the preference relation).

Preference revision is just one of the aspects of legal interpretation. [11,12] propose a defeasible logic framework to model extensive and restrictive legal interpretation. This is achieved by using revision mechanisms on constitutive rules, where the mechanism is defined to change the strength of existing constitutive rules. It is an interesting question whether extensive and restrictive interpretation can be modelled as preference revision operators. An important aspect of legal interpretation is finding the legal rules to be applied in a case, in this work we assumed that the relevant rules have already been discovered, and in case of conflicts, preference revision can be used to solve them.

Closely related to our work are [13,14]. They propose extensions of an argumentation framework and defeasible logic, where the superiority relation is dynamically derived from arguments and rules in given theories. The main difference with these works is that we investigate general conditions under which it is possible to modify the superiority relation to change the conclusions of a theory, while they provide specific mechanisms but no guarantees that a change will happen. [13] is motivated, as us, by legal reasoning, and they use rules to encode the legal principles we mentioned in the introduction. We leave the investigation to the relationships with these works as future research.

Apart from the applications sketched above we shall investigate two limits to the revision operator:

- Revision of preference should not involve minimal defeasible rules. This constraint captures the idea that a rule that wins against all other rules is a basic juridical principle;
- Under given circumstances the revision process should not, for at least a subset of "protected" pairs violate the original preferential order. For instance we should not revise those preferences that are unquestioned because derived by commonly accepted principles or explicitly expressed by the legislator, as discussed in the introduction.

We unashamedly avoided, in this phase, any computational analysis of the introduced operator, but clearly a deeper investigation will include also the definition of that aspects.

Acknowledgements

A previous version of the paper has been presented at the 13th International Workshop on Non-monotonic Reasoning (NMR 2010) [15]. We thank the anonymous referees for NMR 2010 and RuleML 2010 for their valuable comments and feedback.

NICTA is funded by the Australian Government as represented by the Department of Broadband, Communications and the Digital Economy, the Australian Research Council through the ICT Centre of Excellence program and the Queensland Government.

References

1. Katsuno, H., Mendelzon, A.O.: Propositional knowledge base revision and minimal change. Artificial Intelligence 52, 263–294 (1991)
2. Billington, D., Antoniou, G., Governatori, G., Maher, M.J.: Revising nonmonotonic belief sets: The case of defeasible logic. In: Burgard, W., Christaller, T., Cremers, A.B. (eds.) KI 1999. LNCS (LNAI), vol. 1701, pp. 101–112. Springer, Heidelberg (1999)
3. Gordon, T.F., Governatori, G., Rotolo, A.: Rules and norms: Requirements for rule interchange languages in the legal domain. In: Governatori, G., Hall, J., Paschke, A. (eds.) RuleML 2009. LNCS, vol. 5858, pp. 282–296. Springer, Heidelberg (2009)
4. Sartor, G.: Legal Reasoning. Springer, Dordrecht (2005)
5. Governatori, G., Maher, M.J., Billington, D., Antoniou, G.: Argumentation semantics for defeasible logics. Journal of Logic and Computation 14, 675–702 (2004)
6. Antoniou, G., Maher, M.J., Billington, D.: Defeasible logic versus logic programming without negation as failure. J. Log. Program. 42, 47–57 (2000)
7. Antoniou, G., Billington, D., Governatori, G., Maher, M.J.: Representation results for defeasible logic. ACM Transactions on Computational Logic 2, 255–287 (2001)
8. Antoniou, G., Billington, D., Governatori, G., Maher, M.J.: A flexible framework for defeasible logics. In: AAAI, pp. 401–405 (2000)
9. Antoniou, G., Billington, D., Governatori, G., Maher, M.J., Rock, A.: A family of defeasible reasoning logics and its implementation. In: ECAI, pp. 459–463 (2000)
10. Governatori, G., Rotolo, A.: Changing legal systems: Legal abrogations and annulments in defeasible logic. Logic Journal of the IGPL 18, 157–194 (2010)
11. Boella, G., Governatori, G., Rotolo, A., van der Torre, L.: Lex minus dixit quam voluit, lex magis dixit quam voluit. In: A formal study on legal compliance and interpretation. In: AI Approaches to the Complexity of Legal Systems. Springer, Berlin (2010)
12. Boella, G., Governatori, G., Rotolo, A., van der Torre, L.: A logical understanding of legal interpretation. In: Proceedings of KR 2010 (2010)
13. Prakken, H., Sartor, G.: Argument-based extended logic programming with defeasible priorities. Journal of Applied Non-Classical Logics 7 (1997)
14. Antoniou, G.: Defeasible logic with dynamic priorities. Int. J. Intell. Syst. 19, 463–472 (2004)
15. Governatori, G., Olivieri, F., Scannapieco, S., Cristani, M.: Superiority based revision of defeasible theories. In: Meyer, T., Ternovska, E. (eds.) International Workshop on Non-Monotonic Reasoning (NMR 2010). CEUR Workshop Proceedings (2010)

On the Problem of Computing Ambiguity Propagation and Well-Founded Semantics in Defeasible Logic

Ho-Pun Lam[1,2] and Guido Governatori[2]

[1] School of Information Technology and Electrical Engineering
The University of Queensland, Brisbane, Australia
[2] NICTA*, Queensland Research Laboratory, Brisbane, Australia

Abstract. In this paper we present the well founded variants of ambiguity blocking and ambiguity propagating defeasible logics. We also show how to extend SPINdle, a state of the art, defeasible logic implementation to handle all such variants of defeasible logic.

Keywords: Ambiguity Propagation, Well-Founded Semantics, Defeasible logics, Consequences finding.

1 Introduction

Defeasible Logic (DL) [1,2] is a skeptical approach to non-monotonic reasoning. It is based on a logic programming-like language and is a simple, efficient but flexible formalism capable of dealing with many different intuitions of non-monotonic reasoning in a natural and meaningful way [3].

The main advantage of using DL over other non-monotonic formalisms is certainly due to its low computation complexity: Conclusions of DL can be derived in linear time (wrt the size of a theory) [4] and several efficient implementations exist [5,6,7]. Besides, due to its built-in preference handling facilities, it also capable to derive plausible conclusions from incomplete and conflicting information in a declarative way.

Recently, [8] has investigated the relationships among several variants of DL, capturing the intuitions of different reasoning issues, such as ambiguity blocking and propagation, and team defeat. Our focus is on the computational aspect of these variants. We have devised algorithms to compute in linear time the extensions of the ambiguity propagation variants and well-founded semantics of DL. For the well-founded variant we have established a way to compute the unfounded set of a defeasible theory. In addition, by combining the algorithms together, we can handle the well-founded variants of ambiguity blocking and ambiguity propagation of DL maintaining linear complexity.

The outline of this paper is as follows. Section 2 gives a brief introduction and modular construction to the syntax and semantics of defeasible logic. Section 3 and 4 describe the algorithms proposed to compute the ambiguity propagation variant and well-founded semantics of DL respectively, followed by a conclusion.

---

* NICTA is funded by the Australian Government as represented by the Department of Broadband, Communications and the Digital Economy and the Australian Research Council through the ICT Centre of Excellence program.

M. Dean et al. (Eds.): RuleML 2010, LNCS 6403, pp. 119–127, 2010.

2   Basics of Defeasible Logic

In this Section we provide a short outline of DL and the construction of variants capturing different intuitions of non-monotonic reasoning based on a modular and parametrised definition of the proof theory of the logic. For the full details, we refer to [9,10,8].

A defeasible theory D is a triple $(F, R, >)$ where F and R are finite set of facts and rules respectively, and $>$ is an acyclic superiority relation on R. *Facts* are logical statements describing indisputable facts; they are represented by (atomic) propositions (i.e., literals). A rule r describes the relations between a set of literals (the *antecedent* $A(r)$, which can be empty) and a literal (the *consequent* $C(r)$). In writing rules we omit set notation for antecedents. There are three types of rules: *strict* rules $(r : A(r) \rightarrow C(r))$, *defeasible* rules $(r : A(r) \Rightarrow C(r))$, and *defeaters* $(r : A(r) \rightsquigarrow C(r))$. Strict rules are rules in the classical sense, the conclusion follows every time the antecedents hold; a defeasible rule is allowed to assert its conclusion in case there is not contrary evidence to the conclusion. *Defeaters* cannot support conclusions but they provide contrary evidence to them. The *superiority relation* $>$ describes the relative strength of rules, and it is used to obtain a conclusion when there are applicable conflicting rules.

DL is able to distinguish positive conclusions from negative conclusions, that is literals that can be proved and literals that are refuted, in addition it is able to determine the strength of a conclusion, i.e., whether something is concluded using only strict rules and facts or whether we have a defeasible conclusion, a conclusion can be retracted if more evidence is provided. Accordingly, for a literal p we can have the following four types of conclusions, called tagged literals: $+\Delta p$ (p is definitely provable), $-\Delta p$ (p is definitely refuted), $+\partial p$ (p is defeasible provable), and $-\partial p$ (p is defeasibly refuted). At the heart of DL we have its proof theory that tell us how to derive tagged literals. A *proof* is a sequence of tagged literals obeying proof conditions corresponding to inference rules. The inference rules establish when we can add a literals at the end of a sequence of tagged literals based on conditions on the elements of a theory and the previous tagged literals in the sequence.

The structure of the proof conditions has an argumentation flavour:

To prove $+\partial p$
>   Phase 1: There is an applicable rule for p and
>   Phase 2: For every rule for $\sim p$ (the complement of p) either
>> Sub-Phase 1: the rule is discarded, or
>> Sub-Phase 2: the rule is defeated by a (stronger) rule for p

The notion of a rule being applicable means that all the antecedents of the rule are provable (with the appropriate strength); a rule is discarded if at least one of the antecedents is refuted (with the appropriate strength), and finally a rule is defeated, if there is a (stronger) rule for the complement of the conclusion that is applicable (again with the appropriate strength).

The above structure enables us to define several variants of DL by giving different parameters (i.e., this is what we mean 'with the appropriate strength' in the previous paragraph). In particular we address the distinction between ambiguity blocking and ambiguity propagation.

3   Ambiguity Propagation

Intuitively a literal p is *ambiguous* iff there exist two chains of reasoning with one supports the conclusion p is true while another supports the conclusion $\neg p$ is true, one supports the conclusion p is true whereas one supports the conclusion $\neg p$ is true, and the superiority relation does not resolve this conflict.

Example 1. Consider the following theory:

$$\Rightarrow a \qquad\qquad a \Rightarrow c \qquad\qquad\qquad \Rightarrow \neg d$$
$$\Rightarrow b \qquad\qquad b \Rightarrow \neg c \qquad\qquad\qquad \neg c \Rightarrow d$$

Literals c and $\neg c$ are ambiguous, since in both cases we have 'chains' or reasoning leading to them. More specifically, we can prove both $+\partial a$ and $+\partial b$ since there are no rules for their complements, and their rules have empty antecedents, thus the condition that all element of the antecedent are provable is trivially satisfied. At this stage, we have applicable rules for c and $\neg c$. Since the superiority relation is empty we cannot solve the conflict, thus both literals are refuted, i.e., we prove $-\partial c$ and $-\partial \neg c$. Then we have the rule $\neg c \Rightarrow c$ and $\Rightarrow \neg d$. In this case the first rule is discarded since $\neg c$ is refuted. This allows us to conclude $+\partial \neg d$. In this case the ambiguity of c and $\neg c$ is restricted to them and it does not propagate to literals depending on them. we refer to this kind of reasoning as *ambiguity blocking*. On the other hand, one can reason as follows: we have a chain of rules leading to d and none of these rules is overruled by other rules; similarly we have chain of rules leading to $\neg d$, and, again the rules in this chain are not defeated. Thus we have no way to solve the conflict, thus d and $\neg d$ are ambiguous and we have to refute them; in this case we speak of *ambiguity propagation*: there are conflicts in intermediate steps of chains of rules, but these are not defeated. These two lines of reasoning are both valid and appropriate in particular applications. Accordingly, we want to be able to model both of them. The proof conditions described above are suitable for ambiguity blocking. To capture ambiguity propagation one has to make more hard to provide an argument, and easier to give a counter-argument. To this end the notion of support (Σ) is introduced.

A literal p is supported if
    Phase 1: There is a supported rule for p and
    Phase 2: Every rule for $\sim p$ stronger than it is not applicable

Armed with the notion just defined, the ambiguity propagating version of DL is obtained from the same scheme as that of the ambiguity blocking DL, where we stipulate that a rule is *discarded* if at least one of the elements in its antecedent are not supported (according the construction just given). In addition, a rule is *supported* if all the elements of its antecedent are supported.

3.1   Computing Consequences in DL with Ambiguity Propagation

Following the idea of [4] the algorithms to compute the extension of the ambiguity propagation variant of a DL are based on a series of (theory) transformations that allow us to (1) assert whether a literal is provable or not (and its strength) and (2) progressively reduce and simplify a theory. The key ideas rely on the fact that once we have established that a literal is positively provable, we can remove it from the antecedent of rules that contain it without affecting the extension of the theory. Similarly, when it is established that a literal p cannot be proven then those rules with p in their antecedent become inapplicable and the rule can be removed from the theory.

Algorithm 1 computes the consequences of ambiguity propagation variants of DL. In the algorithm, p ranges over literals and s ranges over conclusions. $\mathscr{S}$ holds those proven conclusions that have not been used to derived further consequences; while $\mathscr{K}$ accumulates over the set of conclusions that have been proven and used. $\mathscr{D}$ is the input defeasible theory without superiority relations and defeaters[1].

Algorithm 1. Inference algorithm for ambiguity propagation

Algorithm: *ComputeDefeasibleAP($\mathscr{D}$)*

Data: $\mathscr{D} = (F, R, \emptyset)$: a defeasible theory
Result: $\mathscr{K}_{ap}$: set of defeasible conclusions derived

1 **initialize** $\mathscr{S}$
2 $\mathscr{K}_{ap} = \emptyset$
3 **while** $\mathscr{S}$ *is not empty* **do**
4      $\mathscr{S} = \mathscr{S} \setminus \{s\}$ for some $s \in \mathscr{S}$;
        $\mathscr{K}_{ap} = \mathscr{K}_{ap} \cup \{s\}$
5   **switch** s **do**
6   **case** $+\partial_{ap}p$:
7   **foreach** $r \in R_{sd} : p \in A(r)$ **do**
8   **remove** p from $A(r)$
9   **if** $A(r)$ *is empty* **then**
10                     $h = C(r)$
11   **if** $\neg h \in \Sigma^+$ **then**
12                         $\mathscr{S} = \mathscr{S} \cup \{-\partial_{ap}h\}$
13   **remove**:
                            $\forall r \in R_{sd} : h \in A(r)$
14   **else if** $R_{sd}[\neg h]$ *is null* **then**
15                         $\mathscr{S} = \mathscr{S} \cup \{+\partial_{ap}h\}$
16   **remove**:
                            $\forall r \in R_{sd} : \neg h \in A(r)$
17   **case** $-\partial_{ap}p$:
18   **foreach** $r \in R_{sd} : p \in A(r)$ **do**
19                 $R_{sd} = R_{sd} \setminus \{r\}$
20   **if** $R_{sd}[C(r)]$ *is null* **then**
21                     $\mathscr{S} = \mathscr{S} \cup \{-\partial_{ap}C(r)\}$

The algorithm first starts by initializing $\mathscr{S}$ with the set of conclusions that are know to be defeasibly true: all the facts and the heads of rules with empty antecedent. Then it iterates on $\mathscr{S}$ until $\mathscr{S} = \emptyset$. Whenever a literal p cannot be proved, those rules with p in their antecedent become inapplicable and thus removed from the theory.

For positive defeasible provability, before inserting $+\partial_{ap}$ into the conclusion set, we have to determine whether the complementary literal is in the supporting set. If the complementary literal is in the supporting set, then the literal is refuted and thus $-\partial_{ap}$ is derived. Otherwise, we have to ensure that all rules with $\neg h$ in their head are either refuted or inapplicable, before deriving the $+\partial_{ap}$ conclusion. Consider the case as shown in example 1. Before inserting d in $+\partial_{ap}$, we have to evaluate whether the complement of d, i.e., $\neg d$, is supported or not. Since the complementary literal ($\neg d$ in this case) is supported, we have to conclude that d cannot be proved defeasibly (under ambiguity propagation).

---

[1] Defeasible theories with superiority relations and/or defeaters, can be transformed into equivalent theories without superiority relations and defeaters using the techniques described in [9].

The discussion above shows how definite and defeasible conclusions can be derived from a defeasible theory, which is a bit tedious. However, computing the supported/unsupported set of a defeasible theory is very straight forward.

ComputeSupport (algorithm 2) shows how the *support/unsupport* set of a defeasible theory is computed. The idea behind this algorithm is very simple. Whenever there exists a line of reasoning that would lead us to conclude p, we will say that p is supported irrespective of whether its complementary literal, i.e., $\neg p$, is supported or not.

Algorithm 2. Inference algorithm for Support- and Unsupport-set computation

Algorithm: *ComputeSupport*$(\mathscr{D})$

Data: $\mathscr{D} = (F, R, \emptyset)$: a defeasible theory
Result: Σ^+ - set of supported literals
Result: Σ^- - set of unsupported literals

1 $\mathscr{L}^+ = F \cup \{a \in L \mid \exists r \in R_{sd}[a] : A(r) = \emptyset\}$
2 $\mathscr{L}^- = \{a \in L \mid R_{sd}[a] \text{ is empty}\}$
3 $\Sigma^+ = 0$
4 $\Sigma^- = 0$
5 **while** $\mathscr{L}^+$ *is not empty* **do**
6     $\mathscr{L}^+ = \mathscr{L}^+ \setminus \{l\}$ for some $l \in \mathscr{L}^+$
7     $\Sigma^+ = \Sigma^+ \cup \{l\}$
8   **foreach** $r \in R_{sd} : l \in A(r)$ **do**
9   **remove** l from $A(r)$
10   **if** $A(r)$ *is empty* **then**
11        $\mathscr{L}^+ = \mathscr{L}^+ \cup \{C(r)\}$
12        $R_{sd} = R_{sd} \setminus \{r\}$

13 **while** $\mathscr{L}^-$ *is not empty* **do**
14    $\mathscr{L}^- = \mathscr{L}^- \setminus \{l\}$ for some $l \in \mathscr{L}^-$
15    $\Sigma^- = \Sigma^- \cup \{l\}$
16   **foreach** $r \in R_{sd}, l \in A(r)$ **do**
17      $\mathscr{L}^- = \mathscr{L}^- \cup \{C(r)\}$
18      $R_{sd} = R_{sd} \setminus \{r\}$

The algorithm is similar to the algorithm we discussed before. It starts by initializing two variables: $\mathscr{L}^+$, which stores the set of literals that can be proved definitely, and $\mathscr{L}^-$, which stores the set of literals that are known to be unprovable. The algorithms then iterate on both sets to derive the supported and unsupported set respectively. That is, for each cycle of the iteration, a positively proved literal will be removed from the bodies of all other rules. Whenever the antecedent of a rule becomes empty, its head will then become a new supported literal for future iterations. On the other hand, whenever a literal p found to be negatively provable, then all rules with p in their antecedent will be removed from the theory and their heads will be inserted into the unsupported set. These two steps go on until both $\mathscr{L}^+$ and $\mathscr{L}^-$ become empty.

Executions of the above algorithms can be thought of as execution of transition system on states. As the algorithm proceed, the theory D is simplified and new conclusions are accumulated. The translations for the positive conclusions are based on forward chaining while the negative conclusions are derived by a dual process.

4   Well-Founded Semantics

Well-founded semantics [11] is a fixpoint semantics which was originally developed to provide reasonable interpretation of logic program with negation, but has since been applied to extended logic programs and non-monotonic reasoning. It is a skeptical approximation of answer set semantics such that every well-founded consequences of a logic program P is contained in every answer set of P. Whilst some programs are not consistent under answer set semantics, well-founded semantics assigns a coherent meaning to *all* programs.

Example 2. Consider the following example:

r_1: $\Rightarrow doResearch(John)$ r_2: $doResearch(X) \Rightarrow publishPapers(X)$
r_3: $publishPapers(X), teachAtUni(X) \Rightarrow professor(X)$ r_4: $professor(X) \Rightarrow doResearch(X)$
r_5: $professor(X) \Rightarrow teachAtUni(X)$ r_6: $teachAtUni(X) \Rightarrow highReputation(X)$
r_7: $\Rightarrow \neg highReputation(X)$ $r_6 > r_7$

Given a person *John* who does research at university, we would like to ask if John is a *professor*. To derive *professor(John)* we must derive *publishPapers(John)* and *teachAtUni(John)*. To derive *teachAtUni(John)* we need to check *professor(John)*. And we enter in an infinite loop. Consequently neither could we show *highReputation(John)*.

The notion of *unfounded sets* is the cornerstone of well-founded semantics. These sets provide the basis to derive negative conclusions in the well-founded semantics. Intuitively these are collections of literals with no external support. The only way to prove an unfounded set literal is to use literals that are themselves unfounded.

Definition 1. *Given a theory $\mathcal{D}$, its Herbrand base H, and a partial interpretation I, a set $U \subseteq H$ is an unfounded set with respect to I iff each atom $\alpha \in U$ satisfies the following condition: For each instantiated rule R of $\mathcal{D}$ whose head is α one of the following holds:*

- *Some subgoal of the body is false in I.*
- *Some positive subgoal of the body occurs in U.*

In example 2, the set $\{teachAtUni(John), professor(John), highReputation(John), \neg highReputation(John)\}$ is an unfounded set with respect to the defeasible theory. However, either *highReputation(John)* or *¬highReputation(John)* can be derived if we can remove the loop caused by *professor(John)* (r_3) and *teachAtUni(John)* (r_5). Thus only *professor(John)* and *teachAtUni(John)* constitute an unfounded set under DL.

4.1   Computing Consequences in DL with Well-Founded Semantic

To nullify evidence DL has to be able to disprove rules [12]. This means that the proof system should be able to demonstrate in a finite number of steps that there is no proof of the rule and thus remove them from the theory. As conclusions cannot be derived using circular arguments, *loops detection* plays a crucial role in deriving conclusions under well-founded semantics. *Failure-by-looping* provides a mechanism for falsifying a literal when it is within a loop with no external support. It helps to simplify a theory by removing inapplicable rules and makes theory becomes decisive, i.e., all rules in the theory are either provable or unprovable [13].

Definition 2. *[14] Given a theory $\mathcal{D}$, let $\mathcal{L}$ be the set of literals appear in $\mathcal{D}$. Then a loop in $\mathcal{D}$ is a set of literals $L \subseteq \mathcal{L}$ s.t. for any two literals $p_1, p_2 \in L$ there exists a path from p_1 to p_2 in the literal dependency graph of $\mathcal{D}$ all of whose vertices belong to L.*

In other words, the subgraph of the literal dependcy graph of $\mathcal{D}$ is strongly connected [15]. From the definition of the unfounded set any rule whose head belongs to an unfounded set, or there exists an unfounded literal in their body, is inapplicable. Since unfounded sets are finite, we have the following consequence.

Proposition 1. *[15] Given a theory $\mathscr{D}$, a partial interpretation I, and unfounded set $U_{\mathscr{D}}$ w.r.t. I. If $U_{\mathscr{D}} \neq \emptyset$, we have $L \subseteq U_{\mathscr{D}}$ for some loop L in $\mathscr{D}$ that is unfounded w.r.t. I.*

The above proposition states that any non-empty unfounded set is a super set of some loop that is itself unfounded. Owing to the fact that loops are bounded above by the *strongly-connected-components (SCC)* in the literal dependency graph, algorithm 3 shows the algorithm used to compute the unfounded set of a defeasible theory.

Algorithm 3. Unfounded set computation

Algorithm: *ComputeUnfoundedSet$(l, \mathscr{D})$*

Data: l: a literal in $\mathscr{L}$
Data: $\mathscr{D} = (F, R, \emptyset)$: a defeasible theory
Result: $\mathscr{U}$: set of unfounded literals in $\mathscr{D}$

1 $\mathscr{U} = \{\emptyset\}$
2 $l.id = cnt++$
3 $\mathscr{S}.push(l)$
4 $\mathscr{P}.push(l)$
5 **foreach** $r \in R_{sd} : l \in A(r)$ **do**
6      $c = C(r)$
7   **if** $c.id == -1$ **then**
8          $\mathscr{L} = \mathscr{L} \setminus c$
9          $ComputeUnfoundedSet(c, \mathscr{D})$
10   **else if** $c.groupId == -1$ **then**
11   **while** $\mathscr{P}$ *is not empty and*
               $\mathscr{P}.top().id > c.id$ **do**
12             $\mathscr{P}.pop()$

13 **while** $\mathscr{P} \neq \emptyset$ *and*
     $\mathscr{P}.top().pre > \min(l.pre, \neg l.pre)$ **do**
14     $\mathscr{P}.pop()$
15 **if** $\mathscr{P}.top().id == l.id$ **then**
16     $\mathscr{P}.pop()$
17 **else**
18   **return**

19 **repeat**
20     $t = \mathscr{S}.pop()$
21     $t.groupId = gcnt$
22     $\mathscr{U} = \mathscr{U} \cup \{t\}$
23 **until** $\mathscr{S}$ *is empty or* $t == l$
24 $gcnt++$

In the algorithm, the designated initial situation is that $\mathscr{D}$ is the simplified defeasible theory s.t. $R_{sd} \neq \{\emptyset\}$ but with *no further conclusions can be derived*; and $\mathscr{L}$ is the set of literals that appear in $\mathscr{D}$. $\mathscr{S}$ is a stack used to keep track on the set of processed literals; while $\mathscr{P}$, another stack, containing literals on the search path, is used to decide when to pop the set of SCC from $\mathscr{S}$. The variables *cnt* and *gcnt* store the id of a literal and the group id of the SCC that the literal belongs to respectively. Lastly, $\mathscr{U}$ contains the literals to be extended to an unfounded set.

The algorithm works based on two observations: (1) when we reach the end of the recursive function, we know that we will not encounter any more literals in the same strongly connected set since all literals that can be processed have already been passed (line 5-12); (2) the back links in the graph provide a second path from one literal to another and bind together the SCC (line 13-22).

The algorithm first finds the highest literal reachable based on the literal dependency graph. A literal will be *pushed* onto the stack on entry to the recursive function; and *pops* them (with assigned SCC id) after visited the final member of each SCC. So at the end of the recursive procedure it will return to us all literals encountered since entry that belong to the same SCC, i.e., the set of literals that are unfounded. The algorithm extends the unfounded set through each iteration. That is, to calculate the greatest unfounded set, we have to iterate *ComputeUnfoundedSet* through the set of literals that appear in the defeasible theory $\mathscr{D}$.

As discussed before, failure-by-looping provides a mechanism to remove literals in loops with no external support. That is falsifying all literals in the greatest unfounded set helps to remove loops in the literal dependency graph of a defeasible theory, and thus the well-founded model of the theory can be derived subsequently.

5   Related Works

A number of defeasible logic reasoners and systems have been proposed in the recent year to cover well-founded variants as well as other intuitions of non-monotonic reasoning. The approaches to define a well-founded variant can be classified under three categories: failure-by-loop [1,16,13]; unfounded set [17]; translation to other formalism or extended logic programming [18,6,19].

Nute [2] was the first to propose a form of loop-to-failure, but he did not related the logic to well-founded-semantics, and it was limited to a basic variant, and no implementation was proposed. [16] extended the work, and related the variant to well-founded defeasible logic, but they claim that the resulting variant is ambiguity propagation, and those two notions are entangled. [12] adopts a more sophisticated failure-by-loop algorithm for a clausal variant of defeasible logic (with the consequent increase of the computational complexity).[2]

The unfounded set approach on which the current paper is based was proposed in [17] where a bottom-up approach was presented. The bottom-up approach led to metaprogram representation of defeasible logic and defeasible theories, with the consequent development of the family of defeasible logic framework [20,10].

The meta-program approach is at the foundation of the approaches based on transformation in other formalisms. DR-Prolog [19] provides a Semantic Web enabled implementation of defeasible logic. DR-Prolog directly implements the meta-programs of [20], covering thus various variants, and the well-founded variants are obtained by invoking a well-founded version of a Prolog interpreter. The system is query based and does not compute the extension of a theory.

Other logic formalisms, such as CLIPS or other extended logic programs have been used to implement some variants of the DL [18,6] so that conclusions can be drawn using the underlying reasoning engine. However, most of the systems are query based and do not compute directly the extension of a theory. However transformation based approach may lead to some counterintuitive results [3] as, in most cases, the representational properties of defeasible logic cannot be captured correctly.

6   Conclusions

This paper presents algorithms for computing the consequences of the ambiguity propagation variant and well-founded semantics of defeasible logic. It contributes to the computational aspect of the two variants in a practical approach such that consequences of both variants (as well as their combination) can be computed with linear complexity,

---

[2] See http://www.cit.griffith.edu.au/~arock/defeasible/Defeasible.cgi for a query based reasoner implementing various variants.

which make DL a possible candidate for some computational demanding jobs, or tasks that require immediate response, such as reasoning on the Semantic web.

Recently [8] has studies several variants of defeasible logic based on their abstract presentation of the proof theory. However, the relations between the ambiguity propagation variant, the well-founded semantics, and the well-founded variants of ambiguity propagation is still unclear and further investigation is needed.

References

1. Nute, D.: Defeasible logic. In: Gabbay, D., Hogger, C. (eds.) Handbook of Logic for Artificial Intelligence and Logic Programming, vol. III, pp. 353–395. Oxford University Press, Oxford (1994)
2. Nute, D.: Defeasible logic. In: 14th International Conference on Application of Prolog, IF Computer, Japan, pp. 87–114 (2001)
3. Antoniou, G.: A Discussion of Some Intuitions of Defeasible Reasoning. In: Vouros, G.A., Panayiotopoulos, T. (eds.) SETN 2004. LNCS (LNAI), vol. 3025, pp. 311–320. Springer, Heidelberg (2004)
4. Maher, M.J.: Propositional defeasible logic has linear complexity. Theory and Practice of Logic Programming 1(6), 691–711 (2001)
5. Maher, M.J., Rock, A., Antoniou, G., Billington, D., Miller, T.: Efficient defeasible reasoning systems. International Journal on Artificial Intelligence Tools 10(4), 483–501 (2001)
6. Bassiliades, N., Antoniou, G., Vlahavas, I.: A defeasible logic reasoner for the semantic web. International Journal of Semantic Web and Information Systems (IJSWIS) 2(1), 1–41 (2006)
7. Lam, H.P., Governatori, G.: The making of SPINdle. In: Governatori, G., Hall, J., Paschke, A. (eds.) RuleML 2009. LNCS, vol. 5858, pp. 315–322. Springer, Heidelberg (2009)
8. Billington, D., Antoniou, G., Governatori, G., Maher, M.J.: An inclusion theorem for defeasible logic. ACM Transactions in Computational Logic (2010) (to appear)
9. Antoniou, G., Billington, D., Governatori, G., Maher, M.J.: Representation results for defeasible logic. ACM Transactions on Computational Logic 2(2), 255–286 (2001)
10. Antoniou, G., Billington, D., Governatori, G., Maher, M.J.: A flexible framework for defeasible logics. In: AAAI 2000, pp. 401–405. AAAI/MIT Press (2000)
11. Van Gelder, A., Ross, K.A., Schlipf, J.S.: The well-founded semantics for general logic programs. J. ACM 38(3), 619–649 (1991)
12. Billington, D.: Propositional clausal defeasible logic. In: Hölldobler, S., Lutz, C., Wansing, H. (eds.) JELIA 2008. LNCS (LNAI), vol. 5293, pp. 34–47. Springer, Heidelberg (2008)
13. Billington, D.: A plausible logic which detects loops. In: NMR 2004 (2004)
14. Lee, J.: A model-theoretic counterpart of loop formulas. In: IJCAI 2005, pp. 503–508 (2005)
15. Anger, C., Gebser, M., Schaub, T.: Approaching the core of unfounded sets. In: NMR 2006, pp. 58–66 (2006)
16. Maier, F., Nute, D.: Well-founded semantics for defeasible logic. Synthese (2008)
17. Maher, M.J., Governatori, G.: A semantic decomposition of defeasible logics. In: AAAI 1999, pp. 299–305 (1999)
18. Madalińska-Bugaj, E., Lukaszewicz, W.: Formalizing defeasible logic in cake. Fundam. Inf. 57(2-4), 193–213 (2003)
19. Antoniou, G., Bikakis, A.: DR-Prolog: A system for defeasible reasoning with rules and ontologies on the semantic web. IEEE Trans. Knowl. Data Eng. 19(2), 233–245 (2007)
20. Antoniou, G., Billington, D., Governatori, G., Maher, M.J., Rock, A.: A family of defeasible reasoning logics and its implementation. In: ECAI 2000, pp. 459–463 (2000)

Generating SQL Queries from SBVR Rules

Sotiris Moschoyiannis, Alexandros Marinos, and Paul Krause

Department of Computing, FEPS, University of Surrey,
GU2 7XH, Guildford, Surrey, United Kingdom
{s.moschoyiannis,a.marinos,p.krause}@surrey.ac.uk

Abstract. Declarative technologies have made great strides in expressivity between SQL and SBVR. SBVR models are more expressive that SQL schemas, but not as imminently executable yet. In this paper, we complete the architecture of a system that can execute SBVR models. We do this by describing how SBVR rules can be transformed into SQL DML so that they can be automatically checked against the database using a standard SQL query. In particular, we describe a formalization of the basic structure of an SQL query which includes aggregate functions, arithmetic operations, grouping, and grouping on condition. We do this while staying within a predicate calculus semantics which can be related to the standard SBVR-LF specification and equip it with a concrete semantics for expressing business rules formally. Our approach to transforming SBVR rules into standard SQL queries is thus generic, and the resulting queries can be readily executed on a relational schema generated from the SBVR model.

Keywords: SBVR, SQL, Declarative Programming, Business Rules, Predicate Calculus, Formal Semantics.

1 Introduction

The Business Rules Approach [1] has made significant strides in bridging the spheres of everyday human interactions and information technology. An outgrowth of that movement was the OMG standard Semantics of Business Vocabulary and Rules (SBVR) [2], which brought together research from linguistics, formal logics, as well as practical expertise. SBVR Models are considered constructs that are supposed to help businesses communicate with each other and also business people to communicate with implementers of information technology. Direct transformation of SBVR models into executable code is generally not encouraged and has often resulted in rather harsh compromises of SBVR's meta-model and intended use when attempted [3]. The reason for this mismatch is the chasm between the declarative paradigm implemented by SBVR and the imperative procedural paradigm that is at the heart of most modern programming and business process languages. So thus far, human programmers are needed to interpret and convert the SBVR models into real-world applications. An alternative approach, called Generative Information Systems [4], was presented by the authors of this paper that allowed for real-world systems to be produced by inferring the appropriate reaction directly from a model, without the

M. Dean et al. (Eds.): RuleML 2010, LNCS 6403, pp. 128–143, 2010.

need for an intermediate code generation step, and without the need for explicitly defined business processes. A significant aspect of that model was the method of generating schemas for a relational database from the SBVR Vocabulary, and converting rules into SQL queries to verify the consistency of the data set. This last step, had been only sketched out in the original paper, as the theoretical framework required for this undertaking is significant. This paper addresses precisely these issues and examines in detail the conversion of SBVR rules into SQL queries for the purpose of validating the consistency of a given data set with the SBVR model.

2 Generative Information Systems

This section summarizes the architecture of Generative Information Systems (GIS) in [7] to provide the appropriate context for the rest of the paper. A GIS is based around the concept that the logic of the system is accessible to the owner of the system, and that any change in the logic is immediately reflected in the operation of the system. The architecture as can be seen in Figure 1, specifies that both the RESTful API and the relational database schema (in SQL-DDL) are to be generated from the model.

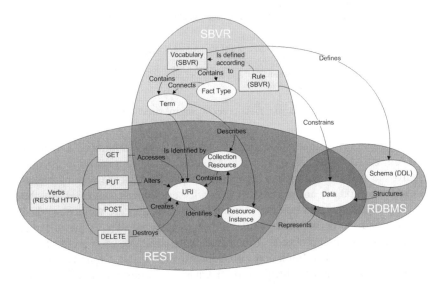

Fig. 1. Connections between REST, SBVR and Relational Databases

The end user can place requests on the system through the API. These requests get evaluated through the ruleset, and if they represent a legal transition and their result is a system in a consistent state, they are applied to the dataset. If not, the inconsistency is presented to the user, who can amend the request to take account of the new information. Through this back and forth negotiation, the user either concludes that the request is fundamentally incompatible with the system, or reaches a formulation of the request that satisfies both the original goal and the system's consistency requirements. This is, in an abstract sense, what many processes achieve. By guiding the user through a sequence of steps, they determine what change needs to be made to the system state to satisfy the user's request while maintaining consistency. We call thus abstract process the 'meta-process'. Its advantage over the traditional process-driven message is that it can respond to unforeseen requests by the user, in contrast to the hardcoded process model which is constrained to the design-time foresight of the developers. More detail on this process can be seen in Figure 2.

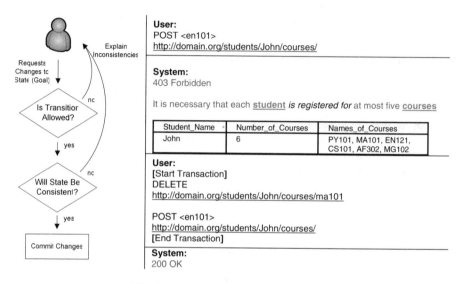

Fig. 2. The meta-process control structure

The way that consistency is currently checked is by performing a sequence of actions on the database as a transactional unit. First, a transaction is initiated. Secondly, the updates are applied to the dataset. If the database schema makes this impossible, the updates are rejected. If it is allowed, the relevant rules are checked against the dataset to make sure they are not violated. If they are violated, updates are rolled back and the details of the violation returned to the user. If the rules are not violated, the transaction proceeds. This mechanism is suitable for a proof of concept, but may have scalability limitations for concurrent systems. Optimizations can be explored that avoid the round-trip to the database. It is however interesting to note that this rough process of adding tentative information to the knowledge base, then checking for consistency, and deleting in case of violation, counterintuitively seems to be the way that the human brain deals with new knowledge. [5] This does not mean that the method is ideal, but it is an interesting parallel that we noted after setting the foundations for Generative Information Systems architecture.

The step in the above process that was left least defined is the one where the updated dataset is checked against relevant rules for consistency. This is done by transforming each rule to an SQL query that requests violations to the rule to be returned (Figure 3). The precise mechanism by which this is carried out is the focus of this paper.

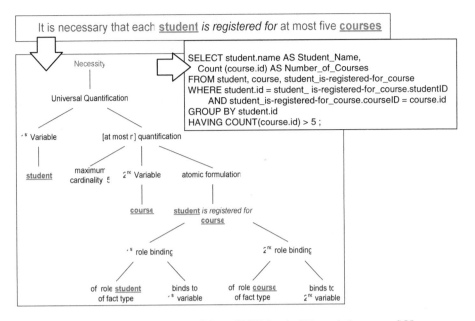

Fig. 3. From SBVR Structured English, to SBVR Logical Formulation, to an SQL query

3 Vocabularies to SQL Schemas

For rules to be validated over a dataset however, first there must be a schema for that dataset. As our starting point is an SBVR model, it is the vocabulary that is the obvious candidate for becoming the scaffold for our schema. The detailed process has been described in our previous work so here we will instead go through an example scenario which we will use throughout this paper. The model for our example can be seen in Table 1. One aspect not covered in previous work is that of primitive data types. We can see that the term Name has a concept type of Varchar(255). This can be read as a reference to a vocabulary of primitive data types that a generative information system is built on. These terms are essentially terminal symbols that get mapped directly onto programming language data types. We use the data types that are fundamental to SQL as this is our target data store. Another novel convention is that since the Name is had by Student, this relation is constrained to a one-to-one cardinality, and Name has no other attributes than its value, we render it an attribute of the table with which it is associated rather than representing it in a separate table, similarly for Code and Title.

The result of converting the vocabulary (and some of the more basic rules) into a schema can be seen in Figure 4.

4 A Predicate Calculus for Advanced SQL DML Constructs

We have seen how an SBVR vocabulary can be used to generate a relational schema. In the remainder of the paper, we are concerned with translating SBVR rules into

Table 1. Example SBVR Model

Terms	Fact Types	Rules
Student	Student *is registered for* course	It is necessary that each **student** *is registered for* at most five **courses**.
Module	Student *is enrolled in* module	
Course	Module *is available for* course	It is necessary that each **student** that *is under probation is registered for* at most three **courses**.
Name Concept-type: **Varchar(255)**	Student *is under probation*	
	Student *has* name	It is obligatory that each **student** *has* exactly one **name**.
Code Concept-type: **Varchar(255)**	Course *has* title	
	Module *has* code	It is obligatory that each **course** *has* exactly one **title**
Title Concept-type: **Varchar(255)**		
		It is obligatory that each **module** *has* exactly one **code**.

```
CREATE TABLE student (id INT NOT NULL AUTO_INCREMENT,name VARCHAR(255),
        is-under-probation BOOL, level INT, primary Key (id));

CREATE TABLE course (id INT NOT NULL AUTO_INCREMENT,
        code VARCHAR(255), primary Key (id));

CREATE TABLE module (id INT NOT NULL AUTO_INCREMENT,
        title VARCHAR(255), primary Key (id));

CREATE TABLE student_is-enrolled-in_module (studentID INT, moduleID INT,
        primary Key (studentID, moduleID),
    foreign Key (studentID) references student(id),
        foreign Key (moduleID) references module(id));

CREATE TABLE student_is-registered-for_course (studentID INT, courseID INT,
        primary Key (studentID, courseID),
        foreign Key (studentID) references student(id),
        foreign Key (courseID) references course(id));

CREATE TABLE course_is-available-for_module (courseID INT, moduleID INT,
        primary Key (courseID, module_id),
        foreign Key (courseID) references course(id),
        foreign Key (moduleID) references module(id));
```

Fig. 4. Resulting SQL DDL Schema

SQL queries. This operational rendering of business rules is more challenging. Thus, we want to prove the correctness of the transformation from SBVR-LF to SQL DML. SBVR-LF has a formal foundation based on first-order or predicate logic, and its variations [2]. SQL has established theoretical foundations [8] and a sound semantics for its basic constructs (SELECT-FROM-WHERE) is based on a tuple relational calculus [6]. This standard semantics however does not cover more advanced SQL DML constructs, such as arithmetic operations, aggregate functions [10], grouping, and grouping on condition. In this section we describe a tuple relational calculus extension that equips such constructs with a clearly defined semantics – this is necessary for operationalising SBVR rules which are more expressive than basic SQL queries (e.g. see running example). The result is a predicate calculus with identity, which establishes a generic mapping between SBVR-LF and SQL DML, as discussed in Section 5. We use the student enrollment example to illustrate our approach.

4.1 Basic Structure of an SQL Query

Our predicate calculus formalisation of SQL DML makes use of tuple variables. A tuple variable is a variable that ranges over a named relation (table). The general form of a query in tuple relational calculus is

$$\{\mathbf{x} \mid F(\mathbf{x})\}$$

where $\mathbf{x}$ is the set of tuples for which the expression $F(\mathbf{x})$ is true. The relation is defined somewhere inside $F(\mathbf{x})$. As we will see, in our approach we make this explicit by separating the filter from the domain.

If only some attributes of $\mathbf{x}$ are of interest, the above expression takes the form

$$\{\mathbf{x} : (x_1, x_2, ..., x_m) \mid F(\mathbf{x})\}$$

where $x_1, ..., x_m$ are attributes of the relation which is the result of the query (i.e. attributes of a tuple $\mathbf{x}$). This set is created by selecting all tuples $\mathbf{x}$ for which $F(\mathbf{x})$ is true, and then projecting those tuples on attributes $x_1, ..., x_m$. The result of a query on a set of tuples (relation) is either a set of tuples matching a certain condition or a value (when using aggregate functions, cf. Section 4.3). For example, the query $\{\mathbf{x} : (name, id) \mid student(\mathbf{x})\}$ returns a set of tuples which contain attributes *name* and *id* from the *student* relation.

A predicate $P(x)$ is a function that maps each element x of a set S to the value 'true' or 'false', i.e., $P : S \rightarrow \{true, false\}$.

Let $x \in N$ - so x is an element of the set of natural numbers. Then the predicate $P_1(x) \equiv x \geq 0$ is true for all x while the predicate $P_2(x) \equiv x < 0$ is false for all x.

Predicates can consist of one expression (as in $x \geq 0$ above) or as a combination of expressions. These combinations arise by combining expressions using the usual first-order or predicate logic operators (e.g. see [9]) given in Table 2.

Table 2. Logical connectives

$\wedge$ (conjunction)	$\vee$ (disjunction)	$\neg$ (negation)	$\Rightarrow$ (implication)

Let $x \in N$, as before. The predicate $P_3(x) \equiv x < 7 \wedge x > 10$ combines the expressions $x < 7$ and $x > 10$ (and is false for all $x \in N$). The predicate $P_4(x) \equiv x \geq 3 \wedge x < 6$ is true for $x = 3, 4, 5$ and false for all other $x \in N$. Predicates can be used to define sets. For example, $S_1 = \{x \mid x \in N \wedge P_1(x)\}$ denotes the set of all x such that x is natural number ($x \in N$) and satisfies the predicate P_1 (where $P_1(x) \equiv x \geq 0$, as before).

We have seen that P_1 is true for all x which means that S_1 is the set of natural numbers, and we can write $S_1 = \{x \mid x \in N \wedge P_1(x)\} = N$. Similarly, we have that $S_2 = \{x \mid x \in N \wedge P_3(x)\} = \emptyset$ where predicate P_1 is as defined before.

The fact that predicates can be used to define sets is well-known in mathematics and is central to our approach – we will be using the set membership to identify relations and the predicate as the selection condition on the tuples of these relations.

If p and q are expressions that valuate to true or false, sometimes called WFFs for Well-Formed Formulae in the literature, e.g. see [6], then the following equations hold. These are standard in first-order logic, e.g. see [9], so we list them here in Table 3 without further explanation. A thorough treatment can be found in [9].

Table 3. Equations on expressions (WWF)

$\neg(\neg p) \equiv p$	$\neg(p \wedge q) \equiv \neg p \vee \neg q$	$\neg(p \vee q) \equiv \neg p \wedge \neg q$
$p \Rightarrow q \equiv \neg p \vee q$	$p \wedge (q \vee r) \equiv (p \wedge q) \vee (p \wedge r)$	$p \vee (q \wedge r) \equiv (p \vee q) \wedge (p \vee r)$

We now turn our attention to the basic structure of a query expressed in SQL DML in our formalization which is an extension to the tuple relational calculus while staying within the predicate calculus semantics – in particular, we will be concerned with setting up formal semantics for transforming SBVR rules to SQL queries based on a predicate calculus with identity.

Since our interest is in transforming SBVR rules to SQL queries on the relational schema generated by the SBVR model, we will be concerned with predicates that define sets of tuples. The general form of a query in our predicate calculus is

$$\{\mathbf{x} | D(\mathbf{x}) \wedge P(\mathbf{x})\}$$

where $\mathbf{x} : (x_1, ..., x_n)$ is the set of tuples from a domain $D(\mathbf{x})$, and $D(\mathbf{x})$ specifies the set of all possible tuples that $\mathbf{x}$ ranges over, i.e. a relation with $x_1, ..., x_n$ attributes, and $P(\mathbf{x})$ is a predicate on the set of all tuples in $D(\mathbf{x})$. For example, $\{\mathbf{x} | student(\mathbf{x}) \wedge student.id = '6081958'\}$ returns the set of all tuples $\mathbf{x}$ from the relation *student* whose attribute *id* has the value 6081958. (Note that *student.id* is a primary key in our schema, given in Section 3, so this expression would return a single tuple.)

The expression $\{\mathbf{x} | D(\mathbf{x}) \wedge P(\mathbf{x})\}$ in the extended predicate calculus considered here is mapped to SQL DML as:

> SELECT   DISTINCT $\mathbf{x}$
> FROM $D(\mathbf{x})$
> WHERE $P(\mathbf{x})$;

The SQL keyword DISTINCT is used to remove duplicates.

If we are only interested in certain attributes $x_1, ..., x_n$ in the result $\mathbf{x}$ and not all attributes $x_1, ..., x_m$ of the relation specified in $D(\mathbf{x})$, then we write for the projection

$$\{\mathbf{x} : (x_1, x_2 .., x_n) | D(\mathbf{x}) \wedge P(\mathbf{x})\}$$

which is mapped to SQL DML as:

> SELECT   DISTINCT $x_1, ..., x_n$
> FROM $D(\mathbf{x})$
> WHERE $P(\mathbf{x})$;

To express the JOIN statements in SQL DML which applies to two or more relations, we need to take a closer look at $D(\mathbf{x})$. In standard tuple relational calculus semantics, it is well known that joining two relations means taking the Cartesian product ($\times$) of the two relations. In our formalization, the join of two relations (tables) is captured in $D(\mathbf{x})$ which is what is used to specify the set of all tuples from which the returned set of tuples $\mathbf{x}$ come from. The join condition, if any, is then added in the predicate $P(\mathbf{x})$ - and that is in addition to the selection condition, if any.

Therefore, if we want to join tuples from relations $\mathbf{y}_1, \mathbf{y}_2, ..., \mathbf{y}_k$ we write

$$\{ \mathbf{x} : (x_1, ..., x_n) \mid D(\mathbf{y}_1) \times D(\mathbf{y}_2) \times \cdots \times D(\mathbf{y}_k) \wedge P(\mathbf{x}) \}$$

where $D(\mathbf{y}_1) \times D(\mathbf{y}_2) \times \cdots \times D(\mathbf{y}_k) = D(\mathbf{x})$. This is mapped onto SQL DML as:

$$\text{SELECT} \quad x_1, .., x_n$$
$$\text{FROM} \quad D(\mathbf{y}_1) \times D(\mathbf{y}_2) \times \cdots \times D(\mathbf{y}_k)$$
$$\text{WHERE} \quad P(\mathbf{x}) ;$$

Note that $\mathbf{y}_1, \mathbf{y}_2, ..., \mathbf{y}_k$ denote relations (sets of tuples) while $x_1, ..., x_n$ is the list of attributes returned after the join of the relations, and this is denoted by $\mathbf{x} : (x_1, ..., x_n)$. It is also worth pointing out that selection conditions on attributes of $\mathbf{y}_1, \mathbf{y}_2, ..., \mathbf{y}_k$ are included in $P(\mathbf{x})$ since they are applied after the Cartesian product on these relations has been applied. For example,

$$\{ \mathbf{x} : (student.id, student.name, COUNT(course.id) \mid D(student) \times D(s\_irf\_c) \times$$
$$\times D(course) \wedge student.id = s\_irf\_c.studentID \wedge s\_irf\_c.courseID = course.id \}$$

is transformed into:

```
SELECT     student.id, student.name, COUNT(student.id)
FROM       student, s_irf_c, course
WHERE      student.id = s_irf_c.studentID AND s_irf_c.courseID = course.id ;
```

We now turn our attention to arithmetic operations and aggregate functions.

4.2 Arithmetic Operations and Aggregate Functions

In SQL, arithmetic operations may appear in the SELECT clause, as in:

```
SELECT     Salary*1.1, EmpID, EmpName
FROM       Employee
WHERE      DeptName = 'Research';
```

which reflects the values of a 10% increase in salaries in the Research department. So we need to apply this arithmetic operation as a function on the returned set of tuples $\mathbf{x}$. For this reason, we write

$$\{ E(\mathbf{x}) \mid D(\mathbf{x}) \wedge P(\mathbf{x}) \}$$

where $E(\mathbf{x})$ is a function on $\mathbf{x}$ that includes addition (+), subtraction (-), multiplication (*), division (/), or a combination of these on one or more attributes of the tuples in $\mathbf{x}$, i.e. tuples from $D(\mathbf{x})$ which satisfy $P(\mathbf{x})$.

Often, arithmetic operations only apply to certain attributes in the set of returned tuples $\mathbf{x}$. So E should be applied to the attributes of $\mathbf{x}$ rather than across $\mathbf{x}$. Thus,

$$\{\mathbf{x}.(E(x_1), E(x_2),..., E(x_n)) \mid D(\mathbf{x}) \wedge P(\mathbf{x})\}$$

where $E(x_i)$, $i = 1..n$, is applied to some attributes, in which case it is one or more of '+', '-', '*', '/' and not applied to others, in which case we have $E(x_i) = x_i$ (identity).

In similar fashion, we can address the aggregate functions in SQL DML, i.e. SUM, AVG, MIN, MAX, COUNT. To take into account the fact that an arithmetic operation may have been already applied to a certain attribute, we define F as a composite function on E so that $(F \circ E)(x_i) = F(E(x_i))$. In other words, F is applied to the output of E, and we write

$$\{\mathbf{x}.(F(E(x_1)), F(E(x_2)),..., F(E(x_n))) \mid D(\mathbf{x}) \wedge P(\mathbf{x})\}$$

Note that if F is the aggregate function COUNT, for some attribute x_i, then $E(x_i)$ must be the identity, i.e. $E(x_i) = x_i$, so that only attribute names are allowed in this case and no arithmetic operations.

This predicate calculus construction is mapped onto SQL DML as

SELECT $F(E(x_1)), F(E(x_2)),..., F(E(x_n))$
FROM $D(\mathbf{x})$
WHERE $P(\mathbf{x})$;

For example,

$$\{\mathbf{x}.(student.id, student.name, COUNT(student.id)) \mid student(\mathbf{x}) \wedge student.level = 3\}$$

is mapped onto the query:

SELECT   student.id, COUNT(student.id)
FROM   student
WHERE   student.level = '3';

and returns the number of final year students in the dataset.

We now turn our attention to grouping and filtering on groups.

4.3 Grouping and Having

The grouping operation on a database comes down to stating the desired grouping attribute(s) and the grouping condition, if any. The grouping condition selects those groups that satisfy the condition and discards those who do not. In our formalisation, the grouping attributes are specified before the projected attributes (and therefore will be mapped onto the SELECT clause in SQL DML) while the grouping condition will be part of the predicate itself. We note that it cannot be included in $P(\mathbf{x})$, like we did for JOIN, because the grouping condition applies to the results of the grouping operation, i.e., once the groups have been formed by the grouping operations.

Therefore, if we want to group a relation by a set of attributes $x_1,...x_m$ (a subset of all the attributes $x_1,...x_n$ of the relation), we write

$$\{\mathbf{x}{:}(x_1,..,x_m\,),\mathbf{x}:(x_1,..,x_n\,)|D(\mathbf{x})\wedge P(\mathbf{x})\}$$

$(x_1,...,x_m\,)$ and $(x_1,...,x_n\,)$ need not be disjoint but both need to be subsets of the set of attributes of $D(\mathbf{x})=(x_1,...,x_n\,)$. Finally, we note that $D(\mathbf{x})$ may be the result of the Cartesian product of a number of relations, as before.

The above expression in our predicate calculus is mapped onto SQL DML as:

SELECT	$x_1,...,x_n$
FROM	$D(\mathbf{x})$
WHERE	$P(\mathbf{x})$
GROUP BY	$x_1,...,x_m$

For example,

$$\{\mathbf{x}:student.id,\mathbf{x}:(student.id,student.name,COUNT(course.id)\,|$$

$$|\,D(student)\times D(s\_irf\_c)\times D(course)\wedge$$

$$\wedge student.id=s\_irf\_c.studentID\wedge s\_irf\_c.courseID=course.id\}$$

returns the number of courses a student has taken, and does this for every student. This translates to the following SQL query:

SELECT	student.id, student.name, COUNT(course.id)
FROM	student, s_irf_c, course
WHERE	student.id = s_irf_c.studentID AND
	AND s_irf_c.courseID = course.id
GROUP BY	student.id ;

Next we may add the grouping condition as an additional predicate $H(\mathbf{x})$ which applies to the result (set of tuples) of the grouping operation, i.e. to the set of attributes in $(x_1,...,x_m\,)\subseteq(x_1,...,x_n\,)$. Therefore, we write

$$\{\mathbf{x}{:}(x_1,...,x_n\,)|\{\mathbf{x}{:}(x_1,...,x_m\,),\mathbf{x}:(x_1,...,x_n\,)|D(\mathbf{x})\wedge P(\mathbf{x})\}\wedge H(\mathbf{x})\}$$

which is mapped onto SQL DML as:

SELECT	$x_1,...,x_n$
FROM	$D(\mathbf{x})$
WHERE	$P(\mathbf{x})$
GROUP BY	$x_1,...,x_m$
HAVING	$H(\mathbf{x})$

Note that this is different to a nested predicate calculus expression because a nested query would simply apply a selection condition to the result of the inner query but could project onto different attributes. In contrast, a grouping condition only filters the groups returned by the grouping operation, and thus cannot apply a further projection. For a nested query we would write

$$\{\mathbf{x}{:}(x_1^{'},..,x_n^{'})\,|\,\{\mathbf{x}{:}(x_1,..,x_m),\mathbf{x}:(x_1,..,x_n)|D(\mathbf{x})\wedge P(\mathbf{x})\}\wedge P^{'}(\mathbf{x})\}$$

which would in turn map onto the following SQL DML:

SELECT	$x_1^{'},..,x_n^{'}$
FROM	(SELECT $\quad x_1,..,x_n$
	FROM $\quad D(\mathbf{x})$
	WHERE $\quad P(\mathbf{x})$)
	GROUP BY $\quad x_1,..,x_m$)
WHERE	$P^{'}(\mathbf{x})$;

It can be seen that $P^{'}(\mathbf{x})$ applies to the result of the inner query, but the result of the nested query as a whole can include a projection on any attributes from $D(\mathbf{x})$.

Going back to our example, if we want to check whether the business rule

It is necessary that each **student** *is registered for* at most five **courses**

expressed in the SBVR model given earlier in Figure 3 is satisfied, we need to restrict to groups (one for each student) who are associated with (registered for) more than five courses. We check for these cases since these are cases where the rule might be violated, and if this happens, the corresponding database operations will need to be executed as a transaction. Taking into account the associated database schema, this rule is expressed in terms of our extended predicate calculus as follows:

$$\{\mathbf{x}: (student.id, student.name, COUNT(student.id))\,|$$

$$|\,\{\mathbf{x}: student.id, \mathbf{x}: (student.id, student.name, COUNT(course.id))\,|$$

$$|\,D(student)\times D(s\_irf\_c)\times D(course)\wedge student.id = s\_irf\_c.studentID \wedge$$

$$\wedge s\_irf\_c.courseID = course.id\}\wedge(COUNT(course.id) > 5)\}$$

which is in turn mapped onto the following SQL DML statements:

SELECT	student.id, student.name, COUNT(course.id)
FROM	student, s_irf_c, course
WHERE	student.id = s_irf_c.studentID
	AND s_irf_c.courseID = course.id
GROUP BY	student.id
HAVING	COUNT(course.id) > 5 ;

It is in this way that we can take rules from an SBVR model and transform them into SQL DML so that we can then check whether they are satisfied on a relational database schema by executing a standard SQL query. In the next section we attempt to generalize this by taking a closer look at both ends, our predicate calculus -based formalisation and the SBVR-LF, and do so at the semantics level.

5 From SBVR-LF to SQL DML

In this section we turn our attention to the SBVR Logic Formulation (SBVR-LF) as defined in the SBVR specification document [2], and describe a mapping onto the predicate calculus foundation for SQL DML which was given in the previous section. The objective is to obtain a generic mapping between rules expressed in SBVR and queries expressed in standard SQL DML, since this would make business rules amenable to immediate validation against a dataset.

Before we embark on the mapping, we define the quantifiers within the predicate calculus semantics in our approach. There are two quantifiers in predicate logic that can be used in an expression (WFF) to find out how many elements of the corresponding set satisfy the expression.

Let $P(\mathbf{x})$ be a predicate (as before). Let $D(\mathbf{x})$ denote the domain of $\mathbf{x}$, i.e. the set of all possible values for the tuple $\mathbf{x}$. To find out if *for at least one* tuple $\mathbf{x}$ from the domain $D(\mathbf{x})$ the predicate $P(\mathbf{x})$ is true, we write

$$(\exists\mathbf{x})(D(\mathbf{x}) \wedge P(\mathbf{x}))$$

which is read as "there is an $\mathbf{x}$ for which $D(\mathbf{x})$ holds, and $P(\mathbf{x})$ is true". The result of this expression is either true or false.

To find out if for all tuples in the domain $D(\mathbf{x})$ the predicate $P(\mathbf{x})$ is true, we write

$$(\forall\mathbf{x})(D(\mathbf{x}) \Rightarrow P(\mathbf{x}))$$

which is read as "for all $\mathbf{x}$ for which $D(\mathbf{x})$ holds, $P(\mathbf{x})$ is true". The result of this expression is true or false.

With reference to the example predicates discussed in the start of Section 4.1, the expression $(\exists x)(x \in N \wedge P_3(x))$ is false. The expression $(\forall x)(x \in N \Rightarrow P_1(x))$ is true.

Note the difference between $(\exists\mathbf{x})(D(\mathbf{x}) \wedge P(\mathbf{x}))$ and $(\forall\mathbf{x})(D(\mathbf{x}) \Rightarrow P(\mathbf{x}))$ which can yield different results (true or false) for the same expression. To avoid such ambiguities the domain $D(\mathbf{x})$ of an expression with a universal quantifier is always placed to the left of the implication logical operator ($\Rightarrow$).

Table 4.

$(\forall\mathbf{x})(P(\mathbf{x})) \equiv \neg(\exists\mathbf{x})(\neg P(\mathbf{x}))$	$(\exists\mathbf{x})(P(\mathbf{x})) \equiv \neg(\forall\mathbf{x})(\neg P(\mathbf{x}))$
$(\forall\mathbf{x})(D_1(\mathbf{x}) \times D_2(\mathbf{x}) \Rightarrow P(\mathbf{x})) \equiv (\forall\mathbf{x})(D_1(\mathbf{x}) \Rightarrow (D_2(\mathbf{x}) \Rightarrow P(\mathbf{x})))$	
$(\forall\mathbf{x})(D_1(\mathbf{x}) \times D_2(\mathbf{x}) \Rightarrow P(\mathbf{x})) \equiv \neg(\exists\mathbf{x})((D_1(\mathbf{x}) \times D_2(\mathbf{x})) \wedge \neg P(\mathbf{x}))$	

Again, drawing upon first-order logic we have that if $P(\mathbf{x})$ is a predicate and $D_1(\mathbf{x})$, $D_2(\mathbf{x})$ are domains (expressions that define relations from the database schema generated by the SBVR vocabulary, as discussed in Section 3, and hence restrict the set of all possible values for a tuple $\mathbf{x}$), then the following equations hold.

We have given these standard equations in terms of predicates that define sets of tuples. In their general form, they apply to an element x rather than a tuple $\mathbf{x}$ and we would also have $\wedge$ instead of $\times$ in the last two.

The specification document of SBVR includes the definition of the Formal Logic and Mathematics Vocabulary [2, pp. 109-118] which provides the logical foundations for SBVR in terms of first-order logic. However, the SBVR specification predefines some numeric quantifiers [2, pp.97-98] in addition to the standard universal and existential quantifiers found in first-order predicate logic. These allow the user to say things like 'exactly one car' or 'exactly two cars' or 'at most 8 and at least 3 cars' or 'at most two cars' and so on. Due to space limitations we do not reproduce the SBVR predefined quantifiers here, and refer the interested reader to the SBVR specification.

The predefined quantifiers can be defined in terms of the quantifiers in our formalization, which were defined earlier in standard predicate logic (Table 4). Drawing upon the definition schemas in [11], also outlined in [2], we may obtain a rewriting of the SBVR predefined quantifiers in our approach.

The *exactly one quantifier* in SBVR-LF, denoted by $\exists^1\mathbf{x}$, can be rewritten as:

$$(\exists^1\mathbf{x})(D(\mathbf{x}) \wedge P(\mathbf{x})) \equiv (\exists\mathbf{x})(D(\mathbf{x}) \wedge P(\mathbf{x})) \wedge (\forall\mathbf{y})(D(\mathbf{y}) \Rightarrow P(\mathbf{y}) \wedge \mathbf{y} = \mathbf{x})$$

The *at most n quantifier* given in SBVR-LF, denoted by $\exists^{0..n}\mathbf{x}$, can be rewritten in terms of our predicate calculus as:

$$(\exists^{0..n}\mathbf{x})(D(\mathbf{x}) \wedge P(\mathbf{x})) \equiv \neg(\exists\mathbf{x})(D(\mathbf{x}) \wedge P(\mathbf{x})) \vee (\exists\mathbf{x}_1)(D(\mathbf{x}_1) \wedge P(\mathbf{x}_1)) \vee$$

$$\vee ((\exists\mathbf{x}_1)(D(\mathbf{x}_1) \wedge P(\mathbf{x}_1) \wedge (\exists\mathbf{x}_2)(D(\mathbf{x}_2) \wedge P(\mathbf{x}_1)) \wedge \neg(\mathbf{x}_1 = \mathbf{x}_2) \vee$$

$$\vdots$$

$$\vee ((\exists\mathbf{x}_1)(D(\mathbf{x}_1) \wedge P(\mathbf{x}_1) \wedge \cdots \wedge (\exists\mathbf{x}_n)(D(\mathbf{x}_n) \wedge P(\mathbf{x}_n)) \wedge \neg(\mathbf{x}_1 = \cdots = \mathbf{x}_n) \wedge$$

$$\wedge (\forall\mathbf{y})(D(\mathbf{y}) \Rightarrow P(\mathbf{y}) \wedge ((\mathbf{y} = \mathbf{x}_1) \vee \cdots \vee (\mathbf{y} = \mathbf{x}_n)))$$

The first disjunction covers the case that there might not exist such a tuple $\mathbf{x}$ (case of 0), the second covers the case there is one such $\mathbf{x}$, the third is for two such $\mathbf{x}$, and so on. The last disjunction says that n such $\mathbf{x}$ may exist, but then there cannot be any more $(n+1)$ tuples that satisfy the predicate.

Similarly, the *at least n quantifier*, denoted by $\exists^{n..}\mathbf{x}$, can be rewritten as:

$$(\exists^{n..}\mathbf{x})(D(\mathbf{x}) \wedge P(\mathbf{x})) \equiv (\exists\mathbf{x}_1)(D(\mathbf{x}_1) \wedge P(\mathbf{x}_1)) \wedge (\exists\mathbf{x}_2)(D(\mathbf{x}_2) \wedge P(\mathbf{x}_2) \wedge \neg(\mathbf{x}_1 = \mathbf{x}_2)) \wedge$$

$$\wedge \cdots \wedge (\exists\mathbf{x}_n)(D(\mathbf{x}_n) \wedge P(\mathbf{x}_n) \wedge \neg(\mathbf{x}_n = \mathbf{x}_1) \wedge \cdots \wedge \neg(\mathbf{x}_n = \mathbf{x}_{n-1})) \wedge$$

$$\wedge((\exists\mathbf{x}_{n+k})(D(\mathbf{x}_{n+k}) \wedge P(\mathbf{x}_{n+k}) \wedge \neg(\mathbf{x}_{n+k} = \mathbf{x}_1) \wedge \cdots \wedge \neg(\mathbf{x}_{n+k} = \mathbf{x}_n)) \vee$$

$$\vee(\forall\mathbf{x}_{n+1})(D(\mathbf{x}_{n+1}) \Rightarrow P(\mathbf{x}_{n+1}) \wedge ((\mathbf{x}_{n+1} = \mathbf{x}_1) \vee \cdots \vee (\mathbf{x}_{n+1} = \mathbf{x}_n))))$$

The first $n-1$ conjunctions refer to each of the n tuples **x** that must exist, must satisfy the predicate. The last conjunction captures the fact that there may be k additional such **x** that satisfy the predicate or no other **x** (apart from the n we already have) may exist that satisfy the predicate.

The *at least n and at most m quantifier* given in SBVR-LF, and denoted by $\exists^{n..m}$**x**, can be obtained by combining the rewriting of the *at least n* and that of the *at most n quantifiers* given earlier.

The intention behind SBVR-LF is to (be able to) capture business facts and business rules formally. Formal statements of business rules may then be transformed into logical formulations that can be read in software tools, or readily adopted in approaches like the one we describe in this paper. An example given in the specification [2, pp.90-91] is the formalisation of a static constraint that says 'each person was born on some date' as the logical formulation:

$$\forall x : person, \exists y : Date, x \text{ was born on } y$$

Going back to our example, the rule in our SBVR model can be written as:

$$\forall \textbf{x} : \underline{student}, \exists^{0..5}\textbf{y} : \underline{course}, \textbf{ x } \textit{is registered for } \textbf{y}$$

With reference to the tree representation of this rule given in Figure 3 earlier, it can be seen that the root is a universal quantification ($\forall$), the 1st variable is **student**, the 2nd variable is **course** and the max cardinality is 5 ($\exists^{0..5}$) while the atomic formulation that completes the [at most n] quantification node is **student** *is registered for* **course** and this binds the 1st variable to x and the 2nd to y.

In fact we are interested in disproving the rule, i.e. identifying students registered for 6 or more courses. This can be encoded by taking the negation of the logical formulation in which case the existential quantifier $\neg\exists^{0..5}$ gives $\exists^{6..}$. Thus, we have

$$\exists \textbf{x} : \underline{student}, \exists^{6..}\textbf{y} : \underline{course}, \textbf{ x } \textit{is registered for } \textbf{y}$$

Now **student** and **course** are relations in our database schema (Figure 4) and so is *is registered for*, thus all three appear in the domain $D(\textbf{x})$ (in a Cartesian product) and consequently in the FROM clause of the resulting SQL query. The primary key of **student** will have to match the foreign key of *is registered for*, similarly for **course**. These join conditions become the predicate $P(\textbf{x})$ and hence appear in the WHERE clause. The cardinality on the existential quantifier (6 or more) is the condition applied to the resulting tuples (per student), hence becomes the predicate $H(\textbf{x})$ and appears in the HAVING clause.

It can be seen that the predicate calculus with identity we presented provides a bridge between SBVR-LF and SQL DML. This means that SBVR rules can be re-written systematically as SQL queries, thus enabling their execution to maintain consistency of a database. The modality of the rule, which has not been addressed explicitly here, is taken into account only in enforcing consistency once a violation is observed. A violation of an alethic rule leads to a direct rejection of the update on the dataset while a violation of a deontic rule can be overridden if authorised by a user with sufficient privileges.

6 Conclusions and Future Work

In this paper we have briefly described the concept of generative information systems, and how rule-based modeling is at their core. We have discussed how an SBVR model (terms, fact types) is transformed into a relational schema that can act as a data store for our information system. By showing how the user interacts with the system, we have demonstrated the need for a formal and rigorous approach to transforming SBVR rules to SQL queries. This transformation allows a rule to be validated against the dataset in much the same way as issuing a query on a database.

The correctness of the transformation has been shown using a predicate calculus with identity, which extends standard relational theory to include provision for aggregate functions and arithmetic operations, and also address SQL DML constructs such as grouping (GROUP BY clause) and grouping on condition (HAVING clause).

The work in [12] is also concerned with generating SQL DML from business rules. However, the rules are expressed in the ORM-based language ConQuer and the transformation is not attempted at the semantic level (at least not through relational theory). The problem of operationalising SBVR business rules is challenging. There are transformations to UML class diagrams [13] and R2ML [14] within an MDA context, as well as the reverse transformation from OCL to SBVR [15]. Instead, we have described the operational rendering of SBVR rules into standard SQL queries, which can then be readily executed to maintain consistency of a database.

To further the research discussed, the transformation needs to be implemented in a tool such that it can be applied to real-world problems. Another possible extension is to add model-checking capabilities to the model execution functionality, described here, such that models with inconsistent, redundant, or needlessly complex rules can be identified and refined accordingly.

Acknowledgements

This work has been supported by the European Commission through IST Project OPAALS: Open Philosophies for Associative Autopoietic Digital Ecosystems (No. IST-2005-034824).

References

1. Ross, R.G.: The Business Rules Manifesto. Business Rules Group. Version 2 (2003)
2. Object Management Group, "Semantics of Business Vocabulary and Rules Formal Specification v1.0, OMG document formal/08-01-02 (January 2008),
   http://www.omg.org/spec/SBVR/1.0/ (accessed: 14/5/2010)
3. Open Philosophies for Associative Autopoietic Digital Ecosystems, Automatic code structure and workflow generation from natural language models (2008),
   http://files.opaals.eu/OPAALS/Year_2_Deliverables/
   WP02/D2.2.pdf (14/5/2010)
4. Marinos, A., Krause, P.: An SBVR Framework for RESTful Web Applications. In: Governatori, G., Hall, J., Paschke, A. (eds.) RuleML 2009. LNCS, vol. 5858, pp. 144–158. Springer, Heidelberg (2009)

5. Gilbert, D., Tafarodi, R., Malone, P.: You can't not believe everything you read. Journal of Personality and Social Psychology 65(2), 221–233 (1993)
6. Date, C.J.: An Introduction to Database Systems. Addison-Wesley, Reading (2004)
7. Marinos, A., Krause, P.: An SBVR Framework for RESTful Web Applications. In: Governatori, G., Hall, J., Paschke, A. (eds.) RuleML 2009. LNCS, vol. 5858, pp. 144–158. Springer, Heidelberg (2009)
8. Codd, E.F.: Relational Completeness of Data Base Sublanguages. In: Dustin, R.J. (ed.) Proc. Courant Computer Science Symposia Series, vol. 6. Prentice Hall, Englewood Cliffs (1972)
9. Huth, A.R.A., Ryan, M.D.: Logic in Computer Science: Modelling and reasoning about systems. Cambridge University Press, Cambridge (2002)
10. Nakano, R.: Translation with Optimization from Relational Calculus to Relational Algebra having Aggregate Functions. ACM Tran. on Database Systems 15(4), 518–557 (1990)
11. Halpin, T.A.: A Logical Analysis of Information Systems: Static Aspects of the Data-Oriented Perspective. PhD Thesis, University of Queensland (1989)
12. Bloesch, A.C., Halpin, T.A.: ConQuer: a Conceptual Query Language. In: Thalheim, B. (ed.) ER 1996. LNCS, vol. 1157, pp. 121–133. Springer, Heidelberg (1996)
13. Kleiner, M., Albert, P., Bezivin, J.: Parsing SBVR-based Controlled Languages. In: Schürr, A., Selic, B. (eds.) MODELS 2009. LNCS, vol. 5795, pp. 122–136. Springer, Heidelberg (2009)
14. Demuth, B., Liebau, H.-B.: An Approach for Bridging the Gaps Between Business Rules and the Semantic Web. In: Paschke, A., Biletskiy, Y. (eds.) RuleML 2007. LNCS, vol. 4824, pp. 119–133. Springer, Heidelberg (2007)
15. Cabot, J., Pau, R., Raventos, R.: From UML/OCL to SBVR Specifications: A Challenging Transformation. Information Systems 35, 417–440 (2010)

Representing Financial Reports on the Semantic Web:
A Faithful Translation from XBRL to OWL

Jie Bao[1], Graham Rong[2], Xian Li[1], and Li Ding[1]

[1] Tetherless World Constellation, Rensselaer Polytechnic Institute
Troy, NY, 12180-3590, USA
{baoj,lix15,dingl}@rpi.edu
[2] Sloan School of Management, Massachusetts Institute of Technology
Cambridge, MA, 02142, USA
grong@sloan.mit.edu

Abstract. We discuss a translation of financial reports from the XBRL format into the Semantic Web language OWL. Different from existing approaches that do structural translation from XBRL's XML schema into OWL, our approach can faithfully preserve the implicit semantics in XBRL and enable the logic model of financial reports. We show that such a translation reduces the risk of redundancy and inconsistency, and enables the quick and useful inference on XBRL based financial reports for better business decisions.

1 Introduction

XBRL (eXtensible Bussiness Reporting Language) is an XML-based standard for exchanging business information, e.g., public company financial reports. XBRL provides considerable benefits in the preparation, analysis and communication of business information. In recent years there has been rapid growth in international adoption of XBRL (cf. a survey as of Apr 2010 [5]).

However, despite its broad acceptance, XBRL remains largely to be a structural model of financial reports, without addressing the *logic model* of these reports. For example, while we can declare the equivalency of two concepts in XBRL using arc roles, there is no means in XBRL to infer new relations from the equivalency relation. Furthermore, its inherited document-oriented nature makes it difficult to process, browse and query data from a large set of XBRL files.

Recently Semantic Web has been argued as a natural choice for complementing XBRL with a logic or semantic data model [6]. This is due to the fact that Semantic Web languages, e.g., RDF and OWL, are inherently built with a graph-based open data model and naturally support integration from different data sources and applications. In addition, these languages are based on formal knowledge representation formalisms thus enable the automatic processing and inference about data.

Garcia and Gil [6] have provided a mapping from XBRL to RDF and OWL. This mapping is based on a structural transformation from XML Schema to OWL. Tthousands of XBRL reports have been published as linked data using this approach. rdfabout.com[1] provides the corporate ownership information derived from SEC filings.

---

[1] http://rdfabout.com/demo/sec/

M. Dean et al. (Eds.): RuleML 2010, LNCS 6403, pp. 144–152, 2010.
© Springer-Verlag Berlin Heidelberg 2010

However, that data is only a partial mapping from financial report data covering individual ownership and subsidiary information for selective companies. Declerck and Krieger [2] translated the XBRL base taxonomy into description logic which is the logic foundation of OWL (2) DL. However, they did not specify how to translate the linkbases in XBRL. None of the above work provides a logic model that faithfully captures the implicit semantics of financial reports in XBRL and enables the automatic inference on XBRL data.

In this paper, we provide an improved semantic data model for XBRL by translating it into OWL. This is done by making explicit the implicit semantic assumptions and constraints in XBRL. Compared with previous work, our contributions include:

- Our model is based on the intended semantic model of XBRL which is currently provided informally as human-readable description in the XBRL specification [3] and is only partially captured in the current XML schema. By encoding these implicit semantics using OWL, we have obtained a more accurate data model for XBRL, that also incorporates domain knowledge.
- To correctly capture the semantics in XBRL, we need to model both ontological constraints and rule constraints. To ensure desirable computational properties of the result, we transform some rules into OWL 2 DL axioms which are known to be decidable, i.e., being able to answer any query in finite time, and have mature tool support. This further enables automatic processing and reasoning of financial data represented using our model.
- Leveraged by the inference capability of OWL, the semantic data model is significantly simplified from the XBRL structural model (as given in the XML schema) without losing information. This reduces both the redundancy in the data model and the risk of data inconsistency.

It is noteworthy, while OWL 2 DL covers a fairly large subset of XBRL's expressivity, there are semantic constraints of XBRL that can only be modeled by other Semantic Web languages, e.g., RIF (Rule Interchange Format) and integrity constraints [7]. These are left as future work.

This paper is accompanied by a technical report [1] with more detailed motivating examples and related work, and additional details of the translation from XBRL to OWL.

2   Representing XBRL Data Model for the Semantic Web: General Issues

In this section, we describe the general issues of the translation of the XBRL data model into Semantic Web representations using OWL (Web Ontology Language). More specifically, we use OWL 2 DL [4] to achieve both the semantic faithfulness of the translation and desirable computation properties (e.g., inference and query complexity) of the resulting knowledge bases (KB). For the sake of readability, we use the OWL 2 Functional-Style Syntax.

The XBRL Specification[2] offers a framework for the definitions of the semantics in business reporting and the production and validation of data from entities that need to communicate business performance. XBRL employs XML Schema and XLink technologies to describe different *taxonomies* for specific domains so that each XBRL document is an instance of an specific XBRL taxonomy. A taxonomy consists of a *taxonomy schema* and a set of *linkbases*. A taxonomy schema defines the reporting *concepts* as XML *elements*. XBRL *instances* contain the *facts* as well as the descriptions of their *contexts* (such as the reporting date of the fact and the currency unit used).

Correspondingly, the translation results in several different types of KBs:

– An XBRL ontology that captures some of the structural constraints defined in the XRBL XML Schema specification, and implicit semantic requirements which are only informally given by the specification or by default assumptions. This ontology will be shared by all translated KBs and its components are identified by the ★ sign in the paper. We assume its URL base name is xbrlo.
– Taxonomy ontologies that correspond to XBRL taxonomy documents.
– Instance ontologies that correspond to XBRL instance documents.

For the naming convention and the URL prefixes used here, please refer to the accompanying technical report [1].

Our translation is based on XBRL 2.0 [3]. The result can be easily extended to XBRL 2.1 as it is an extension to XBRL 2.0.

3 Representing XBRL Concepts

We first describe the translation of XBRL taxonomies into OWL.

Concepts. The <element> tag defines an XBRL *concept* which corresponds to an OWL class. For example, the following is an XBRL element of monetaryItemType and its OWL translation:

XBRL	`<element id="currentAssets"`
	`    name="currentAssets"`
	`    type=xbrli:monetaryItemType`
	`    xbrli:balance="credit"`
	`    substitutionGroup = "xbrli:item"`
	`</element>`

OWL	`Declaration( Class( ex:currentAssets))`
	`SubClassOf(ex:currentAssets xbrlo:monetaryItemType)`
	`SubClassOf(ex:currentAssets xbrlo:credit)`

Note that the substitutionGroup attribute is not translated since it can only have value xbrli:item or xbrli:tuple, which can already been inferred from the type information. The optional id attribute is also not translated as it's usually the same as name.

Elements Types (★). The basic element types in XBRL form a class hierarchy (prefix xbrlo: omitted); every class is disjoint with its siblings (except elementType and balanceType):

---
[2] http://www.xbrl.org

```
elementType                    balanceType
  itemType                        credit
    numericItemType               debit
      monetaryItemType
      sharesItemType
      decimalItemType
    stringItemType
    uriItemType
    dateTimeItemType
  tupleType
```

Each instance of an `itemType` has one and only one value of a particular datatype. For example, an instance of `stringItemType` should have exactly one value of the `xsd:string` type:

```
SubClassOf(xbrlo:itemType DataExactCardinality(1 xbrlo:value))
SubClassOf(xbrlo:stringItemType DataAllValuesFrom(xbrlo:value xsd:string
    ))
```

The type constraint of the item types is summarized in the table below:

monetaryItemType, sharesItemType, decimalItemType	xsd:double
stringItemType	xsd:string
uriItemType	xsd:anyURI
dateTimeItemType	xsd:dateTime

The tuple type will be discussed in the instance document section.

4   Representing XBRL Relations

XBRL relies on Xlink for relating entities defined in the schema, e.g., taxonomies and formulae. The set of xlinkes (called arcs) in an XBRL taxonomy forms its *linkbase*. There are five types of linkbases defined in the XBRL standard: *definition* linkbase, *calculation* linkbase, *presentation* linkbase, *label* linkbase and *reference* linkbase.

Locators. XBRL uses locators to identify a concept (element) in a taxonomy document, e.g., the following defines a locator to the concept `"balanaceSheet.xsd #currentAssets"`.

```
<loc xlink:type="locator" xlink:href="balanaceSheet.xsd#currentAssets"
    xlink:label="loc_currentAssets">
```

Since in OWL we can directly identify a class using its IRI, it's not necessary to use locators. Therefore, the locator `loc_curentAssets` can be replaced by the class `balancesheet.owl#currrentAssets`. Given a locator "L", we use C(L) to denote the class it points to (i.e., the class corresponds to its `xlink:href` property value).

Arcs. Arc-type elements join the resources referenced in their `from` and `to` attributes, for instance:

```
<definitionArc xlink:type="arc"
  xlink:from="loc_assets"      xlink:to  ="loc_currentAssets"
  xlink:show = "replace"       xlink:acuate = "onRequest"
  xlink:title = "From Assets to Current Assets"
  xlink:arcrole = "http://www.xbrl.org/linkprops/arc/parent-child"/>
```

For conciseness, let C(loc_assets)=A and C(loc_currentAssets) = C. An arc is represented as a property in OWL. Since an arc has no name in XBRL, a new property name is introduced for it.

A naive translation approach is to relate the two concepts (elements) using property assertions, such as

```
ObjectPropertyAssertion(ex:arc1 A C )
```

Where ex:arc1 is a new property name for the arc. However, such an approach will result in an OWL 2 Full ontology, hence violates inference termination requirement in OWL 2, since classes A and C are also used as individuals. A better OWL 2 DL translation is:

```
EquivalentClasses(    A  ObjectHasSelf( ex:pA ) )
EquivalentClasses(    C  ObjectHasSelf( ex:pC ) )
SubObjectPropertyOf( ObjectPropertyChain( ex:pA owl:topObjectProperty
    ex:pC ) ex:arc1)
AnnotationAssertion(rdfs:label ex:arc1 "From Assets to Current Assets"^^
    xsd:string))
SubObjectPropertyOf(ex:arc1 xbrlo:definitionArc)
SubObjectPropertyOf(ex:arc1 xbrlo:parent-child)
```

The first three axioms encode the rule ex:arc1(x,y) ← A(x), C(y), where ex:pA and ex:pC are two helper properties. This correctly captures the semantics that the *instances* of A and C have the relation parent-child.

Attributes xlink:actuate which always has value "onRequest", and xlink:show which has value "embed" if the resources linked are in different files and otherwise "replace", are not translated as they can be trivially inferred.

Arc Types. There are 5 arc types which are all subclasses of xbrlo:arc:

- xbrlo:calculationArc[3]: it has an attribute "weight". To obtain an OWL 2 DL translation, we may introduce a helper individual for the arc and associate the weight to that individual so that an XBRL processor can find such information. For example:

  ```
  EquivalentClasses( ObjectOneOf(ex:i1) ObjectHasSelf( ex:arc1 ) )
  DataPropertyAssertion (xbrl:weight ex:i1 "1"^^xsd:decimal)
  ```

- xbrlo:presentationArc: it has an order attribute which can be modeled similarly to calculationArc.
- xbrlo:definitionArc: discussed above.
- xbrlo:labelArc and xbrlo:referenceArc are non-semantic types and their translations are given in [1].

Arc Roles (★). Arc roles have intended semantics. For example, if loc_assets has a child-parent relation to loc_currentAssets, it is expected that loc_currentAssets has a parent-child relation to loc_assets. However,

---

[3] Note that while OWL itself does not provide numeric calculation, there are extensions of OWL that are able to do so, cf. Manchester OWL Arithmetics
http://www.cs.man.ac.uk/~iannonel/owlcalculations/syntax.html

such semantics are left implicit in the XBRL specification, which leads to both the redundancy and the risk of data inconsistency. Thus, for the example above, we have to also add the following content to the XBRL taxonomy document:

```
<definitionArc xlink:type=arc    xlink:from = "loc_currentAssets"
  xlink:to  ="loc_assets"        xlink:show = "replace"
  xlink:acuate = "onRequest"
  xlink:title = "From Current Assets to Assets"
  xlink:arcrole = "http://www.xbrl.org/linkprops/arc/child-parent"/>
```

Leveraging OWL's inference ability, we can eliminate such redundancy by defining the properties of the arc role. For example, the following OWL axioms declare that `parent-child` and `child-parent` are inverse to each other, and that a definition arc is symmetric:

```
InverseObjectProperties(xbrlo:parent-child xbrlo:child-parent)
SymmetricObjectProperty(xbrlo:definitionArc)
```

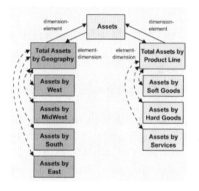

Note that `child-parent` (and similarly `parent-child`) relations in XBRL have different semantic meanings from OWL subclass relations. In XBRL, a `child-parent` relation describes how the *value* of *instances* of the related concepts are related, whereas in OWL a subclass relation means *subset relations between instance sets* of the related concepts.

Similar declarations are added for other arc roles (e.g., `xbrlo:dimension-element` is inverse of `xbrlo:element-dimension`) and arc types. As `xbrlo:dimension-element` indicates equivalency, we require it to be reflexive, transitive and symmetric, i.e.,

Fig. 1. Equivalency relations and child-parent relations

```
ReflexiveObjectProperty(xbrlo:dimension-element)
TransitiveObjectProperty(xbrlo:dimension-element)
SymmetricObjectProperty(xbrlo:dimension-element)
```

Fig 1 shows an example of calculating assets using different dimensions[4]. In XBRL, 18 arcs are required whereas in the OWL translation only 9 arcs are needed; in addition, we can infer that "Total Assets by Geography" and "Total Assets by Produce Line" must have the same value without calculating the value of "Assets".

5   Representing XBRL Instances

Items. Items are actual facts in the report thus are translated into OWL fact assertions. Since they have no name in the XBRL document, they will be mapped to anonymous individuals in OWL. For example, the XBRL fragment:

```
<assets numericContext="c1">300</assets>
```

---

[4] The example is originally from
  `http://us.kpmg.com/microsite/xbrl/train/86/86.htm`

is translated into OWL assertions

```
ClassAssertion(ex:assets _:x1)
ObjectPropertyAssertion(xbrlo:hasContext _:x1 ex:c1)
DataPropertyAssertion(xbrlo:value _:x1 "300"^^xsd:double)
```

where _:x1 is a newly introduced anonymous individual.

Tuples. Tuples are concepts that are used to contain other concepts. The structural relation of a tuple with its component concepts is represented using the xbrlo:tupleValue property, e.g.,

```
<address>
  <street>8th St</street>   ...
</address>
```

is translated to

```
ClassAssertion(ex:address _:x1)
ClassAssertion(ex:street _:x2)
ObjectPropertyAssertion(xbrlo:tupleValue _:x1 _x2)
DataPropertyAssertion(xbrlo:value _:x2 "8th St"^^xsd:string)
```

When the innermost block of a tuple has literal value, we can also use properties to model. For instance, the above example may also be modeled as

```
DataPropertyAssertion(ex:hasAddress _:x1 "8th St"^^xsd:string)
```

Contexts (★). Contexts are used to provide additional information related to the items (facts). A context is an instance of the class xbrlo:numericContext or xbrlo:nonNumericContext, which are both subclasses of xbrlo:context. For example:

```
<numericContext id="c1" precision="12" cwa="true">
  <period><instant>2001-12-31</instant></period>   ...
<numericContext>
```

will be translated into OWL

```
ClassAssetion(xbrlo:numericContext ex:c1)
DataPropertyAssertion(xbrlo:precision ex:c1 "12"^^xsd:integer)
DataPropertyAssertion(xbrlo:cwa ex:c1 "true"^^xsd:boolean)
ObjectPropertyAssertion(xbrlo:period ex:c1 _:x)
ClassAssertion(time:Instant _:x)
DataPropertyAssertion(time:inXSDDateTime _:x "2001-12-31"^^xsd:dateTime)
```

Here we reuse the OWL Time ontology[5] to represent period data.

The xbrlo:context class contains optional components entity, period, unit and scenario. The xbrlo:numericContext class has additional required attributes precision and cwa (closed world assumption)[6]. This requirement can be represented as cardinality constraints in OWL (only two such constraints are shown here)[7]:

---

[5] http://www.w3.org/TR/owl-time/

[6] Note that CWA in XBRL is different from CWA in OWL which models integrity constraints.

[7] All cardinality constraints in our translation should be understood as integrity constraints using the semantics described in [?], i.e., they will be used for data validation but not inference of new knowledge.

```
SubClassOf(xbrlo:context ObjectMinCardinality("0"^^xsd:integer
    xbrlo:entity))
SubClassOf(xbrlo:numericContext ObjectMinCardinality("1"^^xsd:integer
    xbrlo:precision))
```

Only an instance of numericItemType (monetaryItemType, sharesItemType, or decimalItemType) can have an instance of numericContext as its context, therefore we have the constraint:

```
SubClassOf(xbrlo:numericContext ObjectAllValuesFrom(
    ObjectInverseOf(xbrlo:hasContext) xbrlo:numericItemType)
```

We summarize the correspondence of key XBRL and OWL notions in Table 1. Translation of some non-semantic features of XBRL, e.g., annotations, are given in [1].

6   Conclusions

Table 1. Correspondence of Key XBRL and OWL Notions

XBRL	OWL
Taxonomy Document	Axioms
Instance Document	Assertions (facts)
Element	Named class
Datatype	Datatype
Locator	directly identified by the resource's IRI
Arc	Named property
Item	Anonymous individual
Context	Instance (of Context class)
"type" attribute	"SubClassOf" axiom
"name" attribute	local name of the IRI of the resource
"id" attribute	not translated
"title" attribute	rdfs:label annotation

In this paper we provide a semantic data model of XBRL-based financial data by using OWL so as to express the semantics currently described implicitly in XBRL specifications. We show that such a semantic model is able to better capture the domain knowledge related to financial reports, and reduces the redundancy, e.g. relation definition, in the current XBRL models. We also believe such a representation will enhance transparency in financial report filing, as well as the integration of financial reports and other domain knowledge bases.

Our ongoing work includes the modeling of the US GAAP (Generally Accepted Accounting Principles) and the IFRS (International Financial Reporting Standards) taxonomies using Semantic Web languages. Another future work is to publish XRBL data in the SEC EDGAR database as a part of the semantic government data cloud (http://data-gov.tw.rpi.edu) and link it to other government data sets (e.g., bankruptcy data and macroeconomic data).

References

1. Bao, J., Rong, G., Li, X., Ding, L.: Representing financial reports on the semantic web (extended version). Technical report, TW-2010-17, Tetherless World Constellation, RPI, Troy, NY, USA
2. Declerck, T., Krieger, H.-U.: Translating XBRL Into Description Logic. An Approach Using Protege, Sesame & OWL. In: BIS, pp. 455–467 (2006)

152 J. Bao et al.

3. Hampton, L., vun Kannon, D.: Extensible Business Reporting Language (XBRL) 2.0 Specification (December 2001), http://www.xbrl.org/tr/2001/xbrl-2001-12-14.pdf
4. Motik, B., Patel-Schneider, P.F., Parsia, B.: OWL 2 Web Ontology Language Structural Specification and Functional-Style Syntax. World Wide Web Consortium (W3C) Recommendation (2009)
5. O'Kelly, C.: XBRL World Wide Adoption Survey (April 2010),
http://www.slideshare.net/xbrlplanet/
xbrl-world-wide-adoption-survey-april-2010
6. Roberto Garcia, R.G.: Publishing xbrl as linked open data. In: A Unified Approach to Interior Point Algorithms for Linear Complementarity Problems, vol. 538 (2009)
7. Tao, J., Sirin, E., Bao, J., McGuinness, D.L.: Integrity Constraints in OWL. In: AAAI (2010) (in Press)

Transformation of SBVR Compliant Business Rules to Executable FCL Rules

Aqueo Kamada[1,4], Guido Governatori[2], and Shazia Sadiq[3]

[1] CTI, Rod. Dom Pedro I, km 143.6, Campinas, Brazil
[2] NICTA, Queensland Research Laboratory, Brisbane, Australia
[3] The University of Queensland, ITEE, Brisbane, Australia
[4] Unicamp, FT, Limeira, Brazil
aqueo.kamada@cti.gov.br,
guido.governatori@nicta.com.au,
shazia@itee.uq.edu.au

Abstract. The main source of changing requirements of the dynamic business environment is response to changes in regulations and contracts towards which businesses are obligated to comply. At the same time, many organizations have their business processes specified independently of their business obligations (which include adherence to contracts laws and regulations). Thus, the problem of mapping business changes into computational systems becomes much more complicated. In this paper we address the problem by providing an automated transformation of business rules into a formal language capable of directly mapping onto executable specifications. The model transformation is consistent with MDA/MOF/QVT concepts using ATL to perform the mapping. Business rules are compliant to SBVR metamodel, and are transformed into FCL, a logic based formalism, known to have a direct mapping onto executable specifications. Both, source and target rules are based on principles of deontic logic, the core of which are obligations, permissions and prohibitions.

Keywords: Business Contract; Business Rule Transformation; SBVR; FCL; MDA.

1 Introduction

Due to the current dynamic and highly competitive business environment the organizations have to make changes in their computational systems in a much more accelerated rhythm than in past decades. Consequently, the computational solutions for the business problems cannot accompany the speed in which the change necessities appear. One of the main sources of change is response to changes in regulations and contracts towards which businesses are obligated to comply.

Commonly, documents containing contracts, regulations, laws and procedures define the strategies, policies and relationships among organizations and consolidate the organization´s knowledge. From those documents arise the rules that define the behavior of the business processes in the organizations [1]. Hence, the computational systems must be compliant with these business documents. So, ensuring compliance

M. Dean et al. (Eds.): RuleML 2010, LNCS 6403, pp. 153–161, 2010.
© Springer-Verlag Berlin Heidelberg 2010

of business processes with business contracts means ensuring consistency of rules stated in business contracts and rules covering the execution of business processes.

We propose an MDA (Model Driven Architecture) [2] based model to transform SBVR compliant business rules [3] extracted from business contract of services to compliant executable rules in FCL – Formal Contract Logic [4]. Both business rules and FCL rules are based on principles of deontic logic [5] for treating expressions in the form of normative policies, the core of which are obligations, permissions and prohibitions. Deontic constraints express what parties to the contract are required to perform (obligations), what they are allowed to do (permissions), or what they are not allowed to do (prohibitions). We also present a transformation exercise using ATL (Atlas Transformation Language) [6] to transform SBVR compliant rules to FCL rules. We do not go into details about the generation of the predicates of FCL.

The next section provides an overview of the MDA modeling framework and Section 3 discusses aspects on business rules and business contracts formalization. Section 4 presents some requirements on the business contracts edition. Section 5 presents the proposed model transformation and Section 6 discusses some related works and the final section provides a conclusion and discussion on future researches.

2   Foundations on Model Transformation

Model transformation is the process of transforming a model, say Ma, conforming to metamodel MMa into a model, say Mb, conforming to metamodel MMb. QVT (Query/View/Transformation) [7], is an OMG (Object Management Group) standard for performing model transformations in the context of MDA and it can be used to do syntactic or semantic transformation.

The idea of Model Driven Engineering is that, through transformations accomplished on the conceptual model, new models are generated, with abstraction levels more and more specific and the final system is generated automatically. The built models are formals, avoiding ambiguity, so that they can be understood by software systems.

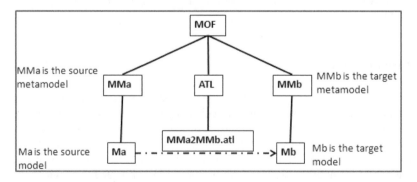

Fig. 1. ATL transformation context

ATL is a model transformation language developed by OBEO and INRIA to answer the QVT Request For Proposal. Considering the Figure 1, an ATL program

(MMa2MMb.atl) will take model Ma.xmi as input and will produce model Mb.xmi as output. Both models may be expressed in the OMG XMI [8] standard. The model Ma conforms to metamodel MMa.km3. Model Mb conforms to metamodel MMb.km3. The KM3 (Kernel MetaMetaModel) notation is a simple and neutral metamodel specification language. The ATL program itself (MMa2MMb**.**atl here) is also a model, so it conforms to a metamodel (the ATL metamodel) not presented here. An ATL program is composed of a header, of a set of side-effect free functions called helpers and of a set of rules.

3   Formalization of Business Rules and Business Contracts

This section presents some foundations on business rules and business contracts and discuss some aspects related to their formalization.

3.1 Business Rules

Although there are a lot of discussion around the definition of what "business rule" means [3], [9] in the context of this work, a business rule is "a rule that can be interpreted by computers, that defines or restricts some aspects of a business, introducing obligations or needs, according to the organization policies."[10]. Following are some business rules in the context of car rental:

- A car must have a registration number.
- A car should not be released to the customer if the credit card was not presented as the payment guarantee.
- A driver of a rental car must be a qualified driver.

The main objective of the SBVR metamodel [3] is to allow business people to define the policies and the rules that drive the organizations in the business people's own language, in terms of the artifacts with which they perform the businesses. Besides, the other objective is to capture those rules in a clear way, without ambiguity, and quickly transformable in other representations, as the representations for business people, for software engineers, and for business rules execution tools.

According to SBVR metamodel a business rule can be expressed formally in statements in a structured English language using a font style convention. There are four font styles with formal meaning: (i) <u>term</u> - the 'term' font is used for a designation for a noun concept (other than an individual concept); (ii) <u>Name</u> - the 'name' font is used for a designation of an individual concept that tend to be proper nouns (e.g., <u>Washington</u>); (iii) *verb* - the 'verb' font is used for designations for fact types — usually a *verb*, preposition, or combination thereof; and (iv) **keyword** - the 'keyword' font is used for linguistic symbols used to construct statements – the words that can be combined with other designations to form statements and definitions (e.g., **'each'** and **'it is obligatory that'**). For example, in the business rule, as shown in the Figure 2, includes three **keywords** or phrases, two designations for <u>noun concepts</u> and one for a *fact type*.

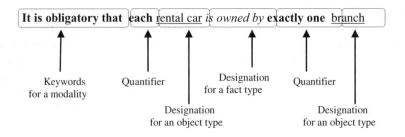

Fig. 2. Business rule elements

3.2 Business Contract of Services

This Section provides some issues related to contract of services formalization based on Formal Contract Logic (FCL). FCL was introduced in [11] for the formal analysis of business contracts and it is based on previous work on formal representation of contracts [12], logic of violations [13], and normative positions based on Deontic Logic with Directed Obligations [14].

A contract is structured in terms of a number of clause groups, each of which contains contract conditions. To save space, consider the following small part of the contract presented in [11] that will be analyzed and formalized in the subsequent sections.

CONTRACT OF SERVICES

This Deed of Agreement is entered into as of the Effective Data identified below.
BETWEEN *ABC Company (To be known as the Purchaser)*
AND *ISP Plus (To be known as the Supplier)*
WHEREAS *(Purchaser) desires to enter into an agreement to purchase from (Supplier) Application Server (To be known as (Service) in this Agreement).*
   NOW IT IS HEREBY AGREED *that (Supplier) and (Purchaser) shall enter into an agreement subject to the following terms and conditions:*
   ...

*5   **Service Delivery***
    5.1 The (Supplier) shall ensure that the (Services) are available to the (Purchaser) under Quality of Service Agreement (http://supplier/qos1.htm). (Services) that do not conform to the Quality of Service Agreement shall be replaced by the (Supplier) within 3 days from the notification by the (Purchaser), otherwise the (Supplier) shall refund the (Purchaser) and pay the (Purchaser) a penalty of $1000.
    5.2 The (Supplier) shall on receipt of a purchase order for (Services) make them available within 1 days.
   ...

Usually a contract comprises two types of clauses: definitional clauses giving the meaning of the terms used in the contract and clauses specifying the normative behaviors (i.e., giving the obligations, permissions, prohibitions the signing parties of the contract are subject to). We will concentrate only on the normative specifications of a contract. Hence, we will ignore all the sections of the contract, except for the section 5. According to the normalization process in FCL [4] give us the following rules:

r5:1 : Service $\vdash$ O$_S$QualityOfService $\otimes$ O$_S$Replace3days $\otimes$ O$_S$Refund&Penalty $\otimes$ P$_P$ChargeSupplier

r5:2 : PurchaseOrder $\vdash$ O$_S$Deliver1day $\otimes$ P$_P$ChargeSupplier

4   Contract of Services Editor Requirements

As in any community, the users of the buyer and seller community use a common terminology, sharing the same understanding about the words, procedures and activities that are part of their daily business routine. To facilitate the task of business contract elaboration, Figure 3 gives an idea of how could be the external interface of an IDE – Integrated Development Environment. It should provide some editors and functionalities to define terms, facts, business rules, contracts and services using that community terminology.

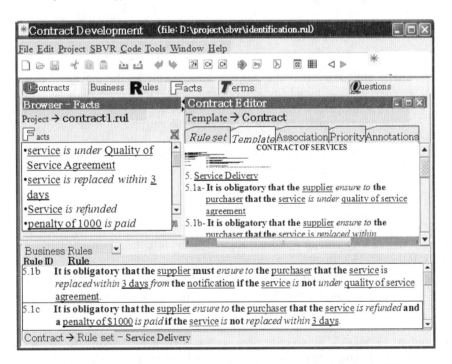

Fig. 3. Interface Prototype for the Business Contract and Business Rules IDE

In this way, <u>supplier</u>, <u>purchaser</u> and <u>service</u> are terms designating concepts, which ultimately represent object types; "<u>service</u> *is replaced within* <u>3 days</u>" and "<u>service</u> *is under* <u>Quality of Service Agreement</u>" are facts; and "**It is obligatory that the** supplier *ensure to* **the** purchaser **that the** service *is refunded* **and a** penalty of $1000 *is paid* **if the** service *is* **not** *replaced within* 3 days" is a business rule. All these elements are meaningful to that community and should be defined using the IDE.

When the business analyst defines terms, verbs, facts and rules contained in a contract of service, they will be stored in the IDE infrastructure.

5   Transformation of SBVR Compliant Rules to FCL Rules

This Section presents the Contract of Services adherent to the SBVR metamodel and provides an example to exercise the proposed model transformation using ATL infrastructure to transform SBVR compliant elements to the FCL elements.

The prior Contract of Services could be represented by using the SBVR metamodel elements, i.e., in terms of terms (designation for object type), Names (designation for Name type), *verbs* (designation for fact type) and **keywords**. To save space, we will concentrate only on the normative specifications of the section 5.1 of the contract, which is divided into 3 business rules to easy understanding.

CONTRACT OF SERVICES

…

5. Service Delivery

5.1 –

    a.**It is obligatory that the** supplier **must** *ensure to* **the** purchaser **that the** service *is under* quality of service agreement (http://supplier/qos1.htm).

    b.   **It is obligatory that the** supplier **must** *ensure to* **the** purchaser **that the** service *is replaced within* 3 days *from* **the** notification **if the** service *is* **not** *under* quality of service agreement.

    c.**It is obligatory that the** supplier *ensure to* **the** purchaser **that the** service *is refunded* **and a** penalty of $1000 *is paid* **if the** service *is* **not** *replaced within* 3 days.

5.2   Model Transformation

Considering just the previous business rules 5.1b and 5.1c they should be transformed to the following FCL rules:

$r_{5:1b}$: ¬ ServiceIsUnderQoSAgreement ⊢ O_SServiceIsReplacedWithin3days

$r_{5:1c}$: ¬ ReplaceServiceWithin3days ⊢ O_SSupplierRefundsService,
    O_SSupplierPaysPenaltyOf$100

According to MDA's perspective we have to define the models for these text fragments. Following is the corresponding model, expressed in XMI, for the SBVR business rules. This model will be the input of the transformation mechanism.

```
<?xml version="1.0" encoding="ISO-8859-1"?>
<xmi:XMI xmi:version="2.0" xmlns:xmi="http://www.omg.org/XMI" xmlns ="Rules">
<Rule ruleId="r51b">
 <keyword keywordLabel="It is obligatory that"/>
```

```
      <keyword kw=" the"/>
      <fact factType="service is replaced within 3 days"/>
      <condition factType="service is not under quality of service agreement "/>
   </Rule>
   <Rule ruleId="r51c">
    <keyword keywordLabel="It is obligatory that"/>
      <keyword kw="the"/>
      <fact factType="service is refunded and penalty of $1000 is paid "/>
      <condition factType="service is not replaced within 3 days"/>
   </Rule>
   </ xmi:XMI >
```

Following is the corresponding model, expressed in XMI, for the FCL rules. This model will be the output of the transformation mechanism.

```
  <?xml version="1.0" encoding="ISO-8859-1"?>
  <xmi:XMI xmi:version="2.0" xmlns:xmi="http://www.omg.org/XMI" xmlns ="FCL Rules">
  <Rule ruleId="r51b">
  <ant_premise>
      <symbol negation="not" />
      <premise a_prem= "ServiceIsUnderQoSAgreement"/>
      </ant_premise>
      <conc_premise>
      <premise c_prem= O_SServiceIsReplacedWithin3days"/>
      </conc_premise>
  </Rule>
  <Rule ruleId="r51c">
   <ant_premise>
      <symbol negation="not" />
      <premise a_prem= "ServiceIsReplacedWithin3days"/>
      </ant_premise>
      <conc_premise>
      <premise c_prem="O_SServiceIsRefunded"/>
      <premise c_prem="O_SPenaltyOf$100IsPaid"/>
      </conc_premise>
  </Rule>
  </xmi:XMI >
```

According to MDA and ATL phylosophy, these two models have to conform to the respective source and target metamodels. Thus, in order to achieve the transformation, it is necessary to provide: (i) a source metamodel in KM3 ("SBVR Rules"), (ii) a target metamodel in KM3 ("FCL Rules"), and (iii) a transformation model in ATL ("SBVR2FCL"). When the ATL transformation is executed the source model (XMI model for SBVR rules) will be transformed into the target model (XMI model for the FCL rules).

6   Related Works

This section discusses some works related to the business contract execution. These works mention the absence of an appropriate treatment so that the business contract clauses and rules can be mapped into executable rules in a collaborative and integrated way with business process mechanisms.

Kabilan [15] proposes an approach to combine contract workflow models with Business Process Modeling Notation (BPMN) models. Business process modelers may model the contract obligation fulfillment process as Contract Workflow Models (CWM) using BPMN diagrams. The weakness of this proposal is that it is not complete in terms normative propositions based on Deontic Logic, for example, it cannot capture all informational aspects and related concepts, likeïprohibitions.

SweetDeal [16] is a rule-based approach to representation of business contracts that enables software agents to create, evaluate, negotiate, and execute contracts with substantial automation and modularity. It builds upon the situated courteous logic programs knowledge representation in RuleML. It combines RuleML with ontologies (DAML+OIL) for a practical e-business application domain. Although it seems to be a good approach, SweetDeal did not show how to incorporate legal aspects of contracts into the approach.

The Edee architecture [17] provides a mechanism for explicitly and uniformly capturing business occurrences, and provisions of contracts, policies, and law. Edee is able to reason about the interactions between organizations and execute business procedures informed by the combined legal effects of the corresponding diverse rules. It deals with both conflict detection and resolution. The weakness of Edee is that it does not show how effectively the business contract issues are translated to the dynamic context of executable business processes.

7   Conclusions and Future Work

The proposed MDA based model transformation makes innovative contributions compared to other initiatives in mapping business contracts to executable code. The model (i) helps business analysts in the definition of contracts and rules, using a language familiar to them, using the terms with which they accomplish their businesses; (ii) can define contracts and rules, using templates, and express them in computation independent models (CIM); (iii) both business rules and FCL rules are based on principles of deontic logic for treating expressions in the form of normative policies, the core of which are obligations, permissions and prohibitions.

Besides, as a proof of concept for the proposed model transformation it is specified some requirements for the IDE to elaborate and edit business contracts, business rules, facts and terms. All these assets should be transformed to computational code, for rules and contract of services, adherent to FCL rules model.

The results indicate that the concepts, ideas and proposed model transformation are promising. Besides business contracts and rules formalization technologies, services (SOA), repositories and ontologies, it seems that the complete solution for the mentioned problems includes the following list of topics that deserve future researches:

- Inclusion of a mechanism in the IDE to contemplate process composition modeling using, for instance, languages such as BPMN and that could make transformation to executable languages like WS-BPEL.

- Proposition of a mechanism to help the business analyst to link business rule actions to Web services. May be considering Web 2.0 application facilities, such as recommendation system linked to trust, preference and rated content to create highly trusted environment for business analyst to decide which Web service is the most adequate in a specific rule action.
- Development of a prototype implementing the IDE, including repository instances for ontologies, adherent to the MOF metamodel, with standardized query and manipulation language.

References

1. Hildreth, S.: Rounding Up Business Rules. ComputerWorld Software. ID (2005)
2. OMG , MDA Guide Version 1.0.1 (2003), http://www.omg.org/cgi-bin/doc?omg/03-06-01 (access in March/2010)
3. OMG Semantics of Business Vocabulary and Business Rules (SBVR), v1.0 OMG Available Specification (2008), http://www.omg.org/spec/SBVR/1.0/PDF/ (access in March/2010)
4. Governatori, G., Milosevic, Z., Sadiq, S.: Compliance checking between business processes and business contracts. In: Proc. The 10th International Enterprise Distributed Object Computing Conference - EDOC, Hong Kong, pp. 221–232 (2006)
5. Beller, S.: Deontic norms, deontic reasoning, and deontic conditionals. Thinking & Reasoning 14(4), 305–341 (2008)
6. ATLAS group, LINA, INRIA, ATL: Atlas Transformation Language ATL User Manual - version 0.7, Nantes (2006)
7. OMG. Meta Object Facility (MOF) 2.0 Query/View/Transformation Specification, version 1.0 (2008)
8. OMG, MOF 2.0/XMI Mapping Specification, v2.1.1 (2005), http://www.omg.org/cgi-bin/doc?formal/2007-12-01/ (access in March/2010)
9. Kamada, Service Execution based on Business Rules, PhD Thesis in Computing Engineering, Unicamp, Campinas, Brazil (2006)
10. Kamada, A.F., Rodrigues, M.: Ontology based Business Rules and Services Integration Environment. In: Ajeeli, A.T.A., Al-bastaki, Y.A.L., Abu-tayeh, J. (eds.) Handbook of Research on E-services in the Public Sector: E-government Strategies and Advancements. Information Science Publishing, United Kingdom (March 2010)
11. Governatori, G., Milosevic, Z.: A Formal Analysis of a Business Contract Language. International Journal of Cooperative Information Systems (IJCIS) 15(4), 659–685 (2006)
12. Governatori, G.: Representing business contracts in RuleML. Int. J. of Cooperative Inf. Sys. 14(2-3), 181–216 (2005)
13. Governatori, G., Rotolo, A.: Logic of violations: A Gentzen system for reasoning with contrary-to-duty obligations. Australasian Journal of Logic 4, 193–215 (2006)
14. Kanger, S.: Law and logic. Theoria 38, 105–132 (1972)
15. Kabilan, V.: Contract Workflow Model Patterns Using BPMN, FORUM 100, Kista, Sweden (2005)
16. Grosof, B.N., Poon, T.C.: Representing Agent Contracts with Exceptions using XML Rules, Ontologies, and Process Descriptions. In: Proc. 12th International Conference on World Wide Web, Budapest, Hungary, pp. 340–349 (2003)
17. Abrahams, D.E., Bacon, J.: An asynchronous rule-based approach for business process automation using obligations. In: Proc. ACM SIGPLAN Workshop on Rule-based Programming, Pittsburgh, USA, pp. 93–103 (2002)

RuleML 1.0:
The Overarching Specification of Web Rules

Harold Boley[1], Adrian Paschke[2], and Omair Shafiq[3]

[1] Institute for Information Technology, National Research Council Canada
Fredericton, NB, Canada
harold.boley@nrc.gc.ca
[2] Freie Universitaet Berlin, Germany
paschke@mi.fu-berlin.de
[3] University of Calgary, AB, Canada
moshafiq@ucalgary.ca

Abstract. RuleML is a family of languages, whose modular system of XML schemas permits high-precision Web rule interchange. The family's top-level distinction is deliberation rules vs. reaction rules. Deliberation rules include modal and derivation rules, which themselves include facts, queries (incl. integrity constraints), and Horn rules (incl. Datalog). Reaction rules include Complex Event Processing (CEP), Knowledge Representation (KR), and Event-Condition-Action (ECA) rules, as well as Production (CA) rules. RuleML rules can combine all parts of both derivation and reaction rules. This allows uniform XML serialization across all kinds of rules. After its use in SWRL and SWSL, RuleML has provided strong input to W3C RIF on several levels. This includes the use of 'striped' XML as well as the structuring of rule classes into sublanguages with partial mappings between, e.g., Datalog RuleML and RIF-Core, Hornlog RuleML and RIF-BLD, as well as Production RuleML and RIF-PRD. We discuss the rationale and key features of RuleML 1.0 as the overarching specification of Web rules that encompasses RIF RuleML as a subfamily, and takes into account corresponding OASIS, OMG (e.g., PRR, SBVR), and ISO (e.g., Common Logic) specifications.

1 Introduction

Rules on the Web come in various formats and with diverse packaging. Often, however, the semantics of Web-distributed rule content are compatible. In such cases, rulebases can be reused with an interchange technology consisting of a family of canonical rule languages and bi-directional translators between canonical languages and the languages to be interchanged. The need for Web rule interchange has been increasing with the amount of business rules (incl. policies, regulations, laws, . . .) in many domains (e.g. finance, engineering, healthcare, . . .) on the Web 1.0, 2.0 (Social), and 3.0 (Social Semantic).

RuleML has been designed for the interchange of the major kinds of Web rules in an XML format that is uniform across various rule languages and platforms. It has broad coverage and is defined as an extensible family of languages, whose

M. Dean et al. (Eds.): RuleML 2010, LNCS 6403, pp. 162–178, 2010.

modular system of XML schemas permits rule interchange with high precision, as follows.

When a rulebase is prepared for interchange by a sender,

- it is translated to RuleML if the source document is not in the RuleML format already,
- the Most Specific Schema (MSS) is determined against which the RuleML document can be validated,
- the Internationalized Resource Identifier (IRI) of the MSS is pointed to from the rulebase or is otherwise transmitted along with the rulebase.

When a rulebase is obtained by a receiver,

- it is validated against the same RuleML schema to exclude any too specific MSS assignments and transmission errors,
- it is converted to the local format if the target document is not to be in RuleML anyway.

The RuleML family constitutes a taxonomy of subfamilies, languages, and sub-languages classified through the syntactic power of rules, as reflected by their XML Schema Definitions (XSDs), and through their semantic power, as reflected by their model-theoretic, proof-theoretic, and operational semantics. Often, more syntactic power leads to more semantic power (e.g., the introduction of Expression syntax pushes Datalog to Horn Logic (Hornlog) models in Section 3.2). Syntactically neutral aspects of semantic power will be expressed by semantic attributes (e.g., by a negation attribute for the semantics of Negation-as-failure in Section 3.5).

Fig. 1, a simplified version of the RuleML taxonomy, shows the semantic subfamilies of *Deliberation* rules for inference and *Reaction* rules for (re)action. Deliberation rules, via *Higher Order Logic (HOL)* and *First Order Logic (FOL)*, subsume *Derivation* rules. Derivation rules subsume Hornlog and Datalog languages and (syntactically) specialize to the condition-less *Fact* and conclusion-less *Query* languages (subsuming *Integrity Constraint (IC)* languages). Reaction rules subsume *Complex Event Processing (CEP)* and *Knowledge Representation (KR)* rules, as well as *Event-Condition-Action-Postcondition (ECAP)* rules. *ECAP* rules specialize to *Event-Condition-Action (ECA)* rules, which themselves specialize to Condition-less *Trigger (EA)* rules and to the rule subfamily of Event-less *Production (CA)* rules. The *RuleML* family also has 'mix-ins' for *Equality* and (oriented) *Rewriting*, as well as for *Naf*. The *Reaction* subfamily has mix-ins for *Event Algebra*, *Action Algebra*, etc.

While not shown in Fig. 1, RuleML languages make use of 'pluggable' libraries of built-ins such as from the Semantic Web Rule Language (SWRL) [HPSB+04] and the Rule Interchange Format (RIF) [PBK10]. There are also entire RuleML languages we cannot further discuss in the confines of this paper, including for uncertainty and fuzzy rules[1] [DPSS08] and for defeasible rules[2] [KBA08].

---

[1] Fuzzy RuleML: http://www.image.ntua.gr/FuzzyRuleML
[2] Defeasible RuleML: http://defeasible.org

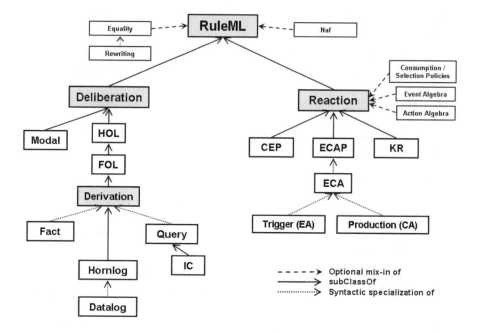

Fig. 1. Taxonomy of RuleML rules

The derivation rule languages have a Datalog language as their kernel. Datalog RuleML is defined over both `Data` constants and `Individual` constants with an optional `iri` attribute for webizing. `Atomic` formulas have n arguments, which can be positional or slotted ($key \rightarrow term$ pairs). Object Oriented Datalog adds optional `types` (sorts) and RDF-like `oids` via IRIs. Inheriting all of these Datalog features, Hornlog RuleML adds positional and slotted `Functional` `Expressions` as terms. In Hornlog – and other languages – with `Equality`, such uninterpreted (constructor-like) functions are complemented by interpreted (equation-defined) functions. This derivation rule branch is extended upward to FOL, including disjunction (`Or`) in conclusions and strong `Negation`.

Reaction RuleML syntactically extends the condition (query) part of Derivation RuleML, whose condition-conclusion rules can be seen as 'pure' production rules with conclusions as actions that just assert derived facts. For a discussion of relationships between active and deductive rules see [Wid93]. Reaction RuleML is based on 'pluggable' ontologies (e.g., algebras) of (complex) actions, events, and – in the KR subfamily – situations. Production RuleML defines condition-action rules. Complex Event Processing (CEP) RuleML defines (complex) events and their efficient processing. Reaction RuleML extends production rules with an event-triggering part, syntactically defining ECA rules, and with further semantic extensions, e.g. for CEP rules.

RuleML rules can combine all parts of both derivation and reaction rules. This allows uniform XML serialization across the rules from the taxonomy. A general `<Rule>` element specifies the kind of rule with a `style` attribute, where shortcuts allow specialized elements such as `<Implies>` and `<Reaction>`.

After its use in SWRL and the Semantic Web Services Language (SWSL) [BBB+05], RuleML has provided input to W3C RIF [BK10a] on several levels. This includes the use of 'striped' XML and the structuring of rule classes into a family of sublanguages with partial mappings between, e.g., Datalog RuleML and RIF-Core [PBK10], Derivation RuleML and RIF Basic Logic Dialect (RIF-BLD), as well as Production RuleML and RIF Production Rule Dialect (RIF-PRD), where RuleML's `<if>` ... `<do>` was adopted as RIF's `<if>` ... `<then><Do>`.

The RIF WG – after having achieved W3C Recommendation status in June 2010 – is scheduled to terminate with the end of September 2010 until an uncertain revival for a possible RIF 2. RIF's standard logic Web rule dialects Core and BLD come with a rigorous model-theoretic semantics, embodying the WG's cascaded design decisions. However, the W3C Core and BLD Recommendations cover only a fraction of the Web rule space and their very rigor gives existing Web rule languages little room for RIF conformance. The RuleML Initiative – whose symposia have been a forum for RIF advances from its beginning – has thus been co-hosting the development of further ("non-standard extensions"[3] or) RIF dialects such as the Core Answer Set Programming Dialect (RIF-CASPD) [HK09] and Semantic Inferencing on Large Knowledge (SILK) [GDK09], using the flexibility-enhancing Framework for Logic Dialects (RIF-FLD) [BK10b], as well as RIF RuleML sublanguages such as Datalog with equality plus externals (Dlex) [Bol09] and the envisioned Reaction Rule Dialect (RRD).

Even languages that will not become ("standard extensions"[3] or) RIF 2 Recommendations themselves can help with Web rule interoperability by consolidating the terrain and acting as connectors to other standards bodies such as OMG and OASIS as well as business rule organizations such as BRF[4] and stakeholders in the private and public sectors. Based on [WATB04] and Production RuleML, members of the Reaction RuleML Technical Group have already contributed to OMG's Production Rule Representation (PRR). RuleML is founding member of the Event Processing Technical Society (EPTS), where it contributes to, and co-chairs, the EPTS Reference Architecture group (ETPS-RA).

This paper, building on our experience with RuleML as the de facto standard for Web rules, discusses the design and definition of RuleML 1.0. As our running example, we will give variations on the discount rule[5] `Implies 1` from the RuleML 1.0 exa directory.[6]

The rest of the paper is organized as follows. Section 2 discusses the design rationale of the overarching RuleML family of languages. Section 3 expands on RuleML 1.0 deliberation rules. Section 4 explains its reaction rules. Section 5 presents selected tools and applications of RuleML. Section 6 concludes the paper. Appendix A gives hints on the RuleML 1.0 XSLTs and XSDs.

---

[3] http://www.w3.org/2005/rules/wg/charter.html

[4] http://www.businessrulesforum.com

[5] http://ruleml.org/lib/discount-variations.ruleml

[6] http://ruleml.org/1.0/exa/Datalog/discount.ruleml

2   Design Rationale for RuleML

The specification of an overarching rule markup family with the primary purpose of rule interchange between platform-specific rule languages as well as between other rule standards for, e.g., Semantic Web rules or production rules, requires the balancing of many (interrelated) design choices with respect to semantics, syntax, and pragmatics. For instance, for a rulebase with advanced constructs such as Naf, a single predefined semantics would limit its use as it becomes impossible for many rule languages to be compliant with this specific semantics. Similarly, a rigorous syntax which does not support extensibility will necessarily lead to problems if more and more major rule types will be included in this overarching rule markup family. The design rationale for RuleML addresses these requirements.

The RuleML syntax strives for the following widely accepted design principles for good language design:

- Minimality: the language provides only the set of needed language features, i.e., except for macro-like extensibility shortcuts and an order-insensitive abstract role syntax, the same construct is not expressed by different syntax.
- Referential transparency: the same language construct always expresses the same semantics regardless of the context in which it is used.
- Orthogonality: the language constructs are pairwise independent, thus permitting their meaningful systematic combination.

RuleML is designed as an extensible family of languages. In each of these languages it provides a minimal set of needed language constructs which can be applied in every meaningful combination in the respective expressiveness class of the language. The language constructs are structured as modules in the XML Schema definitions. This leads to a clear, compact, and precise design which is easily adaptable, manageable, and extensible.

RuleML, as a general interchange format, can be customized for various semantics of underlying (platform-specific) rule languages that should be represented and interchanged. Although a specific default semantics is always predefined for each RuleML language, the intended semantics of a rulebase can override it by using explicit values for corresponding semantic attributes. For instance, a derivation rulebase represented in Datalog RuleML with Naf can be explicitly declared to have Well-Founded (WF) or Answer Set (AS) semantics, with AS as the default (cf. Section 3.5). Moreover, RuleML supports external domain semantics such as ontologies, e.g. RDFS or OWL taxonomies, or class hierarchies, e.g. object oriented models such as UML class models or Java class hierarchies. These can be used as external order-sorted type systems for rule constructs, e.g. variables and constants, giving them an interchangeable and machine interpretable domain semantics. This flexible semantics approach of RuleML allows refining the semantics of a syntactically represented rulebase.

From a pragmatic perspective, the layered RuleML design of Fig. 1 leads to a compact syntax (in terms of language constructs) which is easier to learn, read, understand, and apply by end users, as well as easier to extend in a modular way with new languages and semantics. The modular family of languages also makes it easy for machines to process RuleML, e.g. by translators that map between platform-specific rule languages and an equivalent RuleML language. Additionally, the pluggable-semantics approach supports correct machine understanding and interpretation.

In summary, these design principles allow the overarching RuleML specification to evolve into a standard for rule interchange that provides full coverage of all major rule languages and their underlying semantics while still being an easily usable and further extensible interchange language. A more detailed discussion of the design principles of RuleML and how it compares to other rule markup and Semantic Web languages can be found in [PB09a].

3   Deliberation Rules

This section describes deliberation rules with a focus on derivation rules, proceeding bottom-up from Datalog. The `inference-style Rule` element `<Rule style="inference">` can be equivalently shortcut to the `<Implies>` element.

3.1   Datalog RuleML

Datalog [CGT89] is at the core of many rule languages and is close to relational databases with recursive views. Datalog RuleML is defined over both `Data` constants and `Individual` constants with an optional attribute, `iri`, for webizing. RuleML's `Relational Atoms` have $m + n$ arguments ($m \geq 0$, $n \geq 0$), where m arguments are positional and n are slotted ($key \rightarrow term$ pairs). In Datalog RuleML, terms (e.g. used as positional arguments and slot fillers) can only be constants or `Variables`. Datalog RuleML also has optional RDF-like `type` (on constants and variables) and `oid` attributes via IRIs. It allows for an `Equality` extension, e.g. to call built-ins from 'pluggable' libraries.

To initialize our running example, let us consider Datalog rule `Implies` 1 for deriving discounts, with the ternary `Relation discount` and the unary `premium` and `regular` all being positional. Three versions are given in the columns, where the order of role-tagged children does not matter, and for skipped `<if>/<then>` role stripes the first child is understood as the `<if>` role, the second as `<then>`:

```
<!-- Implication Rule 1:
        Backward notation of 'then' and 'if' roles, as in Logic Programming, and forward notation
        using natural 'if' ... 'then' order, as in textbook logic, with exact same meaning

"The discount for a customer buying a product is 5.0 percent
if the customer is premium and the product is regular."

Notice that the ternary discount relation is applied via an Atom.
Furthermore, a Data constant can syntactically be an entire phrase
like "5.0 percent". It will unify only with variables and with Data
having exactly the same spelling (incl. spaces)
-->
```

```
<Implies>                      <Implies>                        <Implies>
  <then>                         <if>
    <Atom>                         <And>                            <And>
      <Rel>discount</Rel>            <Atom>                           <Atom>
      <Var>cust</Var>                  <Rel>premium</Rel>               <Rel>premium</Rel>
      <Var>prod</Var>                  <Var>cust</Var>                  <Var>cust</Var>
      <Data>5.0 percent</Data>       </Atom>                          </Atom>
    </Atom>                          <Atom>                           <Atom>
  </then>                              <Rel>regular</Rel>               <Rel>regular</Rel>
  <if>                                 <Var>prod</Var>                  <Var>prod</Var>
    <And>                            </Atom>                          </Atom>
      <Atom>                       </And>                           </And>
        <Rel>premium</Rel>       </if>
        <Var>cust</Var>          <then>
      </Atom>                      <Atom>                           <Atom>
      <Atom>                         <Rel>discount</Rel>              <Rel>discount</Rel>
        <Rel>regular</Rel>           <Var>cust</Var>                  <Var>cust</Var>
        <Var>prod</Var>              <Var>prod</Var>                  <Var>prod</Var>
      </Atom>                        <Data>5.0 percent</Data>         <Data>5.0 percent</Data>
    </And>                         </Atom>                          </Atom>
  </if>                          </then>
</Implies>                     </Implies>                       </Implies>
```

A slotted variant of our example uses pairs $key \rightarrow term$ in the conclusion's 3-ary relation, and represents them as metaroles `<slot>`$key\ term$`</slot>` (we will continue the `<then>` ... `<if>` version, in the first column above, and elide the unchanged condition, where slots would not add much to the readability of unary relations):

```
<Implies>
  <then>
    <Atom>
      <Rel>discount</Rel>
      <slot><Data>buyer</Data><Var>cust</Var></slot>
      <slot><Data>item</Data><Var>prod</Var></slot>
      <slot><Data>rebate</Data><Data>5.0 percent</Data></slot>
    </Atom>
  </then>
  <if> . . . </if>
</Implies>
```

A typed variant of our initial example can use `Variables` with the attribute `type`, whose values are IRIs pointing to ontological class definitions on the Web defined in RDFS and OWL:

```
<Implies>
  <then>
    <Atom>
      <Rel>discount</Rel>
      <Var type="http://xmlns.com/foaf/spec/#term_Person">cust</Var>
      <Var type="http://daml.org/services/owl-s/1.0/ProfileHierarchy.owl#Product">prod</Var>
      <Data>5.0 percent</Data>
    </Atom>
  </then>
  <if> . . . </if>
</Implies>
```

3.2   Hornlog RuleML

Horn logic [Mak87] is the pure kernel of Prolog-like rule languages. In RuleML, the corresponding Hornlog sublanguage is regarded as an extension of Datalog RuleML, in particular of its `Atoms`: Besides constants and variables, Hornlog

RuleML allows positional and slotted Functional Expressions as terms in Atoms and, recursively, in other Exprs. Expressions can be uninterpreted, using an attribute per with filler "copy" or interpreted, using it with filler "value". Other per fillers are "effect", for (side-)effectful Expressions, and "modal", for modal Exprs.

We refine the initial example by introducing an uninterpreted Expr representing the constructor term percent[5.0], thus proceeding from Datalog to Horn logic, for XSDs and Herbrand models (we again elide the unchanged condition):

```
<Implies>
  <then>
    <Atom>
      <Rel>discount</Rel>
      <Var>cust</Var>
      <Var>prod</Var>
      <Expr><Fun per="copy">percent</Fun><Data>5.0</Data></Expr>
    </Atom>
  </then>
  <if> . . . </if>
</Implies>
```

3.3 FOL RuleML

First Order Logic (FOL) [End01] has been widely used as a knowledge representation language. FOL RuleML is an extension of Hornlog RuleML mainly adding classical negation and (explicit) quantifiers. An earlier version of FOL RuleML is part of the W3C member submission SWRL FOL.[7]

We modify our initial example as follows:

```
<!--
"A customer receives either a discount of 5.0 percent for buying a product
or a bonus of 200.00 dollar if the customer is premium and the product is regular."

Notice that an 'eXclusive or' is used to shortcut
And(Or(A,B),Not(And(A,B))) to Xor(A,B) in the conclusion.
-->

<Implies>
  <then>
    <Xor>
      <Atom><Rel>discount</Rel><Var>cust</Var><Var>prod</Var><Data>5.0 percent</Data></Atom>
      <Atom><Rel>bonus</Rel><Var>cust</Var><Data>200.00 dollar</Data></Atom>
    </Xor>
  </then>
  <if> . . . </if>
</Implies>
```

3.4 RuleML with Equality

Logics with a distinguished equality predicate [Nie07] have been used for specification languages, where equality has been kept symmetric (via paramodulation) or become oriented (via term rewriting or narrowing). In RuleML, Equality formulas act as an extension to sublanguages such as Datalog RuleML, Hornlog

---

[7] http://www.w3.org/Submission/2005/01

RuleML, and FOL RuleML. `Equal` has an `oriented` attribute whose "no" value is assumed as the default.

We modify our initial example as follows:

```
<!-- Equational Rule 1':
     Conditional oriented equation returns rewritten value of first (left) Equal element
     ('call-by-value'-interpreted binary discount function applied via Expr)
     through second (right) Equal element (an alphanumeric Data value)
-->

<Implies>
  <then>
    <Equal oriented="yes">
      <Expr><Fun per="value">discount</Fun><Var>cust</Var><Var>prod</Var></Expr>
      <Data>5.0 percent</Data>
    </Equal>
  </then>
  <if> . . . </if>
</Implies>
```

3.5   Naf RuleML

Besides strong `Negation` in FOL RuleML (cf. Section 3.3), Deliberation RuleML also allows `Negation-as-failure`, as used in Logic Programming. This Naf RuleML can be parameterized for Answer Set (`AS`) semantics (subsuming stable model semantics) and for Well-Founded (`WF`) semantics, using a semantic attribute, `negation`, on the enclosing `Rulebase`, whose default value is `AS`, accommodating RIF-CASPD [HK09].

The following `Rulebase` example enforces Well-Founded semantics for `Naf`s in the conditions of `discount` rules such as to exclude `late-paying` customers:

```
<Rulebase negation="WF">
  <Implies>
    <then>
      <Atom><Rel>discount</Rel><Var>cust</Var><Var>prod</Var><Data>5.0 percent</Data></Atom>
    </then>
    <if>
      <And>
        <Naf>
          <Atom><Rel>late-paying</Rel><Var>cust</Var></Atom>
        <Naf>
        . . .
      </And>
    </if>
  </Implies>
  . . .
</Rulebase>
```

4   Reaction Rules

Reaction rules are concerned with the invocation of actions in response to events and actionable situations [PB09b]. They state the conditions under which actions must be taken and describe the effects of action executions. In the last decades various reaction rule languages and rule-based event processing approaches have been developed, which for the most part have been advanced separately. The Reaction RuleML subfamily addresses the four major reaction rule types:

- Production Rules (Condition-Action rules) in the Production RuleML sub-family
- Event-Condition-Action (ECA) rules in the ECA RuleML subfamily
- Rule-based Complex Event Processing (complex event processing reaction rules, (distributed) event messaging reaction rules, query reaction rules etc.) in the CEP RuleML subfamily
- Knowledge Representation Event/Action/Situation Transition/Process Logics and Calculi in the KR Reaction RuleML subfamily

The syntax of reaction rules in Reaction RuleML is defined on top of Derivation RuleML by a general rule format which can be specialized in the different Reaction RuleML subfamilies to the four different reaction rule types (and variants of these types).

```
<Rule style="active|messaging|reasoning">

    <oid>      <!-- object id of the rule -->                      </oid>
    <label>    <!- (semantic) metadata of the rule -->            </label>
    <scope>    <!- scope of the rule e.g. a rule module -->       </scope>
    <evaluation>    <!-- intended semantics -->               </evaluation>
    <qualification> <!- e.g. qualifying rule declarations, e.g.
                         priorities, validity, strategy -->  </qualification>
    <quantification> <!-- quantifying rule declarations,
                         e.g. variable bingings -->          </quantification>
    <on>       <!- event part -->                                   </on>
    <if>       <!- condition part -->                               </if>
    <then>     <!- (logical) conclusion part -->                  </then>
    <do>       <!--  action part -->                                </do>
    <after>    <!- postcondition part after action,
                    e.g. to check effects of execution -->       </after>
    <else>  <!- (logical) else conclusion -->                    </else>
    <elsedo>  <!-- alternative/else action,
                    e.g. for default handling -->              </elsedo>
</Rule>
```

The execution style of a reaction rule is defined by the optional attribute style.

- active: 'actively' polls/detects occurred events in ECA and CEP rules or changed conditions in production rules
- messaging: waits for incoming complex event message (inbound) and sends messages (outbound) as actions
- reasoning: logical / inference reasoning as e.g., KR formalisms such as event / action / transition logics (as e.g. in Event Calculus, Situation Calculus, temporal action languages formalizations)

The evaluation semantics (interpretation and/or execution) of reaction rules is defined in the optional role subchild evaluation. This can be used to define rule evaluation semantics such as weak or strong evaluation which defines the "execution lifecycle" of the rule execution.

A rule instance can be uniquely identified by an object identifier <oid>. The metadata <label> is used to annotate the rule with optional metadata. The scope <scope> defines a (constructive) view on the rulebase, e.g. the rule only applies to a module in the rulebase. The qualification <qualification> defines an optional set of rule qualifications such as a validity value, fuzzy value or a priority value. The quantification `<quantification>` is used to define quantifiers such as the typical existential and unversal quantification; it can also be used for extensions such as variable binding patterns to restrict pattern matching in production rules or define other operator definitions.

4.1 Production RuleML

A production rule is a statement of rule programming logic that specifies the execution of one or more actions in case its conditions are satisfied, i.e. production rules react to states changes (not to explicit events). The essential syntax is if *Condition* do *Action*. Accordingly, standard production rules in the Production RuleML subfamily are written as follows (an `active-style` Rule can be shortcut to `Reaction`, which can be stripe-skipped for if as first child and do as second):

```
<Rule style="active">          <Reaction>                  <Reaction>
  <if>...</if>                    <if>...</if>                  ...
  <do>---</do>                    <do>---</do>                  ---
</Rule>                         </Reaction>                 </Reaction>
```

Actions are `Assert` (add knowledge); `Retract` (retract knowledge); `Update` (update/modify knowledge); `Equal` (single-assign term to variable); `Execute` (execute (external) function).

Let us modify our initial example to a production rule which instead of just deriving discounts does an `Assert` of them (`Retract`/`Update` would be similar):

```
<!--  Reaction Rule 1a (Production Rule with "Condition" and "Action"):
      If premium and regular derivable do assert discount for customer -->

<Reaction>
  <if>
    <And>
      <Atom><Rel>premium</Rel><Var>cust</Var></Atom>
      <Atom><Rel>regular</Rel><Var>prod</Var></Atom>
    </And>
  </if>
  <do>
    <Assert>
      <Atom><Rel>discount</Rel><Var>cust</Var><Var>prod</Var><Data>5.0 percent</Data></Atom>
    </Assert>
  </do>
</Reaction>
```

Relationships between Production RuleML and RIF-PRD: Members of the Reaction RuleML Technical Group have co-edited the W3C RIF Production Rule Dialect (RIF-PRD). RIF-PRD with inflationary negation is a less expressive subset of PR RuleML. Syntactically, production rules in RIF-PRD are written in `if-then` syntax instead of PR RuleML's `if-do` syntax, which allows a clear semantic distinction of a conclusion (`then` part) and action (`do` part), when both are allowed for the same rule. Do as a type tag is used in RIF-PRD to syntactically denote a compound action which is a sequence of standard production rule actions (`Assert`, `Retract`, and `Modify`), whereas Reaction RuleML supports expressive complex action definitions using action algebra operators. Quantifying variable binding declarations are supported by RIF-PRD (declare) and by Production RuleML (quantification), which in addition also supports rule qualifications.

Relationships between Production RuleML and OMG PRR: Based on [WATB04] and Production RuleML, members of the Reaction RuleML Technical Group have co-edited the OMG Production Rule Representation (PRR). RuleML is one of the languages whose features are to be covered by PRR on an abstract level. Since PRR is a meta-language, Production RuleML's XML syntax can be used as a concrete expression language instantiating PRR models. That is, OMG PRR provides a way to include rules into the (UML) model of an application at design time and Production RuleML then provides a standard means of translating the model and feeding the executable rules into a PR application at run time.

4.2 ECA RuleML

In contrast to production rules, Event-Condition-Action (ECA) rules define an explicit event part which is separated from the conditions and actions of the rule. Their essential syntax is on *Event* if *Condition* do *Action*. ECA RuleML extends Production RuleML with an explicit `<on>` event part and rich (complex) event and action constructs defined in event/action libraries (the `active Rule` is again shortcut to `Reaction`, but the `<on>`/`<if>`/`<do>` role stripes are kept):

```
<Rule style="active">              <Reaction>
  <on>***</on>                       <on>***</on>
  <if>...</if>                       <if>...</if>
  <do>---</do>                       <do>---</do>
</Rule>                            </Reaction>
```

We modify our example as follows:

```
<!-- Reaction Rule 1c (ECA Rule with "Event", "Condition", and "Action"):
     On receiving premium notification from marketing and if regular derivable
     do send discount to customer -->

<Reaction>
  <on>
    <Receive>
      <from><Ind>marketing</Ind></from>
      <content>
        <Atom><Rel>premium</Rel><Var>cust</Var></Atom>
      </content>
    </Receive>
  </on>
  <if>
    <Atom><Rel>regular</Rel><Var>prod</Var></Atom>
  </if>
  <do>
    <Send>
      <to><Var>cust</Var></to>
      <content>
        <Atom><Rel>discount</Rel><Var>cust</Var><Var>prod</Var><Data>5.0 percent</Data></Atom>
      </content>
    </Send>
  </do>
</Reaction>
```

Variants of this standard ECA rule are, e.g., Event-Action triggers (EA rules) and ECAP rules (ECA rules with Postconditions after the action part).

With its typed logic, RuleML supports the (re)use of external event/action ontologies and metamodels which can be applied in the definition of semantic event/action types. For instance, the following standard library defines a set of typical event and action algebra operators:

```
Event Algebras and Action Algebras

Event Algebra:
    Sequence (Ordered), Or (Disjunction), Xor (Mutal Exclusion),
    And (Conjunction), Concurrent, Not, Any, Aperiodic, Periodic
Action Algebra:
    Succession (Ordered Succession of Actions), Choice
    (Non-Determenistic Choice), Flow (Parallel Flow),
    Loop (Iterative Loop)
```

Furthermore different selection, consumption, and (transactional) execution policies for events and actions can be specified in the complex event/action descriptions. This allows for a highly extensible and flexible Semantic CEP (SCEP) approach which (re-)uses external semantic models.

4.3   CEP RuleML

Complex Event Processing (CEP) is about the detection of complex events and reaction to complex events in near realtime. CEP rules might adopt the style of ECA rules in CEP RuleML, where the <on> event part might be a complex event type definition; or, they might adopt the style of CA producion rules where the complex event patterns are defined as restrictions on the variable binding definitions in the rule quantifications. However, it is also possible to represent serial messaging CEP reaction rules which **receive** and **send** events in arbitrary combinations. A serial (messaging) reaction rule starts either with a receiving event **on** – the trigger of the *global* reaction rule – or with a rule conclusion **then** – the head of the local *inline* reaction rule – followed by an arbitrary combination of conditions **if**, events **receive** and actions **send** in the body of the rule. This flexibility with support for modularization and aspect-oriented weaving of reactive rule code is in particular useful in distributed systems where event processing agents communicate and form a distributed event processing network, as e.g. in the following example:

```
<Rule style="active">
  <on><Receive> receive event from agent 1 </Receive></on>
  <do><Send> query agent 2 for regular products in a new sub-conversation </Send></do>
  <on><Receive> receive results from sub conversation with agent 2 </Receive></on>
  <if> prove some conditions, e.g. make decisions on the received data </if>
  <do><Send> reply to agent 1 by sending results received from agent 2 </Send></do>
</Rule>
```

For better modularization, the sub-conversation can be also written with an inlined reaction rule as follows:

```
<Rule style="active">
  <on><Receive> receive event from agent 1 </Receive></on>
  <if> <!- this goal activates the inlined reaction rule -- see below -->
    <Atom><Rel>regular</Rel><Var>prod</Var></Atom>
  </if>
```

```
<do><Send> reply to agent 1 by sending results received from agent 2 </Send></do>
</Rule>

<Rule style="active">
  <then>
    <Atom><Rel>regular</Rel><Var>prod</Var></Atom>
  </then>
  <do><Send> query agent 2 for regular products in a new sub-conversation </Send></do>
  <on><Receive> receive results from sub conversation with agent 2 </Receive></on>
</Rule>
```

This messaging reaction rule can be translated e.g. into a serial messaging Horn rule and executed in the Prova rule engine.[8]

Relationships between CEP RuleML and EPTS work: RuleML is a founding member of the Event Processing Technical Society (EPTS). Members of the Reaction RuleML Technical Group are contributing to the work on an Event Processing glossary, use cases, reference architectures, and event processing language models. With its flexible and extensible approach, CEP RuleML is a highly expressive rule-based Event Processing Language (rule-based EPL) which can make use of external event and action metamodels / ontologies such as the many existing event ontologies or the planned OMG Event Model Profile. Since CEP RuleML syntactically builds on top of Production RuleML and ECA RuleML – besides flexible (messaging) reaction rules – both major rule types can be used for representing (complex) event processing rules. Moreover, CEP RuleML can adequately represent typical use cases and functionalities in Event-Driven Architectures (EDAs) and (distributed) Event Processing Network (EPN) architectures.

4.4   KR Reaction RuleML

Event/action logics, which have their origins in the area of knowledge representation (KR), focus on the inferences that can be made from the happened or planned events/actions, i.e. they define the inferences of the effects of events/actions on changeable properties of the world (situations, states). KR Reaction RuleML defines syntax and semantics for KR event/action calculi such as Situation Calculus, Event Calculus and Temporal Action Languages etc. Specifically the notion of an explicit *state* (a.k.a. as state or fluent in Event Calculus) is introduced in KR Reaction RuleML. An event/action *initiates* or *terminates* a state. That is, a state explicitly represents the abstract effect of occurred events and executed actions. Such states can be e.g. used for situation reasoning in the condition part of reaction rules.

```
<Rule style="reasoning">
  <on> <Message mode="inbound"> event message </Message> </on>
  <if> <HoldsState> state individual </HoldsState> </if>
  <do> <Message mode="outbound"> action message </Message> </do>
</Rule>
```

---

[8] http://prova.ws

5 RuleML Tools and Applications

Several tools have already been built around RuleML, including rule engines (e.g., OO jDREW[9], Prova[10]), rule editors (e.g., Acumen Business Rule Manager[11], Syntactic-Semantic RuleML Editor (S2REd)[12]), as well as translators such as the Reaction RuleML translator (Web) service framework[13]. Most of these tools contribute to interoperability by making use of translators between presentation syntaxes such as Pure Prolog (or extensions such as POSL[14] and Prova) and RuleML/XML as well as between RuleML/XML and other XML-based languages such as RIF/XML. RIF RuleML interoperation was started with a common subset [Bol09].

RuleML-based multi-agent architectures for distributed rule inference services include Rule Responder[15] [PBKC07] and Emerald[16]. Rule Responder extends the Semantic Web towards a Pragmatic Web infrastructure for collaborative rule-based agent networks implemented as distributed rule inference services, where agents engage in conversations by exchanging messages and cooperate to achieve (collaborative) goals. Rule Responder utilizes messaging reaction rules from Reaction RuleML for communication between the distributed agent inference services. The Rule Responder middleware is based on Enterprise Service Bus (ESB) and Semantic Web technologies for implementing intelligent agent services that access data and ontologies, receive and detect events (e.g. for complex event processing in event processing agent networks), and make rule-based inferences and autonomous pro-active decisions for reactions based on these representations. Rule Responder has become the infrastructure for several Web 3.0 applications (e.g., PatientSupporter[17]).

6 Conclusion

RuleML 1.0 is the unifying family of languages spanning across all industrially relevant kinds of Web rules. It accommodates and extends other languages including W3C RIF. Yet, as shown by this paper, the major RuleML constructs are easy to learn. FOL RuleML deliberation rules could be regarded as an instantiation of the RIF Framework for Logic Dialects. However, for RIF-PRD and Production RuleML no corresponding RIF Framework for Production Rule Dialects exists, and for Reaction RuleML even a RIF instance dialect, RRD, is only envisioned yet, although the ongoing RIF RuleML collaboration should sustain progress here. On the other hand, Modal RuleML deliberation rules could be further developed

---

[9] http://www.jdrew.org/oojdrew
[10] http://www.prova.ws
[11] http://www.acumenbusiness.com
[12] http://sourceforge.net/projects/s2red
[13] http://reaction.ruleml.org/translation.htm
[14] http://ruleml.org/submission/ruleml-shortation.html
[15] http://responder.ruleml.org
[16] http://lpis.csd.auth.gr/systems/emerald/emerald.html
[17] http://ruleml.org/PatientSupporter

in collaboration with corresponding Common Logic extensions, as also needed for Semantics of Business Vocabulary and Business Rules (SBVR).

Object Oriented RuleML's slotted facts and rules can be used to define cases and associated solutions in Case Based Reasoning (CBR). With its optional use of types, which also accommodate finite domains, RuleML is well-prepared for a Constraint Logic Programming (CLP) extension. A related Constraint Handling Rules (CHR) extension could follow next.

Translators between sublanguages of RuleML, RIF, PRR, SBVR, Jess, Prova (ISO Prolog) have been written and further ones are under development. RuleML 1.0 as the overarching specification of Web rules will thus help to unify and drive the development of Web-based rule interoperation.

References

[BBB⁺05]   Battle, S., Bernstein, A., Boley, H., Grosof, B., Gruninger, M., Hull, R., Kifer, M., Martin, D., McIlraith, S., McGuinness, D., Su, J., Tabet, S.: Semantic Web Services Language (SWSL). Release Version 1.0 (May 2005), http://www.daml.org/services/swsf/1.0/swsl/

[BK10a]   Boley, H., Kifer, M.: A Guide to the Basic Logic Dialect for Rule Interchange on the Web. IEEE Transactions on Knowledge and Data Engineering (2010) (forthcoming)

[BK10b]   Boley, H., Kifer, M.: RIF Framework for Logic Dialects, W3C Recommendation (June 2010), http://www.w3.org/TR/rif-fld

[Bol09]   Boley, H.: RIF RuleML Rosetta Ring: Round-Tripping the Dlex Subset of Datalog RuleML and RIF-Core. In: Governatori, G., Hall, J., Paschke, A. (eds.) RuleML 2009. LNCS, vol. 5858, pp. 29–42. Springer, Heidelberg (2009)

[CGT89]   Ceri, S., Gottlob, G., Tanca, L.: What You Always Wanted to Know About Datalog (And Never Dared to Ask). IEEE Trans. on Knowledge and Data Eng. 1(1) (March 1989)

[DPSS08]   Damásio, C.V., Pan, J.Z., Stoilos, G., Straccia, U.: Representing Uncertainty in RuleML. Fundam. Inf. 82(3), 265–288 (2008)

[End01]   Enderton, H.B.: A Mathematical Introduction To Logic, 2nd edn. Harcourt/Academic Press, San Diego (2001)

[GDK09]   Grosof, B., Dean, M., Kifer, M.: The SILK System: Scalable Higher-Order Defeasible Rules. In: Governatori, G., Hall, J., Paschke, A. (eds.) RuleML 2009. LNCS, vol. 5858. Springer, Heidelberg (2009)

[HK09]   Heymans, S., Kifer, M.: RIF Core Answer Set Programming Dialect. W3C RuleML Specification (December 2009), http://ruleml.org/rif/RIF-CASPD.html/

[HPSB⁺04]   Horrocks, I., Patel-Schneider, P.F., Boley, H., Tabet, S., Grosof, B., Dean, M.: Semantic Web Rule Language (SWRL). W3C Member Submission (May 2004), http://www.w3.org/Submission/2004/SUBM-SWRL-20040521/

[KBA08]   Kontopoulos, E., Bassiliades, N., Antoniou, G.: Deploying Defeasible Logic Rule Bases for the Semantic Web. Data Knowl. Eng. 66(1), 116–146 (2008)

[Mak87]   Makowsky, J.A.: Why Horn formulas matter in computer science: Initial structures and generic examples. Journal of Computer and System Sciences 34, 266–292 (1987)

[Nie07]   Nieuwenhuis, R.: A survey of some recent trends in rewrite-based and paramodulation-based deduction (2007)

[PB09a]   Paschke, A., Boley, H.: Rule Markup Languages and Semantic Web Rule Languages. In: Giurca, A., Gasevic, D., Taveter, K. (eds.) Handbook of Research on Emerging Rule-Based Languages and Technologies: Open Solutions and Approaches, pp. 1–24. IGI Publishing (May 2009)

[PB09b]   Paschke, A., Boley, H.: Rules Capturing Events and Reactivity. In: Giurca, A., Gasevic, D., Taveter, K. (eds.) Handbook of Research on Emerging Rule-Based Languages and Technologies: Open Solutions and Approaches, pp. 215–252. IGI Publishing (May 2009)

[PBK10]   Polleres, A., Boley, H., Kifer, M.: RIF Datatypes and Built-ins 1.0, W3C Recommendation (June 2010), http://www.w3.org/TR/rif-dtb

[PBKC07]   Paschke, A., Boley, H., Kozlenkov, A., Craig, B.: Rule Responder: RuleML-Based Agents for Distributed Collaboration on the Pragmatic Web. In: 2nd ACM Pragmatic Web Conference 2007. ACM, New York (2007)

[WATB04]   Wagner, G., Antoniou, G., Tabet, S., Boley, H.: The Abstract Syntax of RuleML – Towards a General Web Rule Language Framework. In: Web Intelligence, pp. 628–631. IEEE Computer Society Press, Los Alamitos (2004)

[Wid93]   Widom, J.: Deductive and Active Databases: Two Paradigms or Ends of a Spectrum? In: Rules in Database Systems, pp. 306–315 (1993)

A   XSLTs and XSDs for RuleML 1.0

The specification of RuleML 1.0 differs from the RuleML 0.91 specification by putting more emphasis on XSLT, besides XML Schema: XSLT translators normalize RuleML 1.0 serializations, so XML Schema Definitions (XSDs) need to validate normal forms only. Normal forms provide an abstract-syntax level, where the equality of arbitrary RuleML 1.0 abstract syntaxes is reduced to the identity of their normal forms. They also simplify the XSDs, e.g., avoiding the permutation of role children. For instance, the normal form for derivation rules uses explicit role tags for <if> and <then> in that order, as shown by the middle-column version of Implication Rule 1 in Section 3.1.

The XSDs of RuleML 1.0 change those of RuleML 0.91 as follows: Type tags Hterm and Con are replaced with Uniterm and Const, respectively. Role tags body and head are replaced with if and then, respectively. Role tags lhs and rhs, with left and right, respectively. Attribute in="no|semi|yes|effect| modal" and respective values are replaced with per="copy|open|value|effect| modal". Attribute uri becomes iri. The online RuleML 1.0 specification is based on *normalidation*, including XSLTs for *normali*zation and XSDs for subsequent vali*dation*.[18] The specification is illustrated by test cases grouped according to sublanguages.[19]

---

[18] http://ruleml.org/1.0 (http://ruleml.org/1.0/xslt and
http://ruleml.org/1.0/xsd)
[19] http://ruleml.org/1.0/exa

Defining Access Control Rules with Conditions

Mark H. Linehan

IBM T.J. Watson Research Center
mlinehan@us.ibm.com

Abstract. The Business Entity method is a new approach for declarative Business Process Modeling. An important aspect of this method is access control rules that determine what users can access what data under what conditions. This paper describes an extension of Semantics of Business Vocabulary and Business Rules (SBVR) for defining these access control rules. A tool supports the creation of these data access control rules by a combination of a matrix format and conditions given in SBVR Structured English. The rules are stored according to the SBVR metamodel, and may be visualized either as individual rules or in a matrix.

Keywords: rules and norms, access control, RBAC, SBVR, Structured English, Business Entity, BPEL4Data, Data4BPM.

1 Introduction

The Business Entity method [1, 2, 3] is an approach to Business Process Management (BPM) that integrates an information model and a lifecycle model of the key business objects ("Business Entities") required in a business system. The information model defines the attributes of the Business Entities. The lifecycle model describes the evolution of the Business Entities, from creation to archiving, through various states according to a finite state machine model. Customer experience [4, 5] suggests that business process models created using the Business Entity method are more abstract and easier to understand than the highly procedural, more detailed models created using other methods such as the Business Process Modeling Notation (BPMN) [6].

The Business Entity method also integrates business rules and user roles. Rules supply two kinds of constraints on Business Entities. One kind limits which state transitions can be made under what circumstances. This author described these rules in detail in [7] and [8]. The other kind of rules control direct access to the Business Entities themselves, meaning read or writes of the attributes of the Business Entities, independent of state transitions. The term "CRUDE policies" is sometimes used collectively to refer to both kinds of rules, where "E" stands for "Execution" rules (the guards on the state transitions), and "CRUD" abbreviates "Create, Read, Update, Delete rules" (data access policies). This paper is about the "CRUD" policies.

CRUD policies are a variant of the well-known "Role Based Access Control" [9, 10] model that integrates consideration of Business Entity states into the access control policies. Data access is conditioned not just by user roles, but also by the state

M. Dean et al. (Eds.): RuleML 2010, LNCS 6403, pp. 179–193, 2010.

of a Business Entity. Each access control rule can also have a "user condition" that provides more precise specification about when access is granted.

The Business Entity method, as described in [1], is agnostic as to what rule language is used to specify access policies. This paper describes a prototype implementation in which the policies are modeled using an extension of the OMG's Semantics of Business Vocabulary and Business Rules (SBVR) [11] specification, supported by a tool that displays the rules in a combination of a matrix format and SBVR Structured English. Benefits of this approach include a simple conceptual model for business users, the ability to customize the access policies with conditions that test any Business Entity attributes, display of the conditions in Structured English, and the potential to map to various runtime execution schemes.

The next section introduces an example as a basis for discussion throughout the paper. The following section describes the prototype tool used to create and edit access control policies, in order to illustrate how users will understand these policies. Section 4 discusses how the rules are modeled using SBVR concepts, and section 5 reviews additional concepts defined in this work to integrate access rules with the Business Entity method. Section 6 discusses an extension of the SBVR meta-model that efficiently solves a scale-up problem that arises with the rules described herein. Section 7 describes the prototype runtime implementation. Section 8 reviews related work by other researchers, and the final section summarizes the paper.

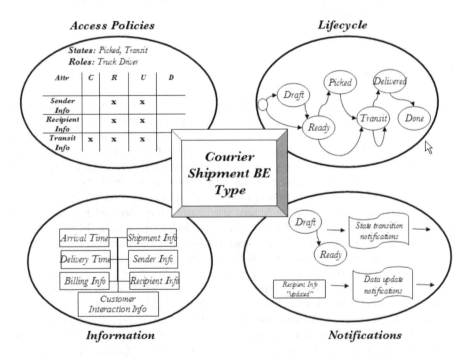

Fig. 1. The Courier Shipment Scenario (figure extracted from [1])

2 Running Example

This paper adopts and extends the "Courier Shipping" use case (Fig. 1) from [1] as a running example.

The top-left quadrant of this shows the "CRUD matrix", which in this case grants the "Truck Driver" user role access to several attributes of the "Courier Shipment" Business Entity when that Entity is in the "Picked" or "Transit" states. The matrix columns are labeled "C" for "create", "R" for "read", "U" for "update", and "D" for "delete". The rows identify individual "Courier Shipment" attributes such as "Sender Info" and "Recipient Info". The "x" marks in the cells specify that the user role has the access type of the column to the attribute of the row when the Business Entity is in any of the specified states. In this example, the "Truck Driver" role can read and update all three attributes shown when the "Courier Shipment" is in the "Picked" or "Transit" states, but can create only the "Transit Info" attribute.

The top-right quadrant of Fig. 1 shows the lifecycle of the "Courier Shipment" Entity. The named ovals identify the Entity states, such as "Picked" and "Transit". In this example, the "Courier Shipment" initially enters either the "Draft" or "Ready" state, and then proceeds through various transitions to the "Picked" and "Transit" states, eventually reaching "Delivered" and then "Done". Note that these are domain-specific states name chosen to be meaningful to business users; they are not generic.

The lower-left quadrant summarizes some of the attributes of the Business Entity. Typically in SBVR, these would be defined by a pair of glossary entries, one for the attribute as a concept, and one to relate the attribute to the "Courier Shipment" concept. For example:[1]

Delivery Time
    Concept Type: role
    Definition: date time when the Courier Shipment is delivered to the recipient
Courier Shipment **has** Delivery Time

This is equivalent to defining a UML class for "Courier Shipment" with a property called "Delivery Time" of type "date time".

The lower-right quadrant of Fig. 1 shows notifications that can be generated as the "Courier Shipment" Entity transitions among the lifecycle states shown in the upper-right quadrant.

3 Tool

This paper describes a prototype tool (Fig. 2) for creating and editing access policies as in the top-left quadrant of Fig. 1. This prototype is targeted to business users, meaning business people who are interested in business needs rather than IT staff focused on implementation concerns.

---

[1] Here and elsewhere in this paper, SBVR examples use the SBVR Structured English convention of showing nouns in underlined green, verbs in *italic blue*, and keywords in **red**. This paper uses **bold font** for the keywords to make them standout in black and white.

In this tool, access policies are grouped in named "Access Sets". The one shown in Fig. 2 is called "Truck Driver Access Policy", as shown in the upper left corner. The Business Entity name, "Courier Shipment" is displayed in the middle. The user roles and the Business Entity states addressed by this access set are shown below the access set name. This particular access set applies to the "Truck Driver" role and the "Picked" and "Transit" states. The edit button between the "User Roles" area and the "States" area opens a popup window in which one can add and delete role and state names. An access set can apply to one or multiple roles, or to all roles in an application. Similarly, an access set can apply to one or multiple states, or to all states of a Business Entity.

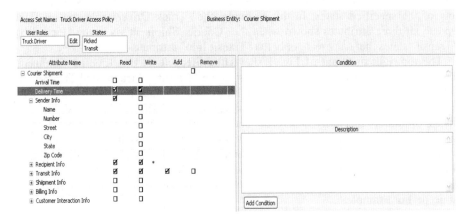

Fig. 2. CRUD Matrix Tool

The matrix below the user roles and states shows the structure of the Business Entity addressed by the access policy, in this case "Courier Shipment". The left column, showing the Business Entity attributes, can be expanded or collapsed to show child attributes to any level of detail. The figure shows the "Arrival Time", "Delivery Time", "Sender Info", and other attributes of "Courier Shipment", and also shows the expansion of "Sender Info".

This prototype labels the other columns of the matrix "Read", "Write", "Add", and "Remove", rather than "CRUD" as show in Fig. 1, on the belief that these labels may be more understandable to business users. "Read" means that attributes may be viewed or queried. "Write" means that they may be set or changed. "Add" and "Remove" mean that attributes may be added or deleted from attribute collections, meaning attributes that have cardinality greater than 1.

The symbols within the matrix show how the access policy applies to each combination of attribute and access type. A checked box indicates that the access type of the column is granted to the attribute of the row. Unchecked boxes show that access is denied. Tool users can check or uncheck these boxes as desired.

Users may give access to all the attributes of a structure as a group. For example, the check mark in the "Read" column of the "Sender Info" attribute means that the entire "Sender Info" structure can be read. The tool automatically "blanks out" some matrix cells to prevent conflicting policies between parent structures and child attributes. For example, the "Read" column is blank for the child attributes of "Sender Info" ("Name", etc.) because read access is already granted for the entire "Sender Info" structure. It would make no sense to permit users to grant or deny access to the child attributes when access is already given to the entire parent structure. Similarly, the "Read" column is blank for the "Courier Shipment" Entity itself because read access is individually given, or not, to specific child attributes of "Courier Shipment".

The "Add" and "Remove" columns are blank for singleton attributes since adding and deleting only applies to those attributes that are collections. In this example, "Add" and "Remove" applies only to the "Transit Info" attribute.

Access to the Business Entity as a whole can be granted if individual access to child attributes is not chosen. In Fig. 2, selecting the "Remove" entry for the "Courier Shipment" line at the top of the matrix would permit Truck Drivers to remove any "Courier Shipments" that are in "Picked" or "Transit" state.

To the right of the access matrix are two boxes titled "Condition" and "Description". They give details associated with the currently-selected access matrix cell, which is indicated by a filled-in box. In Fig. 2, the cell at the intersection of the "Write" column and the "Delivery Time" row is currently selected. Neither a condition nor a description exists for that particular cell.

An asterisk identifies each cell that has a condition, for example in the "Write" column for "Recipient Info". A condition specifies an additional constraint on the access given in the cell, beyond just the user role and Business Entity state.

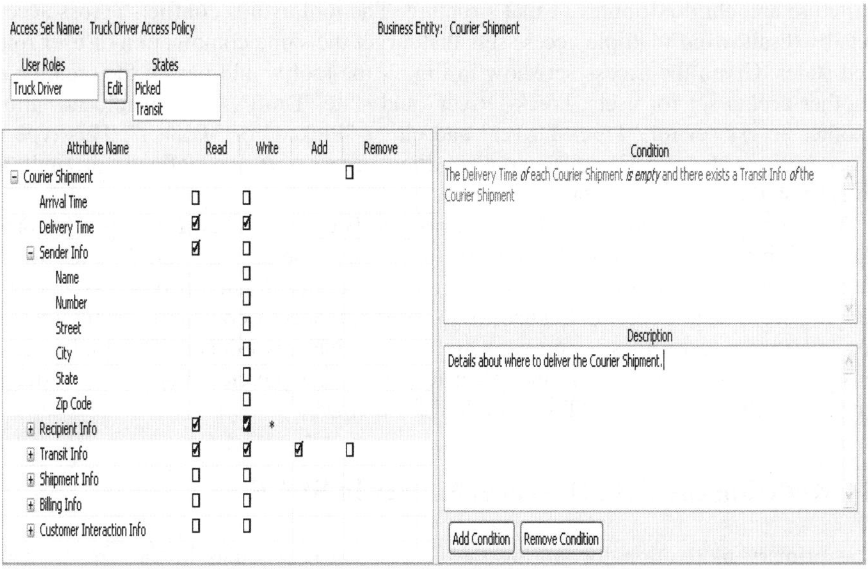

Fig. 3. Example of a condition and description

Fig. 3 shows a user condition and a description for the write access to "Recipient Info". The description is simply unprocessed text. The condition is shown in SBVR Structured English to make it easy for business users to understand.

The effective access control is the conjunction of the access matrix entry and the user condition. In the figure, the user condition, in combination with the selected row in the matrix, means that write access to the "Recipient Info" by the "Truck Driver" role when the "Courier Shipment" is in "Picked" or "Transit" state is permitted only when the "Delivery Time" attribute is empty and there is at least one element of the "Transit Info" attribute collection.

The "Add Condition" button at the bottom of the right-hand side of Fig. 3 initiates a multi-step popup wizard for creating conditions. This wizard is a minor variant of the rule creation wizard described in [8], and is not described again here.

This tool supports access control policies across a wide range of sophistication. A simple policy design could use just two access sets that apply to all roles. One access set might give write, add, and delete access in some states, and another access set might give read access in other states. The access could be given to the Business Entity as a whole. A much more sophisticated policy design might use multiple access sets to give different access for different roles in different states. These access sets could grant access to individual attributes of the Business Entity. They could use conditions to restrict access by more than the Business Entity states and user roles. In summary, this single tool design smoothly support a range of sophistication in access policy management.

One concern that arises with such a tool is the potential for conflicting access policies. Within a single access set, conflicts are prevented by the design of the tool. For example, the tool does not permit users to specify access for both a parent structure and child attributes of that structure. The tool avoids conflicts across access sets by disallowing multiple access sets that target the same combination of user roles and states. Given the access set show in Fig. 2, the tool would permit the creation of another access set for user "Truck Driver" and state "Draft", but it would not allow another access set for "Truck Driver" and either "Picked" or "Transit". This type of cross access-set validation also applies when access sets are defined for multiple roles, or for all roles or all states.

The underlying philosophy of this tool is that Business Entity access is a business data governance issue of direct concern to business users. Who can do what to the data is a business policy issue, not just an IT security detail. In business domains ranging from health care to finance to government, access control decisions make a real difference to business operations and to customer confidence. This tool enables business users to directly view and evaluate their access policies at any level of detail, rather than depending upon IT staff to do it for them.

4   Modeling the CRUD Access Matrix in SBVR

The primary motivation for storing the access matrix as rules in the SBVR meta-model is rich support for user conditions. SBVR provides for logical formulae that use standard predicate and propositional calculus, and enables the display of these formulae in an English-like format. This permits complex user conditions to be shown in English, as illustrated in Fig. 3.

An access matrix is modeled in SBVR as follows: each column of the access matrix shown in Fig. 2 is converted by the tool to an SBVR rule according to the

SBVR meta model with extensions. Cells with conditions are generated separately. For example, the "Write" column of Fig. 2 (except for the "Recipient Info" cell) is generated as:

> **Truck Driver Access Policy:** It is permitted that each <u>Truck Driver</u> *write* the <u>Recipient Info</u> *of* each <u>Courier Shipment</u>, and the <u>Delivery Time</u> *of* the <u>Courier Shipment</u>, only if the <u>Courier Shipment</u> *is Picked* or the Courier Shipment *is Transit.*

In SBVR terms, this is a "restricted permission" rule that permits the consequence that Truck Drivers may write the "Recipient Info" and "Delivery Time" attributes with the antecedent that the "Courier Shipment" is in state "Picked" or "Transit". Note that multiple Business Entity attributes are included in the antecedent by conjunction.

Restricted permission rules are equivalent to conditional prohibition statements where the condition is negated. The rule given above could be stated as:

> **Truck Driver Access Policy:** It is prohibited that each <u>Truck Driver</u> *write* the <u>Recipient Info</u> *of* each <u>Courier Shipment</u>, and the <u>Delivery Time</u> *of* the <u>Courier Shipment</u>, if the <u>Courier Shipment</u> *is* not *Picked* or the Courier Shipment *is* not *Transit.*

Each cell that contains a condition is handled as a separate rule that uses a conjunction to combine the user-specified condition with tests of the Business Entity state. For example, the condition for write access to "Recipient Info", as shown in Fig. 3, is modeled as:

> **Truck Driver Access Policy:** It is permitted that each <u>Truck Driver</u> *write* the <u>Recipient Info</u> *of* each <u>Courier Shipment</u>, only if the <u>Courier Shipment</u> *is Picked* or the <u>Courier Shipment</u> *is Transit* and the <u>Delivery Time</u> *of* the <u>Courier Shipment</u> *is empty* and there exists a <u>Transit Info</u> *of* the <u>Courier Shipment</u>.

Both rules are named to match the access set name, to facilitate associating the rules with each other and with the access set.

The tool builds these access rules according to this template:

> It is permitted that each <role$_1$> [and role$_2$]* {*read* | *write* | *add* | *remove*} each <attribute$_1$> *of* each <business entity> [and each <attribute$_2$> *of* the <business entity>]* [, only if the <business entity> *is* <state$_1$> [and the <business entity> *is* <state$_2$>]* [and <condition>]].

This pattern permits an individual rule to mention any number of roles, attributes, or Business Entity states. This helps avoid an explosion in the number of rules. In principle, there could be a rule for each cell of the access matrix. With this design, and ignoring user conditions, there are no more than four rules per access set.

Users can define access sets that apply to all roles, all states, and/or all attributes of a business entity. For access sets that apply to all roles, the tool substitutes the general concept <u>user role</u> for the " Each <role$_1$> [and role$_2$]*" portion of the template given above. This is motivated by the fact that domain-specific user roles, such as "Truck Driver" are modeled as subtypes of user role, as described below.

The tool omits the "the <business entity> *is* <state₁> [and the <business entity> *is* <state₂>]*" part of the template for access sets that apply to all states. If an access matrix cell also has no condition, then the tool omits the antecedent completely. (In SBVR, such rules are technically called "advice" rather than "rules" since they constrain nothing.) Thus, the rules generated for access sets that apply both to all roles and all states, and have no user conditions, follow this pattern:

> It is permitted that each user role {*read* | *write* | *add* | *remove*} each <attribute₁> *of* each <business entity> [and each <attribute₂> *of* the <business entity>]*.

If an access policy applies to all the attributes of a Business Entity, the tool omits the " each <attribute₁> *of*" component of the rule template. For example, here is a policy that Recipients may read the entire "Courier Shipment" entity when it is in "Delivered" state:

> It is permitted that each Recipient *read* each Courier Shipment, only if the Courier Shipment *is Delivered*.

Considering all the combinations of 0, 1, or multiple roles, 0, 1, or multiple states, 0, 1, or multiple attributes, and 0 or 1 user condition, there are 54 patterns of access rules. The complexity of all these combinations is completely hidden by the tool, which offers a lot of power in a simple user paradigm.

5   Business Entity Metamodel Vocabulary

The rules are enabled by a Business Entity vocabulary that goes beyond the SBVR metamodel to address Business Entity concepts. This vocabulary formally defines the following concepts:

Business Entity
Definition:	noun concept that *has* a lifecycle
Example:	Courier Shipment

user role
Definition:	noun concept that *is* a category of users
Example:	Truck Driver

attribute
Definition:	noun concept that *is of* a given business entity
Example:	Arrival Time *of* Courier Shipment

user role *reads* attribute
Definition:	the user role reads or queries the attribute

<u>user role</u> ***writes*** <u>attribute</u>
    Definition: the <u>user role</u> sets or updates the <u>attribute</u>

<u>user role</u> ***adds*** <u>attribute</u>
    Definition: the <u>user role</u> adds an <u>element</u> to the <u>attribute</u>

<u>user role</u> ***deletes*** <u>attribute</u>
    Definition: the <u>user role</u> deletes an <u>element</u> from the <u>attribute</u>

<u>state</u>
    Definition: <u>characteristic type</u> that *is of* a <u>business entity</u>
    Example: The extension of the state of '<u>Courier Shipment</u>' includes
                         the characteristics '<u>Courier Shipment</u> *is picked*', '<u>Courier
                         Shipment</u> *is ready*', etc.

<u>business entity</u> ***has*** <u>state</u>
    Definition: the <u>state</u> identifies which portion of its lifecycle a <u>business
                         entity</u> has reached
    Necessity: Each <u>business entity</u> *has* exactly one <u>state</u>.

The <u>business entity</u> and <u>user role</u> definitions are straightforward specifications of what would be "classes" in UML. They use a mixture of SBVR vocabulary concepts and unstyled text, such as the word "lifecycle", to define foundational or "ground" concepts for the Business Entity method. The four verb concepts are used in the consequents of the access rules to permit read, write, add, or delete access to Business Entity attributes. '<u>State</u>' is defined as an SBVR characteristic type, which means that <u>state</u> holds one of a choice of values such as "*is picked*" or "*is draft*". Furthermore, a rule can test the <u>state</u> of a <u>business entity</u> via one of the values, such as "… only if the <u>Courier Shipment</u> *is picked*".

These concepts provide the formal basis for defining domain-specific business concepts such as:

<u>Courier Shipment</u>
    Definition   <u>business entity</u> that tracks an actual courier shipment

<u>Truck Driver</u>
    Definition   <u>user role</u> that drives a truck

<u>Courier Shipment</u> *is picked*
    Definition   <u>state</u> that the <u>Courier Shipment</u> has been received by a
                          <u>Truck Driver</u>

The Business Entity method intends that these domain concepts, and the underlying Business Entity vocabulary defined above, should make intuitive sense to business users even though the underlying concepts are quite sophisticated. The expectation is that Structured English rules that incorporate ordinary business terms should be understandable to business users with everyday skills. Furthermore, those users who probe the definitions of the domain concepts should be able to understand how they relate to the Business Entity method.

6 "Quantification Collections"

One issue with SBVR itself arose when designing the consequent part of the access rule template described above. When used with one role and one attribute, the consequent is generated according to a pattern that is equivalent to:

$\forall$ e: business entity, r:user role, $\forall a$:attribute that is of e, <verb>(r, a)...
(where <verb> is one of "read", "write", "add", "remove")

In this pattern, "$\forall$ e: business entity" means universal quantification over business entities, using e as the quantification variable. Similar readings apply to the other two quantifiers. The quantification variable a takes the values of a specified child attribute of the business entity e.

A problem arises when multiple roles or states are specified by an access set, because each use of <verb> can bind to just one role and one attribute using what SBVR calls an "atomic formulation". One solution would be to model multiple rules to represent each combination of user role and attribute. This solution has significant scale problems. In the example shown in Fig. 2, this solution would replace the single rule required for the read column with four rules, one each for reading "Delivery Time", "Sender Info", "Recipient Info", and "Transit Info". If the access set specified 3 roles, then this solution would require 3*4=12 rules, one for the cross-product of each user role and business entity attribute.

To solve this concern, this work designed an extension to the SBVR metamodel called a "Quantification Collection". The name suggests a universal or existential quantifier that can range over a collection of concepts, rather than over just one concept. In this paper, the underlined symbol $\underline{\forall}$ represents a universal quantifier over multiple concepts, defined as follows:

$$\underline{\forall}\ q:\{c_1, c_2, \ldots c_n\} \equiv \forall\ q_1: c_1 \cup \forall\ q_2: c_2 \cup \ldots \cup \forall\ q_n: c_n$$

where "$\forall\ q_1: c_1$" means that quantification variable q_1 ranges over (takes the values of) concept c_1, and the symbol "$\underline{\forall}\ q:\{c_1, c_2, \ldots c_n\}$" means that variable q collectively ranges over the values of the concepts $c_1, c_2, \ldots c_n$. A similar definition applies to existential quantification. Note that when q is bound to a verb in what SBVR calls an "atomic formulation", all the concepts $c_1, c_2, \ldots c_n$ must be of the type expected by the verb.

Using this scheme, the SBVR rule shown at the start of section 4, above, is formulated as:

it is permitted that $\forall e$: Courier Shipment, $\forall r$: Truck Driver, $\underline{\forall} a$: {Recipient Info of e, Delivery Time of e} write(r, a) ONLY IF (isPicked(e) $\vee$ isTransit(e))

As discussed in section 4, an SBVR restricted permission rule is equivalent to a rule given as "it is prohibited <consequent> if not <antecedent>". The implementation uses an abbreviated "ONLY IF" operator (shown above) to directly capture the restricted permission sense. Technically in SBVR, the above should be formulated as:

it is prohibited that $\forall e$: Courier Shipment, $\forall r$: Truck Driver, $\underline{\forall} a$: {Recipient Info of e, Delivery Time of e} $\neg$ (isPicked(e) $\vee$ isTransit(e)) $\rightarrow$ write(r, a)

The Quantification Collection idea permits the information contained in the tool's access matrix to be stored as a limited number of SBVR rules, proportional to the sum of the number of non-blank columns of the access matrix, plus the number of user conditions, rather than the cross-product of user roles and attributes. It enables efficient exploitation of the features of SBVR, such as its logic-based meta-model and the ability to show the user conditions in Structured English.

7   Runtime Execution

Fig. 4 summarizes how the access rule tool described above works with the runtime. The fundamental idea is that a user role can access a Business Entity only if a rule grants access. In the terminology of [14], the CRUD matrix specifies *defeasible rules* in the sense that they defeat an unstated rule that lays a foundation that access is denied if not permitted. As with [14], the matrix is translated to SBVR rules, each of which deny access if a condition is not met.

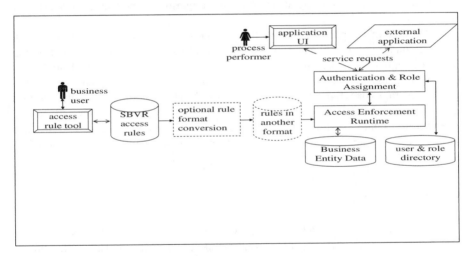

Fig. 4. Tool and Runtime Configuration

The tool produces an XML file containing access rules in an SBVR-based format. Optionally, the rules can be converted to another format, such as XACML [12] or the Business Entity Definition Language (BEDL) of [1]. The runtime access enforcement function on the right-hand side of the diagram reads either the SBVR format or the alternate format and uses them to arbitrate runtime access requests. These requests come from either humans who are using an application user interface to perform business process tasks, or from external applications. In either case, these service requests are first processed by an authentication and role assignment function by reference to a user authentication and role assignment directory, or by rules that determine which requesters get which roles. Both human and external application requests are assigned roles to ensure consistent application of the access controls.

Typically, the authentication and role assignment function is provided by middleware or operating system software.

Requests are of two basic types: directed to a specific business entity instance via an instance identifier, or queries for multiple instances of a particular entity type. To help optimize access enforcement, both request types specify the expected state of the business entities. For requests addressed to specific instances, the access enforcement runtime uses the expected state of the instance and the role of the requester to lookup the appropriate access rule, and rejects the request if no rule grants access. The runtime then compares the expected state against the actual state of the business entity instance. Since different access rules apply to different attributes of an instance, the runtime must check the rules individually for each attribute being read or written.

The processing sequence for queries is somewhat different because the applicable instances are not identified in advance. The runtime first checks that there is a rule that gives access to the business entity type according to the role of the requester and the expected state. The runtime then looks up the business entity instances that have the expected state. Finally, for each queried attribute, the runtime checks that some rule permits read access to the attribute for the requesting user role and current user state.

At the time this paper was written, the runtime supports the access matrix without the user conditions. The planned implementation of user conditions varies depending upon the request type. For reads, writes, and removes, the runtime will apply any condition against the business entity instance data prior to any update so that the request cannot bypass the condition. For queries, the runtime will apply any condition as a filter for the query results. Since each business entity attribute can have a different user condition, this filter must be applied attribute by attribute and instance by instance. Scaling this to work efficiently in the case of many query results is a known challenge.

8   Related Work

As mentioned previously, CRUD policies are a type of Role Based Access control [9, 10]. In terms of Barker's unifying meta-model of access control [14], CRUD policies define a category of user roles and a category of business entities or business entity attributes, and CRUD relationships between these two categories. The addition of a user condition to a CRUD policy effectively subsets the category of business entities or business entity attributes.

This work is similar in some ways to that of Goedertier, *et. al.* [14, 16], which also describes the use of SBVR to model access rules for business process models. The Business Entity vocabulary reviewed in section 5, above, makes the rules described here *process aware*, in the sense of Goedertier. One key difference is that these rules explicitly build upon the concept of Business Entity states, which are not the same as the "business process state space" described in [16]. Business Entity states are the states of a finite state machine, whereas the "business process state space" is the totality of the information associated with a business process.

Another difference arises in the underlying process models. The EM-BrA^{2}CE business model of [16] defines twelve "generic state transitions", such as assignment of a user to an activity, adding a fact, removing a fact, and so forth. In the Business Entity method, states and state transitions are specific to business domains and meaningful to business users. Fig. 1 shows an example.

The policies described here are similar to what Goedertier calls "visibility constraints". The rule structure described here appears to be more general than those of [14] because they support multiple user roles, multiple states, and multiple attributes in one rule.

The work described here models access rules as deontic or behavioral rules, whereas Goedertier uses alethic or structural rules. Alethic rules describe what is true by definition, while deontic rules define what is expected to be true but may in fact not be true. It seems to this author that access control describes expectations of behavior rather than definitions of structure. Hence, access control rules are deontic in the work described here.

Vanthienen [17] describes the Prologa tool, which uses decision tables to visualize a complex set of related rules. This tool is employed in [14] to display access rules. The CRUD visualization described in this paper takes advantage of the Business Entity method semantics to display the access policies in a more compact form. In effect, the CRUD matrix is a specialized decision table that has two fixed conditions that test the user role and business entity state, and an optional third condition specified by the user. The optional user condition, and the ability to specify "all roles" or "all states", relieves the limitations of the two fixed conditions, thus providing flexibility to address any access control use case. Thus the CRUD matrix design addresses the simple cases simply while extending to reach complex cases as required.

Both Prologa and this work convert between decision tables and textual rule sets. An optimization introduced in this paper reduces the number of rules generated in the common situation where the same rule applies to multiple user roles or multiple Business Entity attributes.

9 Summary and Future Work

This work describes an integration of SBVR rules with the Business Entity method of [1] to support data access control rules. It shows how an access rule tool can use a matrix format to display complex data access rules in an easily-understood format. The matrix compactly displays access constraints that would take dozens of lines of text if displayed in an if-then rule format. The matrix format and the use of "Structured English" for user conditions directly support access control management by business users.

Flexibility is provided via fine-grained "user conditions" that may further constrain the access control rules. The rules are captured according to the SBVR meta-model, which enables the user conditions to exploit the richness of SBVR expressions while displaying the conditions in SBVR "Structured English".

A template shows how the matrix form of the access rules is converted to the SBVR meta-model. The template supports 54 different access patterns, considering the possible numbers of user roles, business entity states, and business entity attributes, and the presence or absence of user conditions.

An extension of the SBVR meta-model addresses a scale-up problem that would otherwise result in an explosion in the number of rules. When one access control rule addresses multiple business entity attributes or multiple user roles, the number of equivalent SBVR rules is the product of the numbers of each. In the absence of user conditions, the "quantification collection" extension of the SBVR meta-model reduces the required number of SBVR rules to 1.

The SBVR rules may be implemented directly in a runtime system, or may be converted to another format, such as XACML for execution by an XACML-compliant Policy Enforcement Point. The latter approach combines the advantage of displaying the user conditions in SBVR "Structured English" with the exploitation of existing XACML engines.

Future work is needed in two areas. As mentioned previously, the prototype runtime system needs further development to support user conditions. A particular implementation challenge is handling user conditions in the case of large query results. The second area is end-user testing to make sure the tool design is effective with the intended audience of business users.

Acknowledgements

The original idea for the CRUD matrix was published in [3]. Prabir Nandi promoted the integration of access rules with the Business Entity method. Florian Pinel implemented the runtime access enforcement. Manish Ladda did the initial implementation of the access tool.

References

1. Prabir, N., et al.: Data4BPM Part 1: Introducing Business Entities and the Business Entity Definition Language (BEDL). IBM developerWorks,
   http://www.ibm.com/developerworks/websphere/library/techarticles/1004_nandi/1004_nandi.html
2. Nigam, A., Caswell, N.S.: Business artifacts: An approach to operational specification. IBM Systems Journal 42(3), 428–445 (2003)
3. Nandi, P., Kumaran, S.: Adaptive Business Object: A New Component Model for Business Integration. In: Proceedings of International Conference on Enterprise Information Systems, ICEIS (2005)
4. Kumaran, S.: Model Driven Enterprise. In: Proceedings of Global Integration Summit, Banff, Canada (2004)
5. Hull, R.: Artifact-centric Business Process Models: Brief Survey of Research Results and Challenges. In: Meersman, R., Tari, Z. (eds.) OTM 2008, Part II. LNCS, vol. 5332, pp. 1152–1163. Springer, Heidelberg (2008)
6. Object Modeling Group (OMG): Business Process Modeling Notation Version 2.0 Beta 1,
   http://www.omg.org/spec/BPMN/2.0/
7. Linehan, M.: SBVR Use Cases. In: Bassiliades, N., Governatori, G., Paschke, A. (eds.) RuleML 2008. LNCS, vol. 5321, pp. 128–196. Springer, Heidelberg (2008)
8. Linehan, M.: Ontologies and Rules in Business Models. In: Proceedings of the 2007 Eleventh International IEEE EDOC Conference Workshop, pp. 149–156 (2007)

9. InterNational Committee for Information Technology Standards, Information Technology - Role Based Access Control, ANSI/INCITS 359-2004 (2004), `http://www.techstreet.com/standards/INCITS/359_2004?product_id=1151353`
10. National Institute of Standards and Technology (NIST), Role Based Access Control (RBAC) and Role Based Security, `http://csrc.nist.gov/groups/SNS/rbac/`
11. Object Modeling Group (OMG): Semantics of Business Vocabulary and Business Rules Specification, Version 1.0 (2007), `http://www.omg.org/spec/SBVR/1.0/`
12. OASIS: eXtensible Access Control Markup Language (XACML), version 2.0 (2005), `http://www.oasis-open.org/committees/tc_home.php?wg_abbrev=xacml`
13. OASIS: Core and hierarchical role based access control (RBAC) profile of XACML 2.0 (2005), `http://docs.oasis-open.org/xacml/2.0/access_control-xacml-2.0-rbac-profile1-spec-os.pdf`
14. Barker, S.: The next 700 access control models or a unifying meta-model? In: Proceedings of the 14th ACM Symposium on Access Control Models and Technologies (SACMAT), ACM, New York (2009), `http://portal.acm.org/citation.cfm?id=1542207.1542238&coll=ACM&dl=ACM&CFID=98850045&CFTOKEN=13091977`
15. Goedertier, S., Mues, C., Vanthienen, J.: Specifying Process-Aware Access Control Rules in SBVR. In: Paschke, A., Biletskiy, Y. (eds.) RuleML 2007. LNCS, vol. 4824, pp. 39–52. Springer, Heidelberg (2007), `http://www.econ.kuleuven.be/tew/academic/infosys/RESEARCH/PROLOGA/refsdtpubs/ProcessAwareRules.pdf`
16. Goedertier, S., Vanthienen, J.: EM-BrA2CE v0.2: A vocabulary and execution model for declarative business process modeling. In: ter Hofstede, A.H.M., Benatallah, B., Paik, H.-Y. (eds.) BPM Workshops 2007. LNCS, vol. 4928, pp. 496–501. Springer, Heidelberg (2008)
17. Vanthienen, J., Dries, E.: Illustration of a Decision Table Tool for Specifying and Implementing Knowledge Based Systems. In: Fifth International Conference on Tools with Artificial Intelligence (TAI), pp. 198–205 (1993)

Norm Compliance in Business Process Modeling

Guido Governatori[1] and Antonino Rotolo[2]

[1] NICTA Queensland Research Lab., Australia
guido.governatori@nicta.com.au
[2] CIRSFID, University of Bologna, Italy
antonino.rotolo@unibo.it

Abstract. We investigate the concept of norm compliance in business process modeling. In particular we propose an extension of Formal Contract Logic (FCL), a combination of defeasible logic and a logic of violation, with a richer deontic language capable of capture many different facets of normative requirements. The resulting logic, called Process Compliance Logic (PCL), is able to capture both semantic compliance and structural compliance. This paper focuses on structural compliance, that is we show how PCL can capture obligations concerning the structure of a business process.

1 Introduction

Recent works in business process modeling focus on the concept of norm compliance (see the literature in Section 6). Norm compliance is aimed at ensuring that business processes are in accordance with a prescribed set of norms. More specifically by norm compliance we understand a relationship between two sets of specifications describing the alignment of formal specifications for business processes and formal specifications relevant law and regulations. In other terms compliance is the certification that a process is executed correctly does not result in a breach of the rules governing it. Compliance requirements may stem from legislation and regulatory bodies, standards and codes of practice, and business partner contracts. However, some research issues are still underdeveloped. We focus here on three of them, which are related to the three sources of complexities.

A *first source of complexities* resides in the fact that norms often regulate processes by specifying obligatory actions to be taken in case of breaches of some of the norms, actions which can vary from penalties to the termination of an interaction itself. Obligations in force after some other obligations have been violated correspond to contrary-to-duty obligations (CTDs) [1]. Among them, we have the reparative obligations, which are meant to 'repair' or 'compensate' violations of primary obligations [2]. These constructions identify situations that are not ideal but still acceptable. The ability to deal with violations is an essential requirement for processes where some failures can occur, but they do not necessarily mean that the whole process has to fail. However, these constructions can give rise to very complex rule dependencies, because we can have that the violation of a single rule can activate other (reparative) rules, which, in case of their violation, refer to other rules, and so forth [3].

A *second source of complexities* depends on the fact that processes may be regulated by different types of obligations (see Section 2). We may have obligations requiring (1) to be always fulfilled during the execution of the entire process or of some subpaths of

M. Dean et al. (Eds.): RuleML 2010, LNCS 6403, pp. 194–209, 2010.

it, (2) that a certain condition must occur at least once before the execution of a certain task A of the process and such that the obligations may, or may not, persist after A if they are not complied with, (3) that something is done in a single task [4]. These types of obligation make things more complex when we deal with the compliance of a process with respect to chains of reparative obligations. For example, if the primary obligation is persistent and states to pay before task A, and the secondary (reparative) obligation is to pay a fine in the task B successive to A, the process is compliant not only when we pay before A, but also when we do not meet this deadline, pay later and pay the fine at B. If the secondary obligation rather requires to be always fulfilled for all tasks successive to A, compliance conditions will change.

The *third source of complexities* arises from different types of conditions we have for business processes. We can have normative requirements about the artifacts of a business process, over the activities (tasks) to be performed and over the order on which they are executed, as well as their combinations.

Most of the approaches to business process compliance address only one of these aspects. We propose an approach able to capture compliance requirements through a generic requirements modeling framework, and subsequently facilitate the propagation of these requirements into business process models and enterprise applications, thus achieving *compliance by design*. To achieve this objective we show how to use the language and the algorithm we have proposed in [5] to capture normative conditions on the tasks of a process.

Ensuring automated detection and/or enforcement of compliance requires in this paper to address the following related research tasks. *First*, we have to define in Section 3 a language to represent, and reason about, chains of reparative obligations of the types discussed in Section 2. *Second*, we need a mechanism for normalising a system of norms, namely, identify formal loopholes, deadlocks and inconsistencies in it, and to make hidden conditions explicit; without this, we do not have any guarantee that a given process is compliant, because we do not know if all relevant norms have been considered (Section 3). *Third*, we have to specify a suitable language for business process modeling able to automate and optimise business procedures and to embed normative constraints (Section 4).

2   Normative Constraints: Violations and Types of Obligation

We can distinguish *achievement obligations* from *maintenance obligations* [4]. For an *achievement obligation*, a certain condition must occur at least once before a deadline:

Example 1. Customers must pay before the delivery of the good, after receiving the invoice.

The deadline (before the delivery of the good)—which of course meaningfully applies if the customer is informed about the the maximum timespan within which the good can be delivered—refers to an obligation triggered by receipt of the invoice: such an obligation is persistent. After that the customer is obliged to pay. The obligation terminates only when it is complied with. Note that the obligation persists after the deadline, until it is achieved. But we may have cases where achievement obligations do not persist after the deadline:

Example 2. Once the submissions to RuleML 2010 are made available to RuleML-2010 PC members, the reviewers must send their reports before the notifications are delivered to the authors

Indeed, the obligation to deliver a review does not persist after the deadline, since after the review result has been notified to the authors, the paper has been accepted or rejected on the basis of the other reports delivered in time.

For *maintenance obligations*, a certain condition must obtain during all instants before the deadline:

Example 3. After opening a bank account, customers must keep a positive balance until bank charges are taken out.

By definition, maintenance obligations do not persist after the deadline. In Example 3, the deadline only signals that the obligation is terminated. A violation occurs when the obliged state does not obtain at some point before the deadline.

Finally, *puctual obligations* only apply to single tasks or instants:

Example 4. When banks proceed with any wire transfer, they must transmit a message, via SWIFT, to the receiving bank requesting that the payment is made according to the instructions given.

Punctual obligations apply only to single instants or tasks; mathematically they can be thought as either maintenance obligations or achievement obligations in force in time intervals where the endpoints are equal. Typically punctual obligations must occur at the same time of their triggering conditions, as shown in the above example.

Many norms can be associated with an explicit sanction. Consider

Example 5. Customers must pay before the delivery of the good, after receiving the invoice. Otherwise, an additional fine must be paid.

Example 6. After opening a bank account, customers must keep a positive balance until bank charges are taken out. Otherwise, their account is blocked.

An explicit sanction is often implemented through a separate obligation, which is triggered by a detected violation. Thus, further deadlines can be introduced to enforce the sanctions, leading to a chain of obligations. For instance, the payment of a fine mentioned in Example 5 could be due before the execution of a subsequent task.

We can also distinguish *preemptive obligations* from *non-preemptive obligations*. Suppose that, in Example 1, the price is 200$, and the customer, by mistake, transferred an amount of 200$ to the bank account of the seller before the date of the invoice. In this case, the early transfer may count as a payment and the customer could claim that her obligation to pay the seller is already fulfilled. This is an example of *preemptive* obligation. *Non-preemptive obligations* do not work as above. Consider this example:

Example 7. Executors and administrators of a decedent's estate will be required to give notice to each beneficiary named in the Will within 60 days after the date X of an order admitting a will to probate has been signed.

If an executor gives a notice to the beneficiaries before X, she will have to resend the notification after that. Note that the distinction between preemptive and non-premptive obligations applies only to achievement obligations, while it does not make sense with the maintenance and punctual ones.

What happens if the above types of obligations are combined into chains of reparative obligations? The expression of violation conditions and the reparations is an important requirement for designing subsequent processes to minimise or deal with such violations and also to determine the compliance of a process with the relevant norms. The violation expression consists of the primary obligation, its violation conditions, an obligation generated upon the violation condition occurs, and this can recursively be iterated, until the final condition is reached. We introduced in [3,6] the non-boolean connective $\otimes$: a formula like $OA \otimes OB$ means that A is obligatory, but if the obligation OA is not fulfilled (i.e., when $\neg A$ is the case), then the obligation OB is activated and becomes in force until it is satisfied or violated. However, the violation condition of an obligation varies depending on the types of obligations used. In the next section, we will extend the approach of [3,6] to cover these cases.

3   Process Compliance Language (PCL)

We now provide a formal account of the ideas presented above. Our formalism, called Process Compliance Language (PCL), is a combination of Defeasible Logic (DL) [7] and a deontic logic of violations [6]. PCL significantly extends the logic of [3] with types of obligations discussed in Section 2 and preserves the linear complexity of DL.

PCL formal language consists of a numerable set of propositional letters $p, q, r, \ldots$, intended to represent the state variables and the tasks of a process. Formulas are constructed using the negation $\neg$, the non-boolean connective $\otimes$ (for the reparative operator), and the deontic operators O_y^x, for obligation (where y can be empty). Based on the discussion in Section 2 we have three main classes of deontic operators: punctual obligations (O^p), maintenance obligations (O^m) and achievement obligations (O^a); achievement obligations in turn can be classified based on two orthogonal distinctions: persistent ($O^{a,\pi}$) vs non-persistent ($O^{a,\tau}$), and preemptive ($O_{pr}^{a,x}$) vs non-preemptive ($O_{n-pr}^{a,x}$).

The formulas of PCL are constructed in two steps according to the following formation rules: (i) every propositional letter is a literal; (ii) the negation of a literal is a literal; (iii) if X is a deontic operator and l is a literal then Xl and $\neg Xl$ are deontic literals.

After we have defined the notions of literal and deontic literal we can use the following set of formation rules to introduce $\otimes$-expressions, i.e., the formulas used to encode chains of obligations and violations: (a) every deontic literal is an $\otimes$-expression; (b) if $Xl_1, \ldots, Xl_n$ are deontic literals, then $Xl_1 \otimes \ldots \otimes Xl_n$ is an $\otimes$-expression.

The connective $\otimes$ permits combining primary and reparative obligations into unique regulations. The meaning of an expression like $O_{pr}^{a,\pi} A \otimes O^p B \otimes O^m C$ is that the primary provision is an achievement, persistent, preemptive obligation to do A, but if A is not done, then we have a punctual obligation to do B. If B fails to be realised, then we obtain a maintenance obligation to do C. Thus B is the reparation of the violation of the obligation $O_{pr}^{a,\pi} A$. Similarly C is the reparation of the obligation $O^p B$, which is in force when the violation of A occurs.

Each norm is represented by a rule in PCL like $r : A_1, \ldots, A_n \Rightarrow C$, where r is the id of the norm, $A_1, \ldots, A_n$ is the set of the premises of the rule, and C is the conclusion of the rule. Each A_i is either a literal or a deontic literal and C is an $\otimes$-expression.

PCL is also equipped with another type of rules, called defeaters (marked with arrow $\rightsquigarrow$) and a superiority relation (a binary relation) over the rule set.

In DL, the superiority relation ($\prec$) determines the relative strength of two rules, and it is used when rules have potentially conflicting conclusions. For example, given the rules $r_1 : a \Rightarrow O^m b \otimes O^{a,\pi}_{n-pr} c$ and $r_2 : d \Rightarrow \neg O^{a,\pi}_{pr} c$, $r_1 \prec r_2$ means that rule r_1 prevails over rule r_2 in situations where both fire and they are in conflict.

Defeaters play a peculiar role, as they cannot lead to any conclusion but are used to defeat some rules by producing evidence to the contrary. Thus, defeaters are suitable to model the termination of the persistence of obligations [8]. Consider Example 5:

$$\text{inv}_{init} : \text{invoice} \Rightarrow O^{a,\pi}_{pr} \text{pay} \otimes O^p \text{pay\_fine} \qquad\qquad \text{inv}_{term} : \text{pay} \rightsquigarrow \neg O^{a,\pi}_{pr} \text{pay}$$

Here, compliance is the only condition that terminates the obligation to pay: if not complied with, the obligation in fact persists beyond the deadline (we have still to pay), so failing to meet the deadline is used to signal a violation and trigger a sanction.

Normal Forms. We introduce transformations of a PCL representation of a normative system to produce a normal form of the same (NPCL). The purpose of a normal form is to "clean up" the PCL representation of a normative system, to identify formal properties, e.g., loopholes, inconsistencies, ..., and to make hidden conditions explicit. We first describe a mechanism, based on [6], to derive new conditions by merging together existing normative clauses. Then, we examine the problem of redundancies, and we give a condition to identify and remove redundancies from the formal normative specification. Finally, we discuss how to solve possible conflicts between deontic provisions.

Merging Norms. One of the features of the logic of violations is to take two rules, or norms, and merge them into a new clause.

Consider a norm like (Γ and Δ are sets of premises) $\Gamma \Rightarrow O^m A$. If we have that the violation of $O^m A$ is part of the premises of another norm, for example, $\Delta, \neg A \Rightarrow O^p C$, then the latter must be a good candidate as reparative obligation of the former:

$$\frac{\Gamma \Rightarrow O^m A \qquad \Delta, \neg A \Rightarrow O^p C}{\Gamma, \Delta \Rightarrow O^m A \otimes O^p C}$$

This reads as follows: given two policies such that one is a conditional obligation ($\Gamma \Rightarrow O^m A$) and the antecedent of second contains the negation of the propositional content of the consequent of the first ($\Delta, \neg A \Rightarrow O^p C$), then the latter is a reparative obligation of the former. Their interplay makes them two related norms so that they cannot be viewed anymore as independent. Therefore we can combine them to obtain an expression (i.e., $\Gamma, \Delta \Rightarrow O^m A \otimes O^p C$) that exhibits the *explicit reparative obligation* of the second norm with respect to the first.

Let X, Y, Z be deontic operators. The following is the general rule for merging norms based on [6,2]:

$$\frac{\Gamma \Rightarrow Xa \otimes (\bigotimes_{i=1}^{n} Yb_i) \otimes Zc \qquad \Delta, \neg b_1, \ldots, \neg b_n \Rightarrow Zd}{\Gamma, \Delta \Rightarrow Xa \otimes (\bigotimes_{i=1}^{n} Yb_i) \otimes Zd} \tag{1}$$

Removing Redundancies. It is possible to combine rules in slightly different ways, and in some cases the meaning of the rules resulting from such operations is already covered by other rules. In other cases the rules resulting from the merging operation are generalisations of the rules used to produce them, consequently, the original rules are no longer needed in the specifications. To deal with this issue we introduce the notion of subsumption between rules. A rule subsumes a second rule when the behaviour of the second rule is implied by the first rule. For example, let us consider the rules

$$r : Invoice \Rightarrow O^{a,\pi}_{pr} Pay7Days \otimes O^p PayInterest \qquad r' : Invoice, \neg Pay7Days \Rightarrow O^{a,\pi}_{n-pr} PayInterest.$$

The first rule says that after the seller sends the invoice the buyer has the achievement, persistent and preemptive obligation to pay within one week, otherwise immediately after the violation the buyer has to pay the principal plus the interest. Thus we have the primary obligation $O^{a,\pi}_{pr} Pay7Days$, whose violation is repaired by the secondary obligation $O^p PayInterest$. According to the second rule, given the same set of circumstances *Invoice* and $\neg Pay7Days$ we have the achievement, persistent and non-preemptive obligation $O^{a,\pi}_{n-pr} PayInterest$. However, (a) the primary obligation of r' obtains when we have a violation of the primary obligation of r; (b) after the obligation $O^{a,\pi}_{pr} Pay7Days$ is violated, complying with the secondary obligation $O^p PayInterest$ of r entails complying with the primary obligation $O^{a,\pi}_{n-pr} PayInterest$ of r' (but not vice versa); (c) hence, r is more general than r', and so the latter can be discarded.

In what follows, Definition 4 characterizes subsumption (which refers to Definitions 1, 2, and 3 to establish when the compliance conditions for an $\otimes$-expression cover the compliance conditions of another $\otimes$-expression).

Definition 1. *Let* $X, Y \in \{O^{a,\pi}_{pr}, O^{a,\pi}_{n-pr}, O^{a,\tau}_{pr}, O^{a,\tau}_{n-pr}, O^m, O^p\}$. *Then,* $Y \sqsubseteq X$ *iff*

  (i) if $Y = O^{a,\pi}_{pr}$, *then* $X \in \{O^{a,\pi}_{pr}, O^{a,\pi}_{n-pr}, O^{a,\tau}_{pr}, O^{a,\tau}_{n-pr}, O^m, O^p\}$;

  (ii) if $Y = O^{a,\pi}_{n-pr}$, *then* $X \in \{O^{a,\pi}_{n-pr}, O^{a,\tau}_{n-pr}, O^m, O^p\}$;

  (iii) if $Y = O^{a,\tau}_{pr}$, *then* $X \in \{O^{a,\pi}_{pr}, O^{a,\pi}_{n-pr}, O^{a,\tau}_{pr}, O^{a,\tau}_{n-pr}, O^m, O^p\}$;

  (iv) if $Y = O^{a,\tau}_{n-pr}$, *then* $X \in \{O^{a,\pi}_{n-pr}, O^{a,\tau}_{n-pr}, O^m, O^p\}$;

  (v) if $Y = O^m$, *then* $X = O^m$;

  (vi) if $Y = O^p$, *then* $X \in \{O^p, O^m\}$.

Definition 2. *Let* Xa *be a deontic literal and* Y *any deontic operator. If* $X = \neg Y$, X *is a* negative operator; *if* $X = Y$, *it is a* positive operator.

Definition 3. *Let* $A = \otimes^m_{i=1} Xa_i$ *and* $B = \otimes^n_{i=1} Yb_i$ *be two* $\otimes$-*expressions. Then,* A *deontically includes* B *iff* $m = n$, *and for each* Xa_i, Yb_i *(1)* $a_i = b_i$, *and (2) if* X *and* Y *are positive operators, then* $Y \sqsubseteq X$.

Definition 4. *Let* $r_1 : \Gamma \Rightarrow A \otimes B \otimes C$ *and* $r_2 : \Delta \Rightarrow D$ *be two rules, where* $A = \otimes^m_{i=1} Xa_i$, $B = \otimes^n_{i=1} Yb_i$ *and* $C = \otimes^p_{i=1} Zc_i$. *Then* r_1 *subsumes* r_2 *iff*

1. $\Gamma = \Delta$ *and* A *deontically includes* D; *or*
2. $\Gamma \cup \{\neg a_1, \ldots, \neg a_m\} = \Delta$ *and* B *deontically includes* D; *or*
3. $\Gamma \cup \{\neg b_1, \ldots, \neg b_n\} = \Delta$ *and* $A \otimes \otimes^{k \leq p}_{i=0} c_i$ *deontically includes* D.

Consider, e.g., the obligation $B = O_{n-pr}^{a,\tau}b$. If another obligation A is equal to B, compliance conditions for both are trivially the same. If A is either $O_{n-pr}^{a,\pi}b$, $O^m b$, or $O^p b$, A deontically includes B, because, if both are in force, the compliance of A implies the compliance of B. However, notice that if A is a preemptive achievement obligation, we have no guarantee that its compliance supports the compliance of B: indeed, b could have been obtained before A and B were in force, which is enough for fulfilling only A.

Solving Conflicts. Conflicts often arise in normative systems. However, we have to determine whether we have genuine conflicts between ⊗-expressions or whether such ⊗-expressions admit states where all can be complied with. Suppose that $A = O^p a \otimes O^m b$ and $B = O_{pr}^{a,\pi} \neg a \otimes O^m \neg b$ are in force. The secondary obligations of A and B are in contradiction but their primary obligations do not necessarily lead to a joint non-compliance: if it is now forbidden to pay, and it is obligatory to pay by tomorrow, I can comply with both obligations by simply paying tomorrow.

Therefore, we have first to identify what ⊗-expressions do conflict with one another. First of all, let us define when two single obligations are in conflict:

Definition 5. *Let l, Xl, and Y be a literal, a deontic literal, and a positive operator, respectively. The complement $\sim l$ is $\neg p$ if $l = p$, and p if $l = \neg p$. The complement $\sim Xl$ is defined as follows:*

- *If $Xl = Yl$, $\sim Xl = \{Zp | Z$ is positive, $p = \sim l$, either $Z \sqsubseteq Y$ or $Y \sqsubseteq Z\} \cup \{\neg Zq | Z = Y, q = l\}$;*
- *If $Xl = \neg Yp$, $\sim Xl = \{Zq | Z$ is positive, $Z = Y, q = l\}$.*

Definition 6 states under what conditions two ⊗-expressions are in conflict.

Definition 6. *Let $A = \bigotimes_{i=1}^m Xa_i$ be an ⊗-expression. Then, $\sim A = \{B = \bigotimes_{i=1}^n Yb_i | m = n, \forall Xa_i, Yb_i : Xa_i = \sim Yb_i\}$.*

Given a theory consisting of a set of rules R, a set S of facts (literals and deontic literals), and a superiority relation, we can use the inference mechanism of Defeasible Logic to compute, in time linear to the size of the theory, the set of its conclusions. This implies to solve genuine conflicts by resorting to the superiority relation over the rules. Once we have defined when two ⊗-expressions are in conflict (Definition 6), we can simply use the same reasoning mechanism described in [2].

Normalisation Process. The PCL normal form of a normative system provides a representation of normative specifications in a format that can be used to check the compliance of a process. This consists of the following steps:

1. Starting from a formal representation of the explicit clauses of a set of normative specifications we generate all the implicit conditions that can be derived from the normative system by applying the merging mechanism of PCL.
2. We can clean the resulting representation by throwing away all redundant rules according to the notion of subsumption.
3. Finally we detect and solve normative conflicts.

In general the process at step 2 must be done several times in the appropriate order as described above. The normal form of a set of rules in PCL is the fixed-point of the above constructions. A normative system contains only finitely many rules and each rule has finitely many elements. Notice that the operation on which the construction is defined is monotonic [6], so by set theory results the fixed-point exists and is unique.

4   Process Modeling

A business process model (BPM) describes the tasks to be executed (and the order in which they are executed) to fulfill some objectives of a business. A language for BPM usually has two main elements: tasks and connectors. Tasks correspond to activities to be performed by actors and connectors describe the relationships between tasks: a minimal set of connectors consists of sequence (a task is performed after another task), parallel –AND-split and AND-join– (tasks are to be executed in parallel), and choice – (X)OR-split and (X)OR-join– (at least (most) one task in a set of task must be executed).

Execution Semantics. The execution semantics of the control flow aspect of a BPM is defined using token-passing mechanisms, as in Petri Nets. The definitions used here extend the execution semantics of [9] with semantic annotations in the form of effects and their meaning.

A process model is seen as a graph with nodes of various types –a single start and end node, task nodes, XOR split/join nodes, and parallel split/join nodes– and directed edges (expressing sequentiality in execution). The number of incoming (outgoing) edges are restricted as follows: start node 0 (1), end node 1 (0), task node 1 (1), split node 1 ($>$1), and join node $>$1 (1). The location of all tokens, referred to as a *marking*, manifests the state of a process execution. An execution of the process starts with a token on the outgoing edge of the start node and no other tokens in the process, and ends with one token on the incoming edge of the end node and no tokens elsewhere. Task nodes are executed when a token on the incoming link is consumed and a token on the outgoing link is produced. The execution of an XOR (Parallel) split node consumes the token on its incoming edge and produces a token on one (all) of its outgoing edges, whereas an XOR (Parallel) join node consumes a token on one (all) of its incoming edges and produces a token on its outgoing edge.

Annotation of Processes. The starting point of [5] was the methodology proposed by [10] where the task of a process are annotated with the (i) the artifacts or effects of executing and (ii) the rules describing the obligations for the process, where the rules are expressed in PCL. As for the semantic annotations, the vocabulary is presented as a set of predicates P. There is a set of process variables (x and y in Fig. 1), over which logical statements can be made, in the form of literals involving these variables. The task nodes can be annotated using *effects* which are conjunctions of literals using the process variables. If executed, a task changes the state of the world according to its effect: every literal mentioned by the effect is true in the resulting world; if a literal l was true before, and is not contradicted by the effect, then it is still true. We assume that effects in parallel tasks do not contradict each other.

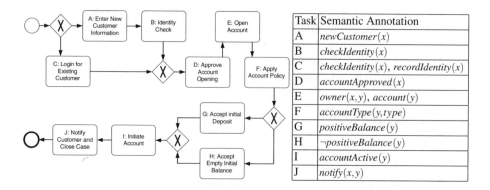

Fig. 1. Example account opening process in private banking, and task annotations

An example of the rules for the process in Figure 1 is "All new customers must be scanned against provided databases for identity checks" (this rule is taken from the Australian *Anti-Money Laundering and Counter-Terrorism Financing Act 2006*)

$$r_1 : newCustomer(x) \Rightarrow O_{pr}^{a,\tau} checkIdentity(x)$$

The predicate *newCustomer*(x) is such that if x is a new customer, we have the obligation to check the data against provided databases. The resulting obligation is non-persistent, i.e., the identity check must be made immediately after we discover that x is a new customer. In addition the obligation is preemptive: if for some reasons the check was already previously performed there is no need to perform it again.

Compliance Checking. Our aim in the compliance checking is to figure out (a) which obligations will definitely appear when executing the process, and (b) which of those obligations may not be fulfilled. PCL constraint expressions for a normative system define a behavioural and state space which can be used to analyse how well different behaviour execution paths of a process comply with the PCL constraints. In [5] we have shown how to adapt the algorithm to check compliance proposed in [3] to take into account the rich ontology of norm types we have discussed in the previous sections. The introduction of the types of obligations allows us to model not only semantic compliance (compliance of the effects of the tasks against a regulation) but also structural compliance, that is, for example, to check the order in which the tasks in a process are executed, and whether two tasks can be executed it the same process.

To check compliance we use the following procedure (for the details see [5]):

Step 1. We traverse the graph describing the process and we identify the sets of effects (sets of literals) for all the tasks (nodes) in the process according to the execution semantics outlined in Section 4.

Step 2. For each task we use the set of effects for that particular task to determine the obligations triggered by the execution of the task. This means that effects of a task are used as a set of facts, and we compute the conclusions of the defeasible theory resulting from the effects and the PCL rules annotating the process. In the same way we accumulate effects, we also accumulate (undischarged) obligations from one task in the process to the task following it in the process.

Step 3. For each task we compare the effects of the tasks and the obligations accumulated up to the task. If an obligation is fulfilled by a task, we discharge the obligation, if it is violated we signal this violation. Finally if an obligation is not fulfilled nor violated, we keep the obligation in the stack of obligations and propagate the obligation to the successive tasks.

5   From Processes to Rules

The aim of this section is twofold. First we want to show that PCL can be used to express conditions on order of the tasks, the structure of the process, including thus common process control flow patterns, as well as other complex conditions about relationships among tasks in a process. In this way, we can use the same language to express the conditions about the effects or artifacts of a process as well as its tasks and we can combine the two to obtain a more expressive formalism able to capture complex compliance requirements. Second, resorting to the same language to express control flows and compliance requirements allows one to use an appropriate rule engine for multiple functions; in particular, we can check the compliance of a process at design-time, and monitoring compliance at run-time. Actually, we can push this one step forward, as the process can be executed directly by the rule engine, thus the monitoring of compliance coincides with the execution of the process. The advantage of this approach is that a business analyst can continue to model a process in familiar standard graphical languages (e.g., BPMN, EPC, Petri-Nets, YAWL, ...), and integrate it with the compliance requirements, and then the combination of the two is executed directly by one engine (the rule engine). This minimises risks of "lost in translation" issues that occur when both the graphical model and the compliance model have to be translated into an execution language for the (common) execution of the two. The use of executable specifications, as in PCL where the rules can be executed directly by a rule engine like SPINdle [11], greatly reduces these risks. On the other hand the mapping of control flow patterns and other complex constraints offers the opportunity for a fully declarative language for business process modeling. In the remaining of this section we illustrate this idea and we show how to capture the most common and basic control flow patterns. Notice that the technique used does not relay on any specific business process language.

To capture control flows and other complex relationships among the tasks in a process we extend the language of PCL with a set of propositional letters to denote the tasks; in what follows we will use $t, t_1, t_2, \ldots$ to refer to them, and these propositional letters correspond to the names/ids of the tasks in a process. For the execution of the process, these names can correspond to calls to the procedures that implement the tasks. In addition, for the representation of OR-split, we need to introduce auxiliary propositional letters corresponding to structural nodes in a process model (i.e., connectors).

Sequence. A sequence means that tasks are executed one after the other. The standard execution pattern for a sequence operator in process language is that one task is executed immediately after another. Thus the sequence connection in Figure 2 between tasks t_1

and t_2 is that task t_2 is executed after task t_1. The relationship between the two task can be modeled by the rule

Fig. 2. Sequence operator

$$t_1 \Rightarrow O^P t_2$$

After task t_1 has been executed, the literal t_1 triggers the rule that puts the punctual obligation $O^P t_2$ in the stack of obligations to be fulfilled at the next step. Thus, the failure to perform task t_2 in the step following the step in which t_1 completed results in a violation and thus we have a non-compliant execution trace.

After. The pattern after, modeled by the rule schema

$$t_1 \Rightarrow O^{a,\pi}_{n-pr} t_2,$$

is a variant of sequence. The idea is that after task t_1 we have the obligation to achieve task t_2, but not necessarily in the step immediately after the step in which t_1 has been executed. It is worth noting that in this case we have to use a non-preemptive obligation to avoid that an execution of t_2 before t_1 fulfils this obligation. Compare this with the co-occurrence condition below.

Parallel tasks: AND-split, AND-join. An AND-split starts several sub-processes to be executed in parallel. The condition encoding this pattern is modeled by a set of rules,

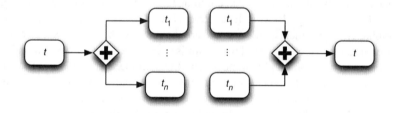

Fig. 3. AND-split and AND-join

$$t \Rightarrow O^P t_1 \quad \ldots \quad t \Rightarrow O^P t_n$$

all of which have the same antecedent, the task t whose completed execution triggers the split. The conclusions of such rules are punctual obligations for the tasks $t_1, \ldots, t_n$ starting the sub-processes to be executed in parallel. This means that the tasks $t_1, \ldots, t_n$ are inserted in the stack of obligations to be executed in the step after task t.

Similarly, an AND-join requires the synchronisation of a number of sub-processes before proceeding to the next task. Accordingly, an AND-join is captured by the rule

$$t_1, \ldots, t_n \Rightarrow O^P t$$

This rule needs all the antecedents to hold to fire, and to conclude the punctual obligation $O^P t$. Hence, all last tasks $t_1, \ldots, t_n$ of the sub-processes to be synchronised have to be completed before we move to the task after the merge of the sub-processes.

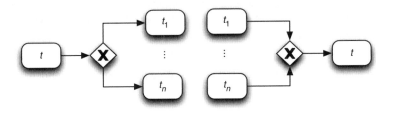

Fig. 4. (X)OR-split and OR-join

Choice: (X)OR split, OR join. An OR-split is intended to capture sub-processes where one has a choice on how to continue a process. For the representation of an OR-split pattern in PCL, we have to use the auxiliary propositional letter. For each OR-split connector in a diagram we establish a one-to-one mapping between the connector and the auxiliary propositional letter. Then the set of rules required to model this pattern is

$$t \Rightarrow O^P(ORsplitID) \qquad t_1 \Rightarrow ORsplitID \quad \ldots \quad t_n \Rightarrow ORsplitID$$

The first rule on the left side tells us that the completion of task t trigger the obligation to fulfill the obligation for $ORsplitID$, where $ORsplitID$ is the propositional letter of the corresponding OR-connector, and the obligation is in the stack of obligations to be fulfilled in the step immediately after the step where we have t. The other rules do not generate normative conclusion, but just factual conclusions. Thus, the meaning of the first rule is that the completion of task t_1 (which we assume to be the first task in one of the outgoing sub-processes after the OR-split) fulfills the obligation, or in other terms that $ORsplitID$ holds.

For an XOR, in addition we need, the rules

$$t_i \Rightarrow \neg t_j \quad i \neq j, 1 \leq i, j \leq n$$

which state that if t_i holds then t_j does not hold, thus it is not possible to have a situation where both t_i and t_j hold. As a consequence, only one of the alternative sub-processes can be executed. This method requires to generate n^2 additional rules for each XOR-split. An alternative encoding of XOR-split, in particular when a default choice is present, is to use a rule with reparative deontic conclusions, thus

$$t \Rightarrow O^P t_1 \otimes O^P t_2 \otimes \cdots \otimes O^P t_n$$

According to the rule above, the best option after t is t_1, but if t_1 is not performed, then the second best option is t_2 and so on. Thus, the above rule determines a total order on the preferences of the alternative choices in an XOR-split. In addition it is possible to combine the above two techniques, so we can have a rule like $t \Rightarrow O^P t_i \otimes O^P ORsplitID$. This gives a default choice over t_i but no preferences over the others sub-processes:

$$t_1 \Rightarrow O^P t \quad \ldots \quad t_n \Rightarrow O^P t$$

Absence. The absence is the condition that establishes that one task cannot be anymore scheduled in the process if another task already happened in the process. This condition can be represented by the rule

$$t_1 \Rightarrow O^m \neg t_2$$

that uses a maintenance prohibition (i.e., $O\neg$) stating that the task t_2 cannot happen after the execution of task t_1.

Co-occurrence. This pattern is designed to check that two tasks, let us say t_i and t_j, occur in the process. This can expressed as follows: if task t_i happens in the process, this should also include task t_j. The idea is similar to the after pattern; the difference is that in after the second task (for the sake of argument, t_j) should occur in a step successive to that including t_i. For the co-occurrence pattern, this restriction is lifted so task t_j can appear anywhere in the process. To express this we use a non-preemptive obligation. Accordingly, the pattern is modeled by

$$t_i \Rightarrow O_{pr}^{a,\pi} t_j \qquad\qquad t_j \Rightarrow O_{pr}^{a,\pi} t_i$$

The first rule on the left says that t_j must occur when t_i occurs, and the second that t_i must occur when t_j does. Thus, depending on the situation, one can use either one of the two rules or both. In case we have only the first rule, an execution trace is non compliant when we have t_i but not t_j, but non-compliance does not occur when we only have t_j (similarly, for the second rule). If both rules are in force, then a trace is compliant if either both tasks are in the trace or none is.

Conditional Occurence. With the previous patters we have examined situations where if one task is included in an execution trace so do other tasks. With this pattern we consider a subtle difference: we consider the case where one task has to be included if another one has to be included as well. This pattern is described by the rule

$$O^x t_1 \Rightarrow O^x t_2$$

The difference with the other patterns is that in the antecedent we have an obligation instead of a factual premise. Most of the considerations regarding the co-occurrence pattern apply to this patter as well; but there is one difference. Suppose that the rule fires, thus we have the obligation of performing task t_1. The obligation to perform task t_2 still exists even if for some reasons task t_1 is not done (for example, let us say there is a situation where it is possible not to execute t_1 provided some compensatory actions are taken).

In Between and Discharge. The aim of this pattern is to model the condition that one task must be executed after another one but before a third one, for example, that task t_j is executed between tasks t_i and t_j. In PCL this can be expressed as

$$t_i \Rightarrow O_{n-tr}^{a,\pi} t_j \qquad t_k \leadsto \neg O^{a,\pi} t_j \qquad t_k \Rightarrow \neg t_j$$

The first rule on the left side is just the rule for the after pattern. The second rule in the middle terminates the obligation to achieve t_j when t_k is performed, in addition the performance of t_k signals that t_j has not been executed. Thus if task t_j is not executed in between the other two task, we have an unfulfilled obligation resulting in a non-compliant situation. Please compare the idea of this pattern with the discussion about deadlines and whether obligations persist after the deadlines.

Loops, Hooks and Loop Termination. Most BPM notations allow us to represent loops (reoccurring sub-processes). PCL is able to represent loops as well, with rules like

$$t_i \Rightarrow O^{a,\tau}_{n-pr} t_i$$

or more in general with rules such as

$$t_i \Rightarrow O^x t_j$$

where t_j is in the dependence graph of t_i.

To avoid infinite loops, a loop termination condition can be expressed by a rule

$$p \rightsquigarrow \neg O^x t_i$$

where t_i is a task involved in a loop (we avoid the discussion about fairness conditions for p and fairness conditions for loop termination for tasks inside OR-split blocks inside loop blocks).

An interesting rule is

$$t_1 \Rightarrow O^m t_2$$

This rule requires task t_2 to be execute in every step following a step where task t_1 successfully completed; the obligation generated by the rule is a maintenance condition. The intuition is that t_2 is a hook task, that is a task that must be executed every time the business process activates another task.

6   Summary and Related Work

Given two tasks t_1, t_2 of a process we can use the types of obligations defined in Section 2 to describe relationships between these two tasks (the types of obligations provide a comprehensive classification of the possible obligations). In particular we have seen that some of them give rise to natural and common control flow patterns in business processes, in particular, even if we limit ourselves to basic relationships, we can express patterns like those in Table 1.

In addition we can represent many more patterns including those that are difficult to express in standard BPM languages, for example,

Table 1. Flow patterns

$t_i \Rightarrow O^p t_j$	sequence
$t_i \Rightarrow O^{a,\pi}_{n-pr} t_j$	after
$t_i \Rightarrow O^{a,\pi}_{pr} t_j$	co-occurrence
$t_i \Rightarrow O^m t_j$	process hook

conditions using tasks from different branches of a process (e.g., in an OR-block), and we can mix information about tasks (task literals) and data conditions. Thus, it seems to us that PCL offers a rich, compact and holistic framework for business process compliance in such a way as we also can use a rule engine for PCL as a process engine. To understand the full extent of the proposed approach we plan a comprehensive comparison with control flow patterns [12], data patterns [13], and the declarative patterns of [14].

A number of works have been devoted to compliance in control modelling. [15] presents the logical language PENELOPE, that provides the ability to verify temporal constraints arising from compliance requirements on effected business processes. [16] develops a method to check compliance between object lifecycles that provide reference models for data artifacts e.g. insurance claims and business process models. [17] provides temporal rule patterns for regulatory policies, although the objective of this work is to facilitate event monitoring rather than the usage of the patterns for support of design time activities. Furthermore, [18] presented an architecture for supporting Sarbanes-Oxley Internal Controls, which include functions such as workflow modeling, active enforcement, workflow auditing, as well as anomaly detection. [19] studies the performance of business contract based on their formal representation. [20] seeks to provide support for assessing the correctness of business contracts represented formally through a set of commitments. The reasoning is based on value of various states of commitment as perceived by cooperative agents. Also, there have been recently some efforts towards support for process modelling against compliance requirements. [10] proposes an approach based on control tags to visualize internal controls on process models. [21] takes a similar approach of annotating and checking process models against compliance rules, although the visual rule language (BPSL) does not directly address the deontic notions providing compliance requirements.

Many works proposed declarative languages to model business processes. [14,22] used a language based on linear temporal logic to model processes to check conformance by symbolic model checking, [23] show how to use Concurrent Transaction Logic to represent the structure of of workflows, while [24] advance a prolog-like language for the same scope. The use of logic and rule based languages to describe business processes is not new. However, most works are restricted to limited patters of tasks, and almost no work uses the same for data (artifact) requirements, nor it address deontic concerns and is able to handle violations and possible compensations for violations.

Acknowledgement

NICTA is funded by the Australian Government as represented by the Department of Broadband, Communications and the Digital Economy and the Australian Research Council through the ICT Centre of Excellence program and Queensland Government.

References

1. Carmo, J., Jones, A.: Deontic logic and contrary to duties. In: Gabbay, D., Guenther, F. (eds.) Handbook of Philosophical Logic, 2nd edn., pp. 265–343. Kluwer, Dordrecht (2002)
2. Governatori, G.: Representing business contracts in RuleML. International Journal of Cooperative Information Systems 14, 181–216 (2005)
3. Governatori, G., Rotolo, A.: An algorithm for business process compliance. In: Sartor, G. (ed.) Jurix 2008, pp. 186–191. IOS Press, Amsterdam (2008)
4. Governatori, G., Hulstijn, J., Riveret, R., Rotolo, A.: Characterising deadlines in temporal modal defeasible logic. In: Orgun, M.A., Thornton, J. (eds.) AI 2007. LNCS (LNAI), vol. 4830, pp. 486–496. Springer, Heidelberg (2007)

5. Governatori, G., Rotolo, A.: A conceptually rich model of business process compliance. In: Link, S., Ghose, A. (eds.) APCCM 2010, CRPIT, ACS (2010)
6. Governatori, G., Rotolo, A.: Logic of violations: A Gentzen system for reasoning with contrary-to-duty obligations. Australasian Journal of Logic 4, 193–215 (2006)
7. Antoniou, G., Billington, D., Governatori, G., Maher, M.J.: Representation results for defeasible logic. ACM Transactions on Computational Logic 2, 255–287 (2001)
8. Governatori, G., Rotolo, A.: Changing legal systems: Legal abrogations and annulments in defeasible logic. The Logic Journal of IGPL 18, 157–194 (2010)
9. Vanhatalo, J., Völzer, H., Leymann, F.: Faster and more focused control-flow analysis for business process models through sese decomposition. In: Krämer, B.J., Lin, K.-J., Narasimhan, P. (eds.) ICSOC 2007. LNCS, vol. 4749, pp. 43–55. Springer, Heidelberg (2007)
10. Sadiq, S.W., Governatori, G., Namiri, K.: Modeling control objectives for business process compliance. [26] 149–164
11. Lam, H.-P., Governatori, G.: The making of SPINdle. In: Governatori, G., Hall, J., Paschke, A. (eds.) RuleML 2009. LNCS, vol. 5858, pp. 315–322. Springer, Heidelberg (2009)
12. van der Aalst, W.M., ter Hofstede, A.H.M., Kiepuszewski, B., Barros, A.P.: Workflow patterns. Distributed and Parallel Databases 14, 5–51 (2003)
13. Russell, N., ter Hofstede, A.H.M., Edmond, D., van der Aalst, W.M.P.: Workflow data patterns: Identification, representation and tool support. In: Delcambre, L.M.L., Kop, C., Mayr, H.C., Mylopoulos, J., Pastor, Ó. (eds.) ER 2005. LNCS, vol. 3716, pp. 353–368. Springer, Heidelberg (2005)
14. Pesic, M., van der Aalst, W.M.P.: A declarative approach for flexible business processes management. [25], 169–180
15. Goedertier, S., Vanthienen, J.: Designing compliant business processes with obligations and permissions. [25], 5–14
16. Küster, J.M., Ryndina, K., Gall, H.: Generation of business process models for object life cycle compliance. [26], 165–181
17. Giblin, C., Müller, S., Pfitzmann, B.: From regulatory policies to event monitoring rules: Towards model driven compliance automation. Technical report, IBM Zurich Lab (2006)
18. Agrawal, R., Johnson, C.M., Kiernan, J., Leymann, F.: Taming compliance with Sarbanes-Oxley internal controls using database technology. In: Liu, L., Reuter, A., Whang, K.Y., Zhang, J. (eds.) ICDE, p. 92. IEEE Computer Society Press, Los Alamitos (2006)
19. Farrell, A.D.H., Sergot, M.J., Sallé, M., Bartolini, C.: Using the event calculus for tracking the normative state of contracts. International Journal of Cooperative Information Systems 14, 99–129 (2005)
20. Desai, N., Narendra, N.C., Singh, M.P.: Checking correctness of business contracts via commitments. In: Proc. AAMAS 2008, pp. 787–794 (2008)
21. Liu, Y., Müller, S., Xu, K.: A static compliance-checking framework for business process models. IBM Systems Journal 46, 335–362 (2007)
22. Rozinat, A., van Der Aalst, W.M.: Conformance checking of processes based on monitoring real behavior. Information Systems 33, 64–95 (2008)
23. Roman, D., Kifer, M.: Reasoning about the behaviour of semantic web services with concurrent transaction logic. In: VLDB, pp. 627–638 (2007)
24. Gregory, S., Paschali, M.: A prolog-based language for workflow programming. In: Murphy, A.L., Vitek, J. (eds.) COORDINATION 2007. LNCS, vol. 4467, pp. 56–75. Springer, Heidelberg (2007)
25. Alonso, G., Dadam, P., Rosemann, M. (eds.): BPM 2007. LNCS, vol. 4714. Springer, Heidelberg (2007)
26. Eder, J., Dustdar, S. (eds.): BPM Workshops 2006. LNCS, vol. 4103. Springer, Heidelberg (2006)

Application of an Ontology-Based and Rule-Based Model to Selected Economic Crimes: Fraudulent Disbursement and Money Laundering

Jaroslaw Bak, Czeslaw Jedrzejek, and Maciej Falkowski

Institute of Control and Information Engineering,
Poznan University of Technology,
M. Sklodowskiej-Curie Sqr. 5, 60-965 Poznan, Poland
firstname.lastname@put.poznan.pl

Abstract. We present an ontology-based and rules-based model of simple, but very typical, economic crimes, namely fraudulent disbursement in combination with money laundering. The extension of the previously proposed ontology model, called the "minimal model", is used to capture the mechanism of the example cases. The conceptual minimal model consists of eight layers of concepts, structured in order to use available data on facts to uncover relations. In comparison to our previous work in which rules were restricted to criminal roles in only one company, where the crime originated, this work is able to capture roles and consequently criminal sanctions throughout the complete chain of conspiring companies. We are able to discover crime activity options (roles of particular type of owners, managers, directors and chairmen) using concepts, appropriate relations and rules. However, due to the varying size of incriminated companies the number of levels of responsibility ranges from one to three, that causes significant increase of necessary rules. These roles are phrased in the language of penal code sanctions. The roles of persons in the crime are mapped into a set of sanctions. We use the Semantic Data Library (SDL) with Jess engine as a reasoning tool to query and infer about crime scheme and sanctions. We present results achieved with our minimal model ontology. Prospects on future capabilities of our tools are presented.

Keywords: Financial crime, money laundering, minimal model ontology, reasoning, penal code.

1 Introduction

Economic crimes are particularly difficult to model [1] and code into an expert system. For example, fraudsters use many types of schemes, techniques and transactions to achieve their goals, so it has seemed impossible to construct a simple conceptual model of any generality. Only recently has the integrated use of semantics expressed by means of ontologies and rules achieved the capability of analyzing large practical problems, such as applying reasoning over legal sanctions on the basis of investigation facts and rules appearing in penal codes.

M. Dean et al. (Eds.): RuleML 2010, LNCS 6403, pp. 210–224, 2010.

In the previous work [2, 3, 4] we presented a model of fraudulent disbursement crime, a subset of asset misappropriation crime. In the 2009 survey [5], such a crime constituted two-thirds of all economic crimes. It is often accompanied by money laundering schemes. In this work we apply our approach to the money laundering thread and present further extensions of the fraudulent disbursement model.

Money laundering is more difficult to model and requires more expressive power. Definition of money laundering differs between jurisdictions [6].

The Polish Penal code defines it in a way similar to the UK law as taking any action with property of any form which is either wholly or in part the proceeds of a crime that will disguise the fact that the property is the proceeds of a crime. Here we restrict the notion to engaging in financial transactions to conceal the identity, source, or destination of illegally gained money.

The model is based on the suitable application of an ontology that forms a "minimal layer" - it contains only necessary concepts that follow the logical order of uncovering a crime [2], [3]. The previous model captured the crime mechanism correctly but was lacking some details. These details concerned rules for taking decisions in companies of various sizes and activities related to transactions and whether persons in these companies formally documented their activities.

Significant extensions made in this work make the model much more realistic. The extended ontology makes it possible to differentiate roles of key people in the crime scheme, and map their crimes into a specific set of penal code articles in a more corrected differentiated ways. The paper is organized as follows. Section 2 presents the Semantic Web Technologies and types of rules which are used in our approach. Section 3 describes our money laundering minimal ontology model compatible with the Hydra case. In Section 4 we analyze law based on the Polish penal code, related to money laundering, and we derive rules that define logical activities appearing in the Penal Code based on physical activities. Conclusions and future work are presented in Section 5.

2 Used Technologies

2.1 Semantic Web Technologies

In information technology, an ontology is the working model of objects (entities) and relations in some particular domain of knowledge. Ontology defines domain knowledge (objects and properties) and also should provide operational knowledge on use (how do we use the objects?, what answers can we get?, and how could we query?). In general, the model represents machine readable projection of a larger domain expressed in a formalized language. We follow less general but more practical bottom-up path. We are interested in legal case description we build hierarchy of objects possessing inheritance, along with their properties such as attributes, and restrictions that apply to the class. One may apply rules to support reasoning.

There are various approaches that construct ontologies based of background knowledge (facts). Notable are approaches [7], [8], that from textual description of case facts select applicable factors. Wyner [8] introduced intermediate concepts that allow differentiating between cases. This approach is more general than ours used in this work, as we mostly concentrate on most precise description of a single case. However, we do not limit ourselves with only facts of the case. We consider also possible variants of the case together with their legal implication. In [7] and [8] levels of intermediate concepts were used in a logical relation rather than lattice-theoretic structure.

The minimal model ontology has been developed in language OWL-DL (Web Ontology Language Description Logic) [9] which supports maximum expressive power without loss of decidability and computational completeness. We define rules in SWRL (Semantic Web Rule Language) [10] language, which, introduces undecidability into our ontology but extends the expressivity of OWL supporting the use of ontology axioms in rules. We also use SWRLB language (SWRL Built-ins) [11] to extend SWRL with additional functions. Generally, we use SWRLB Comparisons to compare variables and to put some constraints on them.

Such a model with ontology and rules needs an appropriate reasoner. There are several of them, for example: Pellet [12] and KAON2 [13]. Our data are stored in a relational database, so we have to use a reasoner which supports querying 'on-the-fly' according to defined semantics and with the use of rules. We decided to use Jess (Java Expert System Shell) [14, 15], a reasoner tool with SDL (Semantic Data Library) [16] which is much more efficient than KAON2 (it also enables 'on-the-fly' querying).

We stress that some of the presented facts, for example *ApprovalOfWorkNotDone(?d)*, will be put into the system by a prosecutor or other person connected with an investigation. We also want to mention that all variables appearing in rules which have different names are treated as having different values. To express that we need to use SWRLB constructions (for example: swrlb:equal ('='), swrlb:notEqual ('!='), swrlb:greaterThan ('>') etc.). But for clarity in this paper we do not use them. Rules are written in SWRL-like notation.

2.2   Types of Rules Used in Approach

Rules play a very important role in the layered architecture of the Semantic Web. They are used for freely mixing of property and class expressions which is not allowed in OWL. Generally, rules in the Semantic Web are needed for:

- inferencing about OWL properties and classes,
- mapping ontologies in data integration,
- transforming data from one to another format,
- querying with the use of complex queries based on OWL, SWRL etc. axioms,
- and many more.

Usually, rules are distinguished into deduction rules, production rules, normative rules, reactive rules, defeasible rules, etc. In our approach we apply two kinds of rules: deduction and production rules. We use deduction rules to infer about facts in the knowledge base. They add new implicit statements about connections between persons, documents, money transfers and legal sanctions. According to them we can discover crime scheme and suggest legal sanctions for people involved in crime. These rules are defined in SWRL language with the use of SWRL Built-ins. Deduction rules are also used for querying Jess engine's working memory. Query rule contains only body part and after hybrid reasoning (executed by SDL with Jess) activations of this rule are obtained as query results [16].

Production rules are used for mapping between ontology axioms (properties and classes) and data stored in a relational database. These rules are defined in Jess language. Their creation is supported by the SDL-GUI module which is the part of the SDL tool. Mapping utilizes simple rule that every "essential" axiom (property or class) has defined appropriate SQL query for mapping. "Essential" means that the instance of this axiom can not be obtained from the taxonomy or rules. It can be obtained only in the direct way (as the result of the SQL query). For example, for the hierarchy of classes *Institution->Company->Buyer*, the *Buyer* class is an "essential" concept, because it is at the bottom of the hierarchy (and there is no rule which defines *Buyer* instance).

We assume that the ontology which is used is properly constructed and defined (the taxonomy is computed and classified; without inconsistencies). The taxonomies of ontology classes and properties are classified by SDL-GUI with Pellet 2.1.1 and presented. User can define SQL query on calculated taxonomies (so the ontology has to be consistent). During reasoning, production rules generate SQL queries and then SDL query relational database. Results are added as RDF triples into Jess working memory.

3 Fraudulent Disbursement and Money Laundering Minimal Ontology Model

The discussion of state-of-the-art legal ontologies and details of our approach has been discussed in [4] and will not be repeated here. Our so-called minimal ontology comes from experience of detailed analysis of descriptions, indictments and sentences of around 10 criminal cases. The most clean case of fraudulent disbursement is so-called *Hydra Case*.

In this case the Chief executive officer (CEO) of company A (*Hydra*) subcontracted construction work. The work is then consecutively subcontracted through a chain of phony companies B, C, and D (Hermes, Dex, Mobex). Each company is getting a commission for money laundering and falsifies documents stating that the contracted work had been done. Actually, what was to be done as "subcontracted construction work" company A did itself.

At the end of the chain, the owner of a single person company D attempts to withdraw cash, and there is a suspicion that this cash reaches the management of company A "under the table". The crime scheme of the Hydra case is presented in Figure 1.

In one of the previous work [3] we considered a simplified version of the Hydra case, such that only the single level of authorization existed. Basically, it meant that once an approval of the construction job was made, the payment for this work followed without further authorization. Consequently, only one person in company A, the CEO was responsible for the crime.

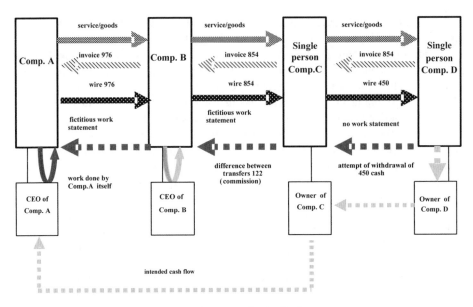

Fig. 1. A basic scheme for the Hydra case

Our ontology is crafted to a task rather that attempting to describe the whole conceivable space of concepts and relations (top ontologies). The methodology consists of several steps:

1. Design of a hierarchical data representation with minimal ontology, constructed in the sequence of uncovering a crime scheme. This means using only necessary concepts that follow in the logical order of uncovering a crime. In the first stage, goods/services transfer data is analyzed with relation to 3 basic flows: money, invoices, and documents (i.e., confirming that the service or goods have been delivered - particularly important for fuel mafia type of crimes). In addition, responsible or relevant people within companies are associated with particular illegal activities.
2. Provision of a framework in which the graph building process and queries are executed.
3. Relating answers to queries with crime qualifications.

This approach is limited, but provides an essential model for evidence-building of a very important class of financial crimes: among them acting to do damage to a company and money laundering.

The major features of the minimal ontology model are the following:

- Only facts contributing to evidence or possible sanctions are kept.
- We leave to a human the answer to difficult questions: for example, deciding that the work has not been done. This requires sending an expert to the field, inspection of construction, taking testimonies, finding that a company that

presumably did the job was a straw company, with no experience in construction, having no equipment, etc. In some cases finding out that the work was underpriced or overpriced is very difficult but a critical issue in a case.

- Reduction of possible relations or attributes. Here we give some examples:

    o   In the case of Hydra, in the first stage it is not necessary to deal with the place of construction. The scheme would be a crime no matter where the construction was taking place (for a given jurisdiction). However, this information has to appear in the indictment.
    o   An invoice can be issued or received. We combine these two relations, the only relation for invoices possible in our model. Invoices may be lost or destroyed, and there will be some cases for which these facts will be of importance, and then possibly we would have to enhance the model.

- The knowledge about the case appears explicit as presented by facts, and implicit – such as regular business procedures. Once the payment is approved, it is then executed and we are not interested who actually did it.
  Such an approach of complementing a scenario with "external knowledge" is similar to that taken in Abraxas project [7]. This spares us expressing a trade code in OWL. In some cases fraudulent disbursement could be perpetrated not by management people but by a lower level officers, For example, a payment authorization could by forged, or a payment could be made without an authorization. In this paper we do not consider such fraudulent mechanisms, but they will be included in a future model.

The minimal ontology model design uses the following methodology:

1. First for a given crime typology we ask questions that are parts of crime mechanism hypothesis. These are constructed with the help of legal experts.
2. We then verify the initially assumed ontology against the appropriate cases.
3. Next decision is taken on granularity (core ontology relevant to all financial crimes, domain typology ontology). It is unrealistic to aim at modeling the whole reality (and this precisely was the weakness of many previous approaches, which although general had to chance to achieve practical results). Some details (and corresponding concepts) are dropped at this stage.
4. Since we do not have enough cases, rules are adopted following experts' experience (such as certain money laundering rules, notably red flag thresholds).
5. In future when more typologies are included hierarchy of concepts should be redesigned.

The questions that lay the ground for our model are:

- Between what entities (companies and people) are the transactions?
- What is a record of business activities and bank accounts of these entities?
- What is a record of tax statements of these entities?
- What are subjects of transactions?
- What was the ground for payments?
- What are documents of transactions?

- What is a hierarchy of management in involved companies?
- What is the decision structure and who (meaning positions, not people) authorizes particular decisions (signs relevant documents) within the structure?
- Which persons can be associated with relevant activities (for a given crime mechanism)?
- Who knew about these activities?
- Who could possibly benefit from a crime?
- What are possibly legal sanctions related to a given crime typology?
- Who are accomplices in wrong doing?
- What were the roles of crime perpetrators (organizers, helping parties, straw companies and straw persons)?

The minimal model consists of eight layers that are structured in order of uncovering the facts (Table 1). The above questions were related to top five levels of ontology. We could ask more detailed questions. For example, what is additional information relevant to sanctions (criminal records, relapse into crime after having served a sentence, coercion on some persons by other perpetrators)? In this work such information belongs to levels 7 and 8 of the ontology structure and was not dealt with in the present model.

Table 1. Layers of concepts for analysis of economic crimes

Type	Concern details
1.	General entities as: Companies, Institutions, Single person companies, levels of authorization, documents having legal meaning. Money transfer between companies.
2.	Invoice flow between companies. Tax statements.
3.	Work/Services flow.
4.	Roles of decisive people in companies who accepted work in the chain of command.
5.	Mapping potential roles coming from positions in companies to particular activities resulting in a financial crime.
6.	People not related to companies but being a part of crimes. Other relations of people.
7.	Information about people, e.g., whether they were sentenced in the last 10 years, their criminal connections; school or business etc., connections.
8.	Additional factors (e.g., learning about averted criminal plans).

Previous model contained fraudulent disbursement crime only, so we need to extend the minimal model ontology presented in [2, 3, 4].

A definition of the minimal model in application to financial crimes, expressed in OWL language using the editor Protégé 4.0 is presented in [16].

This ontology has a modular structure and contains the following modules:

- Person.owl, describing persons as social entities and groups of persons,
- Document.owl, specifying the legal meaning of documents and their content,
- LegalProvision, defining legal acts and sanctions,
- Action.owl specifying activities,
- Object.owl describing other entities, i.e. goods (work or service) ,
- MinimalModel.owl defining general concepts and relations of the minimal model, it also contains rules,
- Institution-Organization.owl describing legal entities (rather than dealing with intentions, it is more important to establish who knew about criminal activities, and whether a crime was perpetrated by a group).

In relational database notation, the most important concepts that are currently functional are the following:

Flow (Money Transfer, Invoice, Goods/Service).
Money Transfer (From Entity, To Entity, Method of Transfer, Date, Value, Title of transfer, i.e. for Goods).
Method of Transfer (Electronic transfer, Cash).

As relates to sanctions there are specified by a certain number of rules that define what are conditions of a given crime, what constitutes evidence and how various activities have to combine to be subjected to a particular sanction.

For example, as is stated in many legal theory texts, fraud must be proved by showing that the defendant's actions involved between five to nine [17] separate elements.

It is important to correctly model a sequence of activities in the company structure that lead to decisions and transactions. We will illustrate this on the example of the three-level structure of authorization (this is easy to generalize to more levels, but the intent is to make it compatible with the Hydra case). The chain of activities is the following: in the Hydra case, acceptance of construction work done by B at a given site is first signed by a manager in A responsible for a work supervision at this site (MiddleLevelManager); this is followed by a signature of the higher level manager – a Director of the company responsible for supervision of all sites. A Director may be authorized to accept invoices and order a payment – technically this is and was done by a written authorization on the back of the invoice. The role if the Principal (the top level of authorization, which however, could have not been exercised) was analyzed in detail in [3], where we modeled all possible options of the Principal's behavior.

The Principal might not have known that the work has not been done. However, he was the one who signed the contract for subcontracting and thus could be implicated.

Had the Principal of company A been a person who on the basis of the work acceptance document had ordered the payment of A to B, upon issuance of an invoice by B, he would be directly implicated.

In order to represent elementary activities, we need to formalize:

1. The concept of complex documents.
2. The Hierarchical chain of responsibility in a company.

Our path of extensions of the minimal model goes through models: I, II, III and IV.

Model I concerned only company A with one level of responsibility but already encompassed the mechanism of fraudulent disbursement [2]. Model II [4] handled a three-level (real) structure of authorization level of responsibility in company A. Model III (this work) deals with all companies in a chain with respective levels of responsibility (fraudulent disbursement and money laundering) and concerns 5 top levels of minimal ontology concepts.
Model IV – full case – will contain model III and will encompass all 8 levels of minimal ontology.

Compared to Model II we have to account for that fact that the varying size of incriminated companies, and consequently the number of levels of responsibility ranges from one to three. The size of companies is measured by number of levels of responsibility, and has nothing to do with revenue or the overall number of workers in companies. For the Hydra case, A is a large company (3 levels of responsibility), B and D are medium size companies (2 levels) and C is a small company. The managers appearing in these companies are the Principal (CEO or Owner) – the top level, a Director for Construction (the middle level) and The MiddleLevelManager responsible for a given construction (the bottom level).

Rules related to consecutive concepts are numbered. These rules are extensions of the ones employed in the fraudulent disbursement only crime [4] and new rules related to money laundering.

Several concepts and rules are defined to achieve ability to describe legal documents:

a. ContractDocument – a document that is drawn up between two parties. This ContractDocument is between two companies, and is signed by principals of these companies. The signature on behalf of the company can be individual or joint, depending on the structure of the company.

The following general rules for the ContractDocument are defined (6 rules); we present only 2 examples here:

1. Rule on a contract between a large and a medium company.

```
Document(?d), CompanysPrincipal(?p1), CompanysPrincipal(?p2),
isSignedBy(?d, ?p1), isSignedBy(?d, ?p2)
→
ContractDocument(?d)
```

2. Rule on a contract between two medium companies.

```
Document(?d), MajorOwner(?p1), MajorOwner(?p2), isSignedBy(?d,?p1),
isSignedBy(?d, ?p2), differentFrom(?p1, ?p2)
->
ContractDocument(?d)
```

b. InternalLegalDocument – a document drawn up in the company that may be authorized in stages up to the highest level of authority. It is signed hierarchically by the persons with different levels of responsibility.

c. ComplexInternalLegalDocument – a virtual hierarchical document which could consist of several physical documents, that together authorize a payment (here

ComplexInternalLegalDocument consists of a construction work acceptance document, and a payment authorization signature on the back of an invoice). The series of authorizations reflects the structure of the company from the lowest to the highest rank of management. ComplexInternalLegalDocument is defined with the following rules:

3. Rule on a complex internal legal document.

```
ApprovalOfWorkDone(?d), Work(?w), Invoice(?i), concerns(?i, ?w),
concerns(?d, ?w), isSignedBy(?i, ?p2), isSignedBy(?i, ?p1),
worksFor(?p1, ?c), worksFor(?p2, ?c), hasLevelOfResponsibility(?p1,
?l1), hasLevelOfResponsibility(?p2, ?l2), lessThan(?l1, ?l2),
differentFrom(?d, ?i)
->
ComplexInternalLegalDocument(?i)
```

4. Rule on a complex internal legal document (it is signed on back of invoice).

```
ApprovalOfWorkDone(?d), Work(?w), Invoice(?i), concerns(?i, ?w),
concerns(?d, ?w), isSignedBy(?i, ?p2), worksFor(?p1, ?c),
isSignedOnBackOfInvoiceBy(?i, ?p2), worksFor(?p2, ?c),
hasLevelOfResponsibility(?p1, ?l1), hasLevelOfResponsibility(?p2,
?l2), lessThan(?l1, ?l2), differentFrom(?d, ?i)
->
ComplexInternalLegalDocument(?i)
```

d. FalsifiedComplexInternalLegalDocument – ComplexInternalLegalDocument with approval of work which was not done.
FalisfiedComplexInternalLegalDocument is calculated with the following rule:

5. The rule defining the falsified complex document consisting of work approving document and accepted invoice. This two documents authorize the payment.

```
ComplexInternalLegalDocument(?d1), ApprovalOfWorkNotDone(?d2),
Work(?w), concerns(?d1, ?w), concerns(?d2, ?w), differentFrom(?d1,
?d2)
→
FalsifiedComplexInternalLegalDocument(?d1)
```

6. This rule refers to the previous one but specifies who signed the two constituent documents.

```
ComplexInternalLegalDocument(?d1), ApprovalOfWorkNotDone(?d2),
Work(?w), concerns(?d1, ?w), concerns(?d2, ?w), isSignedBy(?d1,
?p1), isSignedBy(?d2, ?p2), differentFrom(?d1, ?d2),
differentFrom(?p1, ?p2)
→
FalsifiedComplexInternalLegalDocument(?d1), isSignedBy(?d1, ?p2)
```

e. Transaction – consists of a contract between two companies, the work, an invoice issued for work and payment. It is defined with the following rule:

7. Rule on transaction between two companies.

```
ComplexInternalLegalDocument(?i), ContractDocument(?d), Invoice(?i),
MoneyTransfer(?mt), Work(?w), Company(?c1), Company(?c2),
concerns(?d, ?w), concerns(?i, ?w), flowsFrom(?mt, ?c2),
flowsTo(?mt, ?c1), isIssuedBy(?i, ?c1), isReceivedBy(?i, ?c2)
→
Transaction(?d), hasInvoice(?d, ?i), hasMoneyTransfer(?d, ?mt),
transactionFrom(?d, ?c2), transactionTo(?d, ?c1)
```

If a contract, work or invoice document turns out to be a FalsifiedDocument, then the Transaction will be classified as a FalsifiedTransaction.

f.   We can also define (in the description logic) the MoneyTransfer concept:

```
MoneyTransfer ⊑
                FlowOfMoneyCPTask  ∧
                ∃ flowsFrom.Company ∧
                ∃ flowsTo.Company ∧
                (= 1 occurs ∧∀occurs.TimeInstant)  ∧
                (= 1 hasValue ∧ ∀ hasValue.float) ∧
                ∃ isPaymentFor.Invoice
```

This definition means that a money transfer has one distinctive value, it occurs at exactly one time instant between a pair of companies, and it is connected with paying for some invoice. Additionally, it is a specialization of a top level FlowOfMoneyCPTask concept coming from ontology developed for the PPBW, the Polish Platform for Homeland Security project [16].

It is essential to recognize that documents may require a legal signature by a subset of principals within a company according to a statute. In the Hydra case the board consisted of 5 members, and the chairman of the board was authorized to sign documents without the consent of the others. Since no involvement of the remaining 4 members was found, here the Principal is the CEO.

To model Fraudulent Disbursement in one company of the three-level structure we needed 14 rules [4]. Two of these rules are modified in this work.

4   Rules that Define Logical Activities Appearing in the Penal Code Model

The more detailed model presented here has to be able to define complicity – the knowledge of particular criminal activities. Contrary to many works in legal ontologies, we do not introduce plans and intensions because these are extremely difficult to describe. In further paragraphs in this Section we present money laundering rules.

1.   The rule defining complicity of persons working on behalf of the same company; one person – a construction manager – falsifies ApprovalOfWorkDone document, and the second one approves the payment of the Invoice by signing the back of this document.

```
Company(?c), NoWork(?w), ContractDocument(?d1),
ComplexInternalLegalDocument(?d2), Person(?p1), Person(?p2),
concerns(?d1, ?w), concerns(?d2, ?w), worksFor(?p1, ?c),
worksFor(?p2, ?c), knowsAbout(?p1, ?w), knowsAbout(?p2, ?w),
isSignedBy(?d1, ?p1), isSignedOnBackOfInvoiceBy(?d2, ?p2),
differentFrom(?p1, ?p2), differentFrom(?d1, ?d2)
→
```
inComplicityWith(?p1, ?p2)

2. The rule defining complicity of persons working on behalf of different companies executing a fraudulent transaction.

```
Company(?c1), Company(?c2), NoWork(?w), Transaction(?t),
worksFor(?p1, ?c1), worksFor(?p2, ?c2), knowsAbout(?p1, ?w),
knowsAbout(?p2, ?w), transactionFrom(?t, ?c1),
transactionTo(?t, ?c2), differentFrom(?p1, ?p2),
differentFrom(?c1, ?c2)
→
```
inComplicityWith(?p1, ?p2)

3. The rule defining the MoneyLaundering act committed by the first company in the money laundering chain (if A paid B, this refers to company B; the company A is not indicted). Here A is Hydra and B is Hermes.

```
NoWork(?w), Invoice(?i), Transaction(?t), Company(?c1),
Company(?c2), MoneyTransfer(?mt), hasInvoice(?t, ?i),
concerns(?i, ?w), hasMoneyTransfer(?t, ?mt), flowsFrom(?mt, ?c1),
flowsTo(?mt, ?c2), differentFrom(?c1, ?c2)
→
```
MoneyLaundering (?c2), relatedTo(?c2, ?t)

4. The rule defining the money laundering act committed by next companies in the money laundering chain (e.g. companies C, and D, that is Dex and Mobex).

```
NoWork(?w), Invoice(?i), Transaction(?t), Company(?c1),
Company(?c2), MoneyTransfer(?mt), MoneyLaundering(?c1),
hasInvoice(?t, ?i), concerns(?i, ?w), hasMoneyTransfer(?t, ?mt),
flowsFrom(?mt, ?c1), flowsTo(?mt1, ?c2),
differentFrom(?c1, ?c2)
→
```
MoneyLaundering (?c2), relatedTo(?c2, ?t)

5. The rule defining the sanction PC art. 299 § 1 related to money transfer for work not done (pertains to managers of company B and C).

```
Art_299_1(?a), NoWork(?w), MoneyLaundering(?m), Company(?m),
ApprovalOfWorkNotDone(?d), Transaction(?t), Person(?p),
relatedTo(?m, ?t), worksFor(?p, ?m), knowsAbout(?p, ?w),
concerns(?t, ?w), concerns(?d, ?w), isSignedBy(?d, ?p)
→
```
fallsUnder(?p, ?a)

6. The rule defining the sanction PC art. 299 § 1 when the ApprovalOfWorkDone document does not exist. It happens down the chain that companies do not bother even create documents. In this case there were no documents for fictitious work approval between C and D (Dex and Mobex).

```
Art_299_1(?a), NoWork(?w), MoneyLaundering(?m), Company(?m),
FalsifiedComplexInternalLegalDocument(?d), Transaction(?t),
Person(?p), relatedTo(?m, ?t), worksFor(?p, ?m), concerns(?d, ?w),
concerns(?t, ?w), knowsAbout(?p, ?w), isSignedBy(?d, ?p)
→
```
fallsUnder(?p, ?a)

7. The rule defining the sanction PC art. 299 § 1 when a company accepts laundered money (here Mobex).

```
Art_299_1(?a), NoWork(?w), MoneyLaundering(?m), Company(?m),
Transaction(?t), Person(?p), relatedTo(?m, ?t), transactionTo(?t,
?m), worksFor(?p, ?m), concerns(?t, ?w), knowsAbout(?p, ?w)
→
```
fallsUnder(?p, ?a)

8. The rule defining the sanction PC art. 299 § 5 (since he/she was aware what was the purpose of the scheme and collaborated with others involved – we know this from testimonies and signing relevant documents). This rule is related to persons in the same company.

```
Art_299_5(?a1), Art_299_1(?a2), NoWork(?w),
FalsifiedComplexInternalLegalDocument(?d), Person(?p1), Person(?p2),
fallsUnder(?p1, ?a2), fallsUnder(?p2, ?a2), knowsAbout(?p1, ?d),
knowsAbout(?p2, ?d), knowsAbout(?p1, ?w), knowsAbout(?p2, ?w),
inComplicityWith(?p1, ?p2), differentFrom(?p1, ?p2)
→
```
fallsUnder(?p1, ?a1), fallsUnder(?p2, ?a1)

9. As Rule 8 but related to persons in different companies.

```
Art_299_5(?a1), Art_299_1(?a2), NoWork(?w), Company(?c1),
Company(?c2), ContractDocument(?d), Person(?p1), Person(?p2),
fallsUnder(?p1, ?a2), fallsUnder(?p2, ?a2), knowsAbout(?p1, ?d),
knowsAbout(?p2, ?d), knowsAbout(?p1, ?w), knowsAbout(?p2, ?w),
inComplicityWith(?p1, ?p2), worksFor(?p1, ?c1), worksFor(?p2,?c2),
differentFrom(?p1, ?p2), differentFrom(?c1, ?c2)
→
```
fallsUnder(?p1, ?a1), fallsUnder(?p2, ?a1)

10. The rule defining the sanction PC art. 299 § 5 based on ApprovalOfWorkNotDone for workers in 2 different companies (who did not signed a contract document, as in rules 8 and 9)

```
Art_299_5(?a1), Art_299_1(?a2), NoWork(?w), Company(?c1),
Company(?c2), Person(?p1), Person(?p2), fallsUnder(?p1, ?a2),
fallsUnder(?p2, ?a2), knowsAbout(?p1, ?w), knowsAbout(?p2, ?w),
inComplicityWith(?p1, ?p2), worksFor(?p1, ?c1), worksFor(?p2,?c2),
differentFrom(?p1, ?p2), differentFrom(?c1, ?c2)
->
```
fallsUnder(?p1, ?a1), fallsUnder(?p2, ?a1)

We have verified our ontology with the Pellet 2.1.1 reasoner, which found the ontology to be consistent.

5   Conclusions and Future Work

To our knowledge, the work on mapping of crime activities into criminal law articles has been done [18] only for cyber crimes, which have a much narrower scope. In work [8] OWL ontology was used for only T-Box reasoning (although rules were discussed in a different aspect) , whereas our approach uses ontology and rules.

The minimal model of the fraudulent disbursement combined with money laundering crime (model III), as presented in this work, can be expressed using OWL-DL classes and properties, and a reasonable number of rules.

Strictly, the model III as presented in this work possesses 134 classes, 82 relations, 41 rules. The model II (only fraudulent disbursement and only one company included) 130 classes, 74 relations and 14 rules.

This means that if one restricts himself to only the 5-level concept ontology generalizations of our model to more complex crime one would expect increase of mostly rules. We estimate that we are able to describe around 95% of relevant information for the *Hydra* case.

The most straightforward case to verify this hypothesis would be to model:

- CausingAssetMisappropriation
- CausingDamageToACompany

based on existing CausingFraudulentDisbursement results.

Preliminary verification of the model by selected Polish legal community members suggests two conclusions. First, for the case such as Hydra our system gives better sanction determination than achieved by a an average prosecutor. We hope that with more crime types description the above statement will become acceptable to a wide body of legal community. Second, the reaction of some judges, particularly of the highest level, involves a great deal of suspicion. Judges use statutory interpretation is the process of interpreting and applying legislation. Since statutes are deliberately left open, are often extremely broad, and in most cases, there is some ambiguity or vagueness in the words of the statute that must be resolved by the judge.

It is true that we selected the most favorable crime to be analyzed with our model. Even in Hydra case we would face difficulty, whether in this case a criminal group is an organized criminal group. There is no definition of "an organized criminal group" in the Polish PC. Therefore, inferring the legal qualifications for this case (that is whether Article 258 § 1 applies) is subject to interpretation that has to be provided by legal communities to design appropriate rules. In any case the results of our model have to be verified by leading legal experts.

Increased cooperation between legal community and knowledge engineers would possibly be of great use for society.

First, we demonstrate here reasoning based on all facts for a given case of a selected typology. For practical applications the more interesting case is to uncover facts and choose between several possible typologies. Second, by analyzing many cases and proposed sanctions we could introduce some measure of objectivity into evaluation of prosecutors' work, which could decrease political motivation and corruption in the area. The biggest weakness of our approach is that the population of ontology individuals from the natural language description is so far done manually.

Acknowledgement. This work was supported by the Polish Ministry of Science and Higher Education, Polish Technological Security Platform grant 0014/R/2/T00/06/02.

References

1. Kingston, J., Schafer, B., Vandenberghe, W.: No Model Behavior: Ontologies for Fraud Detection. In: Benjamins, V.R., Casanovas, P., Breuker, J., Gangemi, A. (eds.) Law and the Semantic Web 2005. LNCS (LNAI), vol. 3369, pp. 233–247. Springer, Heidelberg (2005)
2. Jedrzejek, C., Bak, J., Falkowski, M.: Graph Mining for Detection of a Large Class of Financial Crimes. In: 17th International Conference on Conceptual Structures, Moscow, Russia, July 26-31 (2009)
3. Jedrzejek, C., Cybulka, J., Bak, J.: Application Ontology-based Crime Model for a Selected Economy Crime. In: Tadeusiewicz, R., Ligęza, A., Mitkowski, W., Szymkat, M. (eds.) Proc. of 7th Conference on Computer Methods and Systems, CMS 2009, Kraków, ONT, pp. 71–74 (2009)
4. Bąk, J., Jędrzejek, C.: Application of an Ontology-based Model to a Selected Fraudulent Disbursement Economic Crime. In: Casanovas, P. (ed.) AICOL Workshops 2009. LNCS (LNAI), vol. 6237, pp. 113–132. Springer, Heidelberg (2010)
5. PricewaterhouseCoopers Global economic crime survey 2009 (2009), http://www.pwc.com/gx/en/economic-crime-survey/download-economic-crime-people-culture-controls.jhtml
6. Financial Action Task Force (FATF), http://www.fatf-gafi.org
7. Aleven, V.: Using background knowledge in case-based legal reasoning: a computational model and an intelligent learning environment. Artificial Intelligence 150, 183–237 (2003)
8. Wyner, A.: An ontology in OWL for legal case-based reasoning. Artif. Intell. Law 16(4), 361–387 (2008)
9. McGuinness, D., van Harmelen, F.: Owl web ontology language overview. W3C Recommendation (February 10, 2004), http://www.w3.org/TR/owl-features/
10. Horrocks, I., Patel-Schneider, P.F., Boley, H., Tabet, S., Grosof, B., Dean, M.: Swrl: A semantic web rule language combining owl and ruleml. W3C Member Submission (May 21, 2004), http://www.w3.org/Submission/SWRL/
11. SWRL Built-ins, http://www.w3.org/Submission/2004/SUBM-SWRL-20040521/
12. Pellet Reasoner, http://clarkparsia.com/pellet/
13. KAON2, http://kaon2.semanticweb.org/
14. Jess (Java Expert System Shell), http://jessrules.com/
15. Friedman-Hill, E.: Jess in Action. Manning Publications Co. (2003)
16. Bąk, J., Jędrzejek, C., Falkowski, M.: Usage of the Jess engine, rules and ontology to query a relational database. In: Governatori, G., Hall, J., Paschke, A. (eds.) RuleML 2009. LNCS, vol. 5858, pp. 216–230. Springer, Heidelberg (2009)
17. Jedrzejek, C., Cybulka, J.: Minimal Model of financial crimes (In Polish) Definitions In OWL, Technical report PPBW 07/2009 extended 09/2009, http://www.man.poznan.pl/~jolac/MinimalModel/MinimalModel.owl
18. Podgor, E.S.: Criminal Fraud. American Law Review 48(4) (1999)
19. Bezzazi, H.: Building an ontology that helps identify articles that apply to a cybercrime case. In: 2nd International Conference on Software Technology, Barcelona, Spain (2007)

A Contract Agreement Policy-Based Workflow Methodology for Agents Interacting in the Semantic Web

Kalliopi Kravari[1], Grammati-Eirini Kastori[1],
Nick Bassiliades[1], and Guido Governatori[2]

[1] Dept. of Informatics, Aristotle University of Thessaloniki, GR-54124 Thessaloniki, Greece
{kkravari,gkastori,nbassili}@csd.auth.gr
[2] NICTA, Queensland Research Laboratory, Australia
guido.governatori@nicta.com.au

Abstract. The Semantic Web aims at automating Web content understanding and user request satisfaction. Intelligent agents assist towards this by performing complex actions on behalf of their users into real-life applications, such as e-Contracts, which make transactions simple by modeling the processes involved. This paper, presents a policy-based workflow methodology for efficient contract agreement among agents interacting in the Semantic Web. In addition, we present the integration of this methodology into a multi-agent knowledge-based framework, providing flexibility, reusability and interoperability of behavior between agents. The main advantage of our approach is that it provides a safe, generic, and reusable framework for modeling and monitoring e-Contract agreements, which could be used for different types of on-line transactions among agents. Furthermore, our framework is based on Semantic Web and FIPA standards, to maximize interoperability and reusability. Finally, an e-Commerce contract negotiation scenario is presented that illustrates the usability of the approach.

Keywords: semantic web, intelligent agents, e-Contracts, defeasible reasoning.

1 Introduction

The *Semantic Web* (*SW*) [1] is a rapidly evolving extension of the WWW, where the semantics of information and services is well-defined, making it possible for people and machines to understand Web content. Its penetration has transformed the way people satisfy their requests, letting them save time and money. Moreover, SW technologies offer interoperability and, thus, favor *Intelligent Agents* (*IAs*) [2]. Hence, the integration of *multi-agent systems* (*MAS*) with SW technology affects the use of the Web; groups of intercommunicating agents are available to traverse the Web and perform complex actions on behalf of their users in real-life applications. One such application is *Electronic Contracts* (*e-Contracts*), which make transactions simple by effectively modelling and managing the processes involved.

In essence, a contract is an agreement that creates and modifies legal relationshiops (obligations, permissions, prohibitions) between two or more parties and involves several stages, such as information exchange and negotiation. An e-Contract, on the

M. Dean et al. (Eds.): RuleML 2010, LNCS 6403, pp. 225–239, 2010.

other hand, is a contract modelled, specified, executed and enacted (controlled and monitored) by a software system [3]. The main differentiation is that e-Contracts are simply carried out electronically, overcoming the delays and drawbacks of the manual process [4]. Thus, like ordinary contracts, e-Contracts define a set of clauses that must be satisfied by the parties involved.

The execution of an e-Contract involves, as mentioned, several tasks, which can be represented as *workflows* [5]. More specifically, workflow information is extracted from a contract and then the various functions that realize assorted activities within the specified time-bounds are implemented [6]. A workflow is concerned with the automation of procedures, where information is passed between participants according to an overall goal. Thus, the workflow of an e-Contract must be carefully specified and related to meet the contract requirements.

This paper focuses on e-Contracts managed by IAs. Each agent has its own policy, a set of private rules representing its requirements, obligations and restrictions, depending on its role in the e-Contract, as well as its personal data. The e-Contract, on the other hand, has a set of clauses that specify among others how it will be implemented and outlines restrictions on the parties involved. Taking the above into account, a policy-based workflow methodology is proposed that specifies the overall negotiation stages of an e-Contract. The aim of the methodology is to propose a safe, reusable procedure for e-Contract agreements, which could be used for different types of on-line transactions among agents.

Despite the usual issues a contract has to deal with, e-Contracts have to deal with additional issues regarding agents. As agents not necessarily share the same logic or rule representation formalism, this paper presents the integration of the above methodology into a multi-agent knowledge-based framework, called EMERALD. This framework deals with the aforementioned issues proposing the use of trusted, third party reasoning services that can be used in safely exchanging policies with heterogeneous rule formalisms. The provided advantages are, among others, flexibility (each agent can use its own rule formalism; workflow rule sets can vary from empty clauses to large and complex rule programs, etc), reusability (workflow clause sets can be reused in different scenarios and can be shared among agents, since they are modular) and interoperability (agents can use different rule formalisms which can be safely interchanged through external trusted reasoning services) of behavior between agents. Finally, an e-Commerce contract negotiation scenario is presented that illustrates the usability of the approach.

The rest of the paper is organized as follows. In Section 2, we present a policy-based workflow methodology for efficient contract agreement among agents. Section 3 presents the integration of this methodology into the multi-agent Knowledge-based framework. In Section 4, an e-Commerce contract negotiation scenario is presented that illustrates the usability of the approach. Section 5 discusses related work, and Section 6 concludes with final remarks and directions for future work.

2 Policy-based Workflow Methodology

After briefly presenting e-Contracts and the utility of agents in the setting, this section presents the proposed policy-based workflow methodology for contract agreement among agents.

2.1 E-Contracts

E-Contracts, as already mentioned, are agreements between two or more parties to create legal obligations between them, which are modelled, specified and executed by a software system [3]. They consist of at least two parties, here agents, and a number of clauses. Typically, an e-Contract is described by the abstract specification: $EC \equiv \{P, C\}$, where P is the set of parties involved $P \equiv \{P_1, P_2, ..., P_n\}$, $n \geq 2$ and C is the set of clauses $C \equiv \{C_1, C_2, ..., C_m\}$. Each party possesses a well-defined role, specified in the e-Contract. For example, in an on-line e-commerce transaction the parties involved may be defined either as buyers or as sellers. In this study, we assume that there are two agents $P \equiv \{P_1, P_2\}$ that want to make a contract agreement; agent P_2 sets out the agreement rules and agent P_1 negotiates over these rules.

Generally speaking, an agreement between parties is legally valid if it satisfies the requirements of the e-Contract. This intention is proven by their compliance with the clauses of the e-Contract, which, can actually be divided into stages of information exchange and negotiation. More specifically, an e-Contract can be divided into groups of tasks forming special categories; for example, each e-Contract has to contain a stage, in which the involved parties negotiate the terms of agreement, by means of an offer and acceptance that the e-Contract refers to. This natural categorization in stages is considered very useful for all parties involved, as they can better understand the e-Contract steps and, thus, organize their policy accordingly.

2.2 Intelligent Agents

Agents involved in an e-Contract actually act on behalf of their users, thus, they have to contract an agreement efficiently and without human intervention. In order to achieve this, each agent possesses arguments that describe its requirements, preferences and restrictions. These arguments usually include data and rules that comprise the agent's policy and characterize its behavior. A careful consideration would reveal that these policies can, like e-Contracts, be divided into groups of rules, such as personal data restriction rules. Thus, taking advantage of this analogy could lead to an automation of e-Contract procedures.

However, the variety in representation and reasoning technologies is one of the main issues in agent interoperability. An IA (Intelligent Agent) does not necessarily have to oblige to other agents' logic, nor is it essential for the agents to understand each other's rule representation format. In fact, intercommunicating agents usually "understand" different (rule) languages. Thus, it will be essential not only to come up with an automation methodology for e-Contract procedures, but also to provide the suitable framework that will overcome the above issues in real-life applications.

2.3 E-Contract Agreement Workflow Automation Methodology

E-Contracts reduce costs, save time, speed up customer response and improve service quality by reducing paperwork, thus increasing automation. As mentioned, the implementation of an e-Contract involves several groups of tasks, which can be represented as workflows. However, the workflow of an e-Contract must be carefully specified, in order to meet the contract requirements. Thus, taking into account that both e-Contract clauses and participants' policies can be divided in stages, this paper proposes a policy-based workflow methodology, which divides the overall process of an e-Contract agreement in stages.

More specifically, we propose the specification of an e-Contract to be extended to an 8-tuple $EC \equiv \{P, C, N_{STG}, STG, N_{STP}, STP, C_{STP}, COND_{STP}\}$, where N_{STG} is the number of stages of the policy workflow, which in our case is five, STG is the set of stages $STG \equiv \{stg_l, 1 \leq l \leq N_{STG}\}$, N_{STP} is the set of the number of steps for each stage $N_{STP} \equiv \{N^l_{STP}, 1 \leq l \leq N_{STG}\}$, STP is the set of steps for each stage $STP \equiv \{stp_k^l, 1 \leq k \leq N^l_{STP}: stg_l \in STG\}$, C_{STP} is the set of contract clauses for each step $C_{STP} \equiv \{C_k^l: stp_k^l \in STP \wedge C_k^l \subseteq C \wedge (\forall l,k,l',k' \; C_k^l \cap C_k^{l'} = \emptyset \vee (k=k' \wedge l=l'))\}$, and $COND_{STP}$ is the set of step transition conditions $COND_{STP} \equiv \{cnd_k^l: stp_k^l \in STP\}$, which decide if the transaction can proceed from one step to the next and it is part of the agent's internal policy.

Notice that the difference between contract clauses and transition conditions is that the former refer to conditions of the contract that are publicly known, whereas the latter refer to conditions of the state of the workflow that are private to the contracting agents. In general, transitions between stages and steps are sequential, but the parties involved can disagree at any step, terminating the negotiation without agreement. Thus, in order to end in a state of agreement and eventually execute the e-Contract, each stage and step has to be successful, i.e. the set of clauses and conditions of each step should be satisfied.

Our methodology involves at each step: (a) the exchange of the agent's P_i clauses $_iC_k^l$ to the agent P_j, (b) the evaluation of the $_iC_k^l$ clauses using agent's P_j personal data $_jD_k^l$, and (c) the exchange of the results/conclusions $_jE_k^l = \mathcal{I}(_iC_k^l \cup _jD_k^l)$ of step (b) from agent P_j back to agent P_i, in order to test if the clauses of the contract are satisfied so that the contract negotiation workflow can continue. The workflow transition decision is taken by the following algorithm:

$$\textbf{if } _jE_k^l \neq \emptyset \textbf{ and } \mathcal{I}(_icnd_k^l \cup _jE_k^l) \neq \emptyset$$
$$\textbf{then (if } k=N^l_{STP} \textbf{ then } l \leftarrow l+1; \; k \leftarrow 1 \textbf{ else } k \leftarrow k+1)$$
$$\textbf{else } l \leftarrow T \text{ (Termination)}$$

2.4   E-Contract Agreement Workflow Steps

With the automation of e-Contract agreements, e-commerce is expected to improve productivity and competitiveness by providing unprecedented access to an on-line global market place with millions of customers and thousands of products and services. On the other hand, since the e-Contract proposal focuses on an automated environment and not on humans, who take decisions on specific transactions, it is extremely important to avoid any fraud and discrepancy in the contract.

Thus, the first stage refers to *trust* (stg_1). The aim of this stage is to assure that all involved parties are trusted. However, establishing trust is mainly pertained to a problem of authorization and access control [7] [8]. In order to deal with this issue, we propose a policy-based approach, based on a set of policies and credentials (digital certificates). Usually, credentials are sufficient when the agent is convinced either of the other agent's identity or his membership in a sufficiently trusted group. Thus, in stg_1, the agents involved should exchange the appropriate credentials that will enable them to trust each other.

As soon as a satisfying level of trust among agents is established, the procedure can advance to the next stage (stg_2). This stage includes the set of steps that involve the primary data exchange that is required in an e-Contract, in order to specify its context. Thus, in this stage the agents involved could exchange, among others, definition and interpretation data, commencement and completion data or even personal and credit data, which are obligatory in each e-Contract.

The next stage, (stg_3), is assigned with the main body of an e-Contract, which is the negotiation of the e-Contract terms. These terms, mainly, refer to the terms of use and payment of the product or service under negotiation. Thus, after the negotiation and agreement of these terms, the procedure moves to the stg_4 stage. In this stage, the e-Contract is approved and all the extra necessary data are sent. These data may include, among others, technical details, access and credentials, depending on the scope of the e-Contract.

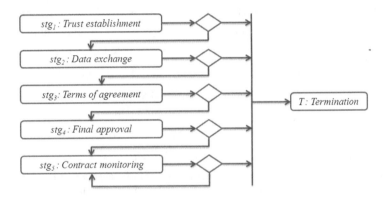

Fig. 1. The overview of the workflow methodology

Finally, the above agreed procedure reaches the stg_5 stage, the contract monitoring stage, during which the e-Contract's content is actually executed and monitored for situations which are out the negotiation phase and involve mechanisms for detecting contract violations, sanction enactment, etc. The overview of the proposed workflow methodology is illustrated in Fig. 1.

3   Knowledge-Based Workflow Model

In this section, we present the integration of the above workflow methodology into a multi-agent knowledge-based framework, called EMERALD [9] [10], providing among others flexibility, reusability and interoperability of behavior between agents. The main advantage of this approach is that it provides a safe, generic, and reusable framework for modeling and monitoring e-Contract agreements, which could be used for various types of on-line transactions among agents. Furthermore, our framework is based on Semantic Web and FIPA standards, to maximize interoperability and reusability.

3.1 The EMERALD Knowledge-Based Framework

In order to model and monitor the parties involved in the e-Contract negotiation, a customizable, knowledge-based agent model, called *KC-AGENTS*, is deployed. Agents that comply with this model are equipped with a Jess rule engine [11] and a knowledge base (KB) that contains environment knowledge (in the form of facts), behavior patterns and strategies (in the form of Jess production rules). Actually, the Jess KB represents the agent's internal policy and implements the workflow transition conditions of each negotiation step cnd_k^l to the next. Examples will be given in Section 4. The use of the KC-AGENTS model offers certain advantages, like interoperability of behavior between agents, as opposed to having behavior hard-wired into the agent's code.

A short description of the abstract specification of this model [9] is presented below for better comprehension. The generic rule format is: *result* $\leftarrow$ *rule* (*preconditions*). The agent's internal knowledge is a set of facts $F \equiv F_u \cup F_e$, where $F_u \equiv \{f_{u1},$ $f_{u2}, ..., f_{uk}\}$ are user-defined facts and $F_e \equiv \{f_{e1}, f_{e2}, ..., f_{em}\}$ are environment-asserted facts. The agent's behaviour is represented as a set of potential actions–rules $P \equiv A \cup S$, where $A \equiv \{a \mid f_e \leftarrow a(f_{u1}, f_{u2}, ..., f_{un}) \wedge \{f_{u1}, f_{u2},..., f_{un}\} \subseteq F_u \wedge f_e \in F_e\}$ are the rules that derive new facts by inserting them into the KB and $S \equiv C \cup J$ are the rules that lead to the execution of a special action. Note that special actions can either refer to agent communication $C \equiv \{c \mid ACLMessage \leftarrow c(f_1, f_2, ..., f_p) \wedge \{f_1, f_2,..., f_p\} \subseteq F\}$ or Java calls $J \equiv \{j \mid JavaMethod \leftarrow j(f_1, f_2, ..., f_q) \wedge \{f_1, f_2,..., f_q\} \subseteq F\}$.

In order to provide a standard communication interface between the Jess KB and the agents, this framework provides a number of Java methods that can be invoked via Jess production rule actions. In addition, the framework provides one more facility, the *AYPS*, a customizable procedure for the *yellow pages service*, both for registered and required services. Its most important feature is that the proper providers are inserted into working memory as Jess facts with a designated format.

Moreover, as agents do not necessarily share a common rule or logic formalism, it is vital for them to find a way to exchange their position arguments seamlessly. Thus, the framework proposes the use of *Reasoners*, which are actually agents that offer reasoning services to the rest of the agent community. This approach does not rely on translation between rule formalisms, but on exchanging the results of the reasoning process of the rule base over the input data. The receiving agent uses an external reasoning service to grasp the semantics of the rulebase, i.e. the set of conclusions of the rule base.

One of these Reasoners (here called *Reasoner*) is the *defeasible logic Reasoner*, based on DR-DEVICE [12], which furthermore assumes an OO RDF data model that treats properties as encapsulated attributes of resource objects, providing more compact representation and property indexing. DR-DEVICE supports two types of syntax for defeasible logic rules: a native CLIPS-like syntax and an OO RuleML [13]-compatible one. The latter deals with extensions regarding rule types, superiority relations among rules and conflicting literals, as well as constraints on predicate arguments and functions. Using the Reasoner, agents communicate with each other, overcoming the fact that they may not comprehend the logic of the other party.

Defeasible reasoning [14] was selected because of its simple rule-based approach for efficient reasoning with incomplete and inconsistent information. Defeasible reasoning can represent facts, rules as well as priorities and conflicts among rules. Such reasoning with conflicts is useful in many applications, such as security policies [15], business rules [16], e-contracting [17], personalization, brokering [18], bargaining and agent negotiations [19], [20], [21]. When compared to mainstream non-monotonic reasoning, the main advantages of defeasible reasoning are enhanced representational capabilities and low computational complexity.

Finally, EMERALD provides an independent agent (called *Timer*) that simulates a time service, in order to synchronize agent transactions, which is used in the following use case paradigm (section 4). Real time could be used equally well.

3.2 Implementing the Workflow Methodology on EMERALD

Following EMERALD's specifications we commit to SW and FIPA standards, thus, we use the RuleML language [22] for representing and exchanging agent policies and e-contract clauses $_iC_k^l$, since it has become a de facto standard and it is very close to the RIF [23] emerging standard for SW rules. In addition, we propose the use of the RDF model for data representation both for the private data $_jD_k^l$ included in agent's P_j internal knowledge and the results $_jE_k^l$ generated during the negotiation steps. The overview of the above proposal is illustrated in Fig. 2.

The agent P_j, in order to start an e-Contract negotiation process with P_i, asks the AYPS service for the latter's default call-for-negotiation requested value (C_0), required formalisms/languages, etc. Thus, P_j sends a call-for-negotiation message (ACL message with *REQUEST* communication-act) to P_i containing C_0. P_i examines the new request and sends back a *REQUEST* message containing part of his clauses $_iC_k^l$ (in RuleML format), waiting for P_j's reply or a termination. P_j, on his behalf, evaluates the receiving $_iC_k^l$ clauses using his own private data $_jD_k^l$ (in RDF format) and informs P_i with a new message (ACL message with *INFORM* communication-act) containing the results $_jE_k^l$ (in RDF format).

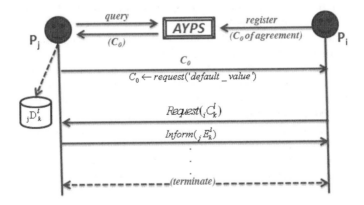

Fig. 2. The workflow implementation

Generally, the negotiation processes is a sequence of exchanged ACL messages; (both) parties use messages with *REQUEST* communication-act in order to ask for valid information and *INFORM* in order to reply. The process can either end successfully with an agreement between the parties or terminate at any step due to disagreement.

4 Use Case: The Wine Club

A Wine Club contract negotiation scenario is presented in order to illustrate the usability of the approach that involves two parties: a) the Wine Club, represented by its agent, that offers a variety of wines, and b) a customer who wishes to become a member of the above Wine Club. In addition, there are two extra agents involved: c) the *Reasoner* an independent third-party service that is responsible for conducting inference on defeasible logic rule bases and produces the results as an RDF file, d) the *Timer* an independent agent that simulates a time service, in order to synchronize agent transactions according to the contract's time schedule.

4.1 The Scenario Overview

First of all, the customer wants to be a member of a wine club, hence, uses the *AYPS* service (via sending an ACL message with *REQUEST* communicate-act) in order to find the appropriate Wine Club, which is registered to the directory. The *AYPS* sends back (via ACL message with *INFORM* communicate-act) the available providers with their default requested value (C_0). Hence, the customer finds the appropriate wine club service and sends a subscription request to it, namely a *REQUEST* message containing C_0 (call-for-negotiation). Since the Club has some terms in order to provide the service, provided by an e-Contract, at this point, a contract negotiation procedure between the Customer and the Wine Club, that follows the aforementioned methodology, begins (Fig. 3).

Following the context of the first stage (stg_1), both the Wine Club's agent, and the Customer have to provide sufficient evidence in order to certify that they can trust each other. Due to Customer's preferences this Wine Club service has to be a member of a trusted third-party organization, such as the *Best Business Bureau* [24], which guarantees that the service satisfies the standard criteria. On the other hand, since it is forbidden to sell alcohol to people under the age of 18, the Customer has to provide credentials that certify his age. Thus, both reveal their credentials, successfully establishing trust among them and, thus, move to the next stage (stg_2).

At the first step of this stage, the Wine Club agent sends part of the e-Contract's clauses ($_2C_1^2$), in defeasible logic, requesting the Customer's personal data. This request includes among others, the Customer's name and e-mail, the credit card number and its date of expiration. The Customer, on the other hand, is willing to reveal a part of his personal data, but internally uses a different type of logic and cannot directly process Wine Club's defeasible logic requirements. Thus, an appropriate defeasible logic *Reasoner*, a trusted third-party reasoning service, is requested, which is retrieved from the directory service (*AYPS*). The Customer communicates with the *Reasoner*, providing both his personal data ($_1D_2^2$), in RDF, and the Club's arguments

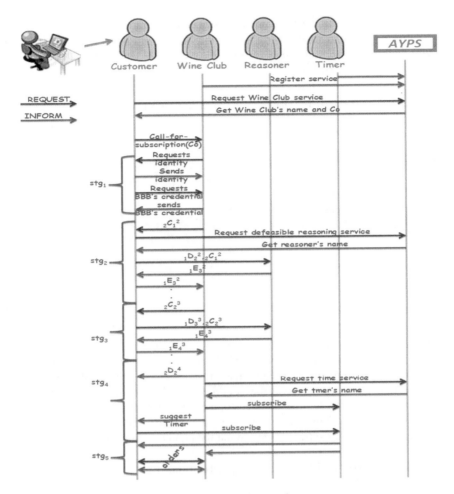

Fig. 3. The scenario overview

($_2C_1^2$), in defeasible logic and in a RuleML format, and waits for a reply. The *Reasoner* conducts inference on these arguments and data and produces the results as an RDF file. Thus, the Customer sends these results, namely his personal information that can be sent ($_1E_3^2$), to the Wine Club agent.

Eventually, the current stage ends successfully and parties move to the next one (stg_3). As soon as the Club's agent receives the required data ($_1E_3^2$), it responds with another part of the e-Contract ($_2C_2^3$), a set of clauses represented in defeasible logic that contain the characteristics of the three available categories of subscription.

The three categories are the "Gold Customer", the "Silver Customer" and the "Bronze Customer", given in Table 1. The Customer communicates again with the *Reasoner*, providing him with both the RuleML file containing these clauses ($_2C_2^3$) and the RDF file which contains his preferences ($_1D_3^3$), such as the minimum price of an order (e.g. 500€) and order frequency (e.g. 1 per four months). Afterwards, the *Reasoner* sends the result ($_1E_4^3$), which suggests the *Silver Customer* category. Thus, the Customer selects the most suitable category ending up the current stage. Eventually, acting in the context of the stg_4 stage, the Wine Club agent saves all the data concerning this customer and approves the subscription by sending him the catalogue of the available Wines $(_2D_2{}^4)$.

Table 1. The characteristics of each customer category

Bronze Customer	Order amount ≥ 200€ & Order frequency ≥ 1 /4 months (at least 1 order per 4 months) & Suspension = 1(in a row) & Delivery_time = 7 days & Discount = 2% (in case of lack in order's products) & Return_fee = 10%
Silver Customer	Order amount ≥ 400€ & Order frequency ≥ 1 /4 months & Suspension = 1(in a row) & Delivery_time = 7 days & Discount = 4% (in case of lack in order's products) & Return_fee = 8%
Gold Customer	Order amount ≥ 600€ & Order frequency ≥ 1 /3 months & Suspension = 2(in a row) & Delivery_time = 5 days & Discount = 8% (in case of lack in order's products) & Return_fee = 6%

At this stage a temporal dimension exists, since the customer has to order once per month (*Silver Customer*); both the Wine Club and the customer have to comply with the environment's common time representation scheme. Thus, the Club's agent finds a suitable time-agent (*Timer*), via the AYPS service, makes a subscription to this service and proposes the service to the customer. The customer, on his behalf, accepts the proposal and subscribes to the Timer's service. Finally, their interaction moves to the stg_5 for the agreed time period, carried out the regular orders, or until a break off.

4.2 Contract Terms and Information Specifications

Both the customer and the Wine Club's agent comply with the KC-Agents model (section 3), thus, they are equipped with a Jess rule engine and a Jess KB. Following this generic specification, the Wine Club agent's description contains facts and rules.

$F_u{}^{wc} \equiv \{categories\}$, $F_e{}^{wc} \equiv \{timer\_name\}$
$C^{wc} \equiv \{(ACLMessage\,(communicative\text{-}act\,REQUEST)$
$\qquad\qquad (sender\,Wine\_Club)(receiver\,Customer)(content\,categories))$
$\qquad\qquad \leftarrow requestCustomerCategory\,(\text{"}COND\text{"})\}$
$J^{wc} \equiv \{\text{"}triples\text{"} \leftarrow (bind\,((new\,java\_class)\,getCustomerCategory\text{"}COND\text{"}\,))\}$

Fact *categories* represent part of his internal knowledge and stand for the *categories characteristics*; part of the associated RuleML file is presented in Fig. 4.

Fig. 4 represents part of the Wine Club's first clause (stg_3) that implements the categories' characteristics (Table 1). Based on these clauses, presented below (in defeasible logic), and his personal preferences (Fig. 5), the customer is able to select the most suitable category. All three rules derive a positive conclusion, only one of which must be true, according to the constraint of the last line (conflicting literals).

```
<rulebase ...>
  <_rbaselab><ind type="defeasible">categories</ind></_rbaselab>
  <imp>
      <_rlab ruleID="r1" ruletype="defeasiblerule"/>
      <_head>    <atom>
                    <_opr><rel><ind>customer-type</ind></rel></_opr>
                    <_slot name="type"><ind>bronze</ind></_slot>
                </atom></_head>
      <_body>
          <atom>
              <_opr><rel><ind>order-pref</ind></rel></_opr>
              <_slot name="amount">
                  <_and>
                      <var>a</var>
                      <function_call name="&ge;">
                          <var>a</var>
                          <ind>200</ind></function_call>
                  </_and></_slot>
              <_slot name="frequency">
                  <_and>
                      <var>f</var>
                      <function_call name="&ge;">
                          <var>f</var>
                          <ind>0.25</ind></function_call>
                  </_and></_slot>
                ...
          </atom></_body></imp>
...
</rulebase>
```

Fig. 4. Part of the Wine Club's RuleML containing categories characteristics (*stg₃*)

r_1: *order-pref(Amount,Frequency,Suspension,Delivery_time,Discount,Return_fee),*
      Amount≥200, Frequency≥0.25, Suspension≤1, Delivery_time≥7,
      Discount≤2,Return_fee≥10

⇒   **customer-type(type→bronze)**

r_2: *order-pref(Amount,Frequency,Suspension,Delivery_time,Discount,Return_fee),*
      Amount≥400, Frequency≥0.25, Suspension≤1, Delivery_time≥7,
      Discount≤4, Return_fee≥8

⇒   **customer-type(type→silver)**

r_3: *order-pref(Amount,Frequency,Suspension,Delivery_time,Discount,Return_fee),*
      Amount≥600, Frequency≥0.33, Suspension≤2, Delivery_time≥5,
      Discount≤8, Return_fee≥6

⇒   **customer-type(type→gold)**

$r_3 > r_2$, $r_2 > r_1$, $r_3 > r_1$

$C(\text{customer-type}(X)) = \{\neg\ \text{customer-type}(X)\} \cup \{\ \text{customer-type}(Y)\ |\ Y \neq X\ \}$

Fact *timer_name* (the Timer's name) is added by the AYPS. Rules "*requestCustomerCategory*" and "*getCustomerCategory*" (*stg₃*) comprise part of the agent's behavior ($_2cnd_k^3$); part of the associated Jess file is presented in Fig. 6.

Fig. 6 presents three of the Wine Club agent's behavior rules; the "*requestCustomerCategory*" rule, as soon as *stg₂* is completed successfully, sends his clauses related to customer categories to the customer and waits; the *getCustomerCategory*" rule receives customer's reply, checks the selected category (bronze, silver, gold) and

```
<rdf:RDF ...>
  <order-pref rdf:about="...">
     <amount rdf:datatype="&xsd;integer">300</amount>
     <frequency rdf:datatype="&xsd;float">0.3</frequency>
     <suspension rdf:datatype="&xsd;integer">1</suspension>
     <delivery_time rdf:datatype="&xsd;integer">10</delivery_time>
     <discount rdf:datatype="&xsd;integer">2</discount>
     <return_fee rdf:datatype="&xsd;integer">10</return_fee>
  </order-pref>
  . . .
</rdf:RDF>
```

Fig. 5. Part of customer's personal data (RDF)

```
....
(defrule requestCustomerCategory "request customer's category"
  (personal_info received);stage 2 completed
  (MyAgent (name ?n))
  (customer ?x) (categories ?cc)
  =>
  (send (assert (ACLMessage (communicative-act INFORM) (sender ?n) (receiver ?x)
                                                       (content ?cc)))))
(defrule getCustomerCategory "get category"
  (customer ?x)
  (customer_personal_info ?x ?p)
  ?z<-(ACLMessage(communicative-act INFORM)(sender ?x)(content ?c))
  (test (or (eq ?c bronze)(eq ?c silver)(eq ?c gold)))
  =>
  (bind ?tt (new Basic))  (bind ?str (?tt extractTriples ?p))
  (batch ?str)))

(defrule find_name
  (triple (subject ?x) (predicate rdf:type) (object sendable))
  (triple (subject ?x) (predicate CustomersName) (object ?name))
  =>
  (assert(name ?name)))
...
```

Fig. 6. Part of the Wine Club's behavior in Jess ($_2cnd_k^3$)

extracts the customer's personal data in RDF triples. Finally, the *"find_name"* rule finds the customer's name using the extracted triples in order to enter this customer in his register.

Similarly, the customer agent's description contains, among others, a fact *personal_data* which is part of his internal knowledge and represents his personal data. Moreover, due to the dynamic environment (AYPS is constantly updating the environment), new facts with the Wine Club's agent name (*Wine_Club*) are added to the working memory. Agent behavior is represented by rules that implement the workflow transition conditions of each negotiation step cnd_k^l to the next; two of these are the *"request"* and *"read"*; the former is used for communication and the latter for Java method calls.

$$F_u^{cust} \equiv \{personal\_data\}, \; F_e^{cust} \equiv \{Wine\_Club\}$$
$$C^{cust} \equiv \{(ACLMessage \, (communicative\text{-}act \, REQUEST)$$
$$(sender \, Customer) \, (receiver \, Wine\_Club) \leftarrow request \, (\text{"}Co\text{"})\}$$
$$J^{cust} \equiv \{ \, personal\_data\_string \leftarrow (bind \, ((new \, java\_class) \, read \, personal\_data)\}$$

5   Related Work

A tightly related approach is the *DR-CONTRACT* [25] architecture for representing and reasoning on e-Contracts in defeasible logic. The architecture captures the notions relevant to monitoring the execution and performance of e-Contracts in defeasible logics. More specifically, the framework deploys the Defeasible Deontic Logic of Violation (DDLV) [17], expressed via a RuleML extension that combines deontic notions with defeasibility and violations. DR-CONTRACT takes as input a DDLV theory, downloads/queries input RDF documents, including their schemata, and translates the RDF descriptions into fact objects. Finally, the conclusions are exported as an RDF/XML document through an RDF extractor.

SweetDeal [26] is another rule-based approach to representing business contracts that enables software agents to create, evaluate, negotiate and execute contracts with substantial automation and modularity. SweetDeal builds upon the Situated Courteous Logic Programs (SCLP) knowledge representation in RuleML that includes prioritized conflict handling and procedural attachments for actions and tests. Process knowledge descriptions are also incorporated, represented as ontologies expressed in DAML+OIL, thereby enabling more complex contracts with behavioral provisions, especially for handling exception conditions (e.g., late delivery or non-payment) that might arise during the execution of the contract.

The ER^{EC} framework [27] is another example for designing, modeling, enacting and monitoring e -Contract processes. The framework centers on an underlying meta-model that bridges the XML contract document with the Web Services-based implementation model of an e-Contract. The ER^{EC} meta-model applies certain constructs for modeling e-Contracts, like clauses, activities, parties, exceptions, contracts and subcontracts. The framework also offers potential for automatic generating and deploying workflows for e-Contract enactment, as well as facilities for analyzing what-if scenarios with respect to e-Contract clause violation.

Another work that automates price negotiations in e-commerce transactions using a rule-based implementation based on JESS utilized in the JADE multi-agent is presented in [28]. However, the focus of our work is e-contract negotiation / argumentation, rather than price negotiation.

Similarly, our approach considers e-Contracts in the Semantic Web, but it is, to the best of our knowledge, the only one that provides a workflow methodology, which models the procedure that can be followed for negotiating and sealing an e-Contract. This methodology divides the overall process of an e-Contract agreement in stages, providing a safe, reusable procedure for e-Contract agreements, which could be used for different types of on-line transactions among agents. Moreover, our approach takes into account trust issues (stg_1 stage), an extremely important issue on on-line transactions. In addition, it is the only approach that is embodied in a multi-agent platform, letting agents easily follow the necessary steps for sealing an e-Contract.

6   Conclusions and Future Work

This paper presented a policy-based workflow methodology for modeling and monitoring e-contract agreements among agents interacting in the Semantic Web. The proposed methodology consists of a sequence of steps, grouped to five stages, which could be used for different types of on-line transactions among agents. In addition, the integration of this methodology into a knowledge-based multi-agent framework is proposed, that provides among others flexibility and reusability. This paper also provides a use case that illustrates the technologies proposed.

As for future directions, it would be interesting to verify our model's capability to adapt to an even wider variety of scenarios. Furthermore, it would be interesting to integrate the representation formalisms of both the public and private agent policies, so that they can interoperate by sharing base and inferred predicates.

Acknowledgements

NICTA is funded by the Australian Government as represented by the Department of Broadband, Communication and the Digital Economy and the Australian Research Council through the ICT Centre of Excellence Program.

References

1. Berners-Lee, T., et al.: The Semantic Web. Scientific American 284(5), 34–43 (2001)
2. Hendler, J.: Agents and the Semantic Web. IEEE Intelligent Systems 16(2), 30–37 (2001)
3. Krishna, P.R., Karlapalem, K., Dani, A.R.: From Contracts to E-Contracts: Modeling and Enactment. Inf. Technol. and Management 6(4), 363–387 (2005)
4. Merz, M., et al.: Supporting electronic commerce transactions with contracting services. International Journal of Cooperative Information Systems 7(4), 249–274 (1998)
5. Chiu, D.K.W., et al.: Workflow View Driven Cross-Organizational Interoperability in a Web-Service Environment. In: Bussler, C.J., McIlraith, S.A., Orlowska, M.E., Pernici, B., Yang, J. (eds.) CAiSE 2002 and WES 2002. LNCS, vol. 2512, pp. 41–56. Springer, Heidelberg (2002)
6. Daskalopulu, A., Dimitrakos, T., Maibaum, T.: E-Contract Fulfilment and Agents' Attitudes. In: ERCIM WG E-Commerce Workshop on The Role of Trust in e Business, Zurich (2001)
7. Winsborough, W., Li, N.: Safety in Automated Trust Negotiation. In: Proceedings of the 2004 IEEE Symposium on Security and Privacy, Oakland, CA, pp. 147–160. IEEE Press, Los Alamitos (2004)
8. Lee, A., Seamons, K., Winslett, M., Yu, T.: Automated Trust Negotiation in Open Systems. In: Secure Data Management in Decentralized Systems. Springer, Heidelberg (2007)
9. Kravari, K., Kontopoulos, E., Bassiliades, N.: Towards a Knowledge-based Framework for Agents Interacting in the Semantic Web. In: 2009 IEEE/WIC/ACM Int. Conf. on Intelligent Agent Technology (IAT 2009), Milan, Italy, vol. 2, pp. 482–485 (2009)
10. Kravari, K., Kontopoulos, E., Bassiliades, N.: A Trusted Defeasible Reasoning Service for Brokering Agents in the Semantic Web. In: 3rd Int. Symp. on Intelligent Distributed Computing (IDC 2009), Cyprus, October 13-14, vol. 237, pp. 243–248. Springer, Heidelberg (2009)
11. JESS, the Rule Engine for the Java Platform, http://www.jessrules.com/
12. Bassiliades, N., Antoniou, G., Vlahavas, I.: A Defeasible Logic Reasoner for the Semantic Web. IJSWIS 2(1), 1–41 (2006)

13. Boley, H.: An Introduction to Object-Oriented RuleML. In: Pires, F.M., Abreu, S.P. (eds.) EPIA 2003. LNCS (LNAI), vol. 2902, p. 4. Springer, Heidelberg (2003)

14. Nute, D.: Defeasible Reasoning. In: 20th Int. Conf. on Systems Science, pp. 470–477. IEEE Press, Los Alamitos (1987)

15. Li, N., Grosof, B.N., Feigenbaum, J.: Delegation Logic: A Logic-based Approach to Distributed Authorization. ACM Trans. on Information Systems Security 6(1) (2003)

16. Antoniou, G., Arief, M.: Executable Declarative Business rules and their use in Electronic Commerce. In: Proc. ACM Symposium on Applied Computing (2002)

17. Governatori, G.: Representing Business Contracts in RuleML. Int. J. of Cooperative Information Systems 14(2-3), 181–216 (2005)

18. Antoniou, G., Skylogiannis, T., Bikakis, A., Doerr, M., Bassiliades, N.: DR-BROKERING: A Semantic Brokering System. Knowledge-Based Systems 20(1), 61–72 (2007)

19. Governatori, G., ter Hofstede, A., Oaks, P.: Defeasible Logic for Automated Negotiation. In: Proceedings of CollECTeR 2000 (2000)

20. Governatori, G., Dumas, M., ter Hofstede, A., Oaks, P.: A formal approach to protocols and strategies for (legal) negotiation. In: Proc. ICAIL 2001, pp. 168–177 (2001)

21. Skylogiannis, T., Antoniou, G., Bassiliades, N., Governatori, G., Bikakis, A.: DR-NEGOTIATE – A System for Automated Agent Negotiation with Defeasible Logic-Based Strategies. Data & Knowledge Engineering 63(2), 362–380 (2007)

22. RuleML, http://ruleml.org/

23. RIF, http://www.w3.org/2005/rules/wiki/RIF_Working_Group

24. Best Business Bureau Organization, http://www.bbb.org/

25. Governatori, G., Hoang, D.P.: A Semantic Web Based Architecture for e-Contracts in Defeasible Logic. In: Adi, A., Stoutenburg, S., Tabet, S. (eds.) RuleML 2005. LNCS, vol. 3791, pp. 145–159. Springer, Heidelberg (2005)

26. Grosof, B.N., Poon, T.C.: SweetDeal: Representing Agent Contracts with Exceptions using XML Rules, Ontologies and Process Descriptions. In: 12th WWW, pp. 340–349. ACM Press, New York (2003)

27. Krishna, P.R., Karlapalem, K., Chiu, D.K.: An ER^{EC} Framework for e-contract Modeling, Enactment and Monitoring. Data Knowl. Eng. 51(1), 31–58 (2004)

28. Badica, C., Ganzha, M., Paprzycki, M.L.: Implementing Rule-Based Automated Price Negotiation in an Agent System. J. of Universal Computer Science 13(2), 244–266 (2007)

Photorealistic Semantic Web Service Groundings: Unifying RESTful and XML-RPC Groundings Using Rules, with an Application to Flickr

Dave Lambert and John Domingue

Knowledge Media Institute
The Open University
Milton Keynes, United Kingdom
d.j.lambert@open.ac.uk

Abstract. Semantic Web services achieve effects in the world through Web services, so the mechanism connecting the ontological representations of services with the on-the-wire messages—the grounding—is of paramount importance. The conventional approach to grounding is to use XML-based translations between ontologies and the SOAP message formats of the services, but these mappings cannot address the growing number of non-SOAP services, and step outside the ontological world to describe the mapping. We present an approach which draws the service's interface into the ontology: we define ontology objects which represent the whole HTTP message, and use backward-chaining rules to translate between semantic service invocation instances and the HTTP messages passed to and from the service. We show how this approach can be used to access the Flickr photo-sharing service through both its RESTful and XML-RPC interfaces.

1   Introduction

The field of semantic Web services uses ontologies to formally model the purpose and operation of Web services such that they can be intelligently used by machines. A crucial part of this is modelling how the Web service is invoked: the message format, and application protocol usage. The major semantic services frameworks—OWL-S [1], WSMO [2], and SA-WSDL [3]—assume services will be implemented using SOAP, and implemented brokers use XML mapping languages to translate between the XML serialisation of the ontology data and the on-the-wire messages exchanged with the Web service. This approach solves only the *data grounding* problem, and even then, solves it only for SOAP services.

Recent trends in Web services have shown that many developers, both on the client and server side, prefer to use techniques other than SOAP or even XML. In particular, XML-RPC is a popular lightweight alternative to SOAP which still uses XML, while RESTful interfaces [4] often eschew XML formats altogether in favour of JSON, or multimedia MIME types. An approach based on SOAP, and therefore XML, does not translate easily to non-SOAP flavours of Web service (Section 2).

M. Dean et al. (Eds.): RuleML 2010, LNCS 6403, pp. 240–250, 2010.
© Springer-Verlag Berlin Heidelberg 2010

In a previous paper [5] we introduced a method where the grounding was described entirely using an ontology language's frames and rules, and demonstrated how it could access Amazon's Simple Storage Service through its RESTful interface. In that paper we made but did not substantiate the claim that our approach could be extended to support other message formats, in particular XML-RPC and SOAP. In the current paper, we show how our technique can be used for XML-RPC. After recapping our approach (Section 3), we develop an ontological model for XML documents and XML-RPC messages (Section 4). We proceed to demonstrate upon Flickr—a popular picture sharing service, which happens to provide interfaces for REST, XML-RPC, and SOAP—presenting descriptions for some of Flickr's XML-RPC and RESTful services (Section 5). We compare our method to the usual approaches (Section 6) and conclude (Section 7).

2   Grounding Web Services

The objective of semantic Web services is to formally model the operation of Web services, so that intelligent agents can reason about them. A key part of the reasoning is concerned with the mechanism of service invocation. A semantic service broker must be able to convert an abstract 'invocation' expressed in terms of ontologies into the correct sequence of bytes sent to the correct network address to cause the service to operate, and to interpret the service's response. The process of translating between the ontological world of domain theories and the on-the-wire data formats and protocols is known as 'grounding' the service. For semantic Web services to be practical, brokers must be able to ground a comprehensive collection of real, actively used Web services.

For most of the lifetime of semantic Web services research, the de facto flavour of Web service was defined by XML [6], SOAP [7], and WSDL [8], which grew into the W3C's Web Services stack, colloquially known as 'WS-*'. As the complexity of the WS-* stack has increased, its popularity has waned, with many services now being offered using lighter weight alternatives. The genuinely simple protocol which inspired SOAP has re-emerged in its own right as XML-RPC [9]. More visibly, REST [4] has gained considerable mind-share: according to Amazon's Web services evangelist Jeff Barr, around 80% of invocations of Amazon's services are made through the REST interface.[1] Yahoo! does not provide a SOAP interface, and has no intention of adding one.[2] Flickr, a popular photo-sharing website, offers its API in SOAP, XML-RPC, and RESTful flavours. The SOAP interface does not have a WSDL description, and none of the the the third-party bindings[3] for the most popular languages target the SOAP variant:

---

[1] http://www.jeff-barr.com/?p=96

[2] http://developer.yahoo.com/faq/#soap

[3] http://www.flickr.com/services/api/

Flickr Binding	Language	API	Flickr Binding	Language	API
Flickcurl	C	REST	Flickr-Upload	Perl	REST
flickrj	Java	REST	phpFlickr	PHP	REST
jickr	Java	REST	flickr.py	Python	REST
FlickrNet	.NET	REST	flickr-ruby	Ruby	REST
Flickr-API	Perl	REST	rflickr	Ruby	XML-RPC

In most cases, the Flickr user is ultimately motivated by the prospect of obtaining a picture. Flickr's API provides only a RESTful means for retrieving the image, requiring the construction of the image's URL in one of several forms, the following being the simplest and most restrictive:

```
http://farm{farm-id}.static.flickr.com/{server-id}/{id}_{secret}.jpg
```

The `farm-id`, `server-id`, `id`, and `secret` parameters are part of a photo's identity, and can be obtained by calling one of several other Flickr services. There is no SOAP mechanism for retrieving images, and no way to couch the URL creation as an XML transformation. Although WSDL 2 [8] and WADL [10] can form URLs based on templates, many of the URLs used in RESTful interfaces are much too complicated for this. For example, the Flickr URL shortening service (similar to the TinyURL service) produces URLs of the form:

```
http://flic.kr/p/{base58-photo-id}
```

where `base58-photo-id` is an algorithmically specified mapping from a photo's details to a base 58 encoded string. RESTful authentication mechanisms also typically produce URLs which are impossible to define with a simple substitution template. A general grounding mechanism must not only support the XML that underlies SOAP, but also describe complex URL schemes, and at least handle, if not manipulate, the multimedia data that constitutes much of the data in the HTTP stream.

3   Ground Rules

We previously introduced our approach to grounding which we believe achieves these objectives [5], and in this section we quickly review the technique. The scheme has been implemented in the Internet Reasoning Service (IRS),[4] a broker based on the Web Services Modelling Ontology (WSMO) [11]. The IRS uses OCML [12] as its knowledge representation language and reasoner. OCML is a frame language with a Lisp syntax and procedural attachment, and is comparable in expressiveness to the Ontolingua and Loom languages. Although we implmented our approach in OCML, the technique is broadly applicable to KR languages with backward-chaining rules.

Our method is to model in ontologies the actual HTTP messages sent and received—including the URL, headers, and the content—and use rules in the ontology language to manage the mapping between those messages and the service invocation objects that the broker deals with anyway in managing the invocation. At a high level, the process of invoking a semantic Web service is:

---

[4] http://technologies.kmi.open.ac.uk/irs/

1. A user invokes a semantic service by calling the broker with a goal description described ontologically.

2. After some processing by mediators, an ontological Web service invocation instance is created. The invocation object holds the service name, input parameters, and slots to hold the return values from the Web service.

3. A rule from the service's semantic description is called to create an HTTP message object based on the service invocation object, with its various slots' values set to reflect the parameters from the the service invocation object.

4. The HTTP message is passed to the broker, which then turns the HTTP object directly into a request on the network.

When the service replies, the same procedure is preformed in reverse. The novelty of our scheme lies in step 3. We define two entry points, or generic rules, which we call `lower` and `lift`. These respectively 'lower' the service request object to an implementation level and 'lift' it back. Concretely, the two rule heads are

```
(lower ?serviceType ?serviceInvocation ?httpRequest)
(lift ?serviceType ?serviceInvocation ?httpResponse)
```

Each Web service description can define its own version of `lift` and `lower`, which the broker distinguishes by unifying on the `?serviceType` parameter that names the service being invoked. The `lower` rule's successful fulfilment leads to the instantiation of `?httpRequest`, which can then be directly interpreted by the broker to call the Web service. When a response is received from the server, the `lift` rule runs on the the newly returned `?httpResponse`, modifying the original `?serviceInvocation` frame to record the return values. The HTTP ontology defines the general form of the HTTP messages in a simple way:

```
(def-class HttpMessage ()
  ((hasHeader :type HttpHeader)
   (hasContent :type String :max-cardinality 1)))
```

with `HttpRequest` and `HttpResponse` subclassed from `HttpMessage`. Our grounding ontologies are relatively simple, being built solely for the purpose of supporting groundings, but they could in principle be general purpose ontologies developed for other uses in the respective domains.

As an example, consider the operation to retrieve an image (Section 2). Recall that this consists of performing an HTTP `GET` operation on a URL of the form:

```
http://farm{farm-id}.static.flickr.com/{server-id}/{id}_{secret}.jpg
```

If an invocation of that service had a `hasPhoto` slot which held the identifying features of the picture, the `lower` rule could be written thus:

```
(def-rule lowerGetFlickrImageService
  ((lower GetFlickrImageService ?invocation ?httpRequest) if
  (hasPhoto ?invocation ?photo)
  (hasFarmId ?photo ?farmId)
  (hasServerId ?photo ?serverId)
  (hasId ?photo ?id)
  (hasSecret ?photo ?secret)
  (= ?httpRequest (new HttpRequest))
  (= ?url (concatenate "http://farm" ?farmId ".static.flickr.com/"
                       ?serverId "/" ?id "_" ?secret ".jpg"))
  (assert (hasUrl ?httpRequest ?url))
  (assert (hasMethod ?httpRequest "GET"))))
```

We use `asserts` here because it is OCML's 'house style' as a mutation-oriented frame language, but we believe the rules would be clearer still in an immutable language. Once `lowerGetFlickrImageService` has succeeded, `?httpRequest` is bound to an instance of `HTTPRequest` whose method field is `GET`, and the URI field is the correctly constructed location of the photo resource.

4   Working with XML and XML-RPC

In many cases, the content of the HTTP messages will be XML, in particular, XML-RPC or SOAP messages. In our lift and lower rules, we could directly manipulate the string representations of XML, but this becomes cumbersome, prone to error, and fails to 'model' in any meaningful way the transformations. Instead, we introduce simple ontologisations of XML and XML-RPC, and using these we can then write simple lifting and lowering rules.

Our ontologies are straightforward. XML is modelled with a `Document` concept, which has a `rootElement` of type `Element`. In turn, `Elements` have children which are `Elements` or `Text`, and they also have lists of `Attributes`. Such structures can be transformed into their corresponding strings, and back again, with the relation `serialiseXml`. The essentials are shown in Figure 1.

```
(def-class Document ()                  (def-class Attribute ()
  ((rootElement :type Element)))          ((name :type string)
                                           (value :type string)))
(def-class Element ()
  ((tag :type string)                   (def-class Contents () ?contents
   (attributes :type Attributes)          :iff-def
   (contents :type Contents)))            (and (listp ?contents)
                                               (every ?contents
(def-class Attributes () ?attributes                 (or Element Text))))
  :iff-def
  (and (listp ?attributes)             (def-class Text ()
       (every ?attributes Attribute)))   ((value :type string)))
```

Fig. 1. XML ontologisation in OCML

An XML-RPC [9] message is a simple serialisation of a remote procedure call, for example:

```
<?xml version="1.0"?>
<methodCall>
   <methodName>examples.getStateName</methodName>
   <params>
      <param><value><i4>41</i4></value></param>
   </params>
</methodCall>
```

The content of an XML-RPC service invocation is a `MethodCall`, comprising a `MethodName` and a list of parameters. Each parameter `Param` has a typed value, which may be a simple scalar, an array, or a structure. These are represented by matching concepts in the ontology, shown in Figure 2.

```
(def-class MethodCall ()
    ((methodName :type MethodName
                 :cardinality 1)
     (params :type ListOfParam)))

(def-class ListOfParam () ?list
    :iff-def (and (listp ?list)
                  (every ?list Param)))

(def-class MethodName ()
    ((value :type string)))

(def-class Params ())

(def-class Param ()
    ((value :type Value)))

(def-class Value ())
```

```
(def-class scalarValue (Value))

(def-class I4 (scalarValue)
    ((value :type integer)))

(def-class Boolean (scalarValue)
    ((value :type boolean)))

(def-class String (scalarValue)
    ((value :type string)))

(def-class Struct (Param)
    ())

(def-class Member ()
    ((name :type string)
     (value :type Param)))
```

Fig. 2. XML-RPC ontologisation in OCML (an illustrative subset only)

The relation xmlrpcToXml deals with mapping from the XML-RPC ontological objects to XML ontological objects, which can then be serialised to a string of XML with serialiseXml.

5 Flickr

We now illustrate the use of rules to create groundings for both RESTful and XML-RPC interfaces to Flickr services. Flickr is a commerical website offering 'freemium' hosting of users' photographs, combined with social-networking facilities for the structured sharing of those images. Flickr provides a sizable API to examine the metadata around the images themselves. We have already seen how an image can be retrieved from Flickr (Section 3), but to do that, we must discover the details about an image required to construct the URL.

We will skip the intricacies of creating an account, setting up API keys and the like, although we have create groundings for those services, too. For this paper, our concern is with *a*) getting a list of recently changed photos in a user's account *b*) getting a list of sizes in which those are available . The relevant services are flickr.photos.recentlyUpdated and flickr.photos.getSizes. The Flickr API provides interfaces for SOAP, XML-RPC, and REST, but for all three, services are defined in terms of a Flickr-specific abstraction for passing arguments. Each method takes a set of name/value pairs, and this is then cryptographically signed to ensure security. The flickr.photos.recentlyUpdated method takes three arguments, api_key, auth_token, and min_date, while flickr.photos.getSizes takes arguments api_key, auth_token, and photo_id. The api_key identifies the application making the request, and the auth_token is obtained when a user grants a particular application access to their account. Figure 3 shows the rule for signing an argument set with an account key, which amounts to taking the MD5 sum of a string which is the concatenation of the application's 'secret' key, and the name/value pairs of the arguments (this ordering is arranged by

```
(def-rule signArguments
    ((signArguments ?flavour ?arguments ?account) if
    (hasSecret ?account ?secret)
    (hasValue ?secret ?secret-string)
    (canonicalArgumentsString ?flavour ?arguments ?canonical-args)
    (= ?to-be-signed (concatenate ?secret-string ?canonical-args))
    (= ?signature (md5sum ?to-be-signed))
    (addArgument ?args "api_sig" ?signature)))
```

Fig. 3. Signing a call

```
(def-rule lower-for-photosRecentlyUpdatedRestService
    ((lower photosRecentlyUpdatedRestService ?invocation ?http-request) if
    (= ?account (wsmo-role-value ?invocation hasAccount))
    (= ?token (wsmo-role-value ?invocation hasToken))
    (= ?min-date (wsmo-role-value ?invocation hasMinimumDate))
    (hasKey ?account ?apikey)
    (hasValue ?apikey ?apikey-string)
    (hasValue ?token ?token-string)
    (= ?args (new-instance Arguments))
    (addArgument ?args "method" "flickr.photos.recentlyUpdated")
    (addArgument ?args "api_key" ?apikey-string)
    (addArgument ?args "auth_token" ?token-string)
    (addArgument ?args "min_date" ?min-date)
    (signArguments rest ?args ?account)
    (argsToRestRequest ?args ?http-request)))
```

Fig. 4. Lowering rule for RESTful `photos.recentlyUpdated`

```
(def-rule argsToRestRequest
    ((argsToRestRequest ?arguments ?http-request) if
    (= ?args (setofall ?pairs
                (and (hasArgument ?arguments ?argument)
                (hasName ?argument ?name)
                (hasValue ?argument ?value)
                (= ?pairs (?name ?value)))))
    (listAsQuery ?args ?query)
    (= ?url (concatenate "http://api.flickr.com/services/rest/?" ?query))
    (rfc2616:set-url ?http-request ?url)
    (rfc2616:set-method ?http-request "GET")))
```

Fig. 5. Translation from an argument set to a RESTful HTTP GET message

the `canonicalArgumentsString` relation, which for brevity is not shown). The `signArguments` rule is used by lowering rules where required.

The lowering rule for the RESTful `flickr.recentlyUpdated` service is shown in Figure 4. The rule is straightforward, with the first half concerned with extracting from the `?invocation` the necessary argument values, and the second half constructing an `Arguments` instance using those values. The last two lines ensure the arguments are signed, and then pack the arguments into an HTTP request. The conversion from an argument set to an HTTP request is handled by the `argsToRestRequest` rule, shown in Figure 5.

`argsToRestRequest` constructs a URL with the arguments in the form

```
param1=value1&param2=value2...
```

and sets the `?http-request` fields appropriately. The lifting rule is shown in Figure 6.

```
(def-rule lift-for-photosRecentlyUpdatedRestService
    ((lift photosRecentlyUpdatedRestService ?http-response ?invocation) if
    (rfc2616:get-content ?http-response ?http-content)
    (xml:serialiseXml ?xml ?http-content)
    (xml:rootElement ?xml ?root-element)
    (xml:elementByName ?root-element ?photos-element "photos")
    (extractXmlPhotoList ?photos-element ?photolist)
    (set-goal-slot-value ?invocation hasPhotoList ?photolist)))
```

Fig. 6. Lifting rule for RESTful `photos.recentlyUpdated`

In lifting the response, we extract the content from the `?http-response`, convert it into an ontological model of the XML, and use a rule `extractXmlPhotoList` (not shown) to extract the appropriate fields and build an ontological list of the contents. With this list of photographs, we are now ready to invoke the second service, `flickr.photos.getSizes`. We will invoke this service in XML-RPC.

```
(def-rule lower-for-photosGetSizesXmlrpcService
    ((lower photosGetSizesXmlrpcService ?invocation ?http-request) if
    (argsForPhotosGetSizes ?invocation ?args)
    (= ?account (wsmo-role-value ?invocation hasAccount))
    (signArguments xmlrpc ?args ?account)
    (argsToXmlrpcRequest ?args ?http-request)))
```

Fig. 7. Lowering rule for `flickr.photos.getSizes`

```
(def-rule argsToXmlrpcRequest
    ((argsToXmlrpcRequest ?args ?http-request) if
    (getArgument ?args "method" ?method)
    (= ?nonmethodargs
    (setofall ?member
            (and (hasArgument ?args ?arg)
                 (hasName ?arg ?name)
                 (not (= ?name "method"))
                 (hasValue ?arg ?value)
                 (= ?member (xmlrpc:Member ?name
                                        (xmlrpc:String ?value))))))
    (= ?xmlrpc
       (xmlrpc:MethodCall ?method
                          (xmlrpc:Param (xmlrpc:Struct ?nonmethodargs))))
    (xmlrpc:mapToXml ?xmlrpc ?xmlmodel)
    (xml:serialiseXml ?xmlmodel ?xmlstring)
    (rfc2616:set-content ?http-request ?xmlstring)
    (rfc2616:set-method ?http-request "POST")
    (rfc2616:set-url ?http-request
                    "http://api.flickr.com/services/xmlrpc/")))
```

Fig. 8. Translation from argument set to an XML-RPC message

Figure 7 shows the lowering rule for this XML-RPC service. This time, the conversion from the invocation object to the argument pairs used by Flickr is done in another rule `argsForPhotosGetSizes` (not shown). The use of a rule for this means we could share the logic between the XML-RPC version shown here, and a REST or SOAP version. The argument set is again signed using `signArguments`, and then passed to a new rule `argsToXmlrpcRequest`, shown in Figure 8.

In `argsToXmlrpcRequest` we see similar machinary to that in `argsToRestRequest` for converting the argument set, but this time we create an XML-RPC message with a `Struct` to hold the pairs, rather than embedding them in a URL.

6   Related Work

WSDL [13] has been the de facto means of specifying Web service interfaces since the birth of Web services. Both OWL-S [1] and WSMO [11] define their groundings by pointing at the WSDL of their targets, but the mapping to the syntactic content of the messages is something of a grey area. The OWL-S WSDL document [14] suggests that OWL-S services should require Web services to use an OWL specific encoding in their implementation. The semantic annotation extensions for WSDL— WSDL-S and then SA-WSDL (Semantic Annotations for Web Service Description Language) [3]—provide a vocabulary to link the WSDL descriptions to mapping schemas to handle the lifting and lowering, but the mechanism of the schemas themselves is not specified, and is XML-centric. The IRS previously used XPath expressions to generate OCML relations which performed the lifting and lowering. Another WSMO based broker, the Web Services Execution Environment (WSMX) uses service-specific 'adaptors', written in Java, to connect to services.

Although the principle of 'lifting and lowering' the XML serialisation is well established, it does not address aspects of the HTTP protocol like the `Authorization` header that many services require for authentication. Moreover, assuming XML translation precludes the use of services that do not employ XML at all. Although WSDL and SOAP are products of the W3C standards, there is significant disquiet amongst developers about their complexity, interoperability, and the way they ignore the Web's architecture. Personal experience has made us skeptical of the quality of WSDL and XSD descriptions, even, or perhaps especially, machine generated ones. Finally, using an XML mapping scheme like XSLT forces the ontology engineer to leave the semantic realm to work on the groundings, and to consider the domain objects in terms of their XML serialisation. In contrast, our groundings unify the lifting and lowering with the management of the HTTP protocol, and are declarative and wholly within the ontology language, modulo the small number of operational primitives such as cryptography functions. Since there are relatively few data encoding and cryptography schemes—many orders of magnitude fewer than there will be Web services—it makes sense to embed them in semantic brokers, and make them available to rules at the ontology level. Such facilities will need to be present one way or another: in our scheme, they are available as reusable primitives, and the number of them therefore kept to a minimum. With these hooks in place, we can encode groundings to a large number of important, real-world Web services in a unified, ontology-based manner.

7   Conclusion

Semantic Web services are about Web services as well as semantics. In this paper, we extended an approach to groundings rooted in ontologies and rules, adding support for XML content and XML-RPC Web services. As an illustration, we described some of the services provided by Flickr, the popular photo sharing site. We have implemented the ontologies discussed in the IRS broker.

We see this approach as a useful low-level implementation platform: it is sufficiently powerful to connect to any kind of HTTP service, and yet is fully accessible from the ontological level. It is general enough, for instance, that it could support multi-part MIME messages. The resulting rules are simple from an engineering perspective, allowing easy reuse of component rules, and declarative description of the necessary operations. For the Flickr services described here, a handful of rules capture the general invocation pattern, and lifting or lowering rules for individual services are compact. Future work will involve a translation to RDF, reusing vocabularies like the W3C's RDF schema for HTTP.[5] We also intend to support SOAP messages directly at the ontological level, in a similar fashion to the XML-RPC support developed here. We intend to create ontologies to model WSDL descriptions, and from there to permit some level of automatic lifting and lowering based on the available information from the WSDL. The same could be done for WADL, and SA-WSDL. Since other semantic Web services work has established XSLT as a means for performing these translations, we should be able to reuse existing XSLT mappings within rules when available.

Acknowledgements

This research was funded by the European Union projects Living Human Digital Library (FP6-026932) and SOA4All (FP7-215219). We thank Marta Sabou and Barry Norton for interesting discussions.

References

1. Martin, D., Burstein, M., Hobbs, J., Lassila, O., McDermott, D., McIlraith, S., Narayanan, S., Paolucci, M., Parsia, B., Payne, T., Sirin, E., Srinivasan, N., Sycara, K.: OWL-S: Semantic Markup for Web Services. W3C member submission, World Wide Web Consortium, W3C (November 2004)
2. Lausen, H., Polleres, A., Roman, D.: Web Service Modeling Ontology (WSMO). W3C member submission, World Wide Web Consortium, W3C (June 2005)
3. Farrell, J., Lausen, H.: Semantic Annotations for WSDL and XML Schema. W3C recommendation, World Wide Web Consortium, W3C (August 2007)
4. Fielding, R.T.: Architectural Styles and the Design of Network-based Software Architectures. PhD thesis, University of California, Irvine (2000)
5. Lambert, D., Domingue, J.: Grounding semantic web services with rules. In: Gangemi, A., Keizer, J., Presutti, V., Stoermer, H. (eds.) Proceedings of the 5th Workshop on Semantic Web Applications and Perspectives (SWAP 2008). CEUR Workshop Proceedings, vol. 426 (December 2008)
6. Bray, T., Paoli, J., Sperberg-McQueen, C.M., Maler, E., Yergeau, F.: Extensible Markup Language (XML) 1.0. W3C recommendation, World Wide Web Consortium, W3C (2008)

---

[5] http://www.w3.org/TR/HTTP-in-RDF/

7. Box, D., Ehnebuske, D., Kakivaya, G., Layman, A., Mendelsohn, N., Nielsen, H.F., Thatte, S., Winer, D.: Simple Object Access Protocol (SOAP) 1.1. W3C recommendation, World Wide Web Consortium, W3C (May 2000)
8. Chinnici, R., Moreau, J.J., Ryman, A., Weerawarana, S.: Web Services Description Language (WSDL) Version 2.0 Part 1: Core Language. W3C recommendation, World Wide Web Consortium, W3C (June 2007)
9. Winer, D.: XML-RPC Specification (June 1999), http://www.xmlrpc.com/spec
10. Hadley, M.J.: Web Application Description Language (WADL). W3C member submission, World Wide Web Consortium, W3C (November 2006)
11. Fensel, D., Lausen, H., Polleres, A., de Bruijn, J., Stollberg, M., Roman, D., Domingue, J.: Enabling Semantic Web Services. Springer, Heidelberg (2006)
12. Motta, E.: An Overview of the OCML Modelling Language. In: 8th Workshop on Knowledge Engineering: Methods & Languages, KEML 1998 (1998)
13. Christensen, E., Curbera, F., Meredith, G., Weerawarana, S.: Web Services Description Language (WSDL) 1.1. W3C recommendation, World Wide Web Consortium (W3C)(2001)
14. Martin, D., Burstein, M., Lassila, O., Paolucci, M., Payne, T., McIlraith, S.: Describing Web Services using OWL-S and WSDL

Towards the Web of Models: A Rule-Driven RESTful Architecture for Distributed Systems

Alexandros Marinos and Paul Krause

Department of Computing, FEPS, University of Surrey,
GU2 7XH, Guildford, Surrey, United Kingdom
{a.marinos,p.krause}@surrey.ac.uk

Abstract. Competing visions have been jostling to define the long-term future of the Web: WS-* Web Services, the Semantic Web, and RESTful Web Services. This paper presents the initial steps towards a Rule-driven, REST-based architecture for the Web that can enable use cases that the Semantic Web and WS-* communities require. The key enabling ingredient is the use of SBVR models as a media type for resource description that allows models to be exposed and consumed. With formal description of data, advanced scenarios such as inference, service composition, and transactions are feasible within an architecture that is backwards-compatible with today's Web.

Keywords: REST, SBVR, Distributed Systems, Web Engineering, Service Composition, Transactions.

1 Introduction

Since its inception, the Web has radically expanded its limits to include ever more people, and cover an ever increasing part of their everyday activities. While initially based on a very straightforward architecture, the aspirations of its users soon exceeded the limits of what was possible within it. So a number of parties started extending that architecture to enable their own use cases. The architecture was gradually revised to include more and more of the low-hanging fruit, and reached a stable point with the release of HTTP 1.1, URI (RFC 3305) and HTML 4. Recent efforts to revise that architecture tend to be practitioner-driven in their approach, intending to enable new uses and standardize widespread practices, without causing deep changes to the way the Web works. Examples of this are HTML 5 and the HTTPbis efforts. At the same time, at least three camps have been jostling to define the long-term vision for a Web where machines will be able to participate as users just as humans do on today's Web. In this paper we examine the competing visions and propose criteria for a way forward. Based on these criteria, we propose an architecture built on RESTful Web Services, Semantics of Business Vocabulary and Rules (SBVR) [1] as a modelling language, and proceed to show how a number of advanced use cases can be built upon this minimal foundation.

M. Dean et al. (Eds.): RuleML 2010, LNCS 6403, pp. 251–258, 2010.

2 Visions for the Future Web

The competing approaches are Representational State Transfer (REST), the Semantic Web and Linked Data, and WS-* web services. Each one descending from a different tradition, using divergent vocabularies to emphasise different use cases and considerations.

The WS-* web services efforts [2], also known as Big Web Services [3] are rooted in enterprise systems vendors and the history of that industry. Starting out as vendor-specific Remote Procedure Call (RPC) technologies, many of these consolidated in the 90's leaving CORBA and DCOM as the only major competitors in this space. With the introduction of SOAP, the companies in both camps worked together in building up the WS-* standards. The focus of these efforts was in service description, discovery, composition and transactions, as well as governance and reliability. The work of Jim Waldo [4] already in 1994 however, stressed the problems with RPC-based approaches to distributed computing. In recent years most of the implementation of WS-* technologies has been limited to the interior of the corporate firewalls.

The Semantic Web[6] and more recently the Linked Data[7] movement have been focusing on expressing or annotating data on the web with machine-readable semantics. With a strong Artificial Intelligence and Formal Methods background, the Semantic Web community has a focus on ontology and aims for novel inferences to arise from this Web of Data. Like the WS-* effort, they have produced a stack of standards such as RDF, RDFS, OWL, OWL-S which until recently have had relatively limited adoption. The effort by W3C to recast HTML into XHTML which would have allowed for more natural integration with the Semantic Web efforts has recently been abandoned in favour of HTML 5. Similarly, the early versions of RSS, based on the Resource Description Framework (RDF) have been rejected in favour of plain XML-based approaches. Controversial elements are the assumption that all RDF triples in a graph are equally trustworthy, as well as the use of HTTP as a read-only protocol, both very limiting in multipurpose distributed systems like the Web. Recently, Linked Data has achieved some success with owners of large data sets such as government organizations, and there are now vast collections of interlinked triplets, forming what is called the Web of Data.

Representational State Transfer is an approach that focuses on the principles behind the architecture of the Web. As such, its ambition may appear limited at first, compared to the other two visionary approaches. Its focus is on scalability, loose coupling, linkability and ease of maintenance [3]. It is a direct result of the work of Roy Fielding in developing HTTP, as described in his doctoral dissertation [5]. What sets REST apart is that its focus is not on novel technologies as much as on a principled use of those already available, mainly HTTP, URI, and the various hypermedia formats. The principles are well defined as a set of architectural constraints that are reflected in the operation of these standards. These are: Naming of resources, the uniform interface, statelessness and self-descriptive messages, manipulation of resources through representations, and use of hypermedia as the engine of application state. Each of these can and has been used on today's Web with great effect. The result has been a large recent shift in interest away from WS-* standards and towards RESTful Web Services on the part of web practitioners, especially when publishing services on the open Web. Perhaps the most well known usage of REST as a machine-to-machine interaction paradigm is the increasing use of feeds (RSS, ATOM) not only for their native blog subscription scenarios, but also as a generic mechanism to communicate updates between services. Recent advances include podcasting and real-time feeds.

An immediate comparison can be made between the granularities of the three approaches. WS-* web services are the most coarse grained with the fundamental element being a 'service endpoint'. Knowing the historical background helps to explain this, but in the context of the Web, limitations such as not being able to use hyperlinks becomes a big drawback. REST focuses on the concept of a 'resource' as identifying a unit that the service deems important enough to name with a URI. A RESTful web service can and usually does break down to multitude of interconnected resources. Finally, the Linked Data approach is to focus on the RDF triple as its primitive element. While this is arguably more granular than a resource, there has been very little work on addressing individual triples. As a result, HTTP is used to read collections of triples, and SPARQL [8] and the newer SPARQL Update [9] being used as means to make queries and updates on collections of triples at SPARQL endpoints. The SPARQL concept of an 'endpoint' is reminiscent of the 'service endpoint' of the WS-* approach, and can even be described with WSDL as a web service. This brings us back to the service level of granularity in terms of linkable entities.

Table 1. Comparing the Visions for the Future Web

Approach	Community Background	Target Properties	Primitive Object	Use Cases	Key Standards
Semantic Web	AI, Formal Logics	Data accessibility, Semantic annotation	Predicate (RDF Triple)	Data analysis, Automated reasoning	RDF, RDFS, OWL, SPARQL
WS-* Web Services	Enterprise Systems	Governance, Reliability, Security	Service / Procedure	Service Composition, Transactions	SOAP, WSDL, UDDI,
RESTful Web Services	Distributed Systems, Software Architecture, Web Development	Scalability, Evolvability, Loose coupling, Linkability	Resource	Web Sites, Feeds, Search Engines	HTTP, HTML, URI, ATOM

To judge any competing proposals for the future of the Web, a consistent set of criteria must be applied. Our specific agenda is in supporting openness and agility in the development and evolution of web services. A parsimonious set of criteria for assessing the viability of any approach in supporting this agenda is the following:

- *Compatibility*: It must be backwards compatible with today's Web to the greatest extent possible.
- *Simplicity*: It must place the least amount of overhead to adoption for developers and users alike.

- *Completeness*: It must allow the different communities to implement as many of their critical use cases as possible.

This short paper places the work of [11] in the broader context of enabling use cases that the Semantic Web and WS-* communities require. In many cases, concepts and even technologies from all three approaches can be used together under the architectural principles of REST to reach these goals.

3 Media Types

One area where the Semantic Web and WS-* approaches have put a lot more effort is that of service description. WSDL and OWL-S focus on exactly this task. Contrary to common perception, there is a place for descriptions in REST, and that is the media type. Roy Fielding in his seminal PhD dissertation writes:

> "The data format of a representation is known as a media type. A representation can be included in a message and processed by the recipient according to the control data of the message and the nature of the media type. Some media types are intended for automated processing, some are intended to be rendered for viewing by a user, and a few are capable of both." [5]

In the course of a sequence of RESTful interactions, media types should contain all the information that is not being communicated through HTTP. When there is a human driving the interaction, the semantics of the resource can be discerned from the content. When however machines need to act as clients, the semantics of a novel type of resource are not clear. This seems to be the canonical use case for the Semantic Web, and thus we can identify the media type as the appropriate place to communicate the semantics of the resource type. This is supported by modern uses of media types, such as ATOM, which use the media type designation to imply not only syntactic information but also semantic information by linking to the appropriate specification.

We propose the introduction of a single new high-level media type (*application/vnd.sbvr-described+xml*) that enables resources that use it to describe themselves at run time. The *+xml* suffix should be replaceable with *+json* or other equivalents if necessary. This allows clients that implement it to react to unforeseen types of resources, in keeping with the general spirit of the Web. In fact, in the spirit of trying to eradicate out-of-band information, this approach would offer a drastic step forward, as it would offer an in-band way to communicate information that was not known to the designers of the client. In a previous publication [11] the potential of an SBVR-described media type was first discussed with the example of a student record resource. Here, we discuss how the media type *application/vnd.sbvr-described+xml* covers four types of information that a media type can convey: syntax; meta-model; schema; and, semantics.

The syntax is covered by the specification of XML as a serialisation format. If one considers SBVR to be the semantic meta-model, then that is specified directly by the media type also. This leaves schema and semantics. Firstly, the vocabulary gives us the terms that are allowed to occur. Secondly, the fact types define which terms can appear directly below or above which other terms. We can start to see the formation of a tree. Other, more structured pieces of information can be requested by following the hyperlinks provided. Finally, constraints allow the client to have specific expectation with regard to the cardinality of elements that it expects to find.

Finally, SBVR models contain definitions for each term. This is a link to semantic information that can be used by the client. Some of these definitions resolve to other terms, some to natural language, and some to outside sources. Unfortunately exposing semantics for novel concepts in an automated fashion is an open problem, but this approach removes all other layers of complexity and exposes this problem directly, making it accessible to various lines of investigation.

We have thus far shown how media type information can be communicated with the introduction a new SBVR-enabled media type, and how this media type can cover the possible requirements that a media type may have to cover. This is not to say this media type can cover all possible needs, but a large spectrum of previously hard use cases is indeed made much more accessible.

Once we can have resources exposing models, or fragments of an overall model, as a description, the question of consuming the exposed models arises. We refer to our earlier paper [11] and the related paper at this conference [16] for more information on this.

4   Model Propagation

The previous section discussed ways of exposing and consuming rule-based descriptions of resources. Thus far we have not made assumptions about the internal operation of the nodes, but this architecture has been developed as an interaction paradigm for Generative Information Systems (GIS), which use SBVR as their internal modelling language as well as external resource description language. It is important to note that while GIS are the canonical example, in the spirit of backward compatibility, anything that can be done in a GIS can be done in a conventional information system. The internal architecture of a GIS simply allows it to do so more efficiently, utilising the full strength of the new paradigm.

It is important to note that our concept of information system is as a two-tiered system, where both model and data are dynamic [11]. The model exposes itself to others that can incorporate it into their service models, and it can change when the models it itself depends on change. This is usual behaviour for data, but highly unusual for models which are supposed to be fixed at design time and need long and involved development cycles to be revised.

5   Service Composition and Transactions

Having covered resource description, model incorporation and model propagation, we have the building blocks to discuss the higher-level use cases that are common topics in the Semantic Web and WS-* communities. Having incorporated logic-based rules into our architecture it is relatively simple to see how an inference engine would operate over the information in this system. In fact, inference is fundamental to the way the Generative Information Systems operate in determining whether an update is allowed and whether it will leave the node in a consistent state. Inference however, can be thought of as a special case of service composition.

According to [13], service composition can be subdivided into three categories: Fulfilling Preconditions; Generating Multiple Effects; and, Dealing with Missing Knowledge. A typical example of service composition is the well-known travel scenario where flight and hotel can be booked independently but must be coordinated. Once the correct combination of services is found, the execution must be made in a transactional manner.

In our case, we can describe an augmented travel scenario that allows us to explore the potential of model propagation and the meta-process described above. To begin with, we assume various service businesses (airlines, hotels, taxi agencies, sightseeing services) that offer their products as resources in a RESTful ecosystem, and expose them through SBVR descriptions. A Travel agent service can select quality providers, import their resources and expose them as resources available from its own API. Also, it can create higher-level 'travel package' resources which can act as a container for a number of provider resources (flight, taxi booking, hotel reservation) but also add extra business logic, concerning the consistency between the items in a travel package. So for instance all the items have to be related with the same destination, there is a single starting date for the trip, etc. Further, we can suppose that the travel agency services businesses that make the 'travel package' resource available to their employees. To do that they simply import the travel package resource description from the travel agency. However, each business has its own set of regulations about travel. Some may disallow certain locations, others may place limits on the total budget. These additional constraints can be added to the model such that an employee cannot book a non-compliant travel package through the API of the business. Through this example we can see three levels of business logic nesting which happens naturally.

In order to see how such a scenario would work out in real life, it is necessary to examine the behaviour of the meta-process when operating recursively. Being in a distributed environment, model propagation is also in effect. So, if a number of resources are being written to as part of a travel package, once the business logic of the organization whose employee is making the booking is satisfied, the changes are propagated to the travel agency. It is important to note that the organisation's API does not return success at that point but waits for the response of the travel agency's API. Given that this is a RESTful environment, depending on the semantics of the operation applied, HTTP provides a number of options to deal with the case of no timely response, and these can be taken advantage of by our architecture. Also, HTTP responses such as `202 Accepted` allow the server to acknowledge receipt of the data and defer producing the result.

Once the request reaches the server of the travel agency, the meta-process gets executed again, this time at the travel agency's node, with the organisation's node as a client. The agency's logic is checked for violations, and again the prospect of success or failure is opened. One possible failure mode is that the service has changed its internal logic so the client (the organizational client in this case) is operating on a stale cached copy. In this case, the violated rule is returned as an error, and the client can inform their users. At the same time the client knows that it needs to update the description of the relevant resources it's using. In every case, the updates can then be propagated further until all relevant nodes in this 'web of models' are aware of the new rules. The other alternative is that the request has violated a non-public rule. In that case a generic response is returned.

The in the case where a request that is submitted to the travel agency succeeds, it will be broken down into parts and each provider will receive the sub-request that is relevant to them. But since the travel agency is interfacing with multiple providers, it needs to make sure that the requests either all succeed or all fail. To guarantee this, a transaction model is required, and since our architecture is RESTful the transaction model needs to operate within the Web Architecture's constraints also. To this end, the authors of this paper have developed RETRO [14], A RESTful Transaction Model, capable of atomic transactions across distributed HTTP systems.

This description of a service composition scenario is a smaller but updated version of previous work done by the authors on declarative service composition with SBVR [15].

6 Conclusions and Future Work

In this paper we have brought together concepts and use cases from the three leading schools of thought regarding the future of the Web and constructed an outline of a novel step forward for Web Architecture paradigm. We have used the concept of resource orientation, hypermedia, and constrained distributed interaction from REST, the ideas of service description, transactions, and the use case of service composition from WS-* and the idea of using formal logic semantics and the use case of knowledge integration from the Semantic Web community. All these are brought together into a coherent whole that is backwards compatible with the REST-based architecture of today's web. This short position paper should be read in conjunction with [16] which expands on the current technical work that is in progress to realise this vision.

Overall, we feel that this unique combination of traits and use cases can genuinely contribute to the discussion about the future of the Web and highlight rule-based approaches in general and SBVR in particular as a powerful paradigm that can act as a unifying force and expose new avenues for exploration.

Acknowledgements

This work has been supported by the European Commission through IST Project OPAALS: (No. IST-2005-034824).

References

1. Object Management Group, Semantics of Business Vocabulary and Rules Formal Specification v1.0, OMG document formal/08-01-02 (January 2008), http://www.omg.org/spec/SBVR/1.0/ (accessed 11/6/2010)
2. World Wide Web Consortium, Web Services Architecture", W3C Working Group Note (February 11, 2004), http://www.w3.org/TR/ws-arch/ (accessed: 11/6/2010)

3. Richardson, L., Ruby, S.: RESTful Web Services. O'Reilly Media, Inc., Sebastopol (2007)
4. Waldo, J., Wyant, G., Wollrath, A., Kendall, S.: A note on distributed computing, Technical Report SMLI TR-94-29, Sun Microsystems Laboratories, Inc. (November 1994)
5. Fielding, R.T.: Architectural Styles and the Design of Network-based Software Architectures. University of California, Irvine (2000)
6. World Wide Web Consortium, W3C Semantic Web Activity, http://www.w3.org/2001/sw/ (accessed: 11/6/2010)
7. Berners-Lee, T.: Linked Data (2006), http://www.w3.org/DesignIssues/LinkedData.html (accessed: 11/6/2010)
8. World Wide Web Consortium, SPARQL Query Language for RDF, http://www.w3.org/TR/rdf-sparql-query/ (accessed: 11/6/2010)
9. World Wide Web Consortium, SPARQL Update: A language for updating RDF graphs (2008), http://www.w3.org/Submission/SPARQL-Update/ (accessed: 11/6/2010)
10. Gregorio, J., De Hora, B.: The Atom Publishing Protocol, Internet RFC 5023 (October 2007), http://www.ietf.org/rfc/rfc5023.txt (accessed: 11/6/2010)
11. Marinos, A., Krause, P.: An SBVR Framework for RESTful Web Applications. In: Governatori, G., Hall, J., Paschke, A. (eds.) RuleML 2009. LNCS, vol. 5858, pp. 144–158. Springer, Heidelberg (2009)
12. Lee, D., Chu, W.W.: Comparative analysis of six XML schema languages. ACM SIGMOD Record 29(3), 76–87 (2000)
13. Kuster, U., Stern, M., Konig-Ries, B.: A Classification of Issues and Approaches in Automatic Service Composition. In: Intl. Workshop WESC, vol. 5 (2005)
14. Marinos, A., Razavi, A., Moschoyiannis, S., Krause, P.: RETRO: A (hopefully) RESTful Transaction Model, Technical Report CS-09-01, University of Surrey, Guildford, Surrey (August 2009)
15. Marinos, A., Krause, P.: Using SBVR, REST and Relational Databases to develop Information Systems native to the Digital Ecosystem. In: IEEE Conference on Digital Ecosystems Technologies 2009, DEST 2009 (2009)
16. Marinos, A., Moschoyiannis, S., Krause, P.: Generating SQL Queries from SBVR Rules. In: Dean, M., Hall, J., Rotolo, A., Tabet, S. (eds.) RuleML 2010. LNCS, vol. 6403, pp. 128–143. Springer, Heidelberg (2010)

Visualizing Logical Dependencies in SWRL Rule Bases

Saeed Hassanpour, Martin J. O'Connor, and Amar K. Das

Stanford Center for Biomedical Informatics Research,
Stanford, CA 94305, U.S.A.
{saeedhp,martin.oconnor,amar.das}@stanford.edu

Abstract. Rule bases are common in many business rule applications, clinical decision support programs, and other types of intelligent systems. As the size of the rule bases grows and the interrelationships between rules become more complex, understanding dependencies among rules can be quite difficult. To address this challenge, we propose a novel approach for modeling logical dependencies among rules and for discovering patterns based on these dependencies. Our method uses rules bases written in the Semantic Web Rule Language (SWRL); we exploit SWRL's logical relationship with OWL to incorporate these semantics in our analysis. We couple this analysis with visualization techniques that create a rule dependency graph. We group nodes into layers based on their dependencies and cluster nodes within a layer if they have similar dependencies. We have evaluated our approach by applying it to two independently developed, publicly available ontologies containing SWRL rules. We show how our analysis and visualization approach can allow users to quickly examine patterns of logical relationships in such rule bases.

Keywords: Rule base management, Rule base visualization, Rule dependency, Ontology, SWRL, OWL.

1 Introduction

The Semantic Web Rule Language (SWRL; [1]) has become the *de facto* standard rule language for developing rule bases on the Semantic Web. SWRL is based on the Ontology Web Language (OWL; [2]) and shares its strong formal underpinnings yet is relatively easy to learn and use. However, in common with many rule languages, as the number of rules in a rule base increases the resulting rule bases can become difficult to comprehend and manage. Methods to assist users in dealing with this complexity can help users and developers to comprehend and manage large rule bases. In particular, methods to detect the underlying logical structure of rule bases and to visualize those structures can enable rapid user comprehension and assist developers in detecting patterns in their own rule bases.

In earlier work [3], we used syntactic analysis to detect similar rules and then clustered them based on their similarity. While this approach performed well on some rule bases, it was limited. Since the semantics of the terms used in the rules was not considered, the method effectively performed a surface analysis only and as a result its cluster formation results were often quite coarse. The method was also relatively

M. Dean et al. (Eds.): RuleML 2010, LNCS 6403, pp. 259–272, 2010.

brittle: A small structural change in a rule could cause it to be removed from its initial cluster. If we can consider the semantics of the terms used in a rule, we can exploit knowledge of these terms from the associated OWL ontology and have an opportunity to more robustly detect similarites between rules. In this paper, we outline a method that uses semantic analysis to detect dependencies between rules. This dependency analysis is based on more than a simple term analysis; it also considers the semantic relationships between the terms used in the rules and the strength of those relationships. We use the results of this dependency analysis to create a method that divides the rule base into logical layers and then detects fine grained clusters within those layers. A range of user-customizable display strategies are also provided to support visualization of the analysis results.

2 Background

SWRL has become the *de facto* standard OWL rule language. It has some attractive properties that have encouraged its adoption. In addition to being simple to learn and use, it provides formal mechanisms for performing reasoning with OWL ontologies. An OWL reasoner that supports SWRL can guarantee the logical consistency of a SWRL rule base. These reasoners can check SWRL rule bases for internal rule inconsistencies, inter-rule inconsistencies, and for inconsistencies between the rules and the underlying OWL ontology. Despite these strong formal underpinnings, rule base comprehension can be a challenge. Interactions between rules and their associated OWL ontology, and between the rules themselves, can be complex, and reasoners do not typically provide mechanisms for exploring these interactions.

Consider, for example, the following five SWRL rules relating to drug recommendations for hypertensive and diabetic adult patients (a detailed description of individual SWRL constructs is provided in Section 4):

Rule A: `Person(?p) ^ hasSystolicBloodPressure(?p, ?sbp) ^`
`hasDiastolicBloodPressure(?p, ?dbp) ^`
`swrlb:greaterThan(?sbp, 140) ^ swrlb:greaterThan(?dbp, 90)`
`→ hasDiagnosis(?p, Hypertension)`

Rule B: `Person(?p) ^ hasBloodSugarLevelBeforeMeal(?p, ?bsl) ^`
`swrlb:greaterThan(?bsl, 126) → hasDiagnosis(?p, Diabetes)`

Rule C: `hasCondition(?p, Hypertension) ^ hasCondition(?p, Diabetes) ^`
`→ prescribedDrug(?p, ACEInhibitor)`

Rule D: `Person(?p) ^ hasAge(?p,?age) ^ swrlb:greaterThan(?age,17) ^`
`hasInsurance(?p, ?i) → InsuredAdult(?p)`

Rule E: `InsuredPerson(?p) ^ prescribedDrug(?p, ?d) → CoPayEligible(?p)`

As can be seen, rules A and B independently produce diagnoses of hypertension and diabetes using the values of data property values associated with persons. Rule C does not initially seem to be dependent on either rule but if the underlying OWL ontology declares that hasCondition and hasDiagnosis are equivalent properties then there is a dependency. Similarly, Rule E is not obviously dependent on rule D because it does not directly use any terms asserted by D. However, if InsuredAdult is declared to be a subclass of InsuredPerson then a dependency can be inferred. Rule E is clearly dependent on Rule C through the direct use of the prescribedDrug property. Furthermore, if the ontology also declares that the domain of the hasCondition and hasDiagnosis properties is of type Person then it can also be inferred that rule C is a rule concerning persons even though that is not directly stated in the rule. This knowledge can indicate its possible dependency on other rules that generate inferences about persons.

As these examples show, even a simple rule set can produce a variety of inter-rule dependencies. Determining these dependencies requires a detailed manual inspection of the rules. This inspection must use knowledge about the underlying ontology and requires a methodical examination of the use of OWL classes and properties that may be indirectly related through their positions in class or property hierarchies. The domains and ranges of properties must also be considered in this analysis. As a rule base grows, these dependencies can become increasingly difficult to detect.

Detailed examination of these dependencies can reveal the underlying logical layers usually present in rule bases. Such layers are typical and reflect a common design pattern of developing sets of rules at successively higher levels of abstraction, with upper layers using the inferences produced by layers below them. Methods that automatically detect and display these dependency layers, in addition to basic inter-rule dependencies, can greatly facilitate rule base comprehension.

3   Related Work

Many rule management tools provide some sort of graphical support for editing and displaying rules. For example, SAMOS, an object-oriented database management system, provides a graphical rule editor and browser for managing Event-Condition-Action-rules in databases [4]. The browser allows users to graphically navigate through rule bases and provides runtime tools for visualizing activities performed during rule execution. It presents a fairly simple view of a rule base, however, and provides no mechanisms for showing the relationships or dependencies between rules.

In recent work, researchers use UML state diagrams to visually represent business rules and their interdependencies [5]. This approach can be used to visualize some types of dependencies between rules, but the overall approach does not provide a full rule representation language because of incompatibilities between rule modeling and the essentially object-oriented paradigm of UML. An extension of UML called UML-Based Rule Modeling Language (URML) addresses some of these limitations [6]. It provides new visual metaphors that can be integrated with UML class diagrams. A rule is represented graphically as a circle with a rule identifier. Incoming arrows represent rule conditions or triggering events; outgoing arrows represent rule conclusions or produced actions. The approach supports the modeling of derivation rules, production rules and reaction rules. The overall approach is focused primarily on representing event triggering and event production rather than displaying the relationships between rules themselves.

With the increasing use of rules in ontology-based systems, some recent work has concentrated on the development of rule dependency analysis techniques [7]. These dependencies can be used to detect anomalies in rule bases. The anomalies can be caused by conflicts between the rules and their associated ontologies or inconsistencies in the rules themselves. For example, these techniques can be used to detect circular dependencies between rules or redundancies between rules and ontology assertions. Other work has investigated visualization techniques to provide explanations of defeasible theories and to display the structure and dependencies between rules in these theories [8, 9]. In general, however, these approaches have not concentrated on exploring these dependencies to produce visualizations of overall rule base structure.

In recent work by the authors, a rule management tool called Axiomé was developed for managing rule bases developed using SWRL [3]. This work used a rule analysis technique to categorize, visualize, and paraphrase SWRL rules. The categorizations attempted to cluster rules into common groups based on their syntactic structure and their shared use of ontology terms. The associated visualizations allowed users to graphically display rules and the dependencies between them. Although this tool worked well in capturing coarse patterns in rule bases, the method was limited because it does not incorporate the semantics of the underlying relationships. Capturing the semantics of these relationships can allow significantly more granular analyses of the types of relationships between rules and thus support more robust methods for rule clustering and visualization.

4 Methods

SWRL's formal OWL underpinning allows the relationship between a rule and the associated OWL ontology to be examined in a principled way. Unlike many rule languages, SWRL is not general purpose and is designed to be used only with OWL ontologies. All entities referred to in a SWRL rule must exist in the OWL ontology that the rules are developed in. SWRL provides six main types of SWRL atoms that govern the interaction between SWRL and OWL (see Table 1). The rules themselves have a simple Horn-like rule structure with a *body* and a *head*, each of which contain conjunctions of atoms.

Table 1. The six main types of SWRL atoms defined by the SWRL Submission together with examples of each. All entity names, such as `Person` and `hasSibling`, refer to OWL classes or properties.

SWRL Atom Type	Example Atom
Class atom	`Person(?x), Female(?y)`
Individual property atom	`hasSibling(?x, ?y)` `hasSister(?x, ?y)`
SameAs/DifferentFrom atom	`sameAs(?x, ?y)` `differentFrom(?x, ?y)`
Data valued property atom	`hasName(?x, "Joe")` `hasAge(?x, ?g)`
Built-in atom	`swrlb:notEqual(?state, "CA")` `swrlb:lessThan(?g, 18)`
Data range atom	`xsd:double(?x)`

Of the six main SWRL atom types, class and object property atoms are the primary sources of potential inter-rule dependencies. These atoms refer to OWL classes, which capture classification information about individuals, and OWL object properties, which relate those individuals to each other. Atoms containing data properties can also cause dependencies by producing data value assertions in a rule that can be used by other rules. However, these dependencies are typically based on the value of data properties generated during the inference process and these actual values cannot typically be determined outside this process. Since our method does not perform a run-time analysis of rules, we do not consider such dependencies. For the same reason, we also do not consider built-in and data range atoms because they also deal with data properties whose values can only be determined during inference.

4.1 Analyzing Dependencies among Rules

The first step in our method involves analyzing the dependencies among rules in a SWRL rule base. This dependency analysis is based on two tasks: (1) an analysis of references to the same OWL classes and object properties in different rules; and (2) an analysis of the domain and range of object property atoms to determine if any resulting object property assertions about OWL individuals can produce dependencies. Both of these approaches are extended to incorporate the hierarchical and equivalence relationships between the matched OWL classes and properties that are specified in the underlying ontology.

The co-occurrence of an OWL class or property in the head of one rule and in the body of another can indicate that one rule can potentially trigger another. For example, if the body of a rule references an OWL class that is also referenced in the head of another, a possible dependency between the rules can be assumed. The hierarchies of these OWL classes and properties can also be considered when computing this dependency. That is, statements about particular classes or properties can also be considered to be statements about their sub classes and properties. Similarly, OWL equivalent class and property assertions in an ontology can also be considered. Each class or property used in a rule can thus be expanded to include entities related to it in an ontology by considering sub type and equivalency relationships. In this way, the dependency method can consider not just the entity names but also knowledge about those entities that can be extracted from the OWL ontology that contains them.

The next step involves examining the arguments to SWRL class and object property atoms to infer possible dependencies between rules. These atom arguments represent OWL individuals. Using the information from the associated OWL ontology, the possible types of these arguments can be automatically inferred. By using this type information it is possible to determine if assertions made by one atom can be used by atoms in other rules, which is a link that indicates a dependency. Our method attempts to enumerate the types of all individuals passed to class and object property atoms and to use this information to detect inter-rule dependencies. Again, the method considers only class and object property atoms since they are the only two atoms that deal with type information for OWL individuals.

SWRL class atoms specify an OWL class and take a single argument representing an OWL individual. When used in the body of a rule, class atoms effectively indicate a membership test for its argument individual. When used in the head of a rule, the atom effectively asserts that the argument individual is a member of the specified class. The intersection of these classes can be considered as the multiple types of each individual. This list can automatically be expanded to include the subclass and equivalent class relationships of these classes to produce an exhaustive list of the possible types of each argument individual.

We use a similar approach with the arguments of object property atoms. SWRL object property atoms specify a named OWL object property and take subject and predicate arguments representing two OWL individuals. When used in the body of a rule, this atom acts as a test to determine if two individuals are related through the specified property; when used in the head of a rule, it asserts that they are. Using the domains and ranges of the specified properties of these atoms, the possible class membership of the argument individuals can automatically be inferred. For example, the domain of the object property specified in an object property atom can be used to construct the possible types of the subject argument individuals. The range can be used in a similar way for the object argument. Again, these types can be expanded using sub class and equivalent class axioms specified in the OWL ontology to produce a comprehensive list of all the possible types of the argument individuals.

Our method thus scans the class and object property atoms of all rules in a rule base and builds a table to record the types of all argument individuals that can be inferred from their use in class and object property atoms. We then use this table to check on dependencies between rules by tracking the common use of these types.

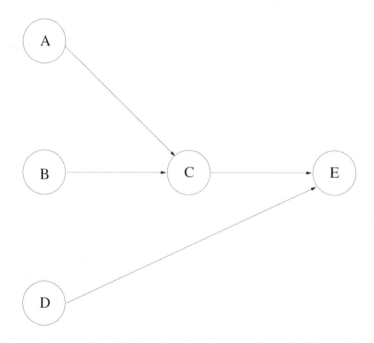

Fig. 1. A dependency graph showing the dependencies among five rules. This graph shows rule C depending on rule A and B, with rule E depending on rules C and D.

4.2   Generating a Rule Dependency Graph

After these dependencies are identified, a dependency graph is constructed. In this graph, each rule is represented as a node and edges represent dependencies between them. A dependency between one rule and another indicates that the rule can be triggered by the other rule in the inference process. Figure 1 shows an example dependency graph for the rules presented earlier. We build an adjacency matrix to save the specification and structure of this dependency graph. In addition to rule connectivity, the types of the dependencies between rules are saved and are encoded as the type of each edge. The method can thus discriminate between connections that are based on classes or object properties. The dependency graph is also checked for potential cycles using Floyd's cycle detection algorithm [10]. The presence of these cycles may indicate logical flaws in a rule base that can cause indefinite inference. If a cycle exists in the dependency graph, the method highlights it and returns the graph to the user for revision. The further dependency analysis in our method relies on the assumption that there are no cycles.

4.3   Generating Rule Layers from the Dependency Graph

Once a dependency graph is built, it can be used for further rule base analysis. As a first step, our method uses the dependency graph to group rules into layers based on the strength of their dependencies. This clustering process produces a multi-layered representation of a rule base and attempts to automatically detect the logical layers of the rules that it contains.

To perform this analysis, the rules are first ordered into a sequence where each rule is before all of its dependent rules. In a directed acyclic graph there may be many possible orderings that satisfy this property. Since the graph has already been checked to ensure that it does not contains cycles, such a reordering is always possible. Our method uses a topological sort algorithm to produce such an ordering for rules. This algorithm [11] is as follows:

```
L ← Empty list that will contain the sorted nodes
S ← Set of all nodes

function visit(node n)
  if n has not been visited yet then
    mark n as visited
    for each node m with an edge from n to m do
      visit(m)
    add n to L

for each node n in S do
  visit(n)
```

After sorting the rules topologically, the method then attempts to group the rules into layers based on their dependencies. To form these layers we use a greedy algorithm that guarantees the minimum number of layers. The algorithm is as follows:

```
L ← List of topologically sorted nodes
Layers ← Empty list of nodes in each layer

for each node n in L do
   P is the list of n's parents
   if P is empty then
      add n to Layers(0)
   else
      maxLayer ← The largest layer number of nodes in P
      add n to Layers(maxLayer+1)
```

This algorithm thus assigns each rule to a layer, producing an overall representation of the layers of rules in a rule base.

4.4   Clustering Rules with Similar Dependencies

As a final step after breaking the rules into dependency layers, the method further clusters the rules within each layer into subgroups of similar rules based on the strength of their dependencies. This clustering can give the user a better understanding of rule dependencies within each layer. This clustering is performed using the semantic distance between pairs of rules. This semantic distance is based on their strength of their dependencies. To compute the semantic distance between rules the methods first builds the sets of most closely related rules for each rule in a rule base. This set is termed the *relevant* rules and is defined as the union of parent rules, which directly depend on that rule, and the set of child rules, which are directly dependent on the rule. So in a dependency graph for a rule a, we have:

$$\text{relevant}(a) = \text{parents}(a) \cup \text{children}(a)$$

Using the relevant sets for two rules a and b, the distance between them can be computed using the formula:

$$\text{Distance}(a, b) = 1 - \frac{|\text{relevant}(a) \cap \text{relevant}(b)|}{|\text{relevant}(a) \cup \text{relevant}(b)|}$$

This number can be used as a normalized representation of the distance between two rules in a single dependency layer and provides a distance measure to capture their similarity. It varies from zero for rules with identical dependencies to one for rules where their relevant rules do not have anything in common. Since rules in a single dependency layer do not depend on each other directly, this approach effectively provides an indirect approximation of their similarity based on their relationship to rules in other layers.

Once the distance measure for rules in each layer is computed, the rules can then be clustered. We use a hierarchical clustering method for this task. Hierarchical clustering provides a simple and intuitive way to cluster the rules with similar dependencies. It involves building a hierarchical tree to represent varying levels of clustering of rules in a layer. In this work, we apply a single-linkage hierarchical clustering algorithm to cluster the rules [12]. The single-linkage algorithm starts with an individual cluster for each rule in the layer and represents them as the leaves of a tree. It then iterates, and at each iteration merges the two closest clusters together. In our method, the distance between two clusters is calculated from the distance between the nearest neighbors from both clusters. If no stopping criteria are specified, hierarchical clustering continues merging clusters until a single cluster is formed (Figure 2).

In order to obtain clusters that meaningfully represent clusters of related rules in a layer, a critical decision is to find a stopping criterion that represents a suitable point to stop merging. In general, there is no universal answer to this question. In many cases, users and experts test different options and choose the best option for their particular use case. In our approach, for example, users can control the cluster formation by setting an upper limit for the distance between two clusters that can be merged.

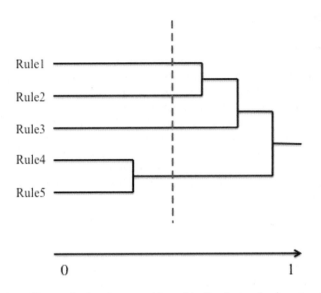

Fig. 2. Illustration of how rules in a layer are hierarchically clustered using stopping criteria to vary the clustering level. Hierarchical clustering starts with each rule in a single cluster and builds a cluster hierarchy by merging the nearest neighbors. The x axis is the stopping criteria and represents a normalized range of the upper limits for the distance of two clusters that can be merged. The dashed line indicates an arbitrary point where the algorithm stops merging clusters.

We provide two heuristic criteria to automatically decide when to terminate the clustering process. The first criterion, which is very common in hierarchical clustering analysis, attempts to find the most stable clustering. The most stable clustering is generally defined as the set of clusters that remains unchanged for the largest range of the stopping criteria. To find such a clustering, we range the maximum merging limit from zero, the smallest possible value, to one, the largest, and find the largest range over which there is no change in the set of associated clusters. We return this set as a candidate clustering for the rules in that layer.

The second stopping criteria attempts to ensure that rules clustered at a particular iteration of the clustering process are significantly related and that their similarity is more than that of two unrelated rules. To guarantee this property, the method computes the median distances for each pair of rules in a layer and uses this number as the maximum distance for which two clusters are to be merged. This process ensures that each two merged clusters are closer than at least half of the rules in the rule base.

Both of these criteria are heuristic suggestions for the challenging problem of automatically finding the stopping criterion in hierarchical clustering. We believe that these criteria give users a sensible estimate of a reasonable clustering for rule base layers. For further analysis, the user can be specify the stopping criteria for merging rule clusters is each layer, so users can experiment and choose between different scenarios.

4.5 Rule Base Visualization

We use a variety of visualization strategies to present the results of these analyses to the user. A basic rule graph visualization is first provided, with each node in a graph representing a rule and dependencies between them indicated by edges. This graph can then be visually separated into the layers determined by the method. In addition to showing the inferred layers, the visualization approach also generates layouts that show rule clusters within layers. We used the JUNG visualization framework [13] to automatically generate a variety of layouts. Five automated layout generation algorithms are supported, each of which supports a particular style of layout strategy. Depending on the characteristics of the underlying rule base, a particular layout may be more appropriate. In addition, a search facility is provided to allow users to visually highlight particular rules matching user-supplied terms.

5   Results

To evaluate the usefulness and efficacy of our techniques, we applied our method to two publicly available OWL ontologies containing SWRL rules bases. Each of these ontologies was developed as part of a medical application and was designed by a knowledge engineer or a domain expert who was not one of the authors.

The first rule base was created to specify medical treatment rules for patients with hypertension, or elevated blood pressure. These rules detected temporal patterns where patients were not treated according to recommended guideline plans for a particular institution. The automated identification of such patterns can lead to interventions to improve the quality of care. The rule base was defined using a patient management ontology that consisted of a disease management ontology, a patient data ontology, and a plan violation taxonomy [14]. Instances in the ontology were populated from an electronic medical record. The developers of the ontology-based application wrote nineteen SWRL rules to represent a set of auditing rules of clinical practice. The ontology and rule base are available online [15].

Figure 3 shows sixteen rules from this rule base. The isolated rules in the rule base, which were not connected to any other rules, are not considered in this figure. As is shown, two dependency layers were detected in this rule base. An examination of the rule base revealed that the rules in the first layer generate basic standalone inferences about patients (e.g., a diagnosis of diabetes); rules in the second layer use these basic inferences to determine if patients meet more complex criteria. Furthermore, our hierarchical clustering method detected two clusters in the first layer and five clusters in the second layer by using the median stopping criteria. The five rules in the first cluster were examined and were discovered to relate to basic medical diagnosis; the two rules in the second cluster use more complex temporal criteria to determine if patients were prescribed anti-hypertensive drugs during particular intervals. One cluster of six rules was detected in the second layer, again using the median stopping criteria. The remaining four rules in this layer did not get assigned to a cluster. An examination of the six clustered rules revealed that four of the six concern blood pressure measurements; none of the non clustered rules does.

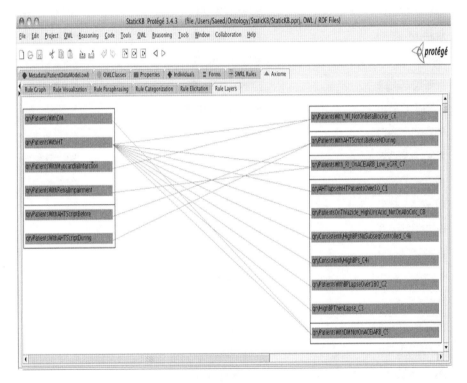

Fig. 3. Screen shot of the Axiomé plug-in showing its visualization of the dependency layers for rules from a medical treatment rule base. In each layer, rules in the same clusters are indicated by gray lines surrounding them.

The second rule base used in the evaluation is contained in an ontology that encodes family relationships [16]. This rule base is composed of 146 rules that define possible relations between people in a family. The ontology and rule base are available online at the National Center for Biomedical Ontology BioPortal [17]. Figure 4 shows a subset of 146 rules in the family history rule base. As is shown, our method organized 146

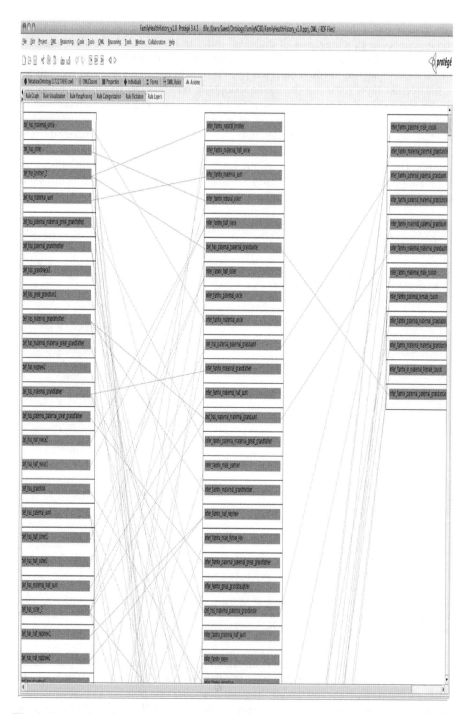

Fig. 4. Screen shot of the Axiomé plug-in showing part of its visualization of the dependency layers for rules from a family history rule base

rules in the rule base in three dependency layers. An examination of the rule base revealed that rules in the first layer define very simple relationships (e.g., has sister); the rules in the second layer use these basic relationships to infer more complex ones (e.g., maternal aunt); the final layer uses a combination of inferences from the second layer to generate even more complex deductions (e.g., paternal paternal grand uncle). An examination of rule name prefixes also revealed the different intentions of the authors, and are reflected in layer assignment: all definition rules in the first layer are prefixed by "def", whereas nearly all rules in the second and third inference layers use the "infer" prefix exclusively. We also clustered the rules in each layer using our hierarchical clustering method with the stability stopping criteria. Very few clusters with multiple rules were detected. A detailed examination of the rule base revealed that each rule aims to model a fairly distinct individual definition and that few meaningful clusters could be detected manually.

6 Discussion

We have developed a novel method that performs a dependency analysis of a SWRL rule base and uses the results of this analysis to generate a summary of the various logical layers it contains. The method then uses clustering strategies to automatically group closely related rules within each layer to further partition the rule base into logical subcomponents. Using the results of these analyses we then use a variety of visualization strategies to conveniently display rule base structure. The primary goal is to help users to quickly explore large unfamiliar rule bases by summarizing their logical structure. Users can rapidly explore a rule base, summarize its structure, and analyze dependencies between rules and groups of rules, thus supporting rapid comprehension.

This approach also supports rule base authors in developing rule bases. New rules can be automatically assigned to a logical layer and then clustered with related rules in that layer. The dependencies and interactions between this new rule and existing rules can thus be quickly identified. The method can also prove useful in detecting inconsistencies, unexpected dependencies, and redundancies in rule bases. It can also assist in identifying repeated logical patterns that may benefit from the development of more abstract high level rules.

The method leverages the strong formal relationship between SWRL and the OWL ontology language to incorporate not just direct ontology term usage within SWRL rules when performing analysis but to also consider the underlying OWL semantics of those terms. This ontology-based analysis supports the detection of logical relationships between rules, far richer than a simple term-based analysis would allow. It also allows semantic similarities between rules to be identified with greater precision, thus allowing related rules to be automatically grouped. The method builds on our earlier work that used term usage and a syntactic analysis of rules to identify relatedness between rules.

We are currently developing additional graphical techniques that will enhance the display of the logical dependencies between layers and clusters of rules. We will be evaluating further the usefulness of our visualization method with domain experts who are developing a rule base or inspecting an unfamiliar one. We believe that the dependency analysis we have undertaken can also help user to understand how results were derived when the SWRL rules were executed. In future work, we are planning to create methods to support explanation of results based on the visualization techniques we have presented here.

Acknowledgements

This research was supported in part by National Institutes of Health grants R01LM009607 and R01MH87756.

References

1. SWRL Submission, http://www.w3.org/Submission/SWRL/
2. Ontology Web Language, http://www.w3.org/TR/owl-features/
3. Hassanpour, S., O'Connor, M.J., Das, A.K.: Exploration of SWRL Rule Bases through Visualization, Paraphrasing, and Categorization of Rules. In: Governatori, G., Hall, J., Paschke, A. (eds.) RuleML 2009. LNCS, vol. 5858, pp. 246–261. Springer, Heidelberg (2009)
4. Dittrich, K.R., Fritschi, H., Gatziu, S., Geppert, A., Vaduva, A.: SAMOS in hindsight: experiences in building an active object-oriented DBMS. Information Systems 28, 5 (2003)
5. Kulakowski, K., Nalepa, G.J.: Using UML state diagrams for visual modeling of business rules. In: IMCSIT 2008, pp. 189–194 (2008)
6. Lukichev, S., Wagner, G.: Visual rules modeling. In: Long, F. (ed.) Software Engineering Environments. LNCS, vol. 467, pp. 467–673. Springer, Heidelberg (1990)
7. Baumeister, J., Seipel, D.: Anomalies in ontologies with rules. Web Semantics 8, 1 (2010)
8. Kontopoulos, E., Bassiliades, N., Antoniou, G.: Visualizing Defeasible Logic Rules for the Semantic Web. In: Mizoguchi, R., Shi, Z., Giunchiglia, F. (eds.) ASWC 2006. LNCS, vol. 4185, pp. 278–292. Springer, Heidelberg (2006)
9. Avguleas, I., Gkirtzou, K., Triantafilou, S., Bikakis, A., Antoniou, G., Kontopoulos, E., Bassiliades, N.: Visualization of Proofs in Defeasible Logic. In: Bassiliades, N., Governatori, G., Paschke, A. (eds.) RuleML 2008. LNCS, vol. 5321, pp. 197–210. Springer, Heidelberg (2008)
10. Knuth, D.E.: The Art of Computer Programming, vol. Seminumerical Algorithms, vol. II, p. 7. Addison-Wesley, Reading (1969)
11. Cormen, T.H., Leiserson, C.E., Rivest, R.L., Stein, C.: Introduction to Algorithms, 2nd edn. Section 22.4, pp. 549–552. MIT Press and McGraw-Hill (2001)
12. Romesburg, H.C.: Cluster Analysis for Researchers, pp. 9, 119–140. Lulu Press (2004)
13. Java Universal Network/Graph Framework, http://jung.sourceforge.net
14. Mabotuwana, T., Warren, J.: ChronoMedIt – A Computational Quality Audit Framework for Better Management of Patients with Chronic Conditions. Journal of Biomedical Informatics (2009)
15. Clinical treatment auditing ontology, http://www.cs.auckland.ac.nz/~thusitha/aiim09/
16. Peace, J., Brennan, P.F.: Instance testing of the family history ontology. In: Proceedings of the American Medical Informatics Association (AMIA) Annual Symposium, Washington, DC, 1088 (2008)
17. National Center for Biomedical Ontology BioPortal, http://www.bioontology.org

An XML Format for Association Rule Models Based on the GUHA Method

Tomáš Kliegr and Jan Rauch

University of Economics, Prague, Dept. Information and Knowledge Engineering,
Nám. Winstona Churchilla 4, 130 67 Praha 3, Czech Republic
tomas.kliegr@vse.cz, rauch@vse.cz

Abstract. This paper proposes the GUHA AR Model, an XML Schema-based formalism for representing the setting and results of association rule (AR) mining tasks. In contrast to the item-based representation of the PMML 4.0 AssociationModel, the proposed expresses the association rule as a couple of general boolean attributes related by condition on one or more arbitrary interest measures. This makes the GUHA AR Model suitable also for other than apriori-based AR mining algorithms, such as those mining for disjunctive or negative ARs. In addition, there are practically important research results on special logical calculi formulas which correspond to such association rules. The GUHA AR Model is intended as a replacement of the PMML AssociationModel. It is tightly linked to the Background Knowledge Exchange Format (BKEF), an XML schema proposed for representation of data-mining related domain knowledge, and to the AR Data Mining Ontology ARON.

1   Introduction

In recent years, the advent of service oriented data mining have been decreasing the costs of advanced analysis for the end user, while semantic technologies and stronger orientation towards the web have opened up new possibilities for post-processing and sharing data mining results. At the same time, the pace of innovations in data mining algorithms is increasing. In this situation, a strong need arose for a generally accepted and maintained standard for exchange of mining models, which was filled by the XML-based Predictive Model Markup Language (PMML) from the DMG consortium. Its latest version 4.0 released in June 2009 supports twelve types of mining models, including association rules.

Although PMML is a widely accepted standard, its AssociationModel (further AR Model) as of its current version 4.0 lacks support for new types of association rule mining algorithms stifling their deployment into industry. For example, the PMML AR Model does not standardize representation of disjunctive association rules (e.g. [13,14]), global constraints as needed e.g. in local mining of association rules [15], new interest measures [23] and constraints involving multiple arbitrary interest measures as e.g. used in [4].

In this paper, we suggest for discussion in the data mining community a new format for representation of association models that covers features mentioned

M. Dean et al. (Eds.): RuleML 2010, LNCS 6403, pp. 273–288, 2010.

above, among others. Our proposal is based on the GUHA ASSOC data mining procedure, therefore we call it GUHA Association Rule (AR) Model.

This paper is organized as follows. Section 2 discusses the demands on model representation format resulting from new AR mining algorithms. Section 3 introduces the GUHA ASSOC procedure. The GUHA AR Schema is presented in detail in Section 4. Section 5 discusses the compatibility and interoperability issues. The conclusions give account of deployments of the GUHA AR Model.

2   Related Research

The term association rule was coined by R. Agrawal in connection with his proposal of the *apriori* algorithm in the early 90s. The idea of association rules was later generalized to any data in the tabular, field-value form. An association rule is understood as the relation between conjunctions of attribute-value pairs (categories) called *antecedent* and *consequent*. There are two basic characteristics of an association rule – *support* and *confidence*.

We must emphasize that the concept of association rule in the form of a relation between two conjunctions of predicates was introduced and studied already in 1960' within the framework of the development of the GUHA method of mechanized hypothesis formation. A milestone in the GUHA method development was the monograph [6], which introduces the general theory of mechanized hypothesis formation based on mathematical logic and statistics. Association rules defined and studied in this book are relations between two general boolean attributes derived from the columns of an analyzed data matrix. Various types of relations of boolean attributes are used including relations corresponding to statistical hypothesis tests. However, these relations between boolean attributes are not called association rules even if the GUHA procedure for mining them is called ASSOC. The concept of association rules has been used for patterns mined by the GUHA ASSOC procedure since the term association rule was introduced in the 90s.

Multiple association rule mining algorithms were proposed since the advent of apriori. While many papers focus on performance enhancements (e.g. all cited in survey [8]), the notion of association rule has undergone evolution, too. According to the on-line annotated bibliography on association rule mining[1], the main research efforts are a) mining association rules (using support and confidence), b) alternative interest measures, c) mining without support, d) constraint-based mining, e) mining sequential, generalized, quantitative or causal rules, f) concise representations of frequent itemsets, g) using association rules to build classifiers, h) evolution of association rules over time, i) theoretic considerations, j) sampling and evaluation and k) efficient implementation of rule mining algorithms.

Out of these research efforts (b), (c), (d), (f), (h) affect the very notion of an association rule and thus put new demands on formats for representation of AR models. To the best of the authors knowledge, the GUHA ASSOC procedure is

---

[1] http://michael.hahsler.net/research/bib/association_rules/, update 14 Oct 2009, accessed June 7, 2010

the only single association rule mining algorithm with significant contributions in all of these research areas: paper [18] introduces classes of association rules by studying the properties of the interest measure related to GUHA ASSOC (b), support is treated as an interest measure and can be left out (c), GUHA ASSOC offers very fine ways of constraining the generation of basic and derived boolean attributes separately for antecedent, consequent and condition thus giving the possibility to significantly limit the search space (d), there is a research into induction of prime association rules [19], that is rules which do not immediately follow from another rule (f), there are theoretical results relating to the general GUHA framework [6] as well more recent results focused directly on theory of association rules [16] (i).

Some of the algorithms that fall into research efforts (e) and (h) are only inspired by association rules but cannot be considered as AR mining algorithms, as either their input data or their output is fundamentally different, the most marked example are sequential association rules. On the other hand, there are disjunctive association rules [13,14] and negative association rules [1] that we consider as association rules.

Representation of setting and results of GUHA ASSOC puts high requirements on the exchange format. In a brief survey of possible XML-based formats [12], PMML in its version 2.0 was deemed inappropriate due to lack of expressivity. It was recommended to create either an extension of the RuleML language or an RDF-based format. The semantic web (Topic Map, not RDF) representation was eventually proposed in [9]. There was no marked improvement in the PMML's AssociationModel from version 2.0 to the current version 4.0 apart from the added support for transactional input (see Subsection 5.1).

The most closely related work to the GUHA AR PMML model is an attempt to use first order logic to extend the PMML 1.1 AssociationModel [21]. While this proposal solves some of the PMML shortcomings that persist in PMML 4.0, particularly the inability to include negated literals and items from multiple fields, the proposal does not cover disjunctive association rules, alternative interest measures and mining constraints. Additionally, the proposed syntax is rather bulky. For example, to express item "female" coming from field gender, the approach [21] uses the following syntax:

```
<Term id="3" type="variable" symbol="sex"/>
<Term id="4" type="constant" symbol="female"/>
<Literal id="1" predicate="equal" numberOfParams="2">
  <TermRef termRef="3" position="0"/>
  <TermRef termRef="4" position="1"/>
</Literal>
```

In GUHA AR Model, this is expressed in a more concise form

```
<BBA id="3">
  <FieldRef>gender</FieldRef>
  <CatRef>female</CatRef>
</BBA>
```

The formalism [21] is more general in the way that the `Term` can be also a function. This advantage is however mitigated by the fact that functions including user-defined were introduced into PMML as of its version 3.0. PMML functions are typically applied in the Transformation Dictionary, which is independent of the mining model.

3   GUHA Procedure ASSOC

GUHA procedure ASSOC mines for association rules $\varphi \approx \psi/\chi$ and for conditional association rules $\varphi \approx \psi/\chi$ where φ, ψ and χ are boolean attributes derived from columns of an input data matrix and symbol $\approx$ is a 4ft-quantifier. The 4ft-quantifier corresponds to a condition concerning contingency table of φ and ψ. The boolean attribute φ is called *antecedent*, ψ is called *succedent* and χ is called *condition*.

An example of an input data matrix is data matrix $\mathcal{M}$ in the left part of Figure 1. Informally speaking, columns of data matrix correspond to attributes

$\mathcal{M}$	A_1	A_2	data matrix ...	A_K	$A_1(1)$	Boolean attributes $A_2(2,9)$	$A_1(1) \wedge A_K(2,6)$
o_1	1	4	...	6	1	0	1
o_2	3	9	...	7	0	1	0
$\vdots$	$\vdots$	$\vdots$	$\ddots$	$\vdots$	$\vdots$	$\vdots$	$\vdots$
o_{n-1}	4	2	...	2	0	1	0
o_n	1	6	...	1	1	0	0

$\mathcal{M}$	ψ	$\neg\psi$
φ	a	b
$\neg\varphi$	c	d

Data matrix and examples of boolean attributes $4\mathrm{ft}(\varphi, \psi, \mathcal{M})$

Fig. 1. Data matrix, Boolean attributes and 4ft-table $4\mathrm{ft}(\varphi, \psi, \mathcal{M})$

and rows correspond to observed objects, e.g. to patients. There are attributes $A_1, A_2, \ldots, A_K$ in data matrix $\mathcal{M}$. The possible values of attributes are called *categories*.

Basic boolean attributes are created first. The Basic Boolean Attribute is an expression $A(\alpha)$ where $\alpha \subset \{a_1, \ldots a_t\}$ and $\{a_1, \ldots a_t\}$ is the set of all categories of the attribute A. The set α is called a *coefficient* of the basic boolean attribute $A(\alpha)$. Basic boolean attribute $A(\alpha)$ is true in row o of $\mathcal{M}$ if it is $A(o) \in \alpha$ where $A(o)$ is the value of the attribute A in row o. Derived boolean attributes φ and ψ are created from basic boolean attributes using connectives $\vee$, $\wedge$ and $\neg$ in the usual way. Sometimes, the term *literal* is used to refer to the basic boolean attribute $A(a)$ or its negation $\neg A(a)$ [19].

Expression

$$A_1(1) \wedge A_2(2,9) \approx A_K(2,6)$$

is an example of an association rule.

The association rule $\varphi \approx \psi$ can be true or false in given data matrix $\mathcal{M}$. The conditional association rule $\varphi \approx \psi/\chi$ is verified against data matrix $\mathcal{M}/\chi$, which consists of all rows of data matrix M satisfying χ.

The rule $\varphi \approx \psi$ is verified on the basis of the *four-fold table* $4ft(\varphi, \psi, \mathcal{M})$ of φ and ψ in $\mathcal{M}$, see Figure 1. Here a is the number of the objects (i.e. the rows of $\mathcal{M}$) satisfying both φ and ψ, b is the number of the objects satisfying φ and not satisfying ψ, etc. We write $4\mathrm{ft}(\varphi, \psi, \mathcal{M}) = \langle a, b, c, d \rangle$.

The rule $\varphi \approx \psi$ is *true in the data matrix* $\mathcal{M}$ if the condition associated with $\approx$ is satisfied in the contingency table $4ft(\varphi, \psi, \mathcal{M})$, otherwise $\varphi \approx \psi$ is *false in the data matrix* $\mathcal{M}(/\chi)$. The 4ft-quantifier $\approx$ is defined by a list of *partial 4ft-quantifiers*: $\langle \approx_1, \approx_2, \ldots, \approx_E \rangle$, where $\approx_1, \approx_2, \ldots, \approx_E$ are *partial 4ft-quantifiers*. The rule is true if the conditions corresponding to all its partial 4ft-quantifiers $\approx_1 \ldots \approx_E$ are satisfied in the contingency table $\langle a, b, c, d \rangle$.

There are many partial 4ft-quantifiers defined and studied in relation to GUHA ASSOC. Several examples are shown in Tab. 1, we sometimes use $r = a + b$, $k = a + c$ and $n = a + b + c + d$.

Table 1. Examples of partial 4ft-quantifiers

Partial 4ft quantifier		
Name	Symbol	$\approx (a, b, c, d) = 1$ iff
Founded implication	$\Rightarrow_{p,B}$	$\frac{a}{a+b} \geq p \wedge a \geq B$
Lower critical implication	$\Rightarrow^{!}_{p,\alpha,B}$	$\sum_{i=a}^{r} \binom{r}{i} p^i (1-p)^{r-i} \leq \alpha \wedge a \geq B$
Founded equivalence	$\equiv_{p,B}$	$\frac{a+d}{a+b+c+d} \geq p \wedge a \geq B$
Fisher	$\approx_{\alpha,B}$	$\sum_{i=a}^{\min(r,k)} \frac{\binom{k}{i}\binom{n-k}{r-i}}{\binom{n}{r}} \leq \alpha \wedge a \geq B$
χ^2 quantifier	$\sim^{2}_{\alpha,B}$	$\frac{(ad-bc)^2}{rkls} n \geq \chi^2_\alpha \wedge a \geq B$
Above average dependence	$\sim^{+}_{q,B}$	$\frac{a}{a+b} \geq (1+q)\frac{a+c}{a+b+c+d} \wedge a \geq B$
Support	$\uparrow_S$	$\frac{a}{a+b+c+d}$

GUHA ASSOC has several implementations [5,18,13], and many applications, see e.g. [2].

4   GUHA AR Model

This section introduces the XML Schema used to formalize the GUHA Association Rule Model version 0.1 (GUHA AR Model). The GUHA AR Model is designed as an alternative to the PMML AR Model. As such, for data input and preprocessing it refers to the corresponding parts of the PMML specification.

The core focus of the GUHA AR Model is to describe the set of discovered rules and the setting of the association rule mining algorithm that produced them. The syntactical patterns used in these descriptions come out of GUHA ASSOC procedure introduced in Section 3.

Coming out of the GUHA method brings with it not only a legacy of more than forty years of research but also of terminology, which has in some cases diverged from the mainstream. When a better known synonym to a GUHA ASSOC term exists, the GUHA AR Model opts for it. Table 2 presents a dictionary of most important differences between PMML 4.0, GUHA AR PMML 0.1 Model and GUHA ASSOC. Comments on the changes placed throughout the rest of this paper are typeset in italics.

Table 2. Terminology dictionary

PMML AR Model	GUHA ASSOC	GUHA AR Model
item	basic boolean attribute	basic boolean attribute
item/@value	category	category
itemset	derived boolean attribute	derived boolean attribute
consequent	succedent	consequent
measure of interestingness	partial 4ft quantifier	interest measure
–	4ft quantifier	–
data- derived-field	attribute	(*-)field

Table 3 presents an overview of differences in *model-specific* (only in the PMML AR Model) and *model-independent* (shared between several PMML models) elements between the PMML AR Model and the GUHA AR Model.

Table 3. Model-level correspondence between PMML AR Model and GUHA AR Model

Model Specific		Model Independent	
PMML AR Model	GUHA AR Model	PMML AR Model	GUHA AR Model
Model Attributes	TaskSettings	Output	← *(change in semantics)*
Items	Basic BAs	Mining Schema	← *(no change)*
Itemsets	Derived BAs	ModelStats	← *(no change)*
AssociationRules	← *(redefined)*	LocalTransformations	← *(no change)*

The remainder of this section is organized as follows. Subsection 4.1 introduces representation of boolean attributes. Subsection 4.2 shows how are boolean attributes used to compose association rules. Subsection 4.3 describes the setting of the AR mining task.

This section uses a **running example** to illustrate serialization of a concrete association rule mining model according to the GUHA AR Model. The model describes a mining task on a fictious dataset, where the target is to discover rules predicting loan status based on loan duration, sex and district of bank customers. The running example covers a complete GUHA AR Model, only the fragments are listed in a different order, which is marked by line numbers. The data and their preprocessing steps could be for the sake of brevity omitted as their description would be done within standard PMML `DataDictionary` and `TransformationDictionary` elements.

4.1 Boolean Attributes

Boolean Attribute (BA) in the GUHA AR Model is defined as a conjunction or disjunction of one or more BAs or a negation of one BA or as a *Basic Boolean Attribute*. Basic Boolean Attribute (BBA) has the form of $A(c_1, \ldots, c_n)$ or shortly $A(\sigma)$. The *coefficient* σ is a subset of possible categories of field A. A BA, which is not a BBA, is Derived Boolean Attribute (DBA).

The terms basic boolean attribute and derived boolean attribute substitute the terms item and itemset from PMML. The definition of both BA, BBA and DBA in the GUHA AR Model is identical to the GUHA ASSOC definition presented in Section 3 apart from the fact that the term "attribute" was replaced with the term "field" with category in the BBA definition.

Since both BBAs and DBAs can reoccur in multiple association rules, it is useful to create a "dictionary" of BAs analogically to the "dictionary" of items and itemsets in PMML 4.0. That is, the sequences of `Item` and `Itemset` elements in PMML AR Model are replaced by sequences of `BasicBooleanAttribute` and `DerivedBooleanAttribute` elements respectively.

In PMML association rules are composed of itemsets and items, in the GUHA AR Model they are composed of boolean attributes.

Running Example 1: basic and derived boolean attributes used in discovered rules

```
     <AssociationRules>              75  <BBA id="4">
       <BBA id="1">                        <Text>sex(female)</Text>
         <Text>duration(2y+)</Text>        <FieldRef>sex</FieldRef>
60       <FieldRef>duration</FieldRef>      <CatRef>female</CatRef>
         <CatRef>2y+</CatRef>            </BBA>
       </BBA>                          80  <BBA id="5">
       <BBA id="2">                        <Text>duration(1y)</Text>
         <Text>statusAggregated(good,medium)   <FieldRef>duration</FieldRef>
65       </Text>                            <CatRef>1y</CatRef>
         <FieldRef>statusAgreggated</FieldRef  </BBA>
         >                            85  <DBA id="6" connective="Negation"
         <CatRef>good</CatRef>              literal="true">
         <CatRef>medium</CatRef>            <BARef>3</BARef>
       </BBA>                            </DBA>
70     <BBA id="3" literal="false">      <DBA id="7" connective="Conjunction">
         <Text>district(Prague)</Text>  90  <BARef>1</BARef>
         <FieldRef>district</FieldRef>      <BARef>6</BARef>
         <CatRef>Prague</CatRef>          </DBA>
       </BBA>
```

Both BBA and DBA share the optional element `Text`, which denotes a textual, user-friendly representation of the boolean attribute, and `id`, a unique BA identifier. Element `Text` is used in several other elements. BBAs contain in `FieldRef` the name of a field and in the `source` attribute optionally the dictionary it comes from[2]. One or more of the `CatRef` elements refer by name to categories contained in the coefficient of the BBA. The value of DBA's `Connective` attribute is either `Conjunction` (default), `Disjunction` or `Negation`. Boolean attributes are referenced from a DBA by their `id` with the `BARef` element.

The `literal` attribute is used to distinguish if a boolean attribute is a literal - a basic boolean attribute or its negation. Its value is assigned as follows:

1. *true* on BBA if it is not contained in a DBA that has negation as connective, otherwise *false.*
2. *true* on DBA if it contains a BBA and has negation as connective, otherwise *false.*

---

[2] Although technically PMML asserts that names of DataFields and DerivedFields are unique, this is not verified by the PMML schema. In addition, it is impractical since data mining software does not usually force the user to name derived field differently than its source data field.

In the common case, when negations are not used, the default values of the literal attribute do not have to be explicitly changed. BBAs are by default literals and DBAs are nonliterals.

4.2 GUHA Association Rule

A (conditional) association rule is represented as $\varphi \langle \approx_1 \ldots, \approx_E \rangle \psi(/\chi)$. Here, rule antecedent φ, consequent ψ and the optional condition χ are *boolean attributes* and $\langle \approx_1, \ldots, \approx_E \rangle$ are interest measure thresholds.

The term succedent used in GUHA ASSOC is replaced by the term consequent, which is widely adopted in the association rule community.

In the GUHA XML Schema, this structure is encoded in the following way:

Running Example 2: two discovered association rules

```
    <AssociationRule antecedent="7" consequent="2" condition="4">
      <Text>duration(2y+) ∧ ¬district(Prague) => statusAggregated(good,medium) / sex(
        female)</Text>
 95   <IMValue name="Support">0.55282316777220514479</IMValue>
      <IMValue name="Average_Difference" imSettingRef="2">0.1414</IMValue>
      <IMValue name="Kulczynski" imSettingRef="3">0.8138</IMValue>
      <IMValue name="Confidence" imSettingRef="1">0.66</IMValue>
      <FourFtTable a="3586" b="874" c="768" d="953"/>
100 </AssociationRule>
      <AssociationRule antecedent="5" consequent="2">
      <Text>duration(1y) => statusAggregated(good,medium)</Text>
      <IMValue name="Support">0.1502993043</IMValue>
      <IMValue name="Average_Difference" imSettingRef="2">1.2978</IMValue>
105   <IMValue name="Kulczynski" imSettingRef="3">0.6128</IMValue>
      <IMValue name="Confidence" imSettingRef="1">0.57</IMValue>
      <FourFtTable a="929" b="252" c="1187" d="3813"/>
      </AssociationRule>
    </AssociationRules>
```

Here, `antecedent`, `consequent` and `condition` attributes contain ids of boolean attributes that they refer to. The interest measures associated with the rule are put into elements to foster addition of new interest measures. This is in contrast to PMML AR Model that puts both pieces of information into attributes, recognizing only support, confidence and lift interest measures.

The `IMValue` element has a `name` attribute with the name of the interest measure, its value is stored as a value of the element.

When working with multiple interest measures, it is useful to make a distinction between interest measures that are associated with threshold constraints (e.g. support related to the minimum support setting) and additional informative interest measures that do not act as a constraint. In the GUHA AR Model, this distinction is made by including the optional **IMSettingRef** attribute, which points to the setting of the corresponding threshold for the interest measure. Although this explicit link is not theoretically necessary in cases when the name of the interest measure value equals the name of the corresponding threshold, it easies the processing of the resulting PMML. In the Running Example 5 Support is used as an informative interest measure, while the name of the setting for Average Difference is Above Average Implication.

4.3 Task Setting

The `TaskSetting` element contains interest measure restrictions and syntactical restrictions, which loosely correspond to the quantifier and syntactical restrictions of the GUHA method. Interest measure restrictions contained in the `InterestMeasureSetting` element define a set of interest measures with threshold values. Syntactical restrictions concern the length of the parts of the association rule, occurrence of particular boolean attributes in them, the way boolean attributes are derived from the input data and the connectives used to link boolean attributes into derived boolean attributes. Syntactical restrictions are defined in `BBA-` and `DBASettings` and `Antecedent-`, `Consequent-`, `Condition-` and `GeneralSetting` elements.

The structure of each of the parts of the association rule (`AntecedentSetting`, `ConsequentSetting` and `ConditionSetting`) is defined through reference to one of `BBASettings` or `DBASettings` listed in the beginning of the `TaskSetting`.

Running Example 3: definition of the set of relevant derived boolean attributes

```
     <DBASettings>                              30   <BASettingRef>7</BASettingRef>
       <DBASetting type="Literal" id="5">            <BASettingRef>5</BASettingRef>
         <BASettingRef>3</BASettingRef>             <MinimalLength>2</MinimalLength>
         <LiteralSign>Both</LiteralSign>            <MaximalLength>2</MaximalLength>
25     <LiteralType>Basic</LiteralType>            </DBASetting>
       <EquivalenceClass>NULL</              35  </DBASettings>
             EquivalenceClass>                     <AntecedentSetting>9</
       </DBASetting>                                    AntecedentSetting>
                                                   <ConsequentSetting>8</
        ...                                             ConsequentSetting>
       <DBASetting type="Conjunction" id="11        <ConditionSetting>9</ConditionSetting>
             ">
```

First consider the higher level `DBASetting`. The `type`=*Conjunction, Disjunction, Negation, Literal* attribute asserts that the boolean attribute created according to this setting must be either a DBA created with a logical connective or a *literal*. For the literal type, there are additional settings. The value of the `LiteralSign` element is used to express whether the literal must be positive (*Positive*), negative (*Negative*) or both types are permissible (*Both*). Note that positive literals are represented as BBAs although they are generated according to a DBA setting. The `LiteralType` has two values: value *Basic* expresses that the DBA containing this literal should contain at least one literal marked as *Basic*, literal with type *Remaining* does not have this priority. The optional `EquivalenceClass` is used to assign an arbitrary name of the class of equivalence to which the literal belongs. The data mining software should ensure that in the discovered rule there is maximum one literal present from each class of equivalence.

The `MinimalLength` $\leq$ `MaximalLength` ≥ 1 attributes specify lower and upper limit of the number of boolean attributes referred to by `BASettingRef` that must be present in a boolean attribute matching the `DBASetting`. The default `MinimalLength`= 1 means that at least one of the boolean attributes must be present. If `MaximalLength` is omitted, the largest possible number is assumed. The `BASettingRef` element has also the optional `transactional` attribute (default value *false*) that is used to express that the referenced BA is a BBA defined over transactional input as detailed in Subsection 5.3.

The id attribute gives the DBA/BBASetting a unique id and the Name element an optional name[3]. While the id is for internal use by the XML schema, the name is important to enhance the readability of the XML file.

Running Example 4: definition of the set of relevant basic boolean attributes

```
   <TaskSetting>                                    <BBASetting id="4">
    <BBASettings>                                     <Name>sex(subset[1-1])</Name>
     <BBASetting id="3">                              <FieldRef>sex</FieldRef>
      <Name>district(Praha)</Name>                    <Coefficient>
 5    <FieldRef>district</FieldRef>          15         <Type>Subset</Type>
      <Coefficient>                                     <MinimalLength>1</MinimalLength>
       <Type>One Category</Type>                        <MaximalLength>1</MaximalLength>
       <Category>Praha</Category>                      </Coefficient>
      </Coefficient>                                  </BBASetting>
10   </BBASetting>                           20</BBASettings>
```

The DBASetting ultimately decomposes to BBASettings, which sets a pattern according to which BBAs are created. The FieldRef element points at a field in PMML DataDictionary, TransformationDictionary or LocalTransformations.

BBA coefficient uses the umbrella term "category" to refer to a piece of content of a DataField (Value, Interval) or a DerivedField (DiscretizeBin or a mapped value in MapValues). While the term "value" would be perhaps more intuitive, it is not general enough as it is already reserved in PMML for a single value of an input data field.

The Coefficient defines the type of the coefficient of the BBA. The possible values for Type are Interval – at least min and at most max adjacent categories, Cyclic Interval – same as Interval, but the lowest and highest categories are considered adjacent, Subset – at least min at most max categories in any order, Right Cut – at least min and at most max highest categories, Left Cut – at least min and at most max lowest categories, One Category – one fixed category.

The GeneralSetting element contains constraints applying to a union of BAs from multiple parts of the rule (Antecedent, Consequent or Condition). These rule parts are identified with references to patterns according to which they are created.

There are two types of constraints upon this union. The first type of a constraint is a limit on the count of boolean attributes contained in the union. The second type of constraint is an assertion that a set of boolean attributes conforming to patterns set by Scope must appear among boolean attributes in the union.

The length constraint of the General element ports the lengthLimit attribute of the PMML AR Model to the GUHA AR model, while generalizing it to the new nested rule structure and the optional presence of condition χ. The second constraint has neither backing in GUHA ASSOC nor PMML, but is an essential part of task setting for some algorithms such as [15]. The example does not include any general constraint.

---

[3] E.g. LISp-Miner data-mining system [20] lets the user to name DBA settings, while Ferda [13] dataminer generates the names automatically.

The `InterestMeasureSetting` element contains a sequence of `InterestMeasure Threshold` elements that contain the name of the measure in the `InterestMeasure` child element and the threshold in the `Threshold` child element. Whether this threshold is interpreted as a minimum or maximum depends on the value of the `CompareType` child element. The optional `SignificanceLevel` child element is for statistical interest measures, such as Chi Square of Fisher (refer to Table 1).

Running Example 5: definition of the interest measure thresholds

```
     <InterestMeasureSetting>
40   <InterestMeasureThreshold id="1">
       <InterestMeasure>Support</InterestMeasure>
       <Threshold>0.1</Threshold>
       <CompareType>Greater than</CompareType>
     </InterestMeasureThreshold>
45   <InterestMeasureThreshold id="2">
       <InterestMeasure>Above Average Implication</InterestMeasure>
       <Threshold>0.02</Threshold>
       <CompareType>Greater than</CompareType>
     </InterestMeasureThreshold>
50   <InterestMeasureThreshold id="3">
       <Formula name="Kulczynski">a/2 * (1/(a+c) + 1/(a+b))</Formula>
       <Threshold>0.1</Threshold>
       <CompareType>Greater than</CompareType>
     </InterestMeasureThreshold>
55   </InterestMeasureSetting>
     </TaskSetting>
```

If the interest measure is not listed in the GUHA AR XML Schema as is the case with the Kulczynski [22] measure in the Running Example 5, it can still be used provided that a formula used to compute its value, which is to be compared with the threshold, is placed into the `Formula` element. The formula must be expressed in terms of the frequencies a, b, c, d, r, k, n of the 4ft-table (refer to Table 1). GUHA theory defines several classes of quantifiers, depending on their properties [16]. If interest measures used in the task can be mapped to a quantifier, theoretical results relating to the quantifier's class, such as deduction rules [16], can be applied. For example, confidence and support can be mapped to the Founded Implication Quantifier in Table 1, which falls into a well-studied class of implication quantifiers.

5   AR Model Compatibility and Interoperability

This section covers compatibility with PMML 4.0 and the interoperability of systems with incomplete support of the GUHA AR PMML.

The GUHA AR PMML Model is designed as a new PMML 4.0 *Model* intended to be used alongside the rest of the PMML 4.0 specification. Since PMML 4.0 XML Schema does not allow to define new models, the `PMML4.0 + GUHAARPMML0.1 XML Schema` is an extension of the PMML 4.0 XML Schema with a reference to the GUHA AR model, which itself is placed in a separate file and namespace[4].

The GUHA AR Model is linked with the rest of PMML specification – particularly with `DataDictionary` and `TransformationDictionary` through

---

[4] Changes to PMML are permitted by under the principal condition that a copyright notice is redistributed along with the modified code. The license is at `http://dmg.org/license.html`

boolean attributes as explained in Subsection 4.1. Differences between the PMML AR model and the GUHA AR Model what concerns the integration with `MiningSchema` and `Output` are covered in Subsections 5.2 and 5.1.

Since the GUHA AR PMML Model is a superset of PMML 4.0 Model and both are XML-based specifications, Subsection 5.3 discusses the conditions under which the PMML 4.0 Association Model can be transformed to GUHA AR PMML 0.1 model. Subsection 5.4 briefly covers an XML Schema for description of supported GUHA AR PMML features.

5.1   Mining Schema

In the PMML AR Model, `MiningSchema` contains usually only two fields, the field containing the items and the field which is used to describe which items belong to which transaction [3] – we call this *transactional data* input. The latter field is distinguished with the value `group` of the attribute `usageType`, which was introduced in PMML 2.1. This poses a severe limitation both on the input data (all items need to come from one field[5]) and on the task setting as there is no means of expressing items allowed in the antecedent and in the consequent.

Although PMML's `MiningSchema` is reused unaltered in the GUHA AR Model, it will typically refer to an arbitrary number of fields, although transactional input can still be handled as shown in Subsection 5.3.

5.2   Output Fields

The PMML `Output` element defines the list of `OutputField` elements to be computed by the model. In an AR model, its main purpose is to define when a rule is selected given an input transaction (object in GUHA terminology). There are three simple algorithms for selecting the rule given input transaction: *recommendation*, *exclusiveRecommendation* and *ruleAssociation*. All are defined through the *algebra of sets* [3].

The definitions of these algorithms need to be updated to consider the new condition χ part of rule and the fact that GUHA AR Model rules are based on formulas of *predicate calculus*, not the algebra of sets:

  – input transaction can match a rule only if it satisfies its condition, if present,
  – the correspondence of a rule part (boolean attribute) α with object o is determined based on verification of formulas of *propositional calculus*.

Paper [16] defines how to create a propositional formula $\pi(\phi)$ associated with boolean attribute ϕ[6]. With this propositionalization, we suggest to define the output functions as follows:

---

[5] Technically, the input data can consist of binarized fields - one field per item, the only possibility in PMML 2.0 and older AssociationModels. However, this is impractical due to sparsity of the input data dictionary.

[6] Essentially, $\pi(\phi)$ is created from ϕ such that each BBA $A(\omega), \omega = h_1, \ldots, h_k$ is replaced by propositional disjunction of $\pi(A(\omega)) = A(h_1), \vee \ldots \vee, A(h_k)$.

- `recommendation`: rule is selected if the antecedent (and condition) logically follow from the input object, i.e. $\pi(o) \Rightarrow \pi(\varphi) \wedge \pi(\chi)$ is a tautology.
- `exclusiveRecommendation`: rule is selected if $\pi(o) \Rightarrow \pi(\varphi) \wedge \pi(\chi)$ is a tautology and $\pi(o) \wedge \neg\pi(\psi)$ is a contradiction.[7]
- `ruleAssociation`: rule is selected if $\pi(o) \Rightarrow \pi(\varphi)\wedge\pi(\psi)\wedge\pi(\chi)$ is a tautology.

5.3   Transformation from PMML 4.0

PMML 4.0 input dataset typically contains multiple entries (rows) per object/transaction. GUHA ASSOC does not allow an object to have multiple values in one field, but since this is an important compatibility issue, the GUHA AR Model addresses it.

The following listing shows a fragment of an official DMG example PMML 3.0 Association model[8] converted into the GUHA AR Model. The setting for this task allows a DBA to connect multiple BBAs generated according to one `BBASetting` by setting the `transactional` attribute on `BASettingRef` to *true*.

Comparison Example: a PMML 3.0 file represented in GUHA AR Model

```
<AssociationModel ...>                    <MiningField name="Product" usageType
<TaskSetting>                                ="active"/>
<BBASettings>                             </MiningSchema>
 <BBASetting id="1">                      <AssociationRules>
 <FieldRef>Product</FieldRef>             <BBA id="1">
 <Coefficient>                             <FieldRef>Product</FieldRef>
  <Type>Subset</Type>                      <CatRef>beer</CatRef>
  <MinimalLength>1</MinimalLength>        </BBA>
  <MaximalLength>1</MaximalLength>        <BBA id="2">
 </Coefficient>                            <FieldRef>Product</FieldRef>
 </BBASetting>                             <CatRef>cannedveg</CatRef>
</BBASettings>                            </BBA>
<DBASettings>                             <BBA id="3" literal="false">
 <DBASetting type="Conjunction" id="2     <FieldRef>Product</FieldRef>
      >                                    <CatRef>frozenmeal</CatRef>
  <BASettingRef transactional="true">1    </BBA>
      </BASettingRef>                     <DBA id="4">
 </DBASetting>                             <BARef>1</BARef>
</DBASettings>                             <BARef>2</BARef>
<AntecedentSetting>2</                    </DBA>
    AntecedentSetting>                    <AssociationRule id="1" antecedent="4"
<ConsequentSetting>1</                         consequent="3">
    ConsequentSetting>                     <IMValue name="Support">0.15</IMValue
<InterestMeasureSetting ...>                   >
</TaskSetting>                             <IMValue name="Lift">2.71</IMValue>
<MiningSchema>                             <IMValue name="Confidence">0.87</
 <MiningField name="cardid" usageType=        IMValue>
    "group"/>                             </AssociationRule>...
                                          </AssociationRules></AssociationModel>
```

The advantage of this proposal is that it does not interfere with the syntax of boolean attributes, and it is modular – parts of the rule can be enumerated in the same way as PMML 4.0 items and then used to create DBAs (itemsets). The fact that each value is listed along with its field name allows to prospectively combine multiple fields and transactional input. Nevertheless, it is a matter of further work to determine, whether transactional input can be fully reconciled with observational calculi and GUHA ASSOC method in particular. Additionally, it should be noted that this representation increases the size of PMML files, for the example above this was from 6.2 to 9.2 KB for a complete PMML model with 18 rules.

---

[7] This is one of possible definitions, more detailed discussion is out of the scope of this paper.

[8] http://www.dmg.org/pmml_examples/SHOPPING_ASSOC.xml

Table 4. High-level example of GUHA AR feature documents for three systems

Feature	PMML 4.0	LISp-Miner	Ferda
Connective	⟨ Conjunction ⟩	All	All
Coefficient	⟨ Subset (minLen 1, maxLen 1) ⟩	Yes	Yes
Interest measures	⟨ Lift, Confidence, Support ⟩	⟨...⟩	⟨...⟩
Condition	No	Yes	Yes
Transactional input	Yes	No	No

5.4   Incomplete Support of GUHA AR PMML

Unlike the PMML AR model, which defines only the basic set of features that all AR mining systems are expected to cover, the level of expressivity offered by the GUHA AR Model is such that, to the best of the authors' knowledge, no existing single data mining software is able to exploit it fully.

At the time when the conservative feature policy of PMML was designed, the typical scenario was such that the PMML model was produced by a desktop data mining system and consumed by a scoring system. Since a scoring system needs to be primarily able to read the set of discovered association rules, its function is not dependent on its ability to reproduce the data mining task.

With the emerging shift of the execution of data mining algorithms to the cloud [3] and the related separation of the user interface and the data mining system, the data mining task can be e.g. set up in a universal web-based component that generates PMML based on user input and then sent for execution to a data mining web service.

In order to facilitate the separation of the setting generation component and the data mining service (both PMML producers) while maintaining their interoperability, it is necessary to determine a common set of features that both systems support. In order to facilitate this, the GUHA AR PMML is complemented by the GUHA AR Feature XML Schema. This schema allows an application processing GUHA AR PMML to express supported GUHA AR PMML features. Table 4 presents a high-level example of feature documents for a PMML 4.0 producer, the LISp-Miner system [20] (`lispminer.vse.cz`) and Ferda dataminer [13] (`ferda.sourceforge.net`).

If the GUHA AR document for both communicating applications is available, it can be used to automatically deduce the set of common features supported by both systems and consequently generate a custom `PMML4.0+GUHAAR0.1` XML Schema.

6   Conclusion

The GUHA AR Model XML Schema has the ambition to stir the discussion on updating the data mining standards, particularly PMML. This is vital to allow interoperability between new association rule mining algorithms and Web 3.0 applications. On the running example we have shown how can the GUHA AR Model be used to represent an AR mininig task involving a combination of confidence with the Above Average interest measure and the experimental Kulczynski interest measure, negative literals, disjunctions in coefficients and condition. None of these features could be represented in a PMML 4.0 document without proprietary extensions.

The proposed GUHA AR Model is meant to be interoperable with PMML 4.0. However, it does not attempt to extend the item-based representation of PMML 4.0 Association Model, instead, this paper argues that a representation shared by multiple mining algorithms should have as a basis some general knowledge discovery theory. The GUHA AR Model comes out of such a framework, a subfield of observational calculi [7], which can be viewed as a logic of association rules [16].

The GUHA AR Model is not a solicited effort. As part of the SEWEBAR framework [10] for entailment of semantics into association rule mining, it is complemented by the Association Rule Mining Ontology (ARON) [9], XSLT styles for HTML presentation and ontology conversion and the Background Knowledge Exchange Format (BKEF) XML Schema and Topic Map ontology [11]. Recent theoretical [17] and practical results [10] related to GUHA ASSOC open possibilities to use domain knowledge in the association rule mining process for automatic task setting generation, and in postprocessing for filtering out uninteresting association rules.

An older version of the GUHA AR model presented in this paper was supported since 2009 by academic data mining systems LISp-Miner [20] and Ferda [13], which implement GUHA ASSOC. Over past two years, hundreds of students have used these systems to mine cardiological dataset Adamek [2]. The results are exported in GUHA AR PMML and send via a webservice to the SEWEBAR-CMS, where it is displayed as HTML and accessed by domain experts. For more details visit the project website at sewebar.vse.cz, the student work is presented at sewebar.vse.cz/cardio.

Acknowledgement. The work described here has been supported by Grant No. ME913 of Ministry of Education, Youth and Sports, of the Czech Republic. We would also like to thank Milan Šimůnek (LISp-Miner system) and Martin Ralbovský and Michal Kováč (Ferda dataminer), for implementation of PMML+GUHAAR export and insightful comments. Vojtěch Jirkovský and Tereza Sulanská contributed to the design of XSL transformations and the XML Schema for the GUHA AR Model.

References

1. Antonie, M.-L., Zaïane, O.R.: Mining positive and negative association rules: an approach for confined rules. In: Boulicaut, J.-F., Esposito, F., Giannotti, F., Pedreschi, D. (eds.) PKDD 2004. LNCS (LNAI), vol. 3202, pp. 27–38. Springer, Heidelberg (2004)
2. Berka, P., Rauch, J., Marie, T.: Data mining in atherosclerosis risk factor data. In: Data Mining and Medical Knowledge Management: Cases and Applications, vol. 15, pp. 376–397. IGI Global (2009)

3. Guazzelli, A., Lin, W.-C., Jena, T.: PMML in Action (2010)
4. Hahsler, M., Grün, B., Hornik, K.: Arules - a computational environment for mining association rules and frequent item sets. Journal of Statistical Software 14(15), 1–25, 9 (2005)
5. Hájek, P. (ed.): International Journal of Man-Machine Studies, second special issue on GUHA 15 (1981)
6. Hájek, P., Havránek, T.: Mechanizing Hypothesis Formation. Springer, Heidelberg (1978)
7. Hájek, P., Holeňa, M., Rauch, J.: The GUHA method and its meaning for data mining. Journal of Computer and System Science, 34–38 (2010)
8. Hipp, J., Güntzer, U., Nakhaeizadeh, G.: Algorithms for association rule mining — a general survey and comparison. SIGKDD Explor. Newsl. 2(1), 58–64 (2000)
9. Kliegr, T., Ovečka, M., Zemánek, J.: Topic maps for association rule mining. In: Proceedings of TMRA 2009. University of Leipzig (2009)
10. Kliegr, T., Ralbovský, M., Svátek, V., Šimůnek, M., Jirkovský, V., Nemrava, J., Zemánek, J.: Semantic analytical reports: A framework for post-processing data mining results. In: Rauch, J., Raś, Z.W., Berka, P., Elomaa, T. (eds.) ISMS 2009. LNCS, vol. 5722, pp. 453–458. Springer, Heidelberg (2009)
11. Kliegr, T., Svátek, V., Šimůnek, M., Šťastný, D., Hazucha, A.: XML schema and topic map ontology for background knowledge in data mining. In: The 2nd IRMLES ESWC Workshop (2010)
12. Lín, V., Rauch, J., Svátek, V.: Content-based retrieval of analytic reports. In: Rule Markup Languages for Business Rules on the Semantic Web, Sardinia 2002, pp. 219–224 (2002)
13. Martin, R., Tomáš, K.: Using disjunctions in association mining. In: Perner, P. (ed.) ICDM 2007. LNCS (LNAI), vol. 4597, pp. 339–351. Springer, Heidelberg (2007)
14. Nanavati, A.A., Chitrapura, K.P., Joshi, S., Krishnapuram, R.: Mining generalised disjunctive association rules. In: CIKM 2001, pp. 482–489. ACM, New York (2001)
15. Olaru, A., Marinica, C., Guillet, F.: Local mining of association rules with rule schemas. In: CIDM, pp. 118–124. IEEE, Los Alamitos (2009)
16. Rauch, J.: Logic of association rules. Applied Intelligence (22), 9–28 (2005)
17. Rauch, J.: Considerations on logical calculi for dealing with knowledge in data mining. In: Data Mining: Foundations and Practice, pp. 177–199. Springer, Heidelberg (2009)
18. Rauch, J.: Logical aspects of the measures of interestingness of association rules. In: Advances in Machine Learning II, pp. 175–203. Springer, Berlin (2010)
19. Rauch, J., Šimůnek, M.: An alternative approach to mining association rules. Foundation of Data Mining and Knowledge Discovery 6, 211–231 (2005)
20. Šimůnek, M.: Academic KDD project LISp-Miner. In: Advances in Soft Computing - Intelligent Systems Design and Applications, pp. 263–272. Springer, Heidelberg (2003)
21. Wettschereck, D., Mueller, S.: Exchanging data mining models with the Predictive Model Markup Language. In: Proceedings of the ECML/PKDD 2001 Worksh. on Integr. of DM Decision Supp. and Meta-Learning, pp. 55–66 (2001)
22. Wu, T., Chen, Y., Han, J.: Association mining in large databases: A re-examination of its measures. In: Kok, J.N., Koronacki, J., Lopez de Mantaras, R., Matwin, S., Mladenič, D., Skowron, A. (eds.) PKDD 2007. LNCS (LNAI), vol. 4702, pp. 621–628. Springer, Heidelberg (2007)
23. Zhang, Y., Zhang, L., Nie, G., Shi, Y.: A survey of interestingness measures for association rules. In: International Conference on Business Intelligence and Financial Engineering, pp. 460–463 (2009)

Realizing Integrated Service Delivery through a Language for Collective Understanding of Business Rules

Sietse Overbeek[1], Marijn Janssen[1], and Patrick van Bommel[2]

[1] Faculty of Technology, Policy and Management, Delft University of Technology,
Jaffalaan 5, 2600 GA Delft, The Netherlands, EU
{S.J.Overbeek,M.F.W.H.A.Janssen}@tudelft.nl
[2] Institute for Computing and Information Sciences, Radboud University Nijmegen,
Heijendaalseweg 135, 6525 AJ Nijmegen, The Netherlands, EU
P.vanBommel@cs.ru.nl

Abstract. Integrated Service Delivery (ISD) concerns the cooperation among multiple service providers to make services available as an integrated package. This cooperation requires that providers connect to each other and understand each other. Yet, there is no support for describing and communicating such a complex set of ISD rules. An ISD language is proposed in this paper, founded in the Semantics of Business Vocabulary and Business Rules (SBVR) specification. SBVR is a human-readable language that has the full power of formal languages. 'Basic expressions' are introduced to verbalize ISD rules in SBVR. 'Composed expressions' have been developed to add logical, temporal, and geographical information to business rules to realize ISD. This is necessary to understand how, when, and where services need to be integrated and delivered. Service providers can realize a shared understanding of how to jointly integrate and deliver services by utilizing the foundations.

1 Introduction

Service providers collaborate more and more in networks to meet customer requirements. Contemporary service providers are shifting from purely supplying common, non-electronic services towards more demand-driven and personalized electronic service delivery (see e.g. [3]). Initially, service providers focus on recurring rather than on irregular client needs. As such, assessing and reacting to needs does not provide the flexibility to react to new needs or even changes in the environment. Integrated Service Delivery (ISD) concerns a bundle of services offered by more than one service provider, that matches variable client needs and environmental changes [2]. With ISD, clients perceive a bundle of services provided by various service providers as a whole and do not have to deal with each single provider.

Although there is technological support for creating ISD (see e.g. [6]), the business rules to realize ISD are not well-defined. Business rules have been defined as 'declarations of policy or conditions that must be satisfied' [4]. In this

M. Dean et al. (Eds.): RuleML 2010, LNCS 6403, pp. 289–296, 2010.

case, business rules are those conditions that have to be satisfied to realize ISD. To allow service providers undergo a transition from delivering fragmented services towards delivering integrated services, it should be specified first which rules these organizations should meet to realize ISD. These insights are needed because ISD requires service providers to work together. There is also a need for a shared understanding, because service providers use a variety of terms and definitions, denoting that there is a need for a shared vocabulary that is easy to understand by the organizations involved. Because service providers may not understand each other, there is a risk that they are unable to realize ISD.

A concrete real-life example of a company that will profit from our research is *Portbase*. Portbase is a non-profit organization acting as a neutral hub for the exchange of logistics information in the ports of Rotterdam and Amsterdam, The Netherlands. Portbase was created by a merger between Rotterdam's Port Infolink (est. 2002) and Amsterdam's PortNET (est. 2000). Portbase provides a multitude of services for enabling the exchange of information between companies in the public and private sectors. Examples of services include notification of arrival, veterinary cargo declaration, tracking and tracing of goods. Their aim is to offer a 'green lane' in which to create no delays in the logistic handling due to information exchange problems. The large number and variety of organizations involved demands for explicit business rules to realize ISD. The arrival of vessels, but also of trucks or trains, triggers information exchange between Portbase and those companies involved in the trade lane. For example: the request for customs information, the reservation of stacks for transferring containers from one modality to another modality, the request of trucks for transport, etc. For each container different activities might be necessary to perform, which can be determined by each individual organization when processing the exchanged information. Each organization maintains its own business rules for processing the information, whereas rules described and shared in an ISD language ensures that all participating organizations will understand which business rules have to be complied with in order to realize ISD.

The goal of this paper is to propose foundations for an ISD language to specify rules for enabling ISD. These foundations can be used to generate the rules needed to achieve ISD and are introduced in sections 2, 3 and 4. They have been formalized to offer precise syntax and semantics. The rules that can be formed by using these foundations are verbalized by using the Semantics of Business Vocabulary and Business Rules (SBVR) specification that has been published by the Object Management Group (OMG) recently [5]. SBVR defines the meta model for documenting the semantics of business vocabulary and business rules such as ISD rules. SBVR was selected as it improves readability and prevents ambiguous interpretations among service providers who need to interpret ISD rules, and it is a human-readable language that at the same time has the full power of formal languages. The foundations describe logical, temporal, and geographical information to understand how, when, and where services need to be integrated and delivered. Finally, the conclusions are presented in section 5.

2   Composed Expressions with Logical Operators

SBVR verbalizations can be divided into atomic formulations or *basic expressions* and *composed expressions*. Basic expressions are simply those business rules or verbalizations that consist of a single sentence. A description of such expressions is not repeated here as they can be found in the SBVR specification [5]. Composed expressions are more complex in the sense that basic expressions are combined (and which can be formed recursively by combining composed expressions) by construction operators. A construction operator is a mathematical operator that can be used to assemble basic expressions [7]. Two basic expressions can be assembled by means of a construction operator, resulting in a composed SBVR expression. This can be realized by using the compose equation:

$$\text{Compose} : \mathcal{EX} \times \mathcal{EX} \to \mathcal{CE} \tag{1}$$

The set $\mathcal{EX}$ contains all possible expressions and the set $\mathcal{CE}$ contains composed expressions. The compose equation can assemble basic expressions, but composed expressions can also be assembled recursively. Because $\mathcal{BE}, \mathcal{CE} \subseteq \mathcal{EX}$, it is possible to assemble basic expressions and composed expressions, which always results in a new composed expression. The set $\mathcal{BE}$ is the set of basic expressions. There are four possibilities to create composed expressions:

1. $\exists_{x,y \in \mathcal{BE}} \exists_{z \in \mathcal{CE}} [\text{Compose}(x, y) = z]$
2. $\exists_{x \in \mathcal{BE}} \exists_{y,z \in \mathcal{CE}} [\text{Compose}(x, y) = z]$
3. $\exists_{y \in \mathcal{BE}} \exists_{x,z \in \mathcal{CE}} [\text{Compose}(x, y) = z]$
4. $\exists_{x,y,z \in \mathcal{CE}} [\text{Compose}(x, y) = z]$

This implies that: (1) A composed expression can be formed by combining two basic expressions. (2) A composed expression can be formed by combining a basic expression with a composed expression. (3) A composed expression can be formed by combining a composed expression with a basic expression. (4) A composed expression can be formed by recursively combining two composed expressions. The simplest construction operators to form composed expressions can be the logical operators for conjunction (and), disjunction (or), and negation (not). These operators are also part of the SBVR specification [5] to compose statements. These operators can be used for Boolean composed expressions that result in true or false. For instance, it can be true that <u>actor</u> <u>Jane</u> <u>enacts</u> <u>role</u> <u>vet cargo inspector</u> and <u>actor</u> <u>Jane</u> <u>performs</u> <u>process</u> <u>handle vet cargo declaration</u>. Subsequently, composed expressions may also be used in a set-theoretical context. For example, the following verbalization produces *all* the roles that are enacted by a certain actor <u>Jane</u> and *all* the processes that are performed by that actor: <u>Actor</u> <u>Jane</u> <u>enacts</u> <u>role</u> and <u>actor</u> <u>Jane</u> <u>performs</u> <u>process</u>. The meaning of the logical operators should be clarified in order to use them in composed expressions. In fact, a logical operator combines two basic expressions to form a composed expression. Using the above-mentioned definition of the set $\mathcal{BE}$, the formal signature of the logical operators can be provided as follows:

$$\_\text{and}\_, \_\text{or}\_, \_\text{not}\_ \subseteq \mathcal{BE} \times \mathcal{BE} \tag{2}$$

Thus, x and y means that two basic expressions $x, y \in \mathcal{BE}$ are both true. The definitions of the and, or, and not construction operators are easy to provide by using the common mathematical operators for logical expressions which are trivial and not repeated here. Next, composed expressions can be formed to verbalize time-related rules for ISD.

3   Composed Expressions with Temporal Operators

Construction operators from the temporal domain can be used to express an *instant* of time, a *duration*, or a *period* with regard to a rule. *Allen's operators* [1] provide a point of departure for adding temporal expressiveness to our language for ISD. Construction operators from the temporal domain are not included in the current SBVR specification yet [5]. Therefore, we will introduce such operators in this section to be able to generate SBVR statements that include temporal operators. For instance, the composed expression actor <u>Jane</u> *enacts* role <u>vet cargo inspector</u> after actor <u>Jane</u> *belongs to* organization <u>FCPSA</u> shows that actor 'Jane' became a cargo inspector after becoming employed at the Food and Consumer Product Safety Authority. Allen's operators are 13 mutually exclusive relationships between an ordered pair of closed, proper periods P_1 and P_2, where $P_1, P_2 \subseteq \mathcal{PE}$. The set $\mathcal{PE}$ contains possible proper periods. To use Allen's operators in composed SBVR expressions, we need to understand the meaning of the operators. In our case, we need to understand when a situation verbalized by a basic expression *starts* and when it *ends*. For example, it is only possible to know the meaning of operators like 'before', 'after', or 'equals' if the start and end times of a situation verbalized by a basic expression are known. This allows for clear differentiation between two time periods. The formal signature of the start and end equations can be represented as follows:

$$\mathsf{Start}, \mathsf{End} : \mathcal{BE} \rightarrow \mathcal{PE} \tag{3}$$

For example, $\mathsf{Start}(b) = p$ implies that the start time of the occurred situation expressed by b is p. Next, formal definitions of start and end times are modeled to give meaning to these equations:

$$\mathsf{Start}(b) \triangleq \forall_{b \in \mathcal{BE}} \forall_{p \in \mathcal{PE}} [\mathsf{Start}(b) < p \wedge p \neq \mathsf{Start}(b)] \tag{4}$$

The definition of the start time shows that there are no time instants that can be earlier than instant $\mathsf{Start}(b)$, i.e. the start time.

$$\mathsf{End}(b) \triangleq \forall_{b \in \mathcal{BE}} \forall_{p \in \mathcal{PE}} [\mathsf{End}(b) > p \wedge p \neq \mathsf{End}(b)] \tag{5}$$

The definition of the end time shows that there are no time instants that can be later than instant $\mathsf{End}(b)$. Using the start and end time equations, notations can be introduced for each of Allen's operators [1]. The 'before' operator can be formalized as follows:

$$\_\mathsf{before}\_ \subseteq \mathcal{BE} \times \mathcal{BE} \tag{6}$$

Note that all temporal operators are proper subsets of the Cartesian product of two sets of basic expressions. The notation above is, therefore, not repeated for the remaining operators. The definition of 'before' can be represented as follows, where $x, y \in \mathcal{BE}$:

$$x \text{ before } y \triangleq \text{End}(x) < \text{Start}(y) \tag{7}$$

If x before y, then the end time of a situation expressed in x should always precede the start time of another situation y. Using two basic expressions of the Portbase example mentioned in section 1, a meaningful composed expression can now be formed, such as: Event goods declaration sent *is produced by* actor John before process handle goods declaration *is performed by* actor Jane. The definition of the 'after' operator is comparable to that of the 'before' operator:

$$x \text{ after } y \triangleq \text{Start}(x) > \text{End}(y) \tag{8}$$

The meaning of the 'equals' operator is that the start time and end time instants of two situations verbalized by basic expressions must be exactly equal:

$$x \text{ equals } y \triangleq \text{Start}(x) = \text{Start}(y) \wedge \text{End}(x) = \text{End}(y) \tag{9}$$

When combining two example basic expressions by means of this operator, a meaningful composed expression can be formed: Role vet cargo inspector *is enacted by* actor Jane equals actor Jane *belongs to* organization FCPSA. This composed expression is true if Jane has indeed started working and has also ended working as a cargo inspector at the Food and Consumer Product Safety Authority (without changing jobs at the same company in the meantime). Subsequently, the 'meets' operator can be defined as follows:

$$x \text{ meets } y \triangleq \text{End}(x) = \text{Start}(y) \wedge \text{Start}(x) < \text{Start}(y) \wedge \text{End}(x) < \text{End}(y) \tag{10}$$

The end time instant of a situation verbalized by a basic expression must be equal to the start time instant of another situation if both situations 'meet' each other. Moreover, the start time of a situation that meets another situation must be earlier than the start time of the situation that is met. This also applies to the end times. Two example basic expressions can be assembled by means of the 'meets' operator as follows: Actor John *produces* event goods declaration form signed meets architecture EDSOA *orchestrates* event goods declaration form signed. The definition of the 'met by' operator is now trivial:

$$x \text{ met by } y \triangleq \text{Start}(x) = \text{End}(y) \wedge \text{Start}(x) > \text{Start}(y) \wedge \text{End}(x) > \text{End}(y) \tag{11}$$

The next operators are the 'overlaps' and 'overlapped by' operators. The start time and the end time of a situation that overlaps another situation must be earlier than those of the situation that is overlapped:

$$x \text{ overlap } y \triangleq \text{Start}(y) > \text{Start}(x) \wedge \text{End}(y) > \text{End}(x) \tag{12}$$

$$x \text{ overlapped by } y \triangleq \text{Start}(x) > \text{Start}(y) \wedge \text{End}(x) > \text{End}(y) \tag{13}$$

An example related to Portbase as mentioned in section 1 can be verbalized as follows: Actor <u>John</u> *enacts* role <u>importer</u> overlaps role <u>vet cargo inspector</u> *is enacted by* actor <u>Jane</u>. The operators 'during' and 'contains' can be used to indicate that a situation takes place within the time span of another situation. This can be formalized by the following equations:

$$x \operatorname{during} y \triangleq \mathsf{Start}(x) > \mathsf{Start}(y) \wedge \mathsf{End}(x) < \mathsf{End}(y) \tag{14}$$

$$x \operatorname{contains} y \triangleq \mathsf{Start}(y) > \mathsf{Start}(x) \wedge \mathsf{End}(y) < \mathsf{End}(x) \tag{15}$$

A meaningful expression related to Portbase is easy to find: Actor <u>John</u> *uses* service <u>declare vet goods</u> during actor <u>John</u> *enacts* role <u>importer</u>. Then, the 'starts' and 'started by' operators can be modeled:

$$x \operatorname{starts} y \triangleq \mathsf{Start}(x) \Rightarrow \mathsf{Start}(y) \wedge \mathsf{End}(x) \neq \mathsf{End}(y) \tag{16}$$

$$x \operatorname{started} \operatorname{by} y \triangleq \mathsf{Start}(y) \Rightarrow \mathsf{Start}(x) \wedge \mathsf{End}(y) \neq \mathsf{End}(x) \tag{17}$$

The 'starts' operator can be used to assemble the following basic expressions, for instance: Event <u>goods declaration received</u> *occurs in* organization <u>Portbase</u> starts event <u>goods declaration received</u> *is consumed by* actor <u>Jane</u>. Finally, the last two temporal construction operators are the 'finishes' and 'finished by' operators:

$$x \operatorname{finishes} y \triangleq \mathsf{End}(x) \Rightarrow \mathsf{End}(y) \wedge \mathsf{Start}(x) \neq \mathsf{Start}(y) \tag{18}$$

$$x \operatorname{finished} \operatorname{by} y \triangleq \mathsf{End}(y) \Rightarrow \mathsf{End}(x) \wedge \mathsf{Start}(y) \neq \mathsf{Start}(x) \tag{19}$$

Subsequently, geographical rules can be formed by using *geographical operators*. Like temporal operators, these kind of operators are not part of the SBVR specification yet. Therefore, they are introduced in the next section such that they can be used in SBVR verbalizations to specify ISD rules.

4   Composed Expressions with Geographical Operators

Geographical expressions can be used to form rules regarding the locations of concepts that are related to ISD. For instance, the expression actor <u>John</u> *produces* event <u>goods declaration form signed</u> north of actor <u>Jane</u> *performs* process <u>handle goods declaration</u> shows that John is signing a goods declaration form north of Jane, who performs a process to handle a goods declaration. To work with geographical operators, the *coordinates* of objects that are related to the geographical operator need to be determined. It is possible to reason about the spatial relationships between objects if such coordinates are known. The three-dimensional coordinates of a main concept mentioned in a basic expression can be found by means of the coordinates equation:

$$\mathsf{Coord} : \mathcal{BE} \rightarrow \mathbb{R} \times \mathbb{R} \times \mathbb{R} \tag{20}$$

The coordinates can be plotted on a three-dimensional Cartesian coordinate system, with an origin and three axis lines X, Y, and Z. For example, $\mathsf{Coord}(b) = (3, 1, 4)$ indicates what the coordinates are for a main concept as part of an arbitrary basic expression b. Several geographical operators can be presented and used to form composed expressions based on a spatial relationship between two basic expressions. Some useful geographical operators are 'above', 'under', 'ahead', 'behind', 'north of', 'south of', 'east of', and 'west of'. The signature of these operators can also be formalized in the following way:

$$\_\mathrm{above}\_ \subseteq \mathcal{BE} \times \mathcal{BE} \tag{21}$$

The signatures of the other geographical operators discussed in this section are identical. The 'above' and 'under' operators can be defined as follows:

$$b_1 \text{ above } b_2 \triangleq \exists_{b_1, b_2 \in \mathcal{BE}} \exists_{x_1, x_2, y_1, y_2, z_1, z_2 \in \mathbb{R}} [\mathsf{Coord}(b_1) =$$
$$(x_1, y_1, z_1) \wedge \mathsf{Coord}(b_2) = (x_2, y_2, z_2) \wedge z_1 > z_2] \tag{22}$$

$$b_1 \text{ under } b_2 \triangleq \exists_{b_1, b_2 \in \mathcal{BE}} \exists_{x_1, x_2, y_1, y_2, z_1, z_2 \in \mathbb{R}} [\mathsf{Coord}(b_1) =$$
$$(x_1, y_1, z_1) \wedge \mathsf{Coord}(b_2) = (x_2, y_2, z_2) \wedge z_1 < z_2] \tag{23}$$

A meaningful composed expression that is created by using the 'above' operator can be described as follows: Process handle goods declaration is performed by actor Jane above process trace cargo with vet goods is performed by actor George. Expressions such as these may be useful when, for instance, Jane is searching for additional information on housing benefits while performing her job as a cargo inspector. Knowing that her colleague George is working on a task related to this topic in close proximity (above her in the same building probably) can be helpful. The intention of the 'ahead' and 'behind' operators is to express whether an object is exactly in front of (ahead) or to the rear of (behind) another object. In terms of the three-dimensional coordinates, this implies that the objects have equal coordinates on the Y and Z axes, but a different coordinate on the X axis, or formally:

$$b_1 \text{ ahead } b_2 \triangleq \exists_{b_1, b_2 \in \mathcal{BE}} \exists_{x_1, x_2, y_1, y_2, z_1, z_2 \in \mathbb{R}} [\mathsf{Coord}(b_1) =$$
$$(x_1, y_1, z_1) \wedge \mathsf{Coord}(b_2) = (x_2, y_2, z_2) \wedge x_1 > x_2] \tag{24}$$

$$b_1 \text{ behind } b_2 \triangleq \exists_{b_1, b_2 \in \mathcal{BE}} \exists_{x_1, x_2, y_1, y_2, z_1, z_2 \in \mathbb{R}} [\mathsf{Coord}(b_1) =$$
$$(x_1, y_1, z_1) \wedge \mathsf{Coord}(b_2) = (x_2, y_2, z_2) \wedge x_1 < x_2] \tag{25}$$

When an object is said to be north of another object, it is not important what the coordinates of the objects on the Z axis are, as long as the coordinates on the Y axis are the same and the coordinates on the X axis differ to let one object lie north of another object. This can be formalized as follows:

$$b_1 \text{ north of } b_2 \triangleq \exists_{b_1, b_2 \in \mathcal{BE}} \exists_{x_1, x_2, y_1, y_2, z_1, z_2 \in \mathbb{R}} [\mathsf{Coord}(b_1) =$$
$$(x_1, y_1, z_1) \wedge \mathsf{Coord}(b_2) =$$
$$(x_2, y_2, z_2) \wedge y_1 = y_2 \wedge x_1 > x_2] \tag{26}$$

Because the remaining operators related to the other quarters of the compass can be formalized in similar ways, they are not repeated here. With logical, temporal, and geographical expressions, service providers can understand how, when, and where services need to be integrated and delivered.

5   Conclusions

The research presented here supports the realization of ISD by helping service providers in making the shift from individually supplying common, non-electronic services towards collaboratively supplying integrated, demand-driven and personalized electronic services. Before service providers are able to deliver integrated services they need to have an unambiguous and shared understanding as to which rules should be met to achieve ISD. To meet these demands, foundations for an ISD language have been proposed in this paper for the specification of business rules involved in enabling ISD. We have been able to specify these foundations in SBVR, which consist of basic and composed expressions. Two basic expressions can be assembled by means of a construction operator, resulting in a composed expression. Three types of construction operators have been introduced that allow for the logical composition of basic expressions, as well as making it possible to assemble basic expressions that result in temporal and geographical expressions. By adding this expressive power to the foundations, service providers can understand how, when, and where services need to be integrated and delivered. Relating this to the Portbase example, it can be concluded that shared business rules described in an ISD language will ensure that organizations understand which rules have to be complied with in order to realize ISD.

References

1. Allen, J.: Maintaining knowledge about temporal intervals. Communications of the ACM 26(11), 832–843 (1983)
2. Álvarez Sabucedo, L., Anido Rifón, L., Pérez, R., Santos Gago, J.: Providing standard-oriented data models and interfaces to eGovernment services: A semantic-driven approach. Computer Standards & Interfaces 31(5), 1014–1027 (2009)
3. Chen, H.: Digital government: technologies and practices. Decision Support Systems 34(3), 223–227 (2003)
4. Martin, J., Odell, J.: Object-Oriented Methods: A Foundation – UML Edition. Prentice Hall PTR, New Jersey, NJ, USA (1998)
5. OMG: Semantics of business vocabulary and business rules (SBVR), v1.0. OMG available specification formal/2008-01-02, Object Management Group, Needham, MA, USA (2008)
6. Overbeek, S., Klievink, A., Janssen, M.: A flexible, event-driven, service-oriented architecture for orchestrating service delivery. IEEE Intelligent Systems 24(5), 31–41 (2009)
7. Wondergem, B., Bommel, P.v., Weide, T.v.d.: Combining boolean logic and linguistic structure. Information and Software Technology 43(1), 53–59 (2001)

Authoring Business Rules Grounded in OWL Ontologies

Amina Chniti[1,2], Sylvain Dehors[1], Patrick Albert[1], and Jean Charlet[2,3]

[1] IBM
{amina.chniti,sylvain.dehors,albertpa}@fr.ibm.com
[2] INSERM UMRS 872, Eq 20, 15, Rue de l'école de médecine, 75006, Paris, France
Jean.Charlet@upmc.fr
[3] AP-HP, Paris, France

Abstract. This paper describes an approach in the double context of business rules and techniques of the semantic web, the ontologies. This approach consists of enabling the use of business rules to automate the decisions on domains which semantic is formalized with an ontological language. Our main objective is to enable business users to edit, manage and execute business rules grounded in ontologies without resorting to an expert. The implementation is based on the Business Rule Management System (BRMS) IBM WebSphere ILOG JRules.

1 Introduction

In the context of information systems, ontologies are artifacts that encode a description of a domain (concepts, roles) in formal language (e.g. Resource Description Framework (RDF) [2], Ontology Web Language (OWL) [1]), which is understandable only by experts in the domain. On the other hand, in the context of BRMS, business rules are a description of a business policy, encoded in an pseudo natural "If-Then" format. They define or specify constraints of some aspect of the business. Business rules are understandable by business users and executable by a machine. The main idea of our work[1] consists of managing relations between Ontologies [10] and Business Rules[2] especially in the processes of authoring and execution of rules. Our objective is to develop a prototype that can be used to edit and execute business rules grounded in ontologies. This will allow business users to own and to manage their business knowledge resource, formalized with an ontological language, without resorting to an expert.

There are languages, described in Section 5 that integrate ontologies and rules. These languages mostly use formal rules, which are written in a formal syntax. Hence, business users cannot edit their rules and, for the vast majority, they cannot even read them.

To summarize: we develop a method that allows business users (doctors, lawyers, scientists ...), who do not have any knowledge of Logic Programming or

---

[1] This work is partially supported by the European Commission under the project ONTORULE (IST-2009-231875).

[2] http://www.businessrulesgroup.org/

M. Dean et al. (Eds.): RuleML 2010, LNCS 6403, pp. 297–304, 2010.
© Springer-Verlag Berlin Heidelberg 2010

Description Logic, to author, manage and execute their business rules, grounded in ontologies of a domain formalized using OWL. We focus on importing OWL-DL descriptions, within the IBM WebSphere ILOG JRules[3], or JRules for short, and the mapping of OWL concepts (TBox) into the JRules formalism, the Business Object Model (BOM), which is used to represent the concepts of the domain.

This paper is organized as follows. Section 2 briefly introduces the BRMS JRules. Section 3 describes the methodology used. Section 4 presents the results obtained. Section 5 overviews related work. Section 6 discusses some perspectives and concludes.

2   IBM WebSphere ILOG JRules

JRules is a BRMS; as such, it provides the means to edit, manage, test, and deploy Business Rules.

JRules consists of a set of components allowing business users to author and execute business rules. These components are the following:

eXecutable Object Model (XOM). This is the model enabling the execution of rules. It references the application objects and data, and is the base implementation of the BOM. The XOM can be built from compiled Java classes (Java execution object model) or XML Schema (dynamic execution object model). Through the XOM, the rule engine can access application objects and methods, which can be Java objects or XML data. At runtime, rules that were written via the BOM are run against the XOM.

Business Object Model (BOM). This is an object-oriented model that defines the concepts of a given business. It describes the classes representing the objects of the application domain [5]. A BOM contains a set of classes and each class contains a set of attributes and methods, which the rules act on. It is in turn mapped into the XOM.

Business Rules. The business rules are expressed in a controlled natural language that can be understood and managed by regular business users, for instance:

> *IF the age of the client is between 18 and 25*
> *THEN set the insurance ratio to 125*

This controlled natural language is compiled into a lower-level technical language. Two models supports the definition of the rules in the "business layer" . The business objects of the domain (*e.g.*, *client*, *age*), which are represented in the BOM and the vocabulary model (VOC), which add a layer of terminology on top of the BOM (*e.g.* "*the client*", "*the age of the client*"). This vocabulary, introduced with the VOC is in turn used to compose the text of the rules [5].

---

[3] http://www-01.ibm.com/software/integration/business-rule-management/jrules/

Currently, input to JRules consists of compiled Java classes or an XML Schema file. The method we developed is a means to import OWL ontologies into JRules. Thus, business users can manage their business resource formalized with OWL using the components provided by JRules, without any change.

3 Authoring and Executing Business Rules from Ontologies

Though the BOM approach provides good results as far as applications are concerned, we believe that using formal and normalized notations for the conceptual domain model would bring a lot of value. We have thus started experiments with OWL as it is the result of many years of experiences reaching the status of a W3C recommendation.[4] To integrate OWL ontologies as input in JRules, we developed a plug-in that produces a mapping of an OWL Ontology into the BOM of JRules. Once the OWL ontology has been imported, all of the regular functionalities provided by JRules can be used without any change.

3.1 Authoring Business Rules from Ontologies: OWL to BOM Mapping

As described in Section 2 the BOM is the main component for authoring rules in JRules. There has been a lot of works related to the mapping of OWL ontologies into the Java object-oriented model such as `Kazuki`,[5] `OntoJava`,[6] `Owl2Java`,[7] and *"Automatic Mapping of OWL Ontologies into Java"* [8]. These methods cannot be directly used to generate an effective BOM supporting the authoring of rules. Nevertheless, we have adapted the method described in [8] to our needs.

Due to the differences in knowledge representation between the BOM and OWL, there are some OWL constructs that cannot be mapped into the BOM such as "`disjointWith`", "`complementOf`". However, a large part of the constructs can be mapped. Below is a description of the main transformations of the mapping of OWL to BOM.

Concepts: An OWL concept is mapped into a BOM Class. The hierarchical relations are mapped into the BOM using the subclass relation and, as the BOM supports multiple inheritance, this information is also preserved.

Properties: An OWL property is mapped into an attribute of a BOM class. Functional properties are mapped to single attributes and multi-valued properties are mapped to multiple cardinality attributes. The class of an attribute corresponds to the domain of the corresponding property, and its type corresponds to the range of the property. Nevertheless, a property may have a null or multiple domain (range, respectively). These cases are mapped as follows:

---

[4] http://www.w3.org/TR/2004/REC-owl-guide-20040210/

[5] http://projects.semwebcentral.org/projects/kazuki/

[6] http://www.aifb.uni-karlsruhe.de/WBS/aeb/ontojava/

[7] http://www.incunabulum.de/projects/it/owl2java

- *Null domain:* The attribute is added to all the root classes, *i.e.*which inherit directly from `owl:Thing`.
- *Multiple domain:* The attribute is added to all the classes corresponding to the set of the domains.
- *Range null:* The type of the attribute is inferred as described in the following. If the property has an equivalent property then the type of the attribute will be the range of the equivalent property. Else, if the property has an inverse property then the type of the attribute will be the domain of the inverse property. Otherwise, the attribute will be of type Object.

Restrictions :
- `cardinality` and `maxCardinality` restrictions: when an attribute's cardinality restrictions is equal to 1, it is mapped into a single-valued attribute; otherwise, it is mapped into a multiple-valued attribute;
- `allValuesFrom` restriction: the type of the attribute is the class defined on the restriction;
- `oneOf` restriction: Static values corresponding to the values defined on the collection are attached to the class.

Table 1. OWL to BOM Mapping

OWL	BOM
Class A	Class A
B subClassOf A	Class B extends A
C intersectionOf(A,B)	Class C extends A,B
C unionOf(A,B)	Class A extends C and Class B extends C
A oneOf {x, y, z}	Class A {domain {'x', 'y', 'z'};}
A equivalentClass B	Keep only A, and references to B are reported to A
P(A,B)	Class A {B[ ] P};
P subPropertyOf P'(A,C)	Class A {B[ ] P; C[ ] P';}
P' equivalentProperty P	Class A {B[ ] P; B[ ] p';}
P' inverseOf P	Class B {A[ ] P;}
P functionalProperty	Class A {B P;}
P.cardinality = 1	Class A {B P;}
P.maxCardinality = 1 on P	Class A {B P;}
P allValuesFrom C	Class A {C[ ] P;}

3.2 Executing Business Rules from Ontologies

The process of executing business rules in JRules consists of several steps. Business rules, written in a controlled natural language, cannot be directly executed. First, they are translated into executable rules, which are written in a formal technical rule language. During this translation, the references to the BOM's classes and properties are translated to references into the XOM. When the input provided to JRules is a Java object model, the XOM is built from this model. But in our case, the input provided to JRules is an OWL model.

To execute business rules authored from ontologies, we perform a second mapping of OWL-BOM entities to a XOM using Jena.[8] Jena is a Java framework, including an OWL API which allows generation of Java objects from the entities of the ontology. These Java objects then constitute the XOM.

The use of Jena provides an execution layer for the OWL ontologies. This execution layer provides inference mechanisms on this model and the mapping of OWL concepts, properties, and individuals to a Java object model.

4   Experiments and Results

To validate our results, we used ontologies provided from our partners in the ONTORULE project [6] and also ontologies from the web like `pizza.owl`,[9] `financialOntology.owl`,[10] and `animal.owl`.[11] All these ontologies have been successfully imported into the BOM without any change. This section illustrates the results obtained using the `LoanValidation` ontology, which is used for demonstration purpose. It contains 5 concepts (Borrower,Loan, Bankruptcy, Report), 3 object properties (borrower (Report, Borrower), loan (Report, Loan), spouse (Borrower, Borrower)) and 5 data type properties (age (Borrower, int), yearlyIncome (Borrower, float), yearlyRepayment (Loan, float), message (Report, string), validData(Report, boolean)) that describes entities used in the process of validating of a loan request posted by a Borrower.

4.1   Examples of Business Rules

Below, we give examples of business rules edited from the BOM generated with the LoanValidation ontology.

Rule 1:

> IF the age of the borrower is more than 18 and the age of the borrower is less than 25
> THEN make it false that the report is valid data ; add messages : "The borrower's age is not valid." to the report ;

Rule 2:

> IF the yearly repayment of the loan is at least 0.37 * the yearly income of the borrower
> THEN make it false that the report is approved ; add messages : "Too big Debt/Income ratio: " + the yearly repayment of the loan /the yearly income of the borrower to the report;

---

[8] http://jena.sourceforge.net/

[9] http://www.co-ode.org/ontologies/pizza/2007/02/12/

[10] http://dip.semanticweb.org/documents/D10.3.pdf

[11] http://www.aifb.uni-karlsruhe.de/WBS/meh/foam/ontologies/animalsABMap. owl

4.2   Executing Rules

This section shows the results of executing the rules described in the previous section. Let us define two instances of borrower, John, aged 20 years old who has a yearly income equal to 100000 and Anna aged 17 with a yearly income equal to 9000. These borrowers request a loan of an amount equal to 200000 and a yearly repayment equal to 10000. The result obtained for John will be "Congratulations! Your loan has been approved" and for Anna "The borrower's age is not valid" (the execution is stopped when executing Rule 1)

Another important point in the process of executing rules is the interaction between the classification engine and the rule engine. Here is an example of this kind of interaction as achieved with the system presented in this work. Let us define a subclasss of customer that defines the risky customers as customers who have at least two known payment incidents. Such definition is well captured in an ontology and can then be used in a rule for example:

> *definitions*
> *set grayList to all risky customers ;*
>
> *IF the customer of "the current rental agreement" is one of grayList*
> *THEN set the discount of the offer of "the current rental agreement" to the*
> *discount of the best offer of "the current rental agreement" - 20*

In this example, the type `risky customer` is assigned by the classification engine based on the individuals. Then, the rule engine uses this inferred knowledge to trigger a computation that could not be easily represented in an ontology. In other words, the rule engine asks the classification engine for the type of the customer, then it executes the rule(s) matching with the returned type.

Enabling the coupling of both approaches gives the business user the best of the two worlds. Definitions remain declarative whenever possible with all the interesting properties of ontologies in term of checking and consistency; while the operational definitions are here to cater for necessary business computations.

5   Related Work

Integration of rules and ontologies is a subject of active research especially in the Semantic Web community. There seems to be a broad consensus that the Semantic Web should include rules as well as ontologies. Integration of rules and ontologies has required definition of new languages, their formal syntax and semantics, and the development of reasoning algorithms for these new languages [3]. There are some proposals for integration of rule languages with ontology languages, like Answer Set Programming (ASP) [4], the Semantic Web Rule Language (SWRL) [9], Description Logic Programs (DLP) [7], the Rule Interchange Format (RIF)[12] or the SPARQL RDF query language.[13]

---

[12] http://www.w3.org/2005/rules/wiki/RIFWorkingGroup
[13] http://www.w3.org/TR/2008/REC-rdf-sparql-query-20080115/

These languages use formal rules, *i.e.* rules written with a technical syntax. To assimilate such rules, users must have a clear understanding of Description Logic and Logic Programming, because they are written in formal ontological and/or rule-based languages. As a result, business users are not able to edit, nor even read, their own rules—let alone rules authored by others—since they are not trained as programmers.

Nevertheless, a special case must be made for SPARQL. We chose to bind the BOM model to the Java API provided by Jena. The BOM must be mapped at some points to Java classes for execution so this is a natural way for JRules to deal with models. For example the XSD schemas are also mapped in JRules to specific Java objects. Instead of using the Jena API directly, it is also possible to bind BOM classes to the result of SPARQL queries. For the condition part of the rules this would be equivalent. However, the Java API offers mutable objects, so it is possible to modify the graph in the action part of the rules. This is not possible using SPARQL. Only constructing new graphs would be possible through the CONSTRUCT, but action rules in production rules engines offer the possibility to modify the instances themselves which is outside the scope of SPARQL. However, with the new SPARQL updates, SPARUL, this could become possible.

6   Perspectives and Conclusion

In this paper we have presented a method for authoring and executing Business Rules from ontologies. This enables business users to edit, manage and execute Business Rules over OWL ontologies. The use of JRules and especially the BOM has enabled us to develop successfully our method, which is now used by our partners in the ONTORULE project.

JRules provides a layer allowing business users to manipulate a technical language. It also provides an editor for Business Rules, which are written in controlled natural language, decision tables and decision trees. Also, it is possible to gather rules into rule sets and create a rule flow to orchestrate the execution of rules.

Our approach has been tested using ontologies provided by our partners and from the Web. Business Rules have been edited and executed successfully. Nevertheless, due to the differences of knowledge representation between the ontological model (OWL) and the BOM, there are some constructs in OWL that we could not map into the BOM, like "someValueFrom," "disjointWith," and "complementOf." In our opinion, these restrictions should not have little an impact on the quality of the mapping we made as it is possible to express the negation in a closed world using rules.

As future work, we envisage studying the degree of dependency and of interaction between the concepts of an ontology, the entities of rules and data to detect the impact of modification of the data set with respect to the ontology and the rule set. We focus especially on consistency problems that could be detected either on the ontology layer or in the rule layer.

Acknowledgement

Many thanks to Marcos Didonet Del Fabro, Hugues Citeau, Adil El Gali and particularly to Hassan Aït-Kaci for their reviews.

References

1. OWL, Ontology Web Language (2004), http://www.w3.org/TR/owl-features/
2. Resource Description Framework, RDF (2004), http://www.w3.org/RDF/
3. Antoniou, G., Damasio, C.V., Grosof, B., Horrocks, I., Kifer, M., Maluszyn-ski, J., Patel-Schneider, P.F.: Combining rules and ontologies: A survey. Techni-cal Report IST506779/Linköping/I3-D3/D/PU/a1, Linköping University (2004), http://rewerse.net/publications/
4. Eiter, T., Ianni, G., Polleres, A., Schindlauer, R., Tompits, H.: Reasoning with rules and ontologies. In: Barahona, P., Bry, F., Franconi, E., Henze, N., Sattler, U. (eds.) Reasoning Web 2006. LNCS, vol. 4126, pp. 93–127. Springer, Heidelberg (2006)
5. Del Fabro, M.D., Albert, P., Bézivin, J., Jouault, F.: Achieving rule interoperability using chains of model transformations. In: Paige, R.F. (ed.) ICMT 2009. LNCS, vol. 5563, pp. 249–259. Springer, Heidelberg (2009)
6. El Ghali, A., Dehors, S., Krof, R., Levy, F., Guisse, A.: D2.1 basic integration of on-tology and business rule authoring technology and basic dependency management, ontorule project delivrable (2009)
7. Grosof, B., Horrocks, I.: Description logic programs combining logic programs with description logic. In: WWW, pp. 48–57 (2003)
8. Kalyanpur, A., Jimenez, D., Battle, S., Padget, J.: Automatic mapping of OWL ontologies into Java. In: Maurer, F., Ruhe, G. (eds.) Proc. of the Sixteenth In-ternational Conference on Software Engineering & Knowledge Engineering, SEKE 2004 (2004)
9. Parsia, B., Sirin, E., Cuenca Grau, B., Ruckhaus, E., Hewlett, D.: Cautiously approaching swrl. Elsevier Science, Amsterdam (2005)
10. Sowa, J.F.: Knowledge representation: Logical, philosophical, and computational foundations (2000)

Author Index

Printing: Mercedes-Druck, Berlin
Binding: Stein+Lehmann, Berlin